Regional Development Strategies

A European Perspective

Edited by Jeremy Alden and Philip Boland

Regional Policy and Development Series 15

Jessica Kingsley Publishers
London and Bristol, Pennsylvania

Regional Studies Association
London

First published in the United Kingdom in 1996 by
Jessica Kingsley Publishers Ltd
116 Pentonville Road
London N1 9JB, England
and
1900 Frost Road, Suite 101
Bristol, PA 19007, U S A

with

The Regional Studies Association
Registered Charity 252269

Library of Congress Cataloging in Publication Data
Regional development strategies : a European perspective / edited by Jeremy Alden and Philip Boland.
p. cm. -- (Regional policy and development series : 15)
Includes bibliographical references (p.) and index.
ISBN 1-85302-356-6 (alk. paper)
1. Regional planning--Europe. I. Alden, Jeremy. II. Boland, Philip, 1967– . III. Series.
HT395.E8R423 1996
307.1'2'094--dc20 95-44356
CIP

British Library Cataloguing in Publication Data
A CIP catalogue record for this book is available from the British Library

ISBN 1-85302-356-6

Printed and Bound in Great Britain by
Cromwell Press, Melksham, Wiltshire

Regional Development Strategies

Regional Policy and Development Series

Series Editor: Ron Martin, Department of Geography, University of Cambridge

Throughout the industrialised world, widespread economic restructuring, rapid technological change, the reconfiguration of State intervention, and increasing globalisation are giving greater prominence to the nature and performance of individual regional and local economies within nations. The old patterns and processes of regional development that characterised the post-war period are being fundamentally redrawn, creating new problems of uneven development and new theoretical and policy challenges. Whatever interpretation of this contemporary transformation is adopted, regions and localities are back on the academic and political agenda. *Regional Policy and Development* is an international series which aims to provide authoritative analyses of this new regional political economy. It seeks to combine fresh theoretical insights with detailed empirical enquiry and constructive policy debate to produce a comprehensive set of conceptual, practical and topical studies in this field. The series is not intended as a collection of synthetic reviews, but rather as original contributions to understanding the processes, problems and policies of regional and local economic development in today's changing world.

Contents

List of Tables

List of Figures

Preface

This book represents the output of some of the papers presented to the European conference, 'Regional Futures: Past and Present, East and West', organized by the Regional Studies Association and held in Gothenburg, Sweden, in May 1995. The chapters in this book are based on the contributions related to one of the conference themes, namely regional development strategies, with case studies drawn from Europe and Asia.

The production of this book is very timely in the sense that regional development strategies have become the focus of attention in many countries. Within the European Union, for example, the European Commission's document, *Europe 2000+*, has discussed in some depth the objectives of its strategy for the development of its regions, and the instruments and policies of spatial planning in the Member States. The contributions in this book include those from both Eastern Europe as well as the EU, and the new directions of regional development planning in Japan to provide another international dimension on this subject.

The chapters have been arranged to provide both a conceptual and practice perspective of regional development strategies within a European context. Chapter 1 identifies and discusses some of the main themes associated with the preparation of regional development strategies, drawing upon the objectives of the European Commission which are contained in their document *Europe 2000+*. This is followed by two conceptual chapters, both by Swedish authors, which examine the notion of the term region and the meaningfulness of such a spatial level for purposes of administration and government. The case studies have been selected to illustrate a wide variety of different approaches and practices of regional development strategies. Chapters 4–7 present four UK case studies, covering Merseyside, the English regions, and Wales; and Chapters 8–13 look at the experience of six other European countries, including Ireland, Germany, Belgium, Sweden, Finland, and Central and Eastern Europe. There are clearly a number of exciting developments taking place in Central and Eastern Europe on regional development, as well as in the EU itself. Chapter 14 presents experience of regional development planning in Japan, and likely future directions for policy. The Japanese experience is both interesting and relevant in the sense that, like many of the countries in Europe, Japan is a mature, advanced and modern economy which has had to address regional disparities of a very similar scale. This East and West perspective of regional development was very much part of the theme and title of the RSA 1995 Gothenburg conference. Finally, the concluding chapter provides a comparative analysis of regional development strategies in Europe and a synthesis of the main

The renovated dockland area of Gothenburg, site of the Regional Studies conference from which this book grew

themes and conclusions which emerge from the individual chapters viewed as a whole.

The editors which to acknowledge the invaluable secretarial assistance provided by Adri Stoffaneller and the advice and input of Mark Tewdwr-Jones in the production of this volume.

CHAPTER 1

Regional Development Strategies in the European Union

Europe 2000+

Jeremy Alden

Regional Development Issues in the 1990s

This chapter seeks to provide a European context for considering both current progress and future potential of regional development strategies and policies being prepared by individual countries. In particular, the chapter examines in some detail the European Commission's most recent policy document on regional development, i.e. *Europe 2000+: Cooperation for European Territorial Development* (CEC 1994a). The (former) Commissioner for Regional Policy, in a foreword to the report, emphasized the basic theme of the document, namely that as the European Union (EU) prepares to enter the 21st century, growing interdependence between the regions which make up the EU (and the increased relations with other European countries) requires closer and more systematic cooperation over spatial planning across Europe as a whole.

Europe 2000+ (CEC 1994a) has stressed that there is a growing acceptance of the need for spatial planning at a European level among Member States, as well as in academic and professional circles. The European Parliament, the Economic and Social Committee, the Consultative Council of Regional and Local Authorities, and most recently the Committee of the Regions, have all emphasized the need for increased cooperation on spatial planning issues. The European Commission's (CEC 1994b) Fifth Periodic Report, *Competitiveness and Cohesion: Trends in Regions*, emphasizes how the 1990s have been a difficult period for reducing regional disparities because of the deep recession. The Treaty on European Union,[1] ratified

1 Since this Treaty, the European Community (EC) has become the European Union (EU). Many authors use these terms interchangeably. For example, the European Commission itself, in its May 1995 Press Statement on the new EC Regional Policy, refers to the Community as well as the Union. For the purposes of this book they are regarded as the same entity.

in 1993, confirmed that economic and social cohesion was one of the main objectives of the Union. The European Commission's report, *Europe at the Service of Regional Development* (CEC 1994c) identified the nature and increased scale of the EU Structural Funds. It also reminded Member States how the opening up of frontiers in 1993, following creation of a Single European Market (SEM), had posed a further problem for the most disadvantaged regions.

There was a risk that the SEM would be of most benefit to those regions best placed to attract capital and human resources. This is a major reason why the objective of economic and social cohesion, i.e. the need to reduce regional welfare disparities within the EU, was added to the Treaty of Rome in 1986 and so became an indispensable counterpart to the SEM of 1993. This resulted, in 1989, in a major reform of the EU Structural Funds and a considerable addition to their financial resources. Since Maastricht and the Treaty on European Union, interest has gone beyond just making the SEM work as well as possible within the context of economic and social cohesion, to focus on progress with wider economic and monetary union (EMU). The Structural Funds, which finance most of the EU's structural action, have been allocated 141.5 billion ECU for the period 1994–1999. This is a measure of the increased importance of regional development within the EU for the future.

The Structural Funds focus on the European Regional Development Fund (ERDF), established in 1975 to assist less-favoured regions and support productive investment, infrastructure and small and medium sized enterprise (SME) development; the European Social Fund (ESF) concentrates on vocational training and employment support; the European Agricultural Guidance and Guarantee Fund (EAGGF) promotes the adjustment of agricultural structures and rural development measures; and the Financial Instrument for Fisheries Guidance (FIFG), established in 1993, promotes structural measures in that sector. The purpose of the Cohesion Fund, established under the Maastricht Treaty to work in conjunction with these existing funds, is to prepare the way forward towards EMU for the Member States whose per capita gross domestic product (GDP) is under 90 per cent of the EU average (i.e. currently Greece, Portugal, Ireland and Spain). Some 15.5 billion ECU have been allocated for the Cohesion Fund for the period 1993–1999. Furthermore, under the financial mechanism of the European Economic Area (EEA), the four beneficiary countries of the Cohesion Fund receive solidarity grants from the main members of the European Free Trade Association (EFTA). Finally, the European Investment Bank (EIB), through its loans, also makes a significant contribution towards social and economic cohesion. In 1993, for example, it allocated more than 15 billion ECU for regional development projects. It is within this context of increasing political and financial support that member countries have seen the value of preparing regional development strategies as a means of gaining access to the substantial resources of the EU.

In order to reinforce economic and social cohesion, the EC has defined priority areas by means of five development Objectives for the 1994–1999 programming period, as follows: the four regional Objectives cover regions lagging behind in development (Objective 1), areas in industrial decline (Objective 2), the vulnerable rural zones (Objective 5b) and regions with a very low population density (Objective 6). To these are added Objectives covering all EU territory: Objective 3 (fight against long-term unemployment, youth unemployment and exclusion from the labour market), Objective 4 (preventative adaptation of the workforce to industrial and production systems changes) and Objective 5a (adjustment of agricultural structures and modernization of the fishing industry, within the framework of the Common Agricultural Policy). It can be seen, therefore, that the EU's Structural Funds have a very strong regional component, represented by the designation of Objectives 1, 2, 5b and 6 areas. This leaves Objectives 3, 4 and 5a not being specifically regional objectives, although they do have strong spatial associations due to the nature of their programmes.

The Main Objectives of *Europe 2000+*

As already mentioned, cooperation and funding on spatial planning has been growing in importance and extent. *Europe 2000+* has identified three types of option in terms of cooperation:

1. general options
2. transnational options
3. options for cooperation with neighbouring countries.

It is within the group of general options that the three main objectives of the European Commission's regional development strategy can be identified. These are: (a) the increased competitiveness of areas in an increasingly competitive global economy; (b) a move towards more sustainable economic development; and (c) the reduction of regional disparities and need for greater economic and social cohesion. This three-pronged regional development strategy, therefore, combines issues of both efficiency and equity between areas. However, there is clearly a tension and possible contradiction here between *competition* and *cohesion.* Greater competition implies winners and losers, and it seems inevitable that the European Commission will become more involved in identifying just where the winners and losers are located.

In seeking a more competitive European territory, the European Commission has emphasized the challenge of global competitiveness. This requires continuation and acceleration of the implementation of large-scale trans-European networks in transport, energy, telecommunications and information to exploit the opportunities of the SEM. However, *Europe 2000+* recognizes the risk which arises from the strengthening of the centre to the detriment of the periphery, the increased role of large cities compared to smaller ones, and the trend towards the concentration of decision-making, innovation potential and accumulated know-how in privileged areas.

Under Article 2 of the Maastricht Treaty, a primary objective of the EU is to achieve 'sustained and non-inflationary growth respecting the environment.' The model for sustainable development emphasizes the solidarity required over environmental issues on a transnational scale; the tendency towards excessive tourism in ecologically fragile or remote areas which calls for specific protection measures to preserve the natural heritage and landscape; and the integration of environmental considerations in the planning of urban areas, particularly in large conurbations and other large cities. The message here is quite clear, namely that regional development is more than just creating jobs and securing economic growth.

Economic and social cohesion, identified as one of the three main objectives in the Treaty on European Union,[2] implies action over the long term to reduce inequalities in income and disparities in development between regions. The experience of many Member States, including the United Kingdom (UK), has been that regional development policies are required over the long term to combat persistent regional disparities. The UK was amongst the first European countries to adopt an official regional policy in 1934 with the Special Areas Act. Some sixty years later, in the 1990s, regional policy legislation is still in place, admittedly to a lesser extent, to address issues of regional inequality and competitiveness.

Europe 2000+ has stressed that restoring spatial balance requires the implementation of specific transnational measures in four particular areas. These cover: (a) the development of cross-border cooperation (a phenomenon which has become a focus of attention in all regions of the world and particularly South East Asia on regional development issues); (b) the reduced isolation of peripheral regions; (c) ensuring the balanced development of the urban system; and (d) the preservation of rural areas. The Annex to *Europe 2000+* summarizes the results of the seven transnational studies which were undertaken as part of the *Europe 2000+* programme. These seven transnational study areas comprise the Centre Capitals, the Alpine Arc, the Continental Diagonal, the new German Länder, the Mediterranean, the Atlantic Arc and the North Sea regions.

The EU has developed into a dynamic and growing structure with increased opportunities for cooperation between Member States and neighbouring countries. In the mid-1980s, there were 10 Member States of the EU, which had grown to 12 by the end of the decade, and which have now expanded further to 15 from 1995 with the addition of Finland, Sweden and Austria. Both Norway and Iceland were incorporated into the SEM with the creation of the EEA. Figure 1.1 illustrates the map of Europe and the potential for further cooperation on territorial planning. The countries of Central and Eastern Europe have already begun a process of establishing closer ties with the EU (see Chapter 13), and cooperation or association agreements have been signed by eleven of them, covering Poland, Hungary, the Czech and Slovak Republics, Romania, Bulgaria, Albania, Slovenia and the three Baltic States. The countries of the Eastern and Southern Mediterranean share

2 The other two are the development of trans-European networks in transport, telecommunication and energy; and the protection of the environment (CEC 1994a, p.11).

many common features, particularly the rapid increase in population expected, estimated to be some 145 million by the year 2025, resulting in a large influx of young people into the labour market and posing a major challenge in terms of immigration for EU policy. *Europe 2000+* has put the average level of GDP per capita in these countries at some 26 per cent of the EU average in 1960 and 23 per cent in 1990.

Source: European Marketing Data and Statistics 1993

Figure 1.1 The European context

The main conclusion of *Europe 2000+* is that promoting a European regional development strategy, which seeks to address issues of both efficiency and equity in terms of spatial planning, requires several levels of regional cooperation within a European framework.

Factors Affecting Spatial Development in Europe

Europe 2000+ identified a number of factors which have affected spatial development in Europe and considered a number of spatial planning problems which have arisen from them.

First, trends in the spatial distribution of population and employment have had a marked impact on spatial development. The main population issues have included the growth of spatial disparities in terms of population change; the tendency for large cities to expand and population to move to the outskirts from the centre which has caused spatial and social imbalances; the shift of population to coastal areas and the process of suburbanization which are increasing pressures on open spaces and sensitive natural areas; the growth of particularly large corridors along which major cities and new emerging centres are located; the reversal of population decline in a large number of rural areas; and the small number of border areas losing population. Changes in the age structure of the population and mobility of the working population both have implications for the labour force and labour market. *Europe 2000+* is looking towards regional development strategies containing more cohesion between the location of jobs and the labour force, and achieving a better balance between the location of housing and jobs.

Second, considerable attention is devoted in *Europe 2000+* to the role of foreign direct investment (FDI) for regional development planning. The document includes an analysis of inward and outward investment flows, and the geographical effects of these flows in terms of the integration of Southern Europe and Ireland into the international economy, the strengthening of the role of large cities, and the uneven distribution of FDI and its effects as between regions. Between 1984 and 1991, FDI in the EU, including flows between Member States, averaged just under 1 per cent of EU GDP. Of this, some 45 per cent came from other countries, mainly the USA, Japan and EFTA countries, and 55 per cent was investment from one Member State to another. However, there have been marked differences in the importance of FDI for individual Member States. As might be expected, Germany, France, the Netherlands and Denmark invested more in other countries than they received, whilst Spain, Portugal, Greece and Ireland received considerably more than they invested elsewhere. Moreover, while the scale of FDI relative to GDP may be small for Member States, it is likely to continue to be important for particular regions and sectors.

The structure of FDI has undergone a major change in recent years, with a shift in emphasis from the industrial to the services sector. Through the 1950s, 1960s and 1970s, some of the peripheral countries and regions (e.g. Wales, Ireland and

Scotland) restructured their economies via manufacturing FDI. However, the 1980s saw the growth of FDI in services. Between 1984 and 1991, over 60 per cent of FDI into the EU from all sources was in service activities. FDI in the core regions of the EU is a higher proportion of the total than might be expected because: (a) there is a greater concentration of large cities in core regions conducive to the development of high level services; and (b) a central location has become an important factor for investment in company head offices (strategic planning) and distribution. *Europe 2000+* makes a valid distinction between the distribution of investment flows between countries and regions (the macro-spatial) and the distribution within countries and regions (the micro-spatial). In macro-spatial terms, FDI has contributed both to improving the economic situation in Southern Europe (especially in Spain and Portugal) and to accelerating the industrial restructuring of some older industrial regions (Wales, North of England, Nord-Pas-de-Calais, Lorraine) and has, therefore, assisted economic and social cohesion. At the micro-spatial level, however, FDI has often led to a widening of differentials due to the preference of investors for large cities or the most attractive areas. Finally on FDI, a comment is necessary on unit labour costs. Whilst the unit costs of production relative to elsewhere have been a determining factor in regional FDI, this is not always the case. Foreign investors often locate in regions with relatively high labour costs because of the greater importance of other factors, such as availability of qualified labour, good infrastructure or a high quality economic environment, all of which support high productivity.

A third factor affecting spatial development in Europe which is covered by *Europe 2000+* is the regional effect of trans-European networks. The creation of major infrastructure networks is seen by the European Commission as being one of the key methods for improving the competitiveness of the European economy. The achievement of greater spatial equity within the EU requires an equal choice in different areas for a wide range of infrastructure networks. This is currently far from the case, especially for many regions in the periphery of the EU, as illustrated by the lack of choice between different energy sources because of inadequate access to natural gas supplies in such areas. The two main lines of development associated with trans-European networks concern (a) the development of information and communication networks to accompany changes in systems of production, the organization of work, and patterns of consumption (a 'new European information society' is in the process of being developed), and (b) the construction of trans-European transport and energy networks aimed at strengthening the international competitiveness problem of avoiding over-concentration in the regions which already have an advantage in terms of infrastructure provision.

Fourth, the Treaty on European Union (Article 130 S) has specifically mentioned spatial planning for the first time as an important element in achieving a number of environmentally-related objectives. Two specific areas are identified in *Europe 2000+* to illustrate the important relationship between the environment and spatial planning and land-use planning, and between the pursuit of sustainable development and the concept of environmental networks. These two areas are focused on (a) the preservation of open spaces and (b) the protection of water reserves (groundwater, fresh-water lake and river systems, marine and coastal waters). As mentioned earlier in this chapter, it is important to recognize that regional planning must engage environmental issues as strongly as it does economic oncs.

Section B of *Europe 2000+* examined developments in specific areas, and in particular (a) urban areas (b) rural areas and (c) border areas. Most countries can cite examples of both urban and rural regions, and border regions have assumed increased significance in recent years alongside a new political map of Europe. The EU is the most urbanized region in the world. According to United Nations estimates, in 1992 some 79 per cent of the total population lived in urban areas as compared with 77 per cent in Japan, 76 per cent in the USA, 67 per cent in Central and Eastern Europe, and just 35 per cent in the developing countries. The European Commission's report notes the increased tendency towards the growth of large cities. There are a number of forces cited as favouring the growth of large cities. These include industrial restructuring with a move towards service sector activities, the growing internationalization of the economy, the increasing degree of competition, the rapid rate of technological and product development, and choosing locations which are the most efficient and not necessarily just least-cost. It is important to recognize that the most efficient locations will be those which can combine external economies and where these are at their greatest. These economies will include infrastructure, public services, education and training, a skilled labour force, and access to research and development facilities.

The United Nations, in its 1994 World Investment Report, has emphasized that *geography* still matters in terms of the location of international investment. Despite the operation of powerful forces which have created a higher degree of global integration of economic activities, technological developments in transport and communications have not removed the influence of space. The 1994 World Investment Report also noted that one of the most important recent developments in the international regulatory environment has been the strengthening of regional economic integration, most notably in Europe (as illustrated by the 1993 SEM and subsequent development of the EU).

Europe 2000+ also addressed one of the main topics of debate at the Regional Studies Association's 'Regional Futures' conference in Gothenburg (1995), namely social exclusion and spatial segregation in large cities. Social exclusion is a growing problem for many large cities in Europe, and the phenomenon is associated with high levels of long-term unemployment, widening income differentials, increasing disparities in education and skill levels and job security, concentrations of poor housing, and a rising crime rate. The European Commission analysed in some detail the features of social exclusion in five cities in different parts of the EU, i.e. Liverpool, Rotterdam, Frankfurt, Barcelona and Athens, and presented the findings in Part B of *Europe 2000+*. The document also concluded that given the tendency for economic, social and technological forces to favour the growth of large cities and conurbations to the possible detriment of smaller towns and cities, it was timely to consider a Europe-wide strategy for urban development. Such a strategy would include strengthening the local capacity for the planning and implementation of urban development strategies.

Europe 2000+ recognizes the need for regional development strategies to address the problems and prospects of its rural areas as well as its urban ones. In particular, one of the principal aims of programmes of rural development in Objective 5(b) areas is to diversify activities,[3] including agricultural activities. The document examines not only comparative advantages in agriculture but also potential comparative advantages outside the agricultural sector. Five kinds of potential comparative advantage of rural areas, other than in agriculture, are identified, which could enable them to diversify their economies. The five types of development include attraction for industry, tourism, leisure, residential housing for commuters, and housing for retired people. It is also acknowledged that these advantages are not mutually exclusive. This notion of comparative advantage for regions and localities in Europe, whether rural or urban, is an important one, emphasizing that areas must capitalize on their strengths, and that they all operate within a competitive global environment. The section of *Europe 2000+* on rural areas also includes an assessment of the support available for the less favoured rural areas, which at present do not have sufficient comparative advantages to preserve their populations.

The Institutional and Statutory Framework for Spatial Planning in the EU

Whilst Section A of *Europe 2000+* examines the main factors which determine the spatial distribution of economic, social and environmental activities, and Section B of the document considers developments in specific areas (most notably urban and rural areas), systems of spatial planning and the implementation of regional development strategies are discussed in Section C. The European Commission has undertaken a comprehensive study of the spatial planning systems and policies and the conditions for their implementation in all of the Member States. The second part of Section C examines the spatial impact of public finance and potential effects of a number of fiscal instruments on the distribution of income and resources between regions, which may contribute towards regional disparities in the EU.

Each Member State has developed its own institutional and statutory framework to manage, control and promote the development process at a variety of spatial levels. *Europe 2000+* contains a summary of the spatial planning systems in each of the 12 Member States as at the end of 1994. The main point here is that a rapidly changing European and international context for spatial planning will

3 For an analysis of the EU's rural policy in action see Chapter 8 on Ireland's LEADER programme.

require a responsive and effective planning system. *Europe 2000+* itself has noted that a number of major trends can be observed in all Member States, even though they tend to be stronger and more advanced in those with a long history of spatial planning.

The first major trend identified in *Europe 2000+* is the growing awareness that spatial planning has shifted from a concern for purely physical planning and land-use matters to a wider concern for social, economic, environmental and political issues. This is a return of the importance of strategic thinking in planning. The founding fathers of town planning, like Ebenezer Howard and his work on Garden Cities, had a vision for improving the economic and social conditions of towns, cities and regions, as well as their physical development. There has been a renaissance in the 1990s of the need for more strategic thinking in spatial planning, especially given the importance of cities and regions operating within both the EU and an even wider global economy, where strategic levels of decision-making assume significance.

A second trend in spatial planning examined in *Europe 2000+* has been the need not only to identify specific strategic planning issues, but also to integrate the various strategic issues into a more comprehensive and complex form of spatial planning. Planning at a variety of spatial levels is now concerned with a wider range of issues than hitherto, including economic development, transportation, retailing, tourism, housing, urban regeneration, waste management, water quality, the countryside, and nature protection, and their integration with each other.

Third, there has developed a wider recognition of the need to take account of market forces within the spatial planning process, notwithstanding the importance of public/private sector partnerships in the development process. The attraction of inward investment and a wider choice as regards location for many companies operating in a global economy has increased the need for spatial plans to respond more fully and readily to market circumstances and requirements. This is particularly the case in the EU with increased competition arising from the SEM.

A fourth trend examined by *Europe 2000+* has been the increased decentralization of responsibility for planning policies and controls to regional and local levels of government – Spain, Italy, Belgium and France are cited as examples of Member States which have recently established regional and local systems of spatial planning. The increased interest in urban and regional governance[4] may be seen as an integral component of the desire to achieve greater economic and social cohesion in the EU. There are a number of reasons to suggest that the momentum built up so far for more regional planning will be maintained and further advanced in the years ahead. These pressures within the UK context, for example, come from a variety of sources, including the following:

---

4 For a greater elaboration of the theoretical approaches to urban and regional governance see the introductory of Chapter 4.

1. Recent changes in the development plan system. The 1991 Planning and Compensation Act removed the need for structure plans to be approved by the Secretary of State, and made the statutory development plan the primary consideration when determining planning applications. These changes reflect a shift of decision-making power away from the centre towards local government. The main purpose of the new system of Regional Planning Guidance (RPG) is to provide a framework for these development plans, and local authorities must take account of RPG when preparing their plans. The UK may see RPG develop into statutory regional plans in the same way as county structure plans once operated.
2. Local government reform in both England and Wales requires a strategic view of planning issues at a regional level. Many investment decisions, related to issues such as transport, economic development, FDI and the environment, require determining at a regional rather than a local level, i.e. across local boundaries. In Wales, for example, from April 1996, the 8 county councils and 37 district councils will be replaced by 22 unitary local planning authorities, and there is a growing concern over their capability to make effective strategic decisions on issues which have wider spatial implications beyond their locality.
3. Recent central government reorganization in the UK has seen the creation of new Integrated Regional Offices (IROs) since April 1994. The formerly separate regional aims of departments of the Environment, Transport, Trade and Industry, and Employment now work and are housed together. There is also a Single Regeneration Budget (SRB) for government regeneration resources (see Chapter 6 for more detail).
4. There are also proposals being discussed for new forms of elected government in the regions of the UK alongside the current debate for stronger regional governance within the EU. The most radical scenario for the development of the current system of RPG lies with the possibility of a democratically-elected tier of government at regional level, i.e. regional government. Whilst the current Conservative government is opposed to elected regional assemblies, e.g. Welsh or Scottish assemblies, or for the English regions, the Labour Party has promised to create regional assemblies in Wales and Scotland if they win the next general election, which is likely to be held in 1997. The prospects for some form of regional government in Britain within an expanding EU have, therefore, never looked more promising.
5. Pressures from Europe have reinforced the importance of the regional dimension in governance. The EU programmes for supporting disadvantaged areas already by-pass nation states and operate at a regional level. Local authorities and central government are cooperating within regions to prepare bids to the EU. The new Committee of the Regions was

established within the EU in 1994, and the document *Europe 2000+* emphasizes the need for greater cooperation at regional level.

All these above developments in the institutional and statutory framework for planning in the UK will have important implications for local and regional development strategies in the UK. Similar developments are taking place in other Member States, as illustrated in the case studies contained in *Europe 2000+*.

The European Dimension in Planning Policies

Europe 2000+ identifies the emergence of a European dimension in planning policies. Reference is made to the practice that most Member States are now integrating transnational and cross-border aspects into their national planning policies. Some good examples of this practice are cited as being the Fourth Note of the Dutch Government; the Danish national planning strategy *Towards 2018*; and the German Raumordnungspolitische Orientierungstrahmen (see Chapter 12). These policy documents have all taken the European context as a major starting point for preparing their national spatial policies.

Another specific need is to mesh EU policies, both funding and legislation, into planning systems, and this trend, already evident in individual Member States, can be expected to continue. Of the major EU policies, the Structural Funds, the Cohesion Fund and the Common Agricultural Policy (CAP) each have widespread spatial effects. Each of these funds are mentioned in the following chapters of this book in relation to the individual country and regional case studies. Several Member States (including the Netherlands, Luxembourg, Portugal, the UK and Spain) identified the CAP as a key determinant of spatial planning. Changes in funding under CAP, or the other EU programmes, have important implications for particular regions and localities (urban as well as rural).

Major transport links are also identified in *Europe 2000+* as having a significant impact on spatial planning policies, particularly for high-speed rail and major road projects. A close integration between transport and land-use planning was identified by a number of Member States. For example, Spain's national infrastructure plan for the period 1993 to 2007, to which the Structural and Cohesion Funds are contributing substantial amounts of finance, provides the basis for consideration of major transport projects in spatial plans.

Likewise, a great deal of EU legislation has an impact on spatial planning. This is particularly the case with environmental legislation. It is noted, for example, that most Member States acknowledge that the Environmental Impact Assessment Directive has had a powerful impact on national legislation and policies, which has filtered down to local spatial planning policies.

Conclusions

This chapter has focused upon the current standing of regional development planning in Europe, and in particular on the preparation of regional development strategies in helping to achieve greater economic and social cohesion in the EU. The European Commission's most recent policy document on regional development and spatial planning is *Europe 2000+*. The document has emphasized the emergence of a European dimension in planning policies of Member States, an increasingly important regional dimension of European policies, and an enhanced role for regional development strategies in achieving the objectives of nations, regions and localities in an enlarged EU. The chapter has paid particular attention to the three main objectives of the European Commission's regional development strategy as contained in *Europe 2000+*. These have focused upon (a) increased competitiveness of areas in an increasingly competitive global economy; (b) a move towards more sustainable economic development; and (c) the reduction of regional disparities and need for greater economic and social cohesion.

Many of the issues identified in this chapter are discussed further in subsequent chapters of this book in relation to specific examples of regional development strategies in Member States. *Europe 2000+* has not only produced guidelines for cooperation on the content of regional development strategies, but has also examined the use and relevance of instruments and policies of spatial planning in Member States and those not (yet) members of the EU. This chapter has documented a number of reasons to suggest that the momentum built up so far for more regional planning and cooperation between regions (as well as competition) will be maintained and further advanced in the years ahead. The prospects for a more proactive role for regional development planning in the EU have never looked more promising.

References

Commission of the European Communities (CEC) (1994a) *Europe 2000+: Cooperation for European Territorial Development.* Luxembourg; Commission of the European Communities.

Commission of the European Communities (CEC) (1994b) 'Competitiveness and Cohesion: Trends in the Regions.' *Fifth Periodic Report on the Social and Economic Situation and Development of the Regions in the Community.* Luxembourg: Commission of the European Communities.

Commission of the European Communities (CEC) (1994c) *Europe at the Service of Regional Development.* Luxembourg: Commission of the European Communities.

Commission of the European Communities (CEC) (1995) *The new EC Regional Policy: Objectives, Means and Methods.* Brussels: Commission of the European Communities. May, pp.1–3.

European Marketing Data and Statistics (1993) London: Euromonitor PLC.

United Nations Conference on Trade and Development (1994) *World Investment Report.* New York and Geneva: United Nations.

CHAPTER 2

Theorizing and Conceptualizing Regions

The West Sweden Region – An Idea Searching for a (Re)Form

Christian Jensen and Svante Leijon

Introduction

This chapter is based on research by the authors into the change processes in public organizations in Sweden. A central issue of the research project has been the formation of a West Sweden region. The focus of this chapter is, therefore, the conceptualization of the term *region* and its operation in practice. A particular generalization concerning Swedish public organizations is that they are said to experience different kinds of identity crises with regard to intangible subjects, i.e. political legitimate issues, together with more tangible ones such as economy and efficiency. Running parallel to this has been the current recession in Sweden, comparable only with that of the 1930s, with its increased unemployment and decreased industrial investments. This alone has created a demand for change. When the world changes it moves from one category to another. The introduction and conclusion of such a change is fairly straightforward, but the intermediate period is incredibly difficult due to the fact that it is absolutely essential to include the past when considering the future.

Historically, the West Sweden region has been very dependent on industries concerned with the production of the various means of transport in which dramatic changes have taken place. There is, for example, no longer any large shipbuilding, and car production has also had its share of crisis. The Swedish public sector is now experiencing such a transition due its enormous budget deficit.

Various development processes have been initiated with a view to obtaining a new and sustainable industrial service structure. County and district councils together with local authorities are investigating those at present, often simultaneously as they have things in common. It is also obvious that these developments sever previous geographical boundaries. The main point is that a collective regional body would contribute to a much greater effectivity in the change process. A lot of work is duplicated and this could be avoided and development investments would then be much more effective through the accumulation of greater resources.

In examining the formation of a West Sweden region, it is possible to identify the different actors from the various levels of government, all having different motives, i.e. national, county or local government. They are all politically active in this region where they support horizontal cooperation on the one hand and private organizations' and interest groups' vertical cooperation on the other. It is said that this region will solve problems for the public as well as the private sector, thus making the region competitive, attractive and well known throughout Europe.

The idea of a region is viewed as being purely strategic by many actors. According to Pettigrew (1987) this strategic management includes three overlapping activities. The first is to identify the problem and devise a strategy, i.e. its content. The second is to consider how the strategy can be realized, i.e. the process. Finally, one should also take into account the connection, i.e. the context in which the process progresses. A short description is given above of the content of the regional strategy – to increase coordination of investment resources – although this chapter will have its focus on the argumentative processes that the idea of a West Sweden region gives rise to. These processes have gained increased attention and different organization researchers (Nelson, Megill and McCloskey 1987) have pointed out the importance of language in being able to understand and influence that which occurs. The primary interest, therefore, is to understand how different actors comprehend their situation and connected actions in relation to the general idea of a region. Figure 2.1 illustrates the county boundaries within Sweden, and Table 2.1 provides an overview of the national, regional and local levels of government and administration.

One of the overriding questions in organization theory is: what knowledge is required to manage large, often loosely coupled, social systems operating in turbulent, complex environments in which change is characterized by major discontinuities? The phenomenon that is studied is the creation of a region and the process of transposing a form into a reform to transpose the concept of a region, whatever that might be, into accepting an idea of change and action that the major part of the institution(s) (audience) can agree upon.

The situation is defined as rhetorical, a concept that has been borrowed from Burke (1973). The situation is seen as a social context of persons, events, objects, relations, and an exigence which strongly invites utterance. This invited utterance participates naturally in the situation and is, in many instances, necessary to the completion of the situational activity. Furthermore, they obtain their meaning and rhetorical character by means of their participation in the situation.

The purpose of this chapter is to describe the different actors' arguments about the concept of a region and its intended function in the future. Studies have shown that most of the outcome of the process was determined in the *unfreezing* phase which was a latter process and merely confirmed that which was created as truth

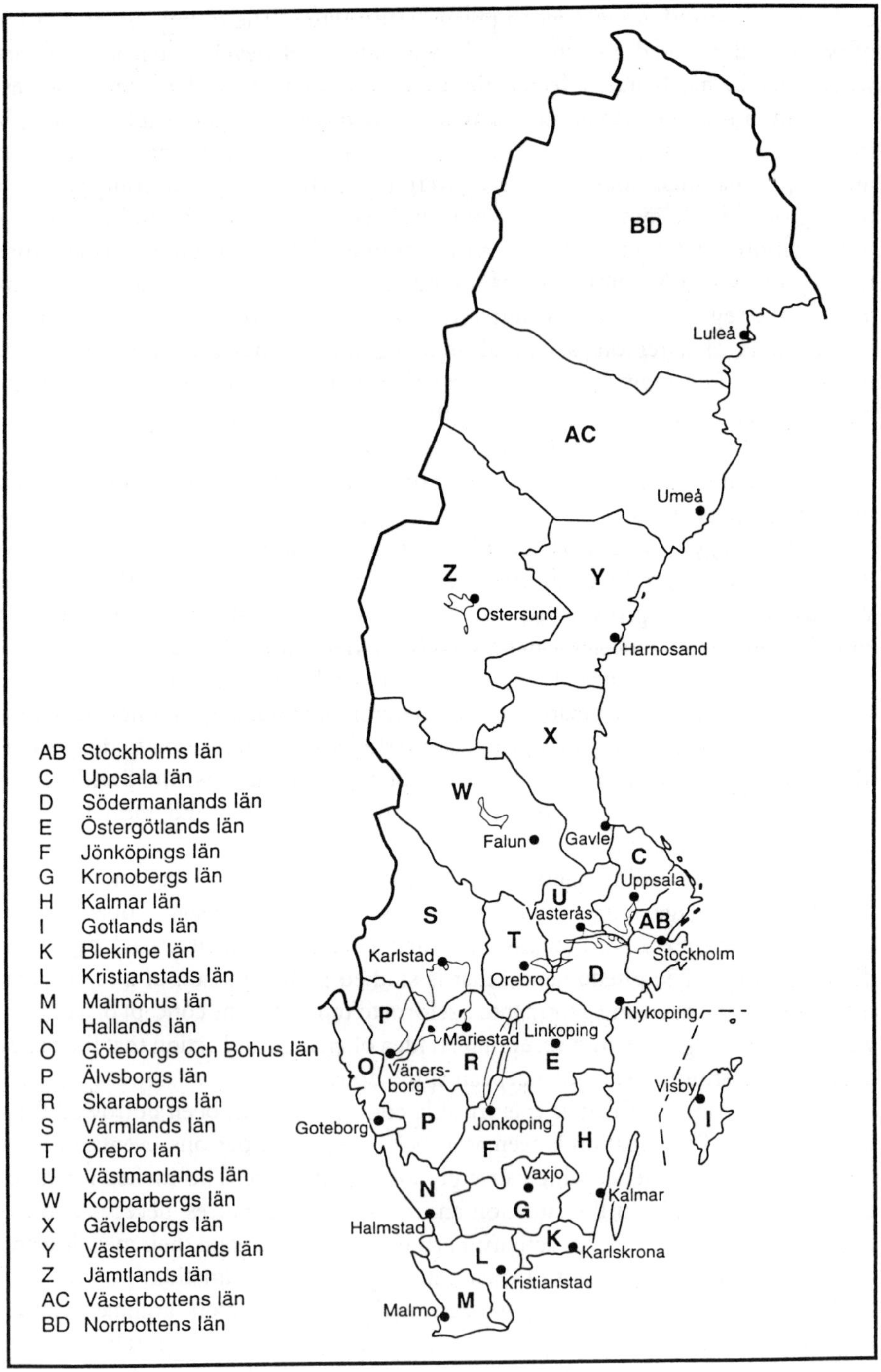

Source: *Statistical Yearbook of Sweden* 1995, p.8

Figure 2.1 The counties and provincial capitals of southern Sweden

Table 2.1 Sweden's political-administrative system

Level	*State*	*County Council*	*Local Authority*
National	Riksdag Government Department	Federation of Swedish County Councils[1]	Association of Swedish Local Authorities[2]
Regional	County Governor	County Council	Local Authority in County
	County Administrative Board[3]	Delegate	
	County Committees	Board	Board
Local	Local Offices, i.e. Committees	Health Care	Local Authority Delegates
	Employment Office (Job Centre)		Boards' Committees

1 Henceforth referred to as the Federation
2 Henceforth referred to as the Association
3 Henceforth referred to as the Board
Source: Compiled by the authors

during the *freezing* phase (see, for example, Flyvbjerg 1991). The tension surrounding organizational change provides us with insights into organizational politics. The authors believe that it is possible to contribute to a greater understanding of organizing inter-organizational reforms, whatever the final decision might be.

Frame of Reference

The first idea that springs to mind when one sees the word *region* is that of a geographically limited area. There are, for example, maps of Europe in which it is divided into a number of regions. Regions, rather than nations, are in many ways understood to be more homogenous units, e.g. for characterizing development possibilities. Densely populated regions within different countries have, for example, greater similarities between them than sparsely populated areas in their own countries.

Thus the important question is: how can a region's natural resources, in the form of population, present commerce and industry, etc., be taken into account in a more effective way by adapting the political organization? Counties, county councils and local authorities' boundaries, and even national ones, can hinder a region's development due to there not being any body/formal organization that can take into account the region's development potential in a unified manner.

It is probably inevitable that at some point in time boundaries will need to be revised especially with regard to, for example, technical development. People are now able to travel over greater distances due to faster communications. A more specialized economic structure combined with that of a highly specialized workforce would cause people to move over greater areas both as producers and consumers. Transformations caused by different material forces make previous boundaries inadequate and stimulate the formation of new ones.

This new formation of a region with an autonomous political structure can be seen to be a much more complicated process than merely adjusting to new material conditions. It is a question of a social process with actors confined by different institutional frameworks. In order to understand the formation it is also necessary to have a frame of reference based on politics as rhetoric and institutional theory.

Parallel with this creation of theory, it appears necessary to include coverage of institutional theory, i.e. how norms are created and recreated within social organizations together with the theory of how organizations are reformed and in this particular case how the concept *region* is organized administratively. The latter theoretic focus leads the way to political theory as seen from a rhetoric perspective.

Rhetorical and Political Action

The crucial first principle is as follows. All intellection is a form of political action (Bernstein 1983; Taylor 1979) and the consequence of this is that all intellection is a form of rhetorical activity. Rhetoric, in turn, is the action of discourse saturated with figures. Figures then constitute the discursive action of political intention.

In classical times, rhetoric occupied a place of prominence in the intellectual realm. Aristotle (1991) defined rhetoric as the faculty of discovery, in the given case, the available means of persuasion. This definition benchmarked an art ranging from the selection of evidence and arguments to the effectiveness of delivery. It made rhetoric a practical art whose proper domain was decision-making under conditions of uncertainty. In particular, Aristotle (1991) regarded rhetoric as the means of deciding public questions determining the right action in the world of practical affairs. It is the knowledge that touches the truth and possibility as opposed to the certain and necessary. Aristotle (1991) is one of the first thinkers to recognize the existence of plural final goods, and therefore to find a need for rhetorical argument to negotiate the practical problems set by this plurality, and that a particular course of action is right is an understanding that can be abandoned with reference to new facts or better suggestions and arguments.

Practical problems of discussion, where it is not possible to ignore the decided content and external conditions and, in addition, are not decided on the particular train of thought to follow due to the non-existence of routines, are resolved by means of argument. Rhetorical argumentation, or enthymeme, differs in two ways from syllogism. In the first place it is characterized by the suppression of premises whose contribution to the argument is in some way obvious and which would be pedantic to include in a speech or text, and these are often held by the audience. The second is that while the syllogisms of logic are directed towards the production of conclusions being indubitably true as premises, the enthymemes of rhetoric are characteristically derived from premises which are true for the most part and inevitably tend to produce conclusions of the same status (Vickers 1988). The 'truth' is in some sense related to the situation.

It should be possible to acknowledge a viewpoint that is commonplace but fundamental in order to clarify rhetoric as essentially related to the situation. Rhetoric is a mode of altering reality, not by direct application of energy to objects, but by the creation of discourse which changes reality through the mediation of thought and action. The rhetor alters reality by bringing in existence a discourse of such a character that the audience, in thought and action, is so engaged that it becomes the mediator of change. Rhetoric is therefore pragmatic; it comes into existence for the sake of something beyond itself. It ultimately functions to produce action or change in the world.

Rhetoric, as mentioned above, is a means of decision-making under conditions of uncertainty, and where you believe that things can be otherwise through discursive action, that situations ought to be other than they are. So rhetoric has its application-area between what is and ought to be or in what ought to be but yet is not. This intersection may be defined as a *rhetorical situation*, a concept which is borrowed from Burke (1973).

Rhetoric has a reputation it does not deserve. Rhetoric is usually understood to be the art of public speaking (oratory) and eloquence where one should represent actual ideas by convincing words. Rhetoric is therefore connected with the concealment of an actual message behind a veil of eloquence.[1] But persuasion does not necessarily mean the manipulation of others through the creation of images. Persuasion could just as well mean a free and open debate where the participants, in mutual understanding, try to clarify and refine the different opinions (Vickers 1988). Thus the discussion inevitably becomes politically active; which in turn presupposes the existence of a public place within which the actors can meet others, thus revealing their identity.

The authors do not believe that the language of politics is a neutral medium that conveys ideas independently formed. This is the interaction between rhetorical action and the use of political language. Politics are an institutionalized structure of meanings that channel political thought and action in certain directions. Thus a more applicable theoretical inspiration or perspective is institutional theory.

Institutional Theory

Institutional theory is a school of thought in whose interest it is to show the repertoire of various norms that occur within a society, organization or group. Its

1 It is the word convince and not persuade, that is in agreement with the meaning of rhetoric in the above paragraph. Nelson, Megil and McCloskey (1987, p.6) write about the nuances between conviction and persuasion. The authors say that authoritarian rhetoric of compelling proof and convincing demonstration usurp the office of sweet reason. *Convincere* means to defeat thoroughly, but *suavis* is the Latin for sweet.

origin is that man functions in an environment the complexity of which is difficult to appraise. The way in which this complexity is dealt with is that man, together with others, develops norms and values that have a durability. This is part of the history in which the individual and the organization act and which is, therefore, difficult to ignore (Berger and Luckmann 1967; Powell and DiMaggio 1991; Selznick 1957). Institutionalized norms are current in organizations and situations where the actual effectivity meant in the sense of the use of resources in order to reach a specific goal is not enough or perhaps does not even exist as a guidance of action. Such norms reflect the collective understanding of the operation's basic aim, its distinctive competence and organizational integrity. The institutionalized action is meant to show how the organizations' work should be performed, thus acting while anticipating the future. Friedland and Alford (1991, p.243) give the following definition of an institution that is conducive to the authors' perspective and very much agrees with how different actor-groups act in relation to the concept of region:

> Simultaneously material and ideal, systems of signs and symbols, rational and transrational...supra-organizational patterns of human activity by which individuals and organizations produce and reproduce their material subsistence and organize time and space...[t]hey are also symbolic systems, ways of ordering reality, and thereby rendering experience of time and space meaningful.

Structure, rules and regulations, as examples of institutionalized activities, are viewed as rational instruments in performing a specific task. A political view of these arrangements, however, suggests that they are better understood as products and reflections of political control.

The concept of institution describes the continuity, but connected to continuity is also change. De-institutionalize and re-institutionalize are two concepts that describe that which happens on both sides of continuity (Oliver 1992). In this regional case it is possible to see the need for change in public organizations as de-institutionalized components and an answer as well as a solution in Sweden's case a region and this will then be the re-institutionalized form. This simple model catches important ingredients in the demand for new organizational forms and reforms, but nevertheless, it gives us a few guidelines as to the direction future re-institution might take. A rhetorical analysis in this instance might give us some answers.

A theoretical summing up and working model for this chapter involves a double focus. First, a linguistic argument describing the proposed organization form for the future alongside a study of the growth and process of new organizational forms, thereby obtaining a more suitable way of dealing with the problems the actors and institutions are experiencing at present or able to foresee within the near future. It is now appropriate, in this connection, to clarify the method to be used in this chapter.

Method

Traditionally, it has been easy for social scientists, politicians and others to reform organizations within modern societies, the process and outcome being supposedly predictable. The conclusion of this discussion, so far, is that there has been a keen debate on the subject where almost all groups concerned have taken part. But apart from this debate no real effort has been made to do anything. Thus, when taking a closer look at the formation of an idea it becomes apparent that the direction is unclear: the only certainty is continuing uncertainty.

Attempts to predict the future often encounter certain tendencies, which in themselves can be clearly formulated, but which people are unable to decide what to do with. Reforming public organizations has, during the past two decades, been accompanied by thoughts about rationality, large-scale production, decentralization, cooperation and competition – development tendencies that, at least on the surface, appear to be incompatible. Despite this impossibility, practice has shown that 'opposite' tendencies can paradoxically continue to work on a parallel. The future does not allow itself to be described as a course where everything is derived from just one beginning. The social reality contains much that can be derived but much more that cannot. Nothing is completely predictable and is in other words seldom that which it was thought to be.

> When we think about the future of the world, we always have in mind its being at the place it would be if it continued to move as we see it moving now. We do not realize that it moves not in a straight line, but in a curve, and that its direction constantly changes. (Wittgenstein 1975, p.10)

On an organizational level – the level where visions materialize and ideas become practice and also where formal politics become current politics – will surely become difficult with the 'muddling through' still being implemented. Here it is the privilege of the formulation of the problem that, to a large extent, decides the context, institutional connection and institutional myths and stories.

It is difficult to predict how the discussion concerning regionalization will develop using present knowledge. There are methods of predicting the path of a projectile and there are trustworthy methods of approximately predicting the result of a parliamentary election, but there is no foolproof way of predicting social development. The popping up of the unexpected is also connected with the difficulties of prognosis and trends. People, events and inventions can change the course of events with their unexpectedness. In this chapter this is referred to as a rhetoric situation.

The material has been collected from official investigations and from interview material with representatives for local authorities, county councils, county administrative boards, the Association, the Federation and representatives of the regional council together with documents collected from actors in West Sweden.

A way of understanding language in an interpretative sense is through the ancient discipline of rhetoric as discussed above. Linguistic data, e.g. interviews, are used extensively in research. But there has been a tendency to believe that the social content of such data can be read without attention being paid to the language itself (Mishler 1986). The tendency is to see language as transparent.

One should not isolate language from social science and reality (Winch 1958; Wittgenstein 1951). A good starting point for an interpretative idea is to see language as multi functional and as language games, e.g. to see texts as simultaneously representing reality, enacting social relations and establishing identities. A specific function is due to the situation or the context. Applying this view of language, it is necessary to reject the idea of the decoupling of action from language and, instead, accept some notion of social being and social identity as being incorporated into each and every knowledge statement about action, agency, and behaviour.

Region – A Way of Discussing General Administrative Problems?

This chapter will present the discussion about the strategy of the West Sweden region that took place between the various actors. The presentation will be in summary form due to limited space but the intention is to highlight the argument of the various representatives. A more extensive exposition is given by Jensen (1995). The discussion will begin with a picture of how the Government Commission of Inquiry (GCI) has dealt with the question of regional coordination. It is the voice of the government that is used in the discussion and will be followed by a presentation of the different voices in the form of arguments for and against the aspiration to organize themselves according to the proposal of a new regional division. Therefore, the next section will make interpretations of the rhetoric processes that have begun due to certain questions being presented in a reformational agenda.

Regional discussion at national level

The question of regions is by no means new in the debate about how public administrations should be organized. During the 1960s investigations were initiated with the aim of investigating the regional structure (SOU 1968:47). The structure dealt mainly with the split in the division of responsibility between the various groups affected together with a geographic division which caused problems in certain parts of Sweden. Since the 1960s this structural problem has been increased and supplemented, e.g. social conditions in the form of housing and work areas are not in agreement with the public organizations' administrative limits. The 1980s brought renewal of the public sector towards a more effective planning of resources. Finally, the 1990s experienced an increased international dependence on, for instance, the European Union's (EU's) Regional Development Funds – thus supposedly increasing the need, it is thought, for coordination between the various sectors and levels of public organizations.

In 1990 a letter was sent to the government on behalf of the Association and the Federation where they requested a collective overview of the public administration's regional development and this was the reason why this particular subject once again appeared on the agendas of these two organizations. The government's reply was to appoint a special commissioner this is referred to as a one-man enquiry for the purpose of producing a perspective study. It was referred to as a regional investigation but the question concerning regions had, as stated above, been approached and looked at in a series of investigations, i.e. County Democratic Committee, SOU (1982:24), and the Municipal Investigation, SOU (1990:36).

The commissioner's results and analysis were presented in 1992 (SOU 1992:63: *Regional Roles – a perspective study*). Various lines of development were given:

1. Government regional development means that the state is responsible for questions of regional development, thus implying that the Board's role as coordinating body is increased.
2. Thus according to the above suggestion this means that, with local authorities working in coordination, the responsibility for regional questions will be passed on to the local government administration. County councils will be redundant but the present role of the county administration board will remain.
3. This final suggestion means that a new regional administrative body should be created. The present county council would be disbanded although it will be simultaneously strengthened due to its being the model on which the regional body is based. This new public authority will use information taken primarily from the Board's data, and the sole function of the Board will be that of a public authority. The local authorities will remain intact.

A separate investigation of West Sweden (SOU 1992:66: *West Sweden – a developing region*) was delivered in connection with the main investigation. The report confirms the first step towards a regional parliament in line with that of the local government administration. It even discusses a long-term amalgamation of the four counties thus making them into one. This suggestion would mean that the more than 300-year-old county division is changed. The Board's responsibility for questions of regional development would be transferred to the proposed regional parliament. This will, according to the investigator, ease the management of future questions as regards development of West Sweden, especially in connection with economic development, communications, higher education and research, the environment, culture, marketing and international cooperation. The proposal has a definite common denominator which is contained in the commissioner's third suggestion, i.e. regional autonomy.

The Conservative government allowed the work of the investigation to continue but in the form of a parliamentary group with representatives from all of the national political parties as well as other interest groups. The GCI's work was presented in June of 1994 but this has since been pushed forward in six-monthly intervals. It seems likely that the GCI will suggest *region-by-trial* where those affected think that the conditions are right.

A representative for the national perspective, who has been a member of the committee for a number of years, describes the regional discussion thus:

> ...the question of regional growth has received another angle since the 1960s, owing to such things, as a declining state economy, increased international dependence and Swedish membership of the European Community. The discussion however, being maintained by the same actors who have a strikingly similar argumentation through the years. (Interview with representative of the Swedish Ministry for Public Administration 2.12.94)

The discussion of region at a regional and local level

This section will focus on how the suggested proposal for West Sweden was received by the various actors in West Sweden together with other interested parties. Here a division is made, partly concerning the understanding about the problem of identification with the present regional organizations and their division, together with the initiating of the West Sweden investigation's (SOU 1992:66: *West Sweden – a developing region*) suggestion of the creation of a regional parliament as a first step towards a future regional local government administration or an elected regional parliament.

WHAT IS THE PROBLEM?

On the whole, the representatives of the local authorities, county councils, the Boards, commerce and industry as well as the various political groups think that there are a few problems in respect of the present division of responsibility and work between central, regional and local levels. A few think that the problem is at a more central level while others thought it to be regional. This is a short presentation of the problems as seen by the various representatives.

Local authorities in the various counties, the local authorities of the county and the Association in West Sweden think that the present county borders are an obstacle to cooperation and the possibility of coming to a definite decision. It is especially noticeable within infrastructural investments in the region. There is also the lack of a mutual authority for West Sweden in questions dealing with commercial development.

County councils in the region share the investigative description of the problems concerning the present West Sweden county divisions as being counteractive to the decision-making processes that strengthen the region as a whole. The county council think that there is the lack of a comprehensive view. The present day situation highlights sector politics, i.e. that a great many sectoral decisions are made without coordination. This benefits the various actors' institutional power because coordination is made difficult in practice.

The four Boards of West Sweden think that the investigation has over-emphasized that the present division alone can be the reason for the problem at a regional level (SOU 1993:97). It must certainly be said that there is a lack of coordination within the region together with an ability to appear to be publicly in agreement. However, this is not reason enough to set an extensive reform in motion, especially as this authority would not be able to exercise a control function in respect to commerce which is one of the most important reasons among the reformists. The Board for Göteborg and Bohus are very much aware of the need and usefulness of a reformation of its borders with Älvsborgs county. They emphasize two arguments in particular for a change in the borders (Dnr 100–1854–92:2):

> In the first place, internationalization and the change in the economic structure which places new quality demands on the infrastructure and requires a particular size for the region in order that it should be able to contain enough competitive power from a Economic Community perspective. And, in the second, the need for effectivity and saving which places a demand on the government on the occasion of extensive reorganizations to review their own administrative divisions. Therefore, as a rule one chooses one's area of activity so that it is greater than that which one has at present.

There is a difference of opinion between and within the various political parties in the above named regions. Most of the political parties' county and local organizations feel that the present county borders are old-fashioned but there are differences between the various parties. Political representatives from Halland and Skaraborg do not agree that the problem of the county borders is the final obstacle for a positive development of the region.

Even actors not belonging to any of the main public institutions still have influence on the course of the reform in specific ways. Commerce in the form of the various Chambers of Commerce participates in the debate about the administrative responsibility at regional level (Andersson and Andersson 1993). The present geographic division made by the authorities is not adequate for the demands that will be made on trade and commerce due to increased international competition. The West Sweden Chamber of Commerce appealed for an improved regional organization that is able to meet the strong infrastructural concentration, i.e. roads as well as education, and work officially for the proposed region thus contributing to the marketing of the region as a whole.

In summarizing this first section it is evident that, in principle, all actors and institutions agree that something has to be done about organizing matters concerning issues which are at present handled at a regional level.

SUGGESTED SOLUTION: THE CREATION OF A REGIONAL PARLIAMENT?

The West Sweden investigation (SOU 1992:66) suggested the creation of a regional parliament. Certain state information is transferred from the Board to a regional parliament, thus making it responsible for questions of regional development. The regional parliament will be seen as a temporary solution due to the investigator being of the opinion that in the future there will be an autonomously elected West Sweden region. The regional parliament suggestion had been included in the GCI report (SOU 1993:97).

The Association is completely against a regional amalgamation, as extended it would become a regional parliament. This would weaken the local authority control, as the regional directives and control would be experienced as domination with the current solution during present conditions. Swedish local authorities are fewer in number although greater in size compared with the local authorities of other countries. This makes the role and importance of the local authority of great importance in Sweden. It is for this reason that the Association believes that there is no scope or work for a new authority between central and local level. They are therefore launching their suggestion about the cooperation of local authorities as an answer to the need for regional coordination (Eriksson 1994). They fear that if a regional parliament is established it will lessen the local authority actors' negotiatory space due to its ability to exercise control over limited resources providing an important source of power between institutions.

Despite this, the local authorities in West Sweden are not negative to a regional parliament being established although this should be in the form of an authority that is publicly able to mobilize the picture of a well coordinated region.[2] There are a number of local authorities in Halland and Skaraborg that are submitting reservations to the proposed solution, probably because they wish to await future investigatory suggestions GCI's and HSU 2000[3] – or with reference to not wishing to prevent further cooperation with representatives outside the proposed region with whom they at present have a number of exchanges.

Local authorities in West Sweden fear that Göteborg as a local authority, and the only municipality in the region, would dominate the development stakes and this is why the peripheral local authorities in West Sweden wish to diminish the influence of Göteborg in connection with questions of regional development. This refers to a quarrel that has existed for a long time in West Sweden between Göteborg and the surrounding local authorities.

Both the local authorities and the Association wish to project local authority autonomy as a vital starting point to the way in which a local coordinating organization should be organized. Local authority autonomy enjoys wide agreement with a bottom-up perspective and principles that are accepted in the debate about how social organizations should be organized.

The Federation has for many years been subject to criticism and views a regional parliament as a new and more attractive role. It therefore supports the proposal

2 A curious feature of the debate surrounding regionalization which should not be underestimated is that it is suggested that a flag should be created for West Sweden. Its function being symbolic for the existence of a region.

3 Reference is made to the extensive health service investigation (HSO 2000) and some argue that they wish to wait for its answer as to see what the future of the health service organization (administrated by the County Council) will look like.

concerning the establishment of a regional amalgamation, and the transformation of the county administrative board's work into an exercise of authority. Although Halland County Council is deferring a decision, this is mainly because they wish to have connections with the county councils in Southern Sweden. Although the Conservative Party is against another formal and elected level being established there are individual Conservative politicians that are in favour of the idea.

As far as the county councils are concerned regions are not responsible for the organization of the health service but are more concerned with the conditions to be found in creating growth in the economy. A regional parliament would provide the arena or social body that keeps the region together and gives the possibility of working in a more decided fashion in relation to other regions and centres within Nordic countries and Europe. The county councils do not feel that there is anyone today who addresses this issue in a purposeful and vigorous way, neither the Boards nor the coordinating local authorities.

The Federation states that various local authority cooperation constellations dealing with vital social questions are not enough. There is a risk that each question will be dealt with individually, each local authority caring for its own and where, according to the county councils, experience has shown that there will be certain questions that no-one will deal with due to the voluntariness of the situation as well as agreements of coordination often including a veto-reservation. But this does not mean that an eventually elected regional authority would control a local authority while simultaneously decreasing its negotiating space. The county council is careful to emphasize this point so that it does prove to be the case (Landstingsförbundet 1994). The county councils will be dealing with tasks received from the Board.

The subsidiary principle that is to be found as a directive given by the government to GCI also refers to this. The government should have more faith in actual regional competence that is closely connected with the conditions of each individual region.

A representative for the Federation stated that 'the county councils have the wind in their sails'. The work that GCI is doing is said to be in line with that of the Federation, and the proposed trial authority with elected decision-making assemblies is now being put together and will be a good beginning to a strong regional concept and it is the county council organizations' institutional future that will certainly be different to the present formation.

The Boards in West Sweden certainly think that there is a need for change but do not believe that a regional authority is necessary or can be established. The conditions for a lot of counties being amalgamated into a multi-county do not exist. The most that can be said is that a few counties will increase cooperation in order to reduce the county limits in the long term. The reason that they do not feel that a change in the direction of a regional parliament exists is found in an identity-creating discourse, i.e. the various counties have differing conditions, they are different with regard to ethnographic factors such as economic structure, history and local identity. This evaluation is often made from a practical understanding of how one conceives the past together with the present.

The difficulty with change is said to depend on the tension to be found between central authorities, civil service departments and public utilities on the one hand and the County Administrative Board on the other. Government utilities and authorities at a regional level have long since been used as an alternative division criterion to counties. The drawing of borders is occasionally in agreement with the county but most often not.

The Board thinks that on the whole they would rather have good experiences of coordination which can then be the criteria for future discussions about change instead of the establishment of a new level within public administration.[4] They believe that the competence disputes between the Board and the respective regional authority can be predicted and that there are no economic bases for the establishment of yet another administrative level. The Board for Göteborg and Bohus still think that there are reasons to review the boundaries with Älvsborg including the concept of a union in the event that the three county councils are united. They suggest administrative coordination between themselves and the reformed county councils' administrative organizations.

There is a consensus between the Federation and the county councils on the one hand and the various Chambers of Commerce on the other. They are appealing for cooperation with a vigorous social partner (Andersson and Andersson 1993). They therefore wish to create a regional parliament that is made up of representatives elected in a general election. The Chambers of Commerce would rather have a parliamentary order.[5]

In conclusion it can be said that the investigatory proposal (SOU 1992: 63, 66; 1993:97) concerning a regional parliament has its basis within the rational-economic and administrative-political frames of reference, and is subject to varying types of queries. These are to a certain extent based upon the conditions contained in the official description but are subsequently given a more situation-specific relevance the effect that the proposal will have on one's own institution and also those that have their bases in other arguments than those referred to above. An example of the latter are historic experiences, culturally and socially based, together with ethnographically oriented arguments. The focus, in this instance, is on the identity of one's own institution.

4 Parallel with the County Administrative Boards efforts for status quo they are also making efforts for the creation of regions to EU's goal-areas for regional politics. External and internal legitimization is, in other words, disconnected, which is not unusual in an organization with many interested parties (Meyer and Rowan 1977).

5 The Federation of County Councils has become involved in the debate about federal forms of social planning (Gidlund 1993), without taking sides for a federation in the same way as the Chambers of Commerce. But it might would bet to much to ask of an institution that is incorporated in the present system. In other words it is easier for the actors who are not part of the present order to suggest radical solutions.

Arguably, these differing comments give a picture of the fact that each institution's argument has its own starting point. One example of this is the answer from the Association to the Federation argument about the fact that in Europe regionalization is taking place at present inadvertently defining the Federation's expectations. But the Association maintains that the European regions' responsibilities are, to a great extent, in line with the Swedish local authorities which indicate a coordination of local authorities. The Association also use the argument contained in the subsidiary principle, i.e. why should the responsibility of the task be placed at a regional and not a local level? This example shows the difficulty in judging the truthfulness of the different statements and arguments.

It has been shown that different actors use different stories about the region and the need to create one. This is done by means of *stories*. Institutions together with actors organize information, transmit understanding and guide judgement. Stories enable the actors to translate impressions of a distant event into a form that allows a listener to grasp the significance. The story is shown by the relatively small number of facts needed to transmit an adequate impression of most events. It provides the framework in which different events are interpreted and the subsequent action taken.

'You Can't See a Region, Because it is an Interpretation of Events'

The previous section described both the picture and arguments used by the government in their investigations that have led to discussions about the ways in which a new regional level can or cannot be established. How different institutional actors meet and translate these thoughts from the specific characteristics that each institute has is a condition of being called an institution. In the general description of the problem it has been seen how the majority think that both the division of work and responsibility is unclear between the different institutions and social levels. There is also a tendency to see this in a – for the individual institution – wider perspective which implies that the discussion includes a dimension that new geographic boundaries would be suitable in dealing with social organization. This would mean, if the ideas of a region were realized, that most of the social institutions would be changed in one way or another.

The purpose of this section is to show how the concept of region functions as a positive myth of alliance and the way in which this has occurred. This will be done primarily by means of a linguistic-rhetoristic focus on the discourse, and where the participants are not individuals but institutions. This insight will be used in the final section in order to provide a particular insight into its importance to the change process.

This analysis has been entitled: 'You can't see a region. Because it is an interpretation of events'. This means that in order to understand the process one must realize that it is not the objective and structural circumstances that make us a region but the interpretations of impressions and events. When using interpretation it is possible to explain why changes of this type can be seen as political processes and how one as an actor and man-about-town cannot ignore them.

The government as well as the county council and local authorities identify the need for new organizational forms when dealing with certain types of new concepts for society and its development. As there are words for describing that which is divided, so there are words for cooperation. The exigence in this case is the complete idea of a region. The situation is an imperfection marked by urgency, that something is waiting to be done, a thing that is other than it should be. But there is more than one option to a solution.

An interpretation can be described as a relationship between constructs and experience. Individuals see and register as experience only that which their constructs, theories and institutionalized norms make available to them. And individuals come to understand constructs only if some experience has provided a basis of meaning. Therefore there is a mutual relationship between constructs and experience.

Just as things are put together and taken apart, so there are words that put things together and words that take things apart. The term 'region' belongs to the former. Even if different actors do not fully agree on what ingredients, policies, strategies and organizational forms constitute a region, it is interesting to note how things more or less follow on by themselves, once the title gives a particular direction. This is implicit in, for example, conference topics such as the naming of political questions and issues or as in the sub-title in one of the government enquiries 'West Sweden – a region in development'. The authors believe that language has a more productive role and therefore directs the audience's attention to topics that are of major interest, or towards that which one can identify with oneself, etc. This is the reason why rhetoric is considered to be a fruitful perspective in analysing political processes in relation to reforms and one of the main reasons why a region is a positive myth of alliance.

Thus, persons attending the negotiations concerning the organizational form and structure of a region may think of themselves as belonging to some special body more or less clearly defined group (institutions, geographic part of the country, political parties or professions, or various combinations of these).[6] In brief, they may identify themselves with such bodies or movements, largely through sympathetic attitudes. This identification is thus also related to some specific norms and values that imply such an identification.

---

6 This complexity is not only on a institutional level. On an individual level the situations are similar. One leading politician in West Sweden is a board member of the Association. He displayed a positive attitude towards creating a regional parliament and by so doing he raised an objection against the Association, which is similar to a criticism levelled against the Association by the other side and he thus risks being accused of being on their side. The Federation's politicians are in the same position. They also argue against the institution's official opinion. Here the tiny first-person plural pronoun *we* has a major impact on identification and hence also of being outside even if one is inside.

Given the great complexities and ambiguity in the situation, actors or institutions may have difficulty in telling their audience just how they can go about carrying out the politics that they stand for. The discussion of a region lacks concrete proposals besides different organizational forms as to how to make the region more competitive and attractive. But they can at least recommend a position antithetically by saying what policies they are against, not least if one has read the local authority and county council's news bulletins. It seems easier to comment and criticize other actors' proposals and this is also a big step towards identification.

But, on the other hand, this section has illustrated the public organizations' structuralization by using the concept of region. Structure is assumed to be both the medium and the outcome of action. Region is a belief and value-structure members employ as they act in the discussion and negotiation with one another. Because it is a generalization applicable across settings, institutions and occasions, region enters into the reproduction of the same systems that it is said to describe. At the same time as region is a medium of action it is also a result. Region is produced by discussion and negotiation, the organizational practices around the different meeting-constellations that continuously push the question ahead. Region will persist only if some aspect of the activity system reproduces it. The concept of a region, then, should be seen as a structure-in-process instead of the static, reified map of beliefs and values shown in the previous, empirical section. This is a factor in making the concept a positive myth of culture.

Thus, on the one hand there are concepts that unite the different actors – region, cooperation, need for change – but alternately these concepts can be translated into individual and institutional experiences, and it is here that it is possible to identify different translations of the concepts. In principle all agree that something should be done, but that agreement does not include exactly what should be done as together they create what can be termed a rhetorical situation. The authors define a rhetorical situation as being a complex of persons, events, objects and relations presenting an actual or potential exigence. It also means that something has to be done to meet demands and claims that the environment creates and directs, for example, shortage of money, membership of the EU and so forth. which may be completely or partially removed from the discourse but when introduced into the situation thus constrain human decision or action resulting in the significant modification of the exigence.

Besides conditions of great need to reform and audience, every rhetorical situation contains a set of constraints made up by the persons, events, objects and relations which are parts of the situation. This is because they have the power to constrain the decision and action necessary to modify the exigence. This study has identified standard sources of constraints, such as beliefs, attitudes, institutionalized norms, traditions, and that which is believed as facts, interests, and motives. All of which are intangible ingredients in the constructing and maintaining of an institution (Friedland and Alford 1991), i.e. different political parties, local authorities versus county councils, pressure groups such as the Association versus the Board, city versus countryside, etc. and also in different combinations of the above.

When an orator (in person or through text) with a back-up of an institution enters the situation, the discourse provides additional important constraints. The actors as persuaders use topics such as *regions of Europe, budget deficit* or *local authority autonomy* persuasively to consolidate their truth and value in the further organizing activity. There is, in other words, an institutionalized rhetoric that is massive in the argumentation.

Use of the Word 'Region'

The first and overall interpretation of the debate about region is the great need for change, both in the division of responsibility and how the borders are drawn geographically. This is considered to be the case by most of the actors involved. This fact, which is not new, has even been connected with latter needs for more cost-effective systems in the form of an increased coordination within social organization as well as a tendency known as increased internationalization where Swedish membership of the EU is a very significant sign. Because the actors consider that what they experience is a change in their environment and this should then correspond to an organizational change because such a change is the best way of adapting to the conditions of the environment and if perceived in this way then the present regional debate is not an unusual one.

The regional debate shows that the proposals for a solution have been various. The government one-man investigation (SOU 1992:64) made three principal proposals of which all can be considered satisfactory by the three actors involved. Increased governmental regional responsibility strengthens the government's role at a regional level. The local authorities in cooperation strengthen the local levels' influence of regional development whilst a regional autonomy strengthens the county councils' role. These proposals have been equated with local experience of the different institutions and today the latter two are strongly supported.

GCI's suggestions concerning three different forms of action and solutions have not eased the work necessary for a definite change. Different institutionalized problems have thus been connected to the various solutions. This makes it difficult, since the whole conversation about a region is not then committed to just one idea concerning the solution, even though on the surface the discussion may appear to be so.

In the province of the intermediate nothing has fixed boundaries, no doors are closed; this means open doors, paths criss-crossed by countless other paths. This chapter has discussed the formation of a region as a rhetorical situation; a complex of persons, institutions, events, objects and relations presenting an actual or potential exigence which can be completely or partially removed if (new) discourses are introduced into the situation. This can further constrain human decision or action as to bring about the significant modification of the exigence. Persons who are able to structure attention on issues who define situations as real thus make their definitions essential to the decision-making process and its consequences.

Central to politics is the ambiguous and relatively open-ended interaction of persons and institutions who share a range of concepts but share them imperfectly and incompletely. Politics are about an ability to cope with uncertainty and this involves a form of interaction in which agents adjust, extend, accommodate, and translate initial differences within a context of partly shared assumptions. Managing meanings assigned to a situation have an influence on how people perceive their realities and hence the way they act.

Most of the institutional actors appear to be in agreement concerning the present formulation of the public organizations' deficiencies in a number of areas. There are many solutions in which the actual problem should be dealt with that may function individually but at the same time promote the status quo. In other words, the difficulty lies in obtaining a consensus concerning the problem and its solutions. There is not much agreement as to how this should be achieved. The facts do not speak for themselves, they must be presented and when new solutions are found they in turn will cause new problems.[7]

Conflicts between institutions occur primarily in rhetorical discussion-fields offered by society and the public sector and where institutions attempt to carve out and maintain 'niches' or domains. But there is also an historical background. Many organizational conflicts become institutionalized in the shape of attitudes, stereotypes, beliefs and other aspects of organizational cultures. In this socialized form, the underlying conflicts can be difficult to identify and break down.

Institutionalized actors, politicians and researchers have realized, from their different perspectives, that the discussion about a region has increased during the past four to five years. The authors believe that every utterance is also a political activity, that the different assessment is a mix between wishful thinking, strict analysis and self-interest depending on who, when and where the statement was given.

In this rhetorical situation, many of the interviewed gave one of the following answers as to how the continued process would end. The answers are radically different. On the one hand there were those who assess that the result will be status quo. The power of the different institutionalized actors will neutralize forces that work for a more 'radical' change. Status quo always has the massive sustaining power of inertia on its side, so they say. Organizations normally change in a way

7 This situation has similarities with what Cohen, March and Olsen (1972) describe as a Garbage Can model and the conversation about a region can be seen as a garbage can. Actors dump both their problems and solution into the can. The idea of a region has been vague, which allows several different problems and solutions to be connected to it. It is therefore easier for the different institutions to identify and exercise their specific problems in the change-process.

that the transition is in agreement with their present identity, culture, values and frames of references. The only way to bring about lasting change, from a managerial perspective, and to foster an ability to deal with new situations is by influencing conditions that determine the interpretation of situations and the regulation of ideas. This is not something that is easily conducted in inter-organizational debates and conflicts as is believed by those who see the future as it is now – especially not when there are many different actors in the future construction.

Alternatively, there were those who believe that Sweden will experience different kinds of attempts and efforts to create a more formalized region, where after a couple of years there will be an evaluation of the endeavour. This opinion can often be connected to those who find the reform well worth a try.

On the basis of the rhetorical analysis it is possible to see that unobtrusive control is built into language, structures of communication, attitudes and procedures and that they exert a decisive impact on decision outcome, which speaks for the last option – that the immediate future will see trial efforts. Perhaps not in the proposed form, or perhaps not even beginning in West Sweden but in other parts of the country.

But parallel with the disputes as to how a regional parliament or less stringent methods of coordination agreement between the Boards, county councils and local authorities are most suitable to deal with today's and tomorrow's problems, a succession of unclear definitions which can hallmark the region arise and, parallel with the quarrel, act as a positive myth of alliance. A series of advantages can be realized by further coordination which would mean that no actor wishes to be left out of the concept or discussion because the concept/myth of region has a strength of its own. What this will mean for future forms of organization is difficult to say but it will probably establish conditions for different forms of experiments where the concept of region functions as a guiding star.

Changes do not occur in a vacuum because every idea is an object for discussion as to how it can be realized practically and where many alternative forms of action can be chosen. This is referred to as reluctance to change by those who support the idea, whilst those who do not support it fail to understand the circumstances. The divergent assumption about the pace of adjustment to new situations and signals is a type of friction in the area between continuity and change. An incremental study will perhaps throw some light on this issue.

Motivating Forces For and Against a Region – Concluding Remarks

This chapter has elucidated that it is the existing institutional forces that are hindering the formation of a region. The different actors, with connections in existing institutions, see the formation of a region with their own institutions as an important part. The formation is advisable and possible only if one's own institution has a main part. The discussion about a region is characterized by a number of runners against something controllably new. But because the runners are not in agreement the result of the discussion becomes the status quo.

Why then does the thought of a region not die? Principally, because there is a motivating force in changing material circumstances. Previous structures do not manage to deal with new economic problems and create motivation for alternative solutions. Regional organization is a possible solution and has its strength in that it really has not been tried before. The illusion of its advantages combined with previous institutions' obvious disadvantages characterizes the rhetoric.

Regional rhetoric as seen from these two force-fields – one conserving the status quo and one seeking a new formation – reflects the twin nature of the actors' problem. They long for something new but cannot let go of the ties that bind them to their own institutions. The solution could be that the new will be a direct extension of that which already exists. The definite cut-off point is when rhetoric is scrutinized very little or not at all.

Rhetoric, if considered externally, reflects the strengths and relations between the social forces, which can be understood as external objective structures and courses of development. The actors' mutual ideas and discussions are a direct reflection of this. If any actor were to defect from the objectivity expected then they would be quickly reprimanded and order restored.

However, the authors believe that there is also a third force namely the discourse itself. A discourse can create its own dynamics due to contact being made between various actors, thus directing attention to possible opportunities etc. It is necessary to re-open the previous discussion about Aristotle's thoughts about the constructive function of rhetoric. This means that the discussion concerning the region can lead to new meanings being created, new alliances being formed, etc. These new meanings can lead to objective relations being considered in another way.

The cooperation between the three force-fields is complicated and, therefore, it is difficult to predict the future formation of the region. West Sweden as a region is, and has been, a point of discussion. The pattern can be repeated but new stages cannot be disregarded due to the increase in the power of transformation. The question is whether the proficiency of rhetoric has increased with the following consequences of either being better supervised by the status quo or in the direction of a constructive re-creation of political structures.

An integral element of the study is to point out the function of rhetoric in respect to the current question of regional roles. Rhetoric reflects but it can also be seen as its own independent motivating force. The authors do not believe that the discourse will finish here and this gives us the possibility of continuing to follow the development with more precise questions surrounding the character of regional rhetoric and its consequences.

Many actors expect that a new West Sweden province will be created from 1999, with the amalgamation of several counties. How this will affect relations between the government, county councils and the local authorities is not known. The present Board organization will be cut and its tasks transferred to the county councils. What this increased strength will mean for the county councils and its relations with the local authorities is not clear as yet. This doubt affects the actors in such a way that, despite the positive association connected with the vision of a region, they adopt an irresolute attitude.

This chapter has indicated the importance of discussion in the realization of the strategy in a new regional organization. The processes can in themselves create a new content – one is not limited by that previously accepted, although we have not been able to identify any previous breakthrough. But what is clear is that in practice it is time that is important. Unfortunately, this is not yet explicit enough to be included in the different change theories.

A clarification of the research question would be to work more explicitly within the time dimension. Time shows itself in many different ways. For example, actors have different interpretations and perceptions of time, or as otherwise expressed, it is time that decides the distances to previous structures. Actors are also replaced over time. When starting with this perspective, the theoretical development should increase our understanding, not just surrounding that which has happened and is happening but even that which will happen.

Acknowledgement

The authors would like to thank Ann McKinnon for her invaluable help with the English language.

References

Andersson, Å. and Andersson, D. (1993) Sveriges regionala organization med svenska handelskammarens förslag till principer för ny regional indelning och beslutsstruktur (Sweden's Regional Organization containing the proposal of the Swedish Chamber of Commerce to the principles of new regional division and decision structure). Trosa Tryckeri AB.

Aristotle (1991) *The Art of Rhetoric.* London: Penguin Books.

Berger, P. and Luckmann, T. (1967) *The Social Construction of Reality. A Treatise in the Sociology of Knowledge.* New York: Doubleday.

Bernstein, R. (1983) *Beyond Objectivism and Relativism: Science, Hermeneutics and Praxis.* Oxford: Basil Blackwell.

Burke, K. (1973) 'The rhetorical situation.' In L. Thayer (ed) *Communication: Ethical and Moral Issues.* New York: Gordon and Breach Science Publishers.

Cohen, M., March, J.G. and Olsen, J.P. (1972) 'A garbage can model of organizational choice.' *Administrative Science Quarterly 17,* 1–25.

Eriksson, S. (1994) Två eller tre nivåer i svensk folkstyrelse (Two or three levels of Swedish autonomy). Svenska Kommunförbundet, Balder AB, Stockholm.

Flyvbjerg, B. (1991) Rationalitet og magt (Rationality and Power). Akademisk Forlag, København.

Friedland, R. and Alford, R. (1991) 'Bringing society back in: symbols, practices, and institutional contradictions.' In W. Powell and P. DiMaggio (eds) *New Institutionalism in Organizational Analysis.* Chicago, IL: University of Chicago Press.

Jensen, C. (forthcoming 1995) Berättelser om regional indelning (Report on Regional Division).

Landstingsförbundet (1994) Regionalt folkstyre, för utveckling, livsmiljö och välfärd, (Regional autonomy, for development, environment and prosperity).

Länsstyrelsen Göteborgs och Bohus Län: DNr 100–1854–92: Betänkande (SOU 1992:66) Västsverige region i utveckling. (Report (SOU 1992:66) West Sweden a developing region; Promemoria 1994 01 25: Skiss till en ny regional organization i Västsverige (Minutes of meeting 25th January, 1994 Regional Organization in West Sweden).

Meyer, J.W. and Rowan, B. (1977), 'Institutionalized organizations: formal structure as myth and ceremony.' *American Journal of Sociology 83,* 340–363.

Mishler, E. (1986) *Research Interviewing, Context and Narrative.* Cambridge, MA: Harvard University Press.

Nelson, J., Megill, A. and McCloskey, D. (1987) *The Rhetoric of Human Sciences Language and Argument in Scholarship and Public Affairs.* Wisconsin: The University of Wisconsin Press.

Oliver, C. (1992) 'The antecedent of deinstitutionalization.' *Organization Studies* 13/4, 563–588.

Pettigrew, A. (1987) 'Researching strategic change.' In A. Pettigrew (ed) *The Management of Strategic Change.* Oxford: Basil Blackwell.

Powell, W. and DiMaggio, P. (1991) *New Institutionalism in Organizational Analysis.* Chicago, IL: University of Chicago Press.

Selznick, P. (1957) *Leadership in Administration. A Sociological Perspective.* New York: Harper and Row.

SOU (1968:47) Förvaltning och folkstyre (Administration and Autonomy). Allmänna förlaget, Stockholm.

SOU (1982:24) Vidgad länsdemokrati (Extended County Democracy). Allmänna förlaget, Stockholm.

SOU (1990:36) Storstadsutredningen (Metropolitan Investigation). Allmänna förlaget, Stockholm.

SOU (1992:63) Regionala roller en perspektivstudie (Regional Roles – a perspective study). Allmänna förlaget, Stockholm.

SOU (1992:64) Utsikt mot framtidens regioner sju debattinlägg (Prospects of Future Regions seven contributions for debate). Allmänna förlaget, Stockholm.

SOU (1992:66) Västsverige region i utveckling (West Sweden a developing region). Allmänna förlaget, Stockholm.

SOU (1993:97) Västsverige och Skåne regioner i förändring (West Sweden and Skåne Regions in Change) Allmänna förlaget, Stockholm.

Statistical Yearbook of Sweden (1995) Statistiska Centralbyrån/Stockholm: Statistics Sweden, p.8.

Taylor, C. (1979) 'Interpretation and the science of man.' In P. Rainbow and W. Sullivan (eds) *Interpretative Social Science, a Reader.* Berkeley, CA: University of California Press.

Vickers, B. (1988) *In Defence of Rhetoric.* Oxford: Clarendon Press.

Winch, P. (1958) *The Idea of Social Science and its Relation to Philosophy.* London: Routledge and Kegan Paul.

Wittgenstein, L. (1953) *Philosophical Investigation.* London: Basil Blackwell.

Wittgenstein, L. (1975) *Philosophical Remarks.* London: Basil Blackwell.

CHAPTER 3

European Developing Regions – Reality or Chimera?

Lars Nordström

Introduction and Background

All organized societies have had some sort of regional grouping, that is, borders to other societies some of which compete. At the beginning, societies were small parts of the geographical surface controlled by a tribe or a monarch. In the course of time the geographical area for influence or control has increased and finally, in our days, we have a world divided into a great number of nations.

Many nation states of today have a very long history while others are products of political decisions or military conflicts during this century. Today's map of Europe differs in many ways from the one we had only ten years ago. New nations have been founded and several old ones have been split up. Nothing indicates that today's picture will remain for a long time. One may simply point at the fact that the Soviet Union no longer exists. Out of this giant empire 25 independent nations have risen, many of which have difficulties in managing their economic situation or feeling a strong inner identity and thus might possibly join a neighbour country. Add to this the civil war in former Yugoslavia, and the future forming of nations is hard to foresee. Perhaps some areas will be split up further while others will merge. It is hazardous to tell with certainty whether Belgium will remain a nation or whether federation will lead to the foundation of two or three new nations. Northern Ireland is another area which might possibly become part of nation, or even a nation in its own right, and so on.

This shows clearly that in reality nation states experience geographical changes and during certain periods this may be extensive. This is particularly true after major wars but also when new political currents emerge. Therefore, the map of Europe will certainly be partly different in 20 years or so from now. To specify in exactly what way is a hazardous path to pursue.

At the same time there is a continuity based on hundreds of years of traditions amongst the people and companies living and working in Europe. Also, in societies experiencing great changes in matters relating to nationality and delimitations, there are preserving elements and cultural patterns bridging over generations.

This chapter analyses different nations' regional grouping from the perspective of whether today's, and even more tomorrow's, new or changed national borders will also lead to the emergence of new regional groupings or rather new regional spheres of influence. It has sometimes been argued that the new Europe will be a 'Europe of Regions', meaning that the real development will take place at the regional and not the national level. The different regions in Europe have hundreds of years of cultural tradition and in many cases a strong feeling of self confidence. Many of these regions, dating back to the fall of the Roman Empire, have been in opposition to the national struggle for unity dominating European politics from the middle of the 19th century.

There is still considerable uncertainty concerning the fundamental traits of development in the change of modern Europe. Many people maintain that modern information technology will hardly make it possible or desirable to strengthen or develop the regional level. As Europe is finally becoming a boundless society one should not try to build new barriers and administrative groupings. Therefore, there is every reason to ask oneself whether the whole issue of regions is a tangible question or a chimera pursued for political reasons by those who wish for another distribution of power, without their wishes being actually realistic. This chapter will discuss the problem from different perspectives and in the light of the changes taking place in trade and industry.

During the past decades a vast volume of literature has been produced in this field, and also before there were empirical as well as theoretical studies treating the regional questions from different perspectives. Lists of current literature have recently been made by Johansson (1994) and Karlsson (1994). Furthermore, one can refer to the extensive conceptual analysis by Gidlund and Sörling (1993).

The European Union and its Supranationality

The geographical changes of nations in Europe are not the only ones to create partly new geographical conditions on the European continent. While large parts of Eastern Europe have changed their economic and political directions dramatically (see Chapter 13), another transformation is taking place in Western Europe with the European Union (EU) becoming more and more nation integrating. All analyses of regional and national changes in Western Europe, and in the long run also in Eastern Europe, must take into consideration the activities in the EU. Therefore it is natural to try to describe some of the changes that have taken or will take place in years to come.

The whole concept of the EU is based upon the thought that an integration of each nation state's economy will result in a more peaceful world with a stronger economic structure (see Chapter 1). This chapter does not aim at making a detailed description of all the integrative steps that the EU and its predecessors have taken. However, there is justification for mentioning some of the components of the EU which are of great importance if we are to understand how the geographical map and the geographical environment will be influenced in the future.

When the Coal and Steel Union was founded in 1951, the urgent problems in Western Europe were strongly related to the effects of the Second World War. The war had shattered large parts of European trade and industry. Furthermore it had once again been made clear that the European countries did not manage to solve their interior problems on their own. Decisive for the outcome of the war was the US entry on the European arena. After the war the American economy was stronger than ever, and the Marshall Aid also made the US economy strategically important in reconstructing Western Europe. The Soviet influence on Eastern Europe had also been heavily strengthened. Western Europe got into a scrape between one apparently ever stronger and richer neighbour in the East and an equally powerful neighbour on the other side of the Atlantic Ocean.

To begin with the Coal and Steel Union, and later the EU, had a strong trade and industry perspective together with a fundamental ambition to create a more peaceful world in Western Europe. From the start these aspirations were considered necessary to pursue through different types of supranational behaviour. The old, or in some cases new, national borders were considered important but at the same time they constituted potential risks for new conflicts, and making the nations less powerful in a gradually stronger world around. Although the EU is an alliance of nations – all decisions are related in some way to the individual member states' governments – there is an inherent suspicion of too strong a nationalism. Nations, for example the UK, which have not fully accepted this approach have had a hard time participating wholeheartedly in the gradual changes of the EU. Others would argue that the UK has been a perhaps necessary brake on a sometimes very fast speeding vehicle.

The gradual enlargement of the EU implies that after decisions made according to the principles of consensus or majority the individual Member States must accept the agreement. To some extent the individual nation loses its sovereign position and plays a somewhat more minor role than if the decisions are made in a more bilateral or recommending way. The supranationality has been considered necessary in order to give the EU the power needed to cope with the superior goals of peace and economic growth. Goals expressed later, like securing a good environment, creating endurable social conditions, fighting criminality and so on, have not in principle changed the basic view on supranationality and the need to revise national borders.

Alongside the expansion of EU activities to include more than its original tasks, that is work for a peaceful development and, by creating a larger market, an increase in European competitiveness, regional issues are obtaining heightened importance. It has unambiguously been made clear that the whole EU area cannot be seen as a homogenous market with similar potential for development. Great differences are to be found in different parts of the EU, as well as within one country and between countries. This has led to the fact that to a greater extent the EU has created different forms of development instruments with clear regional features. It may be favouring the industrial development in old industrial areas or favouring new establishments in thinly populated areas. Also, the upgrading of infrastructure has proved to demand important regional adjustments and different directions in different parts of the EU. In many respects the nation states used to be responsible for these sorts of regional policies and may still feel an inherent responsibility for affording every region within its boundaries the opportunity to develop.

At the same time it is obvious that with the reduced importance of national borders as economic barriers, new or old regional borders within the EU will be more evident, since separate regions are more exposed to competition and regional variations become more obvious. Similar issues have been raised over several years by Porter (1990) and Enright (1992). Also, Andersson (1989) has pointed out the increasing importance of the region in connection with the continuous integration in Europe.

The national levelling between regions in a country has been replaced by a supranational levelling which has not yet obtained the same strength, leading to regional variation becoming more apparent and politically sensitive. Therefore, the EU has had to devote great effort to trying to moderate regional differences through new funds or other support in order to reach a comparable level of economic development in as many parts of the EU as possible. This has been desirable but also very complicated since almost every EU member during the past ten years has fought against large unemployment problems and considerable eliminations of groups of inhabitants from the labour market and maybe also whole geographical areas.

European economic development during recent decades indicates three very important and basic trends. First, the European nation borders have changed dramatically and many factors imply that this will also be the case in the future. National borders and nation states are not the stabilizing factors in the historical development that one might have been led to think. Second, the historical development in Europe has pointed out the need for a compelling supranational decision-making in many issues that were earlier dealt with at the national level. Third, the differences in, for example, economic development have grown very large between separate geographical areas. The geographical variations where some regions have experienced a very rapid growth rate, while others encounter stagnation, indicate that the EU cannot be looked upon as one united homogenous market. In contrast, a great number of areas within the EU develop at different growth rates with widely separated potentials and problems.

These changes direct the spotlight on the central issue of this chapter: are there certain areas in Europe – why not call them regions – with a stable delimitation in time which can be expected to survive today's rapidly changing world? To answer that question a historical and economic/technical perspective must be presented.

The Geographical Structure of Europe in a Historical Context

As mentioned earlier, today's national borders in Europe have in many instances only recently been erected. Perhaps never before have so many new nations been formed as during the past five years. A similar period of major upheaval started with the French Revolution in 1789, lasting until the Congress in Vienna in 1814. At the Congress was decided how large parts of Europe were to be divided into separate nations, and many of the nations that have lately experienced difficulties with their coherent identity were founded at that very moment. Some nations, like France and the England of that time, are much older, but on the whole modern Europe was created during the 19th century. In several of today's countries like Germany and Italy the changes meant that earlier smaller nations voluntarily, or by means of coercion, were united in new states.

The actual reason for the creation and organization of the new nations during the 19th century differs from one country to another, but many factors have played a consistently important role. Language is a good example, that is areas with the same language are tied together under one government. Furthermore, religious and cultural bonds have had a large impact on the formation of nations. There are also factors concerning military and economic policy. Victorious dominions always want to secure their own safety, not allowing the defeated to threaten the winning nation again. Many of the nations of that time had this buffer state role. Perhaps the most famous example is Belgium which the great powers, especially England, thought necessary to create in order to weaken France's influence on the English Channel. Poland has also for a very long time been a buffer state between Russia and different German states.

This short résumé indicates that many factors have directed the delimitation of the nations observable today on the European map. Seldom have popular demands been decisive, even though national feelings have come into play and in many cases been used by different nation founders.

All this has meant that national stability is not as firmly established in the broad national groups as it could have been, provided that the macro-political elements during the creation of nations were not as dominant as was the case. A more detailed discussion about the historical relations with today's structural changes in Europe has been made by Hettne (1994) in a study aiming at explaining the topic of regional currents from ethical as well as micro-political conditions.

From the studies by Hettne and others one can understand that the historical processes of change and the superior structures of decision have sometimes not been firmly established with the masses, leading to other identities becoming more important than those of the nation states. Here language and religion play an important role. People in areas with the same language and religion automatically feel a great solidarity since they can communicate internally and understand each other's way of thinking. Add to this the fact that the geographical mobility during earlier epochs was very limited, implying also that the closest area was the only part of the world that people on a practical basis could feel any affinity with.

For many people in Europe, the nearby area, the common language and religion, have meant and still mean that the old nation states and principalities are at least as important factors of creating identity as are the nations of today. Most nations in Europe have such old, often very old, groupings to fall back upon. They can be areas maintained since the days of the Roman Empire, while others were founded during the Middle Ages. On the whole these old nations, or in current usage, regions, number approximately 200 in Western Europe alone.

During the past decades these old regions have obtained a partly different position connected to the changes in Europe discussed above. At the national level, the anxiety concerning the constantly new or changing national borders and the addition of a strong supranational organization, the EU, has led to a basic crisis of identity in many societies. What shall the individual identify himself or herself with? The new great Europe in a constant process of change? Today's nation states whose borders might change but which are definitely losing influence to the EU and maybe also to other international bodies of decision-making? Without doubt there is a considerable frustration amongst the public as well as the decision-makers. Several of today's nation states have never received the democratic legitimacy a country requires to survive during a longer period of time. In other cases international changes create a pressure from the world around undermining the basis for the foundation of the nation state. Much of the new coming of countries and the changes of the old ones are connected to the radical changes within the old Soviet Union and the new economic systems in Eastern Europe. The uncertainty and the irresolution may be rooted in a doubtfulness about European overall possibilities to meet, powerfully, the challenges from the rapid growing economies, particularly in the Far East.

During the past decades Europe has undergone, and is still undergoing, very large changes creating uncertainty but also potentials for completely new solutions to old national or regional problems. Therefore, it is not unexpected that in times of great changes, many people seek phenomena that have proved to be stable over a long period of time. This expresses itself in a broadened interest in domestic culture, language and history. Another such feature may be to strengthen the bonds with what has turned out to be stable during a long period of time, namely the old regions or provinces.

The current intense discussion about these issues in many European countries originates from a certain misguidance about belonging and what might happen in an ever more changing world. Beside these historical factors and a purely psychological need for community, other factors have changed making it meaningful to speak about a new era which will have a major geographical impact. These changed conditions will now be discussed.

The Geographical Effects of Economic and Technical Development

A characteristic feature in economic development during the past decades is that, in more and more lines of businesses, the whole world constitutes the market for the large companies. The national businesses which in many cases used to have actual local or national monopolies have gradually changed character. Today, within most product areas where international trade is current, companies are operating on a global scale causing trouble for individual nation states. These global companies are spread geographically when it comes to production and may easily move production from one area to another if that would turn out to be profitable or in other ways desirable.

In reality it is a matter of international industry being divided into at least four different levels or segments, namely management, product development, production and, finally, sales. As a result of modern information technology these four segments do not have to be located in the same geographical area. On the contrary, it is advantageous to separate them from one another to exploit cheap labour, land, raw materials, etc.

The management of large companies is often located in the country and the region of origin. This is probably also where the major owners are situated. Hence, in general today's old international Swedish large companies still have their headquarters in Sweden. The same is true of American and maybe to an even larger extent Japanese corporations. The concentration of management functions to metropolitan areas within each country has been delineated in several studies, for example Nordström (1971) and Törnqvist (1994).

The location of a company's research and development activities can be less restricted. Research and development are usually located where the possibilities of recruiting prominent researchers are most favourable, or where the environment is suitable, for example close to a university or research centre. This geographical freedom of localization of the research activities implies a totally new situation of competition within a segment which was not considered movable earlier. The researchers in question may not always feel that the nation state of the company's origin is their geographical residence. Either they want to stay where they are or move to another region independent of country origin as long as the exterior conditions are satisfactory. Since language skills in this group of people are usually good, national borders do not play the same role as for other groups of people who might wish to stay in their country of origin. When it comes to research and product development the competition amongst companies has therefore led to a competition between regions, that is which region can offer the best total living environment and the best potential for development (Andersson and Strömqvist 1988).

When it comes to localization of production a great number of factors are important. Traditionally all large global companies locate an important part of their production in the country of origin. Often there is also a large domestic market for the product. Thanks to a very rapid change in the international transportation market it has, relatively speaking, become cheaper to transport goods long distances. Therefore, major parts of the global demand for a certain product may be met from a few large plants. If these plants are located in low wage countries with good infrastructure and skilled work force a centralized production may be very competitive. However, such great opportunity is usually not available. Other factors must also be taken into consideration. Large production units may be vulnerable and difficult to supply with raw materials. Add to this the fact that a combination of low wages and a highly skilled workforce is rarely possible – it almost invariably involves a question of priorities and a compromise between these two factors. Furthermore, a low wage country may in time develop a higher level of cost than before, which might lead to a need for relocalization of production.

Another factor which has been considered to play a major role in the EU is the fact that companies wish to place production in areas with political stability. Rapid changes of economic and political rules are considered an element of insecurity reducing the incentive for investment, as has been the case in today's East European countries. Localization of industrial production is therefore largely a matter of a combination of purely economic factors and an estimate of the future political development. Since it is impossible to be sure about future economic and political decisions, most global companies have more or less openly chosen a risk-spreading strategy. Companies locate their plants in different nations and in different parts of the world even if, in the short run, it means a more expensive production. From these scattered plants the different markets are provided independently of distance and costs in each individual case.

However, there have been some guiding principles in the large companies' choices of localization for production. Perhaps the most important principle when it comes to risk spreading is to have at least one plant within the EU, one in the USA and one in the Far East. The reason for this strategy is that apart from these areas being large markets, there is a risk of a future trade war between the three. Being located in all three major areas the companies are safeguarded whether protectionism will increase or not.

Regarding the EU, when selecting a location for a Japanese car factory for example, the choice of nation has turned out to be less important. Instead competition has ruled between different regions which can give more or less support to a certain establishment. A lot of this support has naturally passed through the EU, but far from all of it. Regional institutions have often on their own responsibility offered potential companies favourable conditions. Hence the regions in Europe compete with one another and often the competition is between regions within the same country. Once again the national borders have become less important as the decisive factor when global companies choose where to locate their production of goods.

Finally, concerning sales – how the global companies try to influence the market – several interesting trends have occurred during the past few years. There are contradictory ways of development which are not easy to explain.

A general trend is that within many product areas each product is shaped to sell unchanged all over the world. Car models being developed are made to fit widely spread markets, climate areas and environments. The same applies for home electronics and to a certain extent clothes. In other words there has been a global standardization resulting in lower production costs and maybe also a certain equalization. In some cases, the standardization or the sales of branded products have been given an intrinsic value, that is the brand is more important than the product itself. Hence a product can be sold almost anywhere without adjustments to local or national special demands or traditions. Once again, it is clear that certain products no longer have to be adjusted to national preferences. Within the EU one of the most important tasks is to facilitate standardization while national borders and national rules must not create any trade barriers.

Another partly contradictory trend is to adjust the products to the customers so that they correspond to each customer's special wishes and demands. To a large extent modern information technology makes this possible even though it is not appropriate for some more simple products. Regarding capital goods like cars, boats, and larger machines, the development is heading towards a large adjustment of the individual products. Within the car industry many companies only produce the cars they have already sold, and where the customers may have expressed a number of wishes regarding equipment and other special demands. In order to make it technically possible, a rapid transformation of information to the individual subcontractor and a very efficient transportation market are required. These customer adjustments require production located close to the market or in some large region. In many branches, Europe or the USA are such suitable regions. Within each region the different markets may be supplied with only a couple of days of transportation. When it comes to Europe, once again the companies look upon Europe as a common market, the national borders being an obstacle.

On the whole this gives a picture of gradual shift in industrial activities to certain large areas in the world, while within these areas individual regions compete for the localization of research and production. What has been argued about the industrial sector is applicable also to the services sector, although the patterns there are not as absolute (Dunning 1969; Illeris 1989). National monopolies, often state owned, still play an important role. This applies certainly within the field of communication where for example rail companies have a strongly national structure. The same is also true concerning the area of health care and education, though in the latter an internationalization process is taking place.

On the other hand during the past twenty years a very heavy internationalization and in many cases a globalization has taken place in the area of financial services, consulting, advertising, travelling business, information production, news services and so on. Once again for many companies Europe constitutes a common area which can be provided for from one or a couple of places. The biggest issue for national borders is that they are often language borders creating certain problems of harmonization.

This indicates that large parts of the internationally oriented economy today have a small or insignificant connection to the individual nation's delimitations. The companies often consider larger areas or significantly smaller areas as their natural areas of action.

The Competition of the Regions

The nation states are, and will most certainly also be, the legally most important level for international agreements. Within the framework of the nation state individual regions are given, more or less, many possibilities to act independently. The nation state might delegate some tasks to the regional level, or in more federative constitutions the regions let the nation states take care of certain tasks while keeping others at the regional level.

Independent of whether individual nations are to be considered absolute nation states or federations, today there is strong regional self confidence in most European nations. During the past years, as can be understood from the earlier discussion, self confidence has been strengthened by political and economic development. The effects of the increased importance of the regional level have not always attracted enough attention. Therefore, it is necessary to discuss these issues from a future perspective of increased European integration and continued strong international competition.

Today there is rather large unanimity regarding the factors that may explain the development of yesterday's and today's industrial nations. Basically there are three factors which a region should have as an appropriate combination, namely physical production factors, legislative order and method and independent and skilled individuals.

The Industrial Revolution in Europe at the beginning of the 19th century showed that it was possible to create rapid economic growth spreading to other parts of the world. The concept was more or less the same, namely using existing raw materials and increasing the content of the product through gradual refinement. Compared to today's society it is obvious that the transport structure, or rather lack of transport, of those days was a strongly restricting factor. Industrial production took place close to the localization of the heaviest raw materials.

In the course of time, as mentioned before, a real revolution took place concerning the possibility to rapidly transport goods over long distances at low cost. This, together with the fact that technical development has made a bigger part of the industrial sector work within areas where the products have a high value added per unit of weight, has increased geographical mobility dramatically in terms of localization of industrial production (see Johansson and Snickars 1992).

Naturally there has always been a certain competition between different parts of a nation. This was the case during the industrialization in the 19th century and has continued to a greater extent to today. The task of the nation state, apart from the legal institutional function, has been to create a redistribution between rich and poor regions. The means are regional policies but also building up infrastructural resources like transportation networks and educational institutions.

In the Europe growing within the framework of the EU, the function of redistribution has not been easily connected to a system of free inner competition. The risks are considerable that instead of primarily being a redistribution, a regional support may easily in practice become a subvention aiming at favouring a company more than other companies in other countries. Therefore the regional support within the Member States is gradually being conformed to the support system of the EU itself. The nation states then lose their task of redistributing their resources reserved for regional support internally between their own regions.

Every region with growth is to be found in nations with a legislation safeguarding the legal rules of the game for industrial activities, that is the second factor mentioned above. In this area the nation state's task is to take care of the institutional stability while competition acts on a regional level. Also, in this case a shift of power is currently taking place in the EU. Much of the economic policies are coordinated and decided at the EU level. It is a matter of creating similar rules of competition for all companies within the EU.

It has been made clear that the development of the transportation system has resulted in very extensive mobility in production. Furthermore, the institutional stability in Europe is by and large handled by the EU and a harmonization between the member states has taken place. The fact remains that an important means of competition with regional and national differences is one concerning the individual's situation and knowledge.

Competition and development within the internationally influenced sectors of society have turned out to be a matter of the skills, location and ambitions of the workforce. Successful regions are completely dependent on the people in the area and their expertise, from those working in the industry to every single services sector. The functioning of this collected network determines whether a region will develop or stagnate.

The increased content of knowledge in the products in world trade makes education an ever more important factor in explaining the success of certain nations or regions (Nordström 1994). The rapid expansion and high welfare level of California is often used as an example of a region with a combination of a well educated workforce and a high degree of individual freedom. An additional factor is the climate, making it easy to attract people from other parts of the USA or abroad.

The same is true about many regions in Europe which experienced success during the past decades. In each such region there is one or more universities responsible for developing knowledge and for supplying the companies in the region with new ideas and research results (technological transfer). Moreover, these regions always have a well functioning infrastructure with aircraft, highways and rail services, whilst sometimes a shipping system can also be very important.

Hence the traditional localization theory must be complemented with a great number of factors previously considered insignificant. When an international company looks for suitable locations for single work places, ranking lists of regions of interest are being made. A check of these lists shows that beside the traditional factors like level of cost and transportation possibilities other soft variables become more important. For example educational level of the workforce, quality of the educational system, crime rate, continuity in the political system, environment, supply and quality of culture and so on. A common feature is that these elements are not vital, measuring at a national level, but are significant only at a local or regional level. The accessibility of the factors should be on a daily basis, hence influencing everyday life. At the same time, by the overall improvement of the road network, the daily reach has been extended and a daily commuting distance of 150 kilometres can be acceptable in extreme cases. For certain more qualified services even longer distances may be possible.

The picture which appears indicates that much of what was earlier of national importance has been taken over by the EU. On the other hand, in an environment of continuously stronger international competition, regions and their peculiarities have become the new level for industrial and qualified competition. This change and shift of power is most apparent in Europe, but basically the same trends can be traced also in the USA and in several countries in the Far East.

Of course, competition between regions will not be without obstacles. A number of restrictions will appear, not least within the frame of the EU. Otherwise the consequences would be far too drastic with a huge impoverishment of certain parts of Europe. Still it is reasonable to assume that regional competition will characterize the geographical picture of Europe during decades to come. The signs for such a development are very clear and empirical knowledge of how it will happen is vital.

All through, every region tries to find some kind of institutional legacy, for example an elected parliament or an indirectly elected organization. The current debate in Sweden about provincial parliament, or other forms of regional levels of decision-making, accordingly connects well to the European debate on these issues.

Moreover the representatives of the regions strive to develop some kind of strategy for the future. There is a feature of planning which used to be on a national level but turned out to be difficult to pursue in practice. These regional plans contain proposals on higher education, transportation systems, culture and recreation and environment policy. Usually there are also ideas about which industry and services structure the region desires.

Single regions often work with international marketing aimed at companies and decision-makers. Only in Brussels are there a hundred different regional representation and marketing offices. Larger regions are also present in other important centres of decision-making like the USA and the Far East. In this marketing and lobbying activity all modern tools are used and large resources are spent on information material. The purpose is to sell the region to companies and individuals as well as tourists and visitors.

Finally the regions usually try to create a strong inner identity by strengthening the connecting networks. As the former nation states tried to encourage nationalism, the regions now often try to stimulate regionalism. This appears in symbols on flags and logotypes but also in different types of manifestations like cultural arrangements, sports activities, common information and news programmes, mass media companies with regional ownership, etc. This kind of regionalism may cause one region to be favoured over other regions.

Regional Stability or Turbulence?

An inner dynamic and stable structure is a decisive factor for a certain geographical area in the internationally competitive economy in creating a long term and stable labour market. Changed conditions of competition and new demands on the labour force must quickly influence, for example, the school system and other infrastructure. At the same time there must be a continuity in the political structure, enabling potential investors or people thinking of moving to the region to forecast what decisions may be made in the foreseeable future.

Obviously there is a conflict between these two directions which might imply that a certain region will not obtain the development desired. Basically it is due to difficulties in foreseeing all rapid changes that take place in the industrialized world. The former stability, when a company or a public institution could make long-term plans which were often realized, is today partly a past phase. Through the enlargement of information technology and the transportation systems, the speed of economic oscillations has meant that former long-term stable regions have suddenly become problem areas. A former profitable industrial activity can go under in a very short period of time and alternative employment is then not to be achieved rapidly.

There is every reason to believe that this kind of regional structural crisis will be more common during the decades to come. This is due to the fact that in the global competition system different regions will specialize in certain niches where they are highly competent. Also universities and other infrastructure will then be directed towards this specialized trade and industry. If suddenly a whole line of business or part of it turns obsolete, the regional consequences may be very severe.

The basic issue for every specialized region is how much resources should be reserved for creating alternatives to the activity which might have been very successful and still is competitive. In practice it has turned out to be extremely difficult to be prepared in due time to cope with the changes that are not easy to anticipate.

From the development taken place in Europe and in the USA, one may conclude that obsolete regions, for example the old coal areas, in many cases never shift towards a more modern industry. This is not only due to the fact that they may geographically be situated on poor industrial transport networks, but more to purely mental and political conditions. In old industrial regions there is often an inability to meet the changing conditions. In many cases, however, it has proved possible to turn old regions into high technology ones. In the USA, the Boston area and parts of North Carolina are two examples. In Europe, southern Germany and parts of southern France as well as the area around Birmingham in Great Britain are considered regions with a new structure and large modern investing activities. Subsequent chapters in this book take up this theme of regions/nations responding to structural economic decline.

Several factors explain why the regions mentioned above have been successful in their restructuring process. An interesting feature in the transformation is the fact that the political system is seldom the driving factor. There are strong individuals working outside, for example in the case of southern France working in direct conflict with other local or regional politicians. Also the transformation of the Baltimore region is due to individual and private initiatives. In Boston, however, it was a combination of politicians and representatives of the trade and industry that achieved a major restructuring of the whole region.

A common transformation can be observed from both successful and unsuccessful regions, that it is difficult to foresee such rapid destruction of companies as has often been the case. Likewise, regional and local politicians, often in combination with representatives of labour unions, have wished to support unprofitable lines of business. A more intense commitment has been to keep the old industries rather than to aim at something new and insecure. Furthermore, on the whole, it is common in old industrial regions that the understanding of higher education and international competition has not been significant. The preparedness for industrial crisis has been weak and a long time has passed before real action has been taken.

From this one can learn, in today's competition, that important regional crises will be common and new problem areas will emerge in regions which today seem to be very stable and profitable. Furthermore, in the future it will often be politically impossible to mobilize and finance investments aiming at creating flexibility if current advantageous industrial activities are destroyed or put in a position of excessive competition.

On the contrary, the regionalization described earlier – every region wishing to develop its own profile and uphold its interests in competition with other regions – will make it difficult to reserve resources for long-term alternative actions. The proud regional politician trying to put forward his or her region's advantages will find it hard to simultaneously indicate the need for creating alternatives to the development currently being marketed in a positive way.

The two perspectives, pointing at the region's stability and favourable conditions and at the same time emphasizing to the electors and trade and industry the need for flexibility and change, demand a very special way of regional thinking. Perhaps within the framework of a certain renewed interest in regional planning which is noticeable in some European countries, it might be possible to join these two directions of development. In the long run, the ability to combine short-term stabilizing actions and long-term flexibility might be the characteristic feature of the most successful regions.

Conclusions

The rapid transformation of the modern industrial nations including an extensive international competition has led to a completely new situation at the regional level in most industrial countries. This applies particularly within the EU but the same basic changes take place in most industrial nations in other parts of the world.

In the future, how will the geographical surface in major parts of the world be divided? Will there, in conformity with what has been the case during the past 150 years, be distinctly discernible nations with sole and full control of their areas? These nation states create alliances and are responsible for national symbols like currency, defence, foreign policy, etc. In each country certain regional independence will be tolerated, but basically it is a matter of a top-down decentralization.

The appearance of supranational bodies like the EU and its potential adherents in the Far East and maybe on the American continent fundamentally change the bases for the power and importance of nation states. In the long run, the whole world will certainly be divided into nations with well-defined borders. At the same time the nation states' roles and tasks will change. Much will be centralized to the superior institutions.

Simultaneously, as this chapter aims at illustrating, many problems will be solved at a level below the nation states, if they contain geographical areas which each can be defined as functional regions. Striving at, as far as possible, decentralizing power and influence in the public and private sector will turn out to be very hard. This striving is not only a strong trend in the EU but the same repugnance to central decision-making is applicable to the USA and other great nations. Also, in trade and industry with global corporations it has been possible to unite large connected systems with a decentralized decision-making.

While the supranational public level aims both at harmonizing in order to equalize regional differences through different support, and at creating conditions of competition for regions to compete on equal terms, there is a built-in conflict which cannot be completely avoided. Often the contradiction between harmonization and polarization creates such great tensions that the nation's foundation itself may be altered. For example, in today's Belgium harmonizing forces have grown weaker during the past decade while polarization has gained power (see Chapter 9).

In the business world basically the same incentives occur. Naturally the large global corporations aim at utilizing large-scale advantages, thereby reducing costs and increasing market shares. At the same time a real marketing process should be carried out in close relation to the local market. Therefore, divergence from the general corporate strategy must often be allowed. The countervailing forces of the uniformity of the company's actions and the local divergences and adjustments for each market create a tension not easy to explicate. Some corporations clearly work against any local or regional adjustment while others find it an important factor of competitiveness.

In the two sectors in society, the public sector and private trade and industry, conflicting trends are apparent. At the same time it can doubtless be stated that while technology allows a highly harmonized public sector in a nation or large area and while global corporations can be managed in a uniform way, there are still strong counteracting forces. Basically these concern finding close contacts to the market on which each product is dependent for survival. Consumers of public or commercial goods become more and more enlightened, requiring more of the commodity that they have to pay for, wanting it to correspond to their needs. As a result, an adjustment of the general to the local or regional market must always be made.

The whole question of regional development in Europe must be seen in the light of what has been mentioned above. In the public as well as the private sector a dividing up of large geographical areas into smaller regions is taking place. In some cases the old nation states constitute such appropriate areas. Sometimes smaller, sometimes larger areas than today's nations are suitable. At present, however, these regions will be some of the more noticeable areas of competition in Europe.

Regional competition will largely be about competence and knowledge as well as a great number of soft factors previously considered unimportant. This is due to the fact that all modern industrial societies have changed from being tied to heavy production of goods to focusing on highly value-added goods or services. Competition between regions will intensify concurrently with the globalization of production of goods and services. In this context, national or supranational institutions responsible for major parts of public services and authorities will act more and more as equalizing or moderating bodies. However, they will not be able to change the major direction of the future of European regional development.

It is open to discussion whether this development can be considered positive or negative for the individual and the issue should be part of the political sphere. Over time the old nation state will probably have a totally different role while the region will take over some of the nation state's tasks. At the same time the internal structure makes the region a somewhat uncertain creation. In parts of Europe the regions sometimes date back to the Roman Empire. In some regions, Sweden for one, there is a significant misguidance due to the lack of historical background. Will modern creations like West Sweden survive the oscillations of time (see Chapter 2)? Only the future can tell.

However, it should now be obvious that the question put at the beginning of this chapter – whether the regions in Europe constitute a real developing force or whether they are a fiction created by politicians but not established in reality – may now be answered comparatively unambiguously. The analysis of the development trends of the changes in today's Europe made in this chapter, and in the remainder of this book, indicates that regionalization is a true force. This idea is further confirmed by a great number of studies in this field, a notable contribution being the various chapters contained in this volume.

References

Andersson, Å.E. and Strömqvist, U. (1988) *K-samhällets framtid.* Stockholm: Prisma.

Andersson, Å.E. (1989) *Kreativitet – Storstadens framtid.* Stockholm: Prisma och Regionplanekontoret, Stockholms läns framtid.

Dunning, J.H. (1969) 'The city of London.' *Town Planning Review* (40).

Enright, M. (1992) *The Geographic Scope of Competitive Advantage.* Utrecht: VUGS-Congress.

Hettne, B. (1994) *Den europeiska paradoxen.* Stockholm: Nerenius o Santerus förlag.

Gidlund, J. and Sörling, S. (1993) *Det Europeiska Kalejdoskopet.* Stockholm: SNS-förlag.

Illeris, J. (1989) *Service and Regions in Europe.* Aldershot: Gower.

Johannson, J. (1994) *Europeiska regioner.* Stockholm: Svenska Landstingsförbundet.

Johannson, B. and Snickars, F. (1992) *Infrastruktur – Byggnadssektorn i kunskapssamhället.* Stockholm: Byggforskningsrådet T 33:1992.

Karlsson, C. (1994) *Regioner och nätverk i Europa.* Stockholm: Svenska Landstingsförbunet.

Nordström, L. (1971) *Rumsliga förändringar och ekonomisk utveckling.* Göteborg: Regionkonsult AB.

Nordström, L. (1994) *Högskolornas regionala roll.* Stockholm: Svenska landstingsförbundet.

Porter, M.E. (1990) *The Competitive Advantage of Nations.* London: The Macmillan Press.

Törnqvist, G. (1994) *Sverige i Nätverkens Europa.* Stockholm: Liber-Hermods.

CHAPTER 4

Contested Governance

European Exposure in the English Regions

Peter Lloyd and Richard Meegan

Local Economic Development and Issues of Governance

The Schumpeterian Workfare State and Urban and Regional Entrepreneurialism

To set the events which we wish to explore in this chapter in some kind of theoretical framework there is a large and rapidly expanding literature (see, for example, Benko and Dunford 1991; Hirst and Zeitlin 1991; Dunford and Kafkalas 1992; Lipietz 1992; Storper and Scott 1992; Amin 1994). At the macro scale it is becoming almost *de rigueur* to posit that, from a regulation theory perspective, the transition to post-Fordism appears, in the European context at least, to be seeing a move from the Keynesian Welfare State (KWS) to the Schumpeterian Workfare State (SWS) – a move, in crude terms, from a situation in which the state attempts to regulate the economy and bolster social wages to one in which the state actively disengages itself from regulatory activity in the economic sphere and restricts itself to only a minimal *safety-net* role in the social sphere (see, for example, Jessop 1992, 1994a; Macleod 1995).

For the regions and their inhabitants this broad shift toward the prescriptions of the SWS is being conducted within a hegemonic discourse that it is their prime task to *pay their way in the world* (Jessop 1994b, 1995). In concert with this it is the job of all who represent local interests, democratically or otherwise, to deliver *supply-side advantage* (cheap flexible and skilled labour and desirable sites and infrastructure in a climate of entrepreneurship) to businesses and industries capable of holding their own in globalized competition. It is from these roots in competitive businesses across the regions that Europe as an entity must *fight its corner* against the Americas and Pacific Asia (see, for example, Child-Hill 1992; Ohmae 1985; Gertler and Schoenberger 1992). The European Commission's own prescription for global competitiveness is set out in Table 4.1. Much of it clearly resonates strongly with neo-Liberal and Schumpeterian agendas.

Table 4.1 Guidelines for a policy of global competitiveness

Objectives	*Means*
1. Helping European firms to adapt to the new globalized and interdependent competitive situation	• Capitalizing on the Community's industrial strengths • Developing an active policy of industrial cooperation • Establishing a concerted approach to strategic alliances • Targeting measures to ensure the competitive functioning of markets
2. Exploiting the competitive advantages associated with the gradual shift to a knowledge-based economy	• Reforming tax policies so as not to create employment disincentives and to promote incentives for the efficient use of scarce resources • Developing a policy to encourage 'non-physical' investment (training, research, technical assistance) • Bolstering policies to streamline and rationalize rules and regulations • Reviewing the criteria governing the use of public instruments in support of industry so as to enhance their impact on the growth of value-added and employment • Launching à European policy aimed at quality
3. Promoting a sustainable development of industry	• Increasing substantially and coordinating R&D efforts in the field of clean technology • Developing economic incentives to support the diffusion of R&D results into products and processes
4. Reducing the time-lag between the pace of change in supply and the corresponding adjustments in demand	• Demand-side measuresPursuing initiatives aimed at facilitating a concerted revival in consumption at world level • Promoting the emergence of new markets *Supply-side measures* • Encouraging continuing structural adjustment by supporting privatizations • Underpinning the dynamism of SMEs *Measures to improve the relationship between supply and demand* • Facilitating partnerships between large firms and their subcontractors • Improving the interfaces between products and users • Establishing collaboration networks so as to develop clusters of competitive activities

Source: Commission of the European Communities (CEC) 1994a

In the past decade, consistent with the focus on entrepreneurship and effective supply side measures, the role of local authorities in the United Kingdom (UK) has been dramatically changed from being providers and guarantors of a level of welfare provision and supporting infrastructure to their local electorates to being enablers, intermediaries and *change agents.* In Harvey's (1989) terminology, urban governance has shifted from *urban managerialism* to *urban entrepreneurialism.* In this transition local authorities must engage, as part of a local class-alliance or growth coalition, in competition over: the international division of labour (attracting mobile investment and employment); the spatial division of consumption (tourism and consumerism – attracting the consumer dollar); the acquisition of control and command functions (securing high-status activities – corporate headquarters, media and financial decision-makers – in the hierarchial division of labour); and, finally, the redistribution of surpluses by central government (transfer payments, defence expenditure, etc).

Consistent with the Schumpeterian emphasis on entrepreneurship and the pursuit of the new, local authorities and their partners have, then, become infused by a drive to enhance the competitive edge of their cities and city-regions as *core business.* This is conducted against the demands of increasing globalization. The local and regional need to compete is not confined to rivalries within the same national space but is truly international. The drive is to be more successful than competitor cities and city-regions across the world to secure an advantaged place in an urban system which now very distinctly operates at global and transnational levels (Sassen 1994). In parallel there has also been a move to a more loosely defined mode of governance based on more flexible and less formalized systems of bargaining and negotiation in partnerships and coalitions (Hay 1995; Macleod 1995).

Old players with new tasks, new players with old ones

While the move to prioritize local economic development has been gathering pace, neo-Liberal prescriptions for the withdrawal of the central state through the processes described by Macleod (1995) as *de-nationalization* and *de-statization* have thrust a whole range of new players into the policy domain traditionally occupied by the local authorities. Training and enterprise councils (TECs), urban development corporations (UDCs), city challenge bodies, business link and others have been elbowing their way to the table of local governance. They have been joined on this increasingly crowded platform of local governance by such bodies as the health and community care trusts, the newly independent colleges of further and higher education, the privatized former public utilities and public transport providers. All are having to carve out roles for themselves in the new flexible system of governance. What this amounts to is a move by old players to adopt new tasks at the same time as new players are coming in to take over old ones.

Inevitably this is creating a turbulence that would, even without other complications, render local governance an increasingly contested domain. What is also happening in regions which qualify for assistance from Europe is that the drive toward regional entrepreneurship and new forms of governance are becoming heavily influenced by the conflicting ideas and instructions emanating from Brussels and Whitehall. Ideological battles between neo Liberals, neo corporatists and neo-statists (Jessop 1992) are being fought out not just at Maastricht, the council of ministers and in the national assemblies and parliaments of the Member States but also in the partnerships, Monitoring committees and technical panels of the peripheral English regions. While the individuals concerned might not think of their debates in these terms, the policy and legislative context in which they find themselves operating has built into it elements of these grander discourses. What they are doing is converting them into the realms of local realpolitik.

Winners and losers in the drive for competitive advantage

What significantly sharpens the edge of these conflicting ideas locally in the drive to create competitive advantage from place to place across the single european market (SEM) is the inevitable logic that there will be *winners* and *losers* – nations, regions and cities. At every level of spatial resolution the SEM, to which all the Member States of the European Union (EU) unequivocally subscribe, offers the most powerful policy tool to deliver both the advantages of scale and the discipline of untrammelled competition. The price for the SEM and even more so for the European Economic and Monetary Union (EMU) as it emerges will be a sharp increase in spatial inequality. Those *spatial mosaics of unevenness* already visible at every level of resolution from the intra-regional and regional to the national will become more sharply defined (Dunford 1994; Dunford and Perrons 1994). For the entrepreneurial state and the entrepreneurial city-region the *winning option* is the only one to be countenanced. The result is a scramble for competitive position from regional and national circumstances which offer distinctly differing prospects of success. The problem for all is *how to win*. This is a realm of contested ideas not simply about the *how* but also about the relative price to be paid socially and politically for different *how* solutions.

Institutional searching and fiscal stringency

The power of market forces differentially to offer the prospects of development or decline across national, regional and local economic spaces across Europe provokes a conflict at all those levels of governance from which policy leverage can be exerted. This is not just about appropriate jurisdiction or representation or even just about transfer payments and access to resources. The ways in which institutional structures *facilitate* or *obstruct* the development process at the different levels of governance will have a potentially powerful role to play itself in delivering competitive advantage. At the regional level the particular effectiveness of middle-level institutional structures has been a key forum for debate not least in the UK where the availability of the Welsh Development Agency and Scottish Enterprise makes for clear contrasts between them and the English regions (for Wales see, for example, Morgan 1992, Cooke and Morgan 1993; for both Wales and Scotland see Trade and Industry Committee 1995a, b). Institutional frameworks will have a powerful influence on who wins and who loses and it is no surprise that, despite the willingness of the central governments to sign up to abstract concepts of free market forces, daily battles are being fought to erect, at the very least, effective windbreaks against Schumpeterian *gales of creative destruction.*

These debates are, as we have pointed out earlier, being conducted against the backdrop of radical and fast moving changes in the overall nature of local governance in a process fundamentally connected to the way institutional forms can themselves be expected to deliver the holy grail of regional, national and Europe wide competitive edge. The UK, other EU members and the European Commission also have widely differing views on this issue. As the old Chinese curse puts it: we live in interesting times.

It is feature of such times that *institutional searching* is a widely observed phenomenon (Peck and Tickell 1994). Like everything else in the field of contested governance it is a process driven as much from the realm of competing ideas as from the politics of power. In the realm of ideas the Commission and its advisors are a key source of new scripts about the development process – both in the sense of *how to* and in terms of their views on the most appropriate institutional arrangements. These scripts draw upon a vocabulary (including, for example, excluded groups, social partners, social cohesion and regional convergence) which offers, particularly for regions and localities on the losing end of uneven regional development, an appealing antidote to prevailing neo-Liberal discourse. Indeed the European Commission is already a significant policy actor within the less favoured regions of the UK. The powers conferred on the Commission and its Directorates though the Structural Funds and Community Initiatives Regulations (CEC 1994b, c) give it a legitimate seat at the debating table and its perspectives on Euro Regionalism (Millan 1990; Committee of the Regions 1994; CEC 1994d–f) become ever more attractive. Local authorities in particular take every opportunity to explore new ways to foster institutional alliances with such a potentially powerful ally.

For the regional interests in the UK the attractiveness of the Commission and its perspective on regional reconversion is greatly enhanced by the fact that it has become a treasure chest of funds for development at a time of sharp fiscal stringency. While the entrepreneurial mission for local authorities and other regional agencies has become ever more sharply trumpeted by central government, the resources to carry out that mission have been consistently reduced. Structural Funds and Community Initiatives monies have become, for many regions, the only significant new resources available to underpin the drive to out-compete their rivals. Fiscal stringency also brings the new players on board as ferocious bidders for their share of the European regional cake. Struggles for resources and effective control of them are intense.

Europe as a player in contested regional governance

If *many capitalisms* are evolving and being consolidated (as argued, for example, by Hampden-Turner and Trompenaars 1993), the UK and the EU appear to be pursuing significantly different versions. Lord Cockfield's vision in the 1985 White Paper, *Completing the Internal Market*, was to make Europe a robust global competitor by sweeping away all barriers to the free movement of goods, services, capital and labour to create a full and unified market by the end of 1992 (Colchester and Buchan 1990). The next stage ushered in by Maastricht and the Treaty of European Union will continue the process of creating a level European playing field for competition with movement toward a single currency. It is how to deal with the *social price* to be paid for this process of opening up to market forces that traces the outline of one of the major fault lines between some Member States, notably the UK, and the majority view in the EU. The degree of concern about the social price to be paid, despite ideology, is likely to vary with expectations about the outfall of the benefits and disadvantages of the free market among Member States. Some will expect to fare well from the outset, while others will be forced to experience the effects of a major restructuring of their national and regional economies. It is this which is promoting a strong rearguard action, led by the UK, to preserve national leverage over economic and social policy against the strong centrifugal forces of a move toward a more powerful European tier of government.

There will also be a *regional price* to be paid and the regions may not see eye to eye with their central states on either the issue of national sovereignty or the acceptability of accepting the inevitable deleterious effects of the full flow of market forces. From this perspective what is being sharpened is the intensity of competition between regions and a search by those regions themselves for resources and the most profitable alliances to them in delivering the necessary degree of regional competitive advantage. Where these alliances bring them into conflict with their own national governments new fault lines appear, moving the contested terrain from one between nation states and the EU to one between nation states and their own regions.

It is not only at the inter-governmental conferences, therefore, that the fault lines between Britain and Europe are being contested. The designated areas for Structural Funds assistance and the Community Initiatives are no less contested terrains for debates about the nature of regional governance, the acceptable limits to the competitive flexible labour market, and the social costs of economic exclusion. Locally, these debates are conducted at the present time around the regional conversion plans developed for drawing down assistance from the Structural Funds – the so-called Single Programming Documents (SPDs) – and the arrangements for their implementation. The fault lines show up clearly and are caught up in the more localized debates about the democratic deficit and the representative politics of the regions versus the central state (Meegan 1994).

The European Commission is powerfully positioned as an active player in the contest over governance in the UK regions. Its constitutionally founded position with respect to the allocation and administration of the Structural Funds and Community Initiatives offers to these regions a means to challenge the hegemonic discourses of the national state. This comes at a time when the strong hand of the Integrated Regional Offices (IROs) is being played by what one national newspaper describes as 'Regional Viceroys' in the form of Senior Regional Directors appointed by Whitehall (Foster 1995).

The Increasing Relative Importance of the Structural Funds in United Kingdom Regional Policy

The decline of regional policy in the UK

While the commitment of the EU to regionally based policies for economic and social cohesion has tended to remain a central plank of policy strongly reinforced by the Delors package, UK regional policy has all but been dismantled. By 1994 national expenditure on regional policy had fallen to a quarter of its level in the early 1980s (Gudgin 1995). The recent report on regional policy by the House of Commons Trade and Industry Committee clearly reveals the growing relative importance of EU funding for regional policy. In 1993/94 expenditure on regional industrial policy in Great Britain (figures are not given for Northern Ireland) by the Department of Trade and Industry and the Welsh and Scottish Offices had fallen to £286.9 million. Between 1994 and 1996, the UK's share of the EU's funds targeted specifically at regional development (i.e. for Objectives 1, 2 and 5b of the Structural Funds) total £980 million per year, rising to £1115 million if the funding of Community Initiatives is included (Trade and Industry Committee 1995a, p.xvii).

It is not only the shifting balance of resourcing toward European origins that makes the difference. It is the position of the region as a player in the process. By contrast with Europe, the UK's own version of regional industrial policy sees the beneficiary as the *firm* and not the region *per se.* Selective Financial Assistance, the last substantive instrument for regional policy in the UK, is granted to businesses in qualifying areas according to centrally determined criteria. This is consistent with an overarching view which has no concept of the region other than as a *container for programmes* of various kinds operated under the auspices of national government. The EU, in marked contrast, views the regions as *entities in themselves* (see, for example, CEC 1993b; OECD and CEC 1993) and many of its regulations imply the existence of some form of effective regional body – in drawing up the SPDs for example – which can be charged with the responsibility to achieve defined objectives for social and economic development to foster cohesion (CEC 1993b, 1994d–f).

The effects of this contrast in perspectives between the UK and the EU on issues of regional governance cannot be over-emphasized. For the **regions as containers** proposition what is deemed to be needed is *administration* – systems to draw down, spend and account for resources from approved programmes, both national and European. For the **region as a level of governance** what is needed is an effective local *partnership* to determine the nature of the problem and to draw up, within the rules, an effective and coherent programme (plan) to deal with it. As this chapter has shown, current financial stringency gives a sharp cutting edge to this fundamental difference in approach. As a focal point in debates about contested governance there is a strong perception from the Objective 1 and Objective 2 Regions in England that Whitehall is effectively inserting itself between them and resources given specifically to help them carry out the government's mandate to be more flexible and entrepreneurial in building regional competitive advantage.

Institutional issues: the delivery of regional and local economic development policy in England

Consistent with the dominant view from the government that, insofar as regional policy exists in the UK, its purpose is to ensure the *better functioning of markets*, the current institutional framework in England is dedicated to *more efficient delivery of programmes for the regions* (Lloyd 1995) The programmes themselves are nationally determined and those charged with delivering them are accountable in the normal way to Ministers and to Parliament. From this viewpoint resources derived from the EU under the Structural Funds are made to the national exchequer and disbursed to responsible government departments for distribution to the regions concerned strictly in accordance with government prescription. While those departments are, of course, able to take advice from regional and other interests, control by the centre is absolute.

The creation of the IROs, or Government Offices (GOs) as they are more commonly referred to, has been critical in this context (for more detail on the GOs see Chapter 6). Their role is to provide a vehicle by which the wishes of departmental Ministers for the regions are carried out in a more coordinated and efficient manner. Within the structure the key figure is the Senior Regional Director whose local powers far override those of any other individual in the region, provoking, as we have seen, newspaper satire about the new regional viceroys. The *regional* element in the creation of the GO is to **weld together as teams people who are working for the more efficient delivery of programmes for the region**. The wording is revealing. Programmes are external. The job is to deliver them efficiently. The problem to be tackled by the creation of the IROs is deemed to have come from a lack of coherence among the regionally configured multiple arms of the UK Civil Service and not from any weakness in the conceptualization of what regional programmes might have been about.

Paradoxically, however, at another level within the mandate of the GOs, there does exist a concept of places as entities for which coherent, locally sponsored, programmes can be drawn up. This is in the Single Regeneration Budget (SRB) – itself an attempt by the Department of the Environment (DoE) to give coherence to a previously disjointed battery of programmes. The beneficiaries of this policy are identified with particular areas against carefully set out plans. The areas are, however, local in scale rather than regional in scope. Here there exists a philosophy rather closer to the European one than the firm-based perspective of the Department of Trade and Industry (DTI) which has responsibility for the rump of regional policy.

Outside these regional arms of central government in the English regions there exist what the report of the Trade and Industry Committee calls a bewildering profusion of other agencies in the field of local economic development, including local authorities, TECs, regional and local development organizations, Business Links, UDCs, City Challenge partnerships, Chambers of Commerce, universities and other institutions of higher education. In the face of such a confused array, the role of the GOs is to 'help coordinate the activities of other agencies where necessary' (Trade and Industry Committee 1995a, p.li). This help is to be given in a context determined by the dominant ideology of what was described earlier as regions as containers for programmes. Strategy for local economic development, where it exists, is a derivative of national macro-economic policy for the enhancement of competitiveness by removing barriers to the efficient operation of markets. Regional and local agencies can have a role in shaping and delivering policy to meet these overarching national requirements for their areas. What is not countenanced in English policy is a specifically *regional* strategy based on the identification of regional problems and the delivery of coherent regional programmes to address them. This, of course, is precisely what the new, post-1993, Structural Funds Regulations require in the preparation and negotiation of SPDs (CEC 1993b).

More than this, the Structural Funds Regulations place particular emphasis on economic and social partnership based in the regions themselves. The story of the negotiation into place of the six SPDs for which the authors were involved as independent advisors to Brussels shows how the working out of these fundamental tensions in both national/regional and national/European terms had a powerful impact on the outcomes and is continuing to lead to sharp-edged local battles involving the formation of unlikely coalitions dedicated to challenging the hegemony of the GO.

Structural Funds Allocations for the United Kingdom

The Objective 1 regions

Three regions in the UK were designated as being eligible for Objective 1 funding following the 1993 reforms. These were Highlands and Islands (Scotland), Northern Ireland and Merseyside. For each of these the UK authorities were required to submit to the Commission SPDs for the period 1994–1999 on the basis of which negotiations were to proceed. Following a successful outcome the *plans* were to be signed off, with confirmation from Brussels coming in the form of a Community Support Framework (CSF) for each region. A total of some £1850 million has been committed to the three UK-based Objective 1 regions for the period 1994–1999 (figures calculated from CEC 1994g–i). This authority to spend was granted by the Commission on 13 July 1994 after what turned out to be, in all three cases, a protracted series of often acrimonious discussions between Commission officers and their UK counterparts in the DTI and the regional offices of government. The priorities finally agreed as the basis of each reconversion plan are shown in Table 4.2.

Table 4.2 UK Objective 1 regions 1994: the choice of priorities in the SPDs

Merseyside	*Highlands and Islands*	*Northern Ireland*
1. Inward investment and corporate business development	Business development	Economic development and competitiveness
2. Development of indigenous enterprise and local business development	Tourism, heritage, cultural development	Investments in communities and people
3. Knowledge-based industries and advance technologies	Preservation and enhancement of environment	Reducing the effects of peripherality
4. Cultural, media and leisure industries	Primary sector support and related food industries	Development of agriculture, fisheries and the rural economy
5. Action for the People of Merseyside: integration, better housing, community development and a better quality of life	Communications and service networks to support business and community development	Protection and enlargement of the natural and built environment

Source: CEC (1994g–i)

It is worthy of note that all three of the Objective 1 plans for regions in the UK contain specific commitments to **social** as well as economic regeneration consistent with the specific requirement to address the needs of excluded groups. This is a European requirement and not one which the UK authorities would have necessarily elevated to priority status without the specific requirements of the Objective 1 regulations. Concessions were, however, not always made by the UK government to the spirit if not the final legal letter of the Structural Funds Regulations. The UK government has set its face against applying the provisions of Objective 4 within its territory. Similarly, the Objective 1 provisions for programmes of assistance in the areas of pre-vocational education and health were specifically ruled out in the UK.

Negotiating the Merseyside CSF into place

While the authors cannot comment in detail on the programmes for the Highlands and Islands and Northern Ireland, the process of negotiation and agreement for Merseyside provides some valuable insights about the ways in which contested views emerged at various levels about the nature of the SPD and the resultant CSF.[1] For more detail and critical evaluation of the SPD and its operation on Merseyside see Chapter 6.

Perhaps the first point to be made is that there appears to be a willingness among all parties to set ambitious objectives. For Merseyside, for example, the SPD recognizes that to close the economic gap between the region and the European average would require a growth in gross domestic product (GDP) some 5 per cent above the EU average and growth in employment of some 8400 jobs in each of the 5 years of the proposed programme. Given previous historical trends which have left the region's per capita GDP at about 75 per cent of the EU average (a slide which itself prompted the region's eligibility for Objective 1 Status) and involved annual job loss running at 6000 in the past 13 years, the SPD is clearly wise to acknowledge that the closing of the economic gap between Merseyside and Europe as a whole will take longer than its six-year life (CEC 1995). The SPD nevertheless still goes on to claim, on the basis of specially commissioned regional forecasts, that a net increase of some 25,000 jobs can be achieved with the intervention of Objective 1 funding – a growth of 5000 jobs in each of the SPD's 5 years of operation thus neatly replacing the previous annual loss of 6000 jobs in the 13 years preceding its inception. We would argue that, considering the history of the region and the timescale for the SPD, if this forecast is achieved it would represent an almost revolutionary turnaround in the region's fortunes.

---

1 In November 1993 the authors were contracted by Directorate-General XVI of the European Commission to act as independent advisors on the recently delivered SPD for the newly designated Merseyside Objective 1 Region (Lloyd and Meegan 1994). This had been presented to Brussels by the UK government in accordance with the new Structural Funds Regulations promulgated in July 1993 (CEC 1993b).

In order to bring these rather ambitious changes about, the agreed plan concentrates on the five priorities or, as they are referred to in the SPD itself, drivers for change set out in Table 4.2. The process of arriving at these priorities for the Merseyside case is instructive about the nature of the negotiation process.

The original Merseyside 2000 document was submitted to the Commission in November 1993. It was based upon an underlying philosophy that the purpose of the SPD was to draw down, spend and account for the requisite funds from European Regional Development Fund (ERDF) and European Social Fund (ESF) in accordance with the rules set out in the appropriate European legislation (see Figure 4.1). The SPD was not a 'plan', nor did the UK authorities see such an

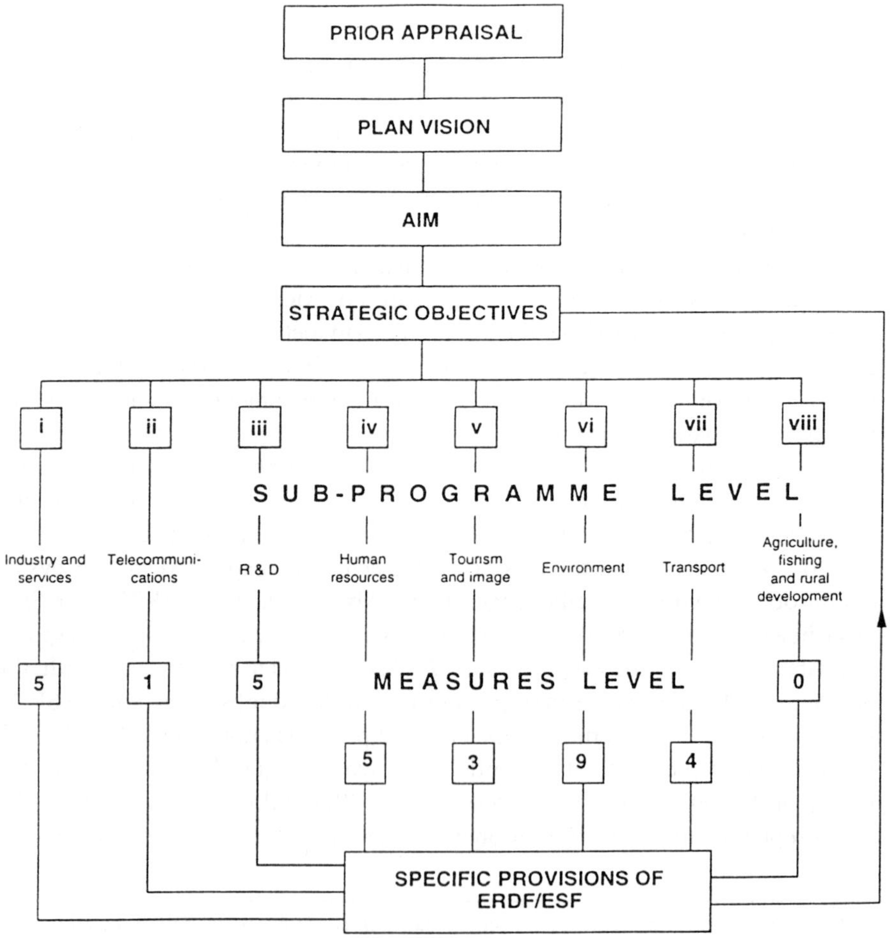

Source: Lloyd and Meegan 1994

Figure 4.1 Merseyside 2000 plan philosophy

approach as appropriate. What was significantly absent was an analysis of the nature of the particular conversion problem of the Merseyside region with a set of proposals to address it (Lloyd and Meegan 1994). This is in accordance with the prevailing Ministerial view in the responsible department (DTI) in the UK that there is no need for a regional plan because 'the great strength of our system is its flexibility' (Trade and Industry Committee 1995a, p.liii). In this context it is revealing that the Government Office for Merseyside (GOM), in its response to the Trade and Industry Select Committee, stated that it had not been asked to prepare a regeneration statement.

The view of the UK government is that to introduce formal statements or strategies setting out priorities for regeneration 'could limit the flexibility of local partnership-building capacity which the IROs are seeking to encourage in order that local needs can be addressed on a more responsive basis' (Trade and Industry Committee 1995a, p.liii). The essence of the view of the UK authorities in the negotiations with Brussels was that planning and strategy was unhelpful and that their focus lay on the primacy of flexible regional responses to market forces. This is, of course, in clear contradiction to the programming principle set out in the Structural Funds regulations which requires that: 'The Member States concerned shall submit to the Commission their regional development plan' (CEC 1993b, p.50).

Such plans are described in detail as including (CEC 1993b, pp.50–51):

1. a description of the current situation with regard to disparities and development gaps
2. a description of an appropriate strategy to achieve the objectives
3. an appraisal of the environmental situation
4. an indicative overall financial table...corresponding to each regional development priority adopted in the context of the plan.

The concepts of appraisal, plan strategy, priority and programme are central to the Commission's view of the regional conversion process.

Given such a fundamental opposition of views on the regional development policy and equally divergent views on the issue of social exclusion and the means of dealing with it, it is hardly surprising that the negotiations were to become protracted. In the event it was July 1994 before the Merseyside CSF was signed and March 1995 before the agreed SPD (CEC 1995) became publicly available. Paradoxically, the bids for the 1994 and 1995 calendar years were already called for and the bid rounds closed before this latter event took place (see Chapter 6).

Interestingly, the plan when it emerged represented a compromise which sought, following a suggested framework in matrix form (see Figure 4.2), to preserve both supply-side and more strategic perspectives on the structure of the overall programme. Supply-side measures for facilitating the operation of market forces across Merseyside were captured by the rows of the matrix. The *driving forces* of the SPD, the verticals, were more strategically conceived as dynamic forces for

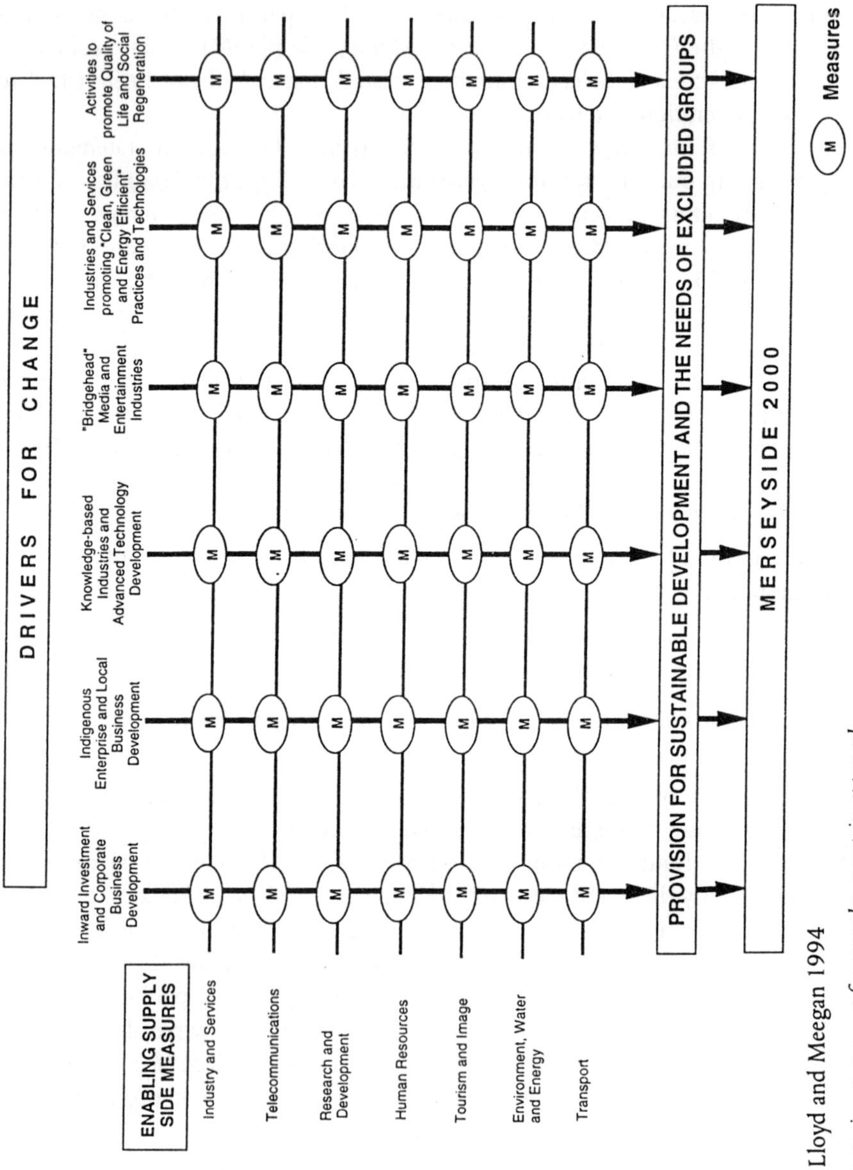

Source: Lloyd and Meegan 1994

Figure 4.2 Strategic management frameworks: a matrix approach

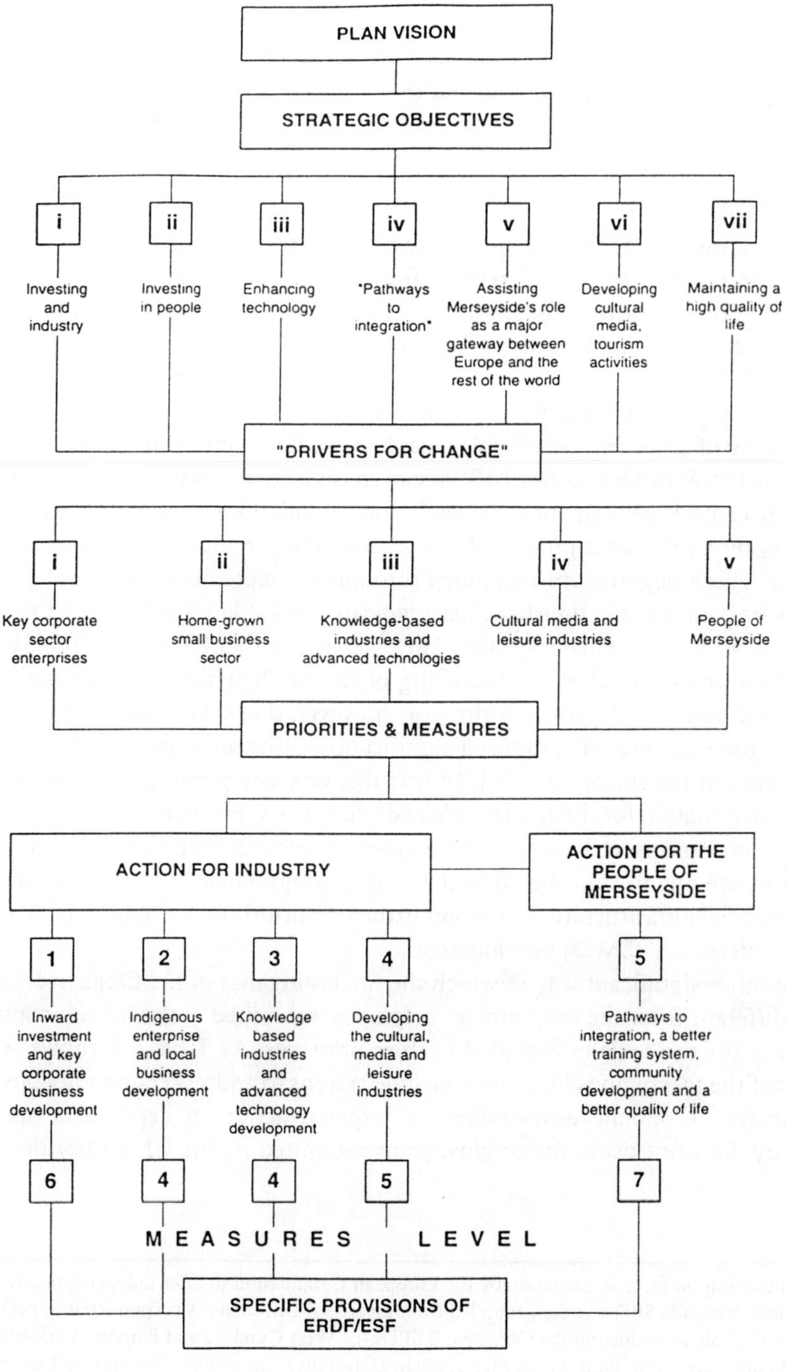

Source: Based on CEC 1995

Figure 4.3 Regional development strategy and structural fund priorities, Merseyside 1994–1999.

change around which a current strategy for economic and social development could be constructed. The structure set out in Figure 4.3 was finally agreed by all parties to provide an appropriate **regional development strategy** (see Chapter 6).

The Objective 2 regions

As with Objective 1, the new general regulations for the Structural Funds were in operation for the Objective 2 regions from July 1993. Following the submission of a list of proposed areas for all Member States, the Commission formally adopted the list of areas eligible under Objective 2 on 21 January 1994 for the period 1994–1996.[2]

With regard to Objective 2, two three-year phases are planned with the possibility of adjusting the eligible areas and the CSFs at the end of the first three years in 1996. In March/April 1994, eleven Objective 2 plans were submitted by the UK central government to Brussels and negotiations continued on what was once again a protracted process of appraisal and negotiation (Bachtler and Michie 1994). These negotiations continued throughout September and October 1994 and were concluded in time to achieve *spend* in 1994. Plans for the UK's Objective 5b areas were on a similar trajectory. However, for neither Objective 2 nor 5b areas was there the comprehensive redrafting of the SPDs which occurred with Merseyside's Objective 1 plan. It is the case, however, that the Objective 2 redrafting and negotiation process produced significantly different plans to the first drafts submitted in the spring of 1994. In part this was as a product of the experience of the negotiation for the Merseyside and other UK Objective 1 plans. One of the biggest changes to emerge was the renewed emphasis from the Commission on plans which aim to shift the Objective 2 SPD programmes from a regional spend on physical infrastructure to *soft* infrastructure priorities for small and medium sized enterprises' (SMEs) development.

Another significant way in which the final outcomes of the Objective 2 SPDs was different from the programmes originally submitted is the introduction of a concern for the socially excluded in their priorities. As Table 4.3 shows, all the plans of the five regions listed now include actions to address community business, community economic development or targeted action in deprived areas. This priority did not exist in the original plans submitted by the UK authorities.

2 Following on from an invitation by the European Commission to offer independent advice on the Merseyside SPD a wider group led from Liverpool University was contracted to perform a similar role in evaluating the Objective 2 SPDs for West Cumbria and Furness; Yorkshire and Humberside (John Shutt, Leeds Metropolitan University); Lancashire; Cheshire and Greater Manchester (Jamie Peck, University of Manchester); the West Midlands (Gill Bentley, Coventry University) and the East Midlands (Graham Haughton and Trevor Hart, Leeds Metropolitan University).

Table 4.3 Final priority policy objectives In five Objective 2 SPDs

Priority measures	*North West England*	*West Cumbria and Furness*	*West Midlands*	*Yorkshire and Humberside*	*East Midlands*
1.	Support for small businesses	Industrial and business development	Develop research and development and encourage technological innovation	Action to support SMEs	To strengthen technological base by stimulating R & D and innovation and SMEs
2.	Action to strengthen and diversify medium-sized enterprises	Development of knowledge-based industries	Support indigenous enterprise and local business	Action to strengthen and diversify mature SMEs	Indigenous enterprise and business and enterprise
3.	Development of knowledge-based industries and advanced technologies	Tourism development	Assisting diversification and new growth	Action to strengthen the knowledge-based industries and develop advanced technology	Diversification of the economy
4.	Action to attract inward investment and to support the key corporate sector	Community economic development	Urban and community regeneration	Action to attract new industry and services	Community economic development
5.	Tourism and cultural industries and image enhancement		Building cultural media and tourist industries	Action to develop the tourism and cultural industries	
6.	Action for community economic development			Targeted action in key deprived areas	

Source: Lloyd *et al.* 1995

Perhaps one of the more interesting features of the five Objective 2 plans as they emerged from the negotiation process is that, despite differences in precise wording, **they are all remarkably similar**. All address inward investment, the SME sector, the knowledge-based industries, and community-based development. All, in fact, have strong priorities for building tourist industries, though this is subsumed in some cases under broader headings. They do, in fact, emerge as relatively orthodox blueprints for development – tackling well tried areas of activity with, for the most part, well tried measures. It was a clear feature of the plans that they were significantly lacking in innovation (Lloyd *et al.* 1995). In part, it can be suggested that this was a product of the way the plan-negotiation process was conducted. The struggle over ideology between Brussels and the UK authorities and the drive for compromise was likely to suppress innovation. From the regional perspective the disappearance of the original plans into the *mincing machines* of those same negotiations meant that little opportunity existed for feedback to generate more creative thinking. Indeed, in true British fashion the entire process was cloaked in secrecy from first to last. From the Commission perspective, the effects of tight timescales, staff changes and sheer weight of work meant that the Objective 2 plans did not receive the same feedback, consultation and scrutiny as there had been in the case of Merseyside.

Issues of Contested Governance: Focal Points for Conflict

While there were many concerns which arose from the *ex-ante* assessments in which the authors were involved (the Merseyside Objective 1 plan and the Objective 2 plans of five English regions) the focus here is on four key issues:

- partnership
- transparency
- additionality
- programming, appraisal and evaluation.

These are particularly important because they represent the *key principles* of the Structural Funds philosophy.

Partnership

The concept of partnership is central to the Structural Funds plan process. 'The partnership shall cover the preparation and financing, as well as the *ex-ante* appraisal, monitoring and *ex-post* evaluation of the operations' (CEC 1993b, pp.48–49). What constitutes the effective partnership in each regional case is, however, rather obscurely defined as follows:

> Community operations shall be such as to complement or contribute to corresponding national operations. They shall be established through close consultations between the Commission, the Member State concerned and

> the competent authorities and bodies – including within the framework of each Member State's national rules and current practices, the economic and social partner designated by the Member State at national, regional, local or other level with all parties acting as partners in pursuit of a common goal. These consultations shall hereinafter, be referred to as the partnership. (CEC 1993b, p.48)

In the case of the English regions the resolution of this requirement for partnership has strongly privileged the position of the new integrated GOs (created during the plan review process). Equally, a considerably less privileged position has been offered to the private sector and to the voluntary sector in each region and, of course, in line with neo-Liberal thinking, none whatsoever to local trades unions. The general mix of key consultees comprised the local authorities, the TECs and the newly privatized public utilities providers along with local quasi-public agencies for inward investment promotion and infrastructure development.

Many of the bodies constituting the partnership – seen by Brussels as a process of consultation as much as a group of partners acting in concert – are long-term beneficiaries of European funding assistance in one form or another. Most were heavily involved in the administration of previous European programmes under Integrated Development Operations or other aspects of the pre-1993 Structural Funds programme. From this perspective it is clear that, beyond the 1993 reforms, there were likely to be forces operating within evolved systems of partnership which would see local and national government interests come together to resist radical change and maintain more traditional flows of funds to projects.

In the case of the Merseyside Objective 1 programme the partnership continued to be dominated by the five local authorities, the TEC, the Merseyside Development Corporation, the Chamber of Commerce and interests from Higher Education. The drivers for change in the agreed SPD gave considerable weight to the importance of the private sector – both corporate business and SMEs – in providing active leadership as the programme developed. In the event, however, the private sector felt itself to be excluded from what it saw as an essentially public sector plan. As a result the SME sector fought to obtain a seat at the table by a vigorous lobbying campaign aimed at Ministers and local popular opinion. 'Merseyside Business and Manufacturing Challenge' came into existence as a vehicle to press private sector claims to a place in the Objective 1 programme against what it saw as the exclusionary tactics of a public sector club (Merseyside Business and Manufacturing Challenge Group 1994). In parallel, the local authority sector fought hard to gain seats for elected council representatives on the key committee charged with monitoring the Objective 1 programme. Also feeling themselves to be on the outer edge of a cosy partnership of a public sector quango and GO interests, the voluntary sector fought hard to obtain a voice – particularly in respect of the Pathways to Integration driver for targeting excluded groups (North West Network 1994).

Across the board, the arrival of £1.6 billion in additional resource through Objective 1 provoked what was, at first, a scramble for a seat at the table of the so-called partnership on Merseyside. Over time, however, the degree of control exercised by the GO and its Director and the effectiveness of the coalition of long-standing partners saw things settle down. Elected members were given seats on the Monitoring Committee but an immediate effect of this was to see much of the decision-making migrate to the lower-level Technical Panels. Here groups of officers from the key boards managed decision-making in relation to the bids forwarded to the programme.

In the contest for local governance the Merseyside experience in relation to Objective 1 is instructive. In the first instance it was the local authority sector which took the initiative through its established European networks to have Merseyside designated although, as with the region's previous experience of securing European aid under the Merseyside Integrated Development Operation, this initiative was not helped by the neo-Liberal inspired reorganization of local government that saw the abolition of the Merseyside County Council in 1986 (Meegan 1994). Subsequently, the UK government took up the bid and pressed the case with Brussels. While local Merseyside interests were closely in tune with Brussels in pressing a *regional* case, the UK government perceived it as an opportunity to recapture resource from the Structural Funds to offset its position as a net positive contributor.

In the preparation and negotiation of the SPD, Merseyside and Brussels interests were close while the relations of both with the UK national authorities were frequently in conflict. In the outcome the drivers for change model seemed to satisfy all parties. However, beyond the signing of the CSF new more localized coalitions and alliances began to emerge around the principle of *take*. In this the interests of GO and key local public sector players began once again to converge, with struggles becoming more localized about shares of resource, while debates about regional versus national perspectives in regional planning receded. At this stage contested governance tended to become reduced to the technical level – issues abut bid scoring systems, the turnaround speed of bid cycles, local qualifying rules for bidders, definitions of appropriate *match* for funding and so on.

Looked at from the outside it appears that the Objective 1 programme, despite its innovative beginnings and the scale of resource applied to it, is now bedding down to become a relatively orthodox traditional programme for drawing down, spending and accounting for European funds. In this it has tended to have in place the pre-existing partners – most of whom are long-standing beneficiaries of Structural Funds. In the face of fiscal stringency and the micro-motives of each individual partner the imperative of *take* has rendered the programme anti-innovative and exclusionary. While higher order debates continue around issues of regional planning versus market forces or a Europe of the regions versus national sovereignty, on Merseyside these now take second place to more pragmatic concerns in attempting to solicit bids, process them and organize spend against a tight timetable.

To a significant degree these experiences of partnership in relation to the Merseyside plan were replicated in the Objective 2 plans. It was a feature of our critique of all the Objective 2 plans offered to DG XVI that, without significant exception, they rolled-forward previous plan frameworks from the previous funding period and were lacking in innovation and imagination (Lloyd *et al.* 1995). In essence, all the plans appeared, once again, to have been framed around a desire to draw down, spend and account for European Structural Funds assistance with a particular emphasis on supporting existing government programmes. This was reflective of past practice with Objective 2 funding. The new opportunities for more integrated and coherent planning through the medium of the SPDs was even less widely grasped in the Objective 2 plans. The nature of the partnerships as defined by the UK authorities denied opportunities for innovative action and a degree of local institutional capacity-building which the new Structural Funds Regulations made possible at the plan preparation stage. Beyond the signing of the CSFs any further prospect for institutional searching tends to come to an abrupt halt as the mechanics of the plan process take over.

In respect of implementation, the Regulation provides for the following: 'Monitoring committees shall be set up within the framework of the partnership, by agreement between the Member State concerned and the Commission' (CEC 1993b, p.68). As has been shown, given the framework of the partnership for the UK regions set out above, the same groups of local stakeholders (primarily GO and local public and ex-public sector agencies) now emerge as the guardians of the implementation process. GOs in every case in the English regions have reserved to themselves the role of Secretariat to manage the on-going operations of the programme. This has had the effect of reinforcing a strong bias toward central government control at every stage. While this may be regarded as essential for the purposes of parliamentary accountability, it would be the view of the authors that opportunities for a strong degree of regional ownership and institutional capacity building are forgone. In particular, the failure actively to engage the private sector, voluntary sector and trade unions more directly seems to deny the entire process an important element of local skill and knowledge.

Transparency

One of the issues surrounding local governance is that concerning access to information. For local partners and agencies to be effective there is a need to tackle asymmetries in available information on key areas of policy. While the traditional approach of the UK Civil Service to this is based upon the importance of confidentiality, the Structural Funds Regulations require transparency. Once again the Objective 1 and Objective 2 planning and negotiation processes provide a sharp edge of conflict in this respect between the UK authorities on the one hand

and regional agencies and Brussels on the other. The Structural Funds Regulations state that 'For the greater effectiveness of the Funds the Commission shall ensure that particular attention is paid to transparency of management in its implementation of them' (CEC 1993b, p.69).

However, for all that the process for preparation of the SPDs for the English regions was often unnecessarily opaque. In the case of Merseyside there was wide publication of the original draft Merseyside 2000 document and a call for comment. Such relative openness was, however, not a feature of the Objective 2 plans. Many were regarded as confidential though there was widespread informal circulation of drafts to key consultees rather than a wider constituency. Even for Merseyside, beyond the *ex-ante* assessment and negotiations stage, the finally 'agreed' plan was kept closely under GO control – with drafts circulating but no definitive document officially available until the end of March 1995 (after the completion of the two rounds of calls for bids against the SPD).

Across the Objective 2 regions there was a good deal of variety in the openness with which the SPDs were treated. In some areas partnerships were relatively open and flexible while in others the SPD was drafted in the GO with very little attempt to let it see the light of day outside.

A particular issue arises with respect of the membership of the Monitoring Committees. Within the twin concepts of partnership and transparency an examination of the composition of these committees provides little evidence of a *transparent* logic for their structure. The issue of elected membership arose in the Objective 1 negotiations with the Commission but the arrangements agreed for Merseyside do not appear to have been replicated in the Objective 2 regions. Similar considerations apply with respect to the membership and definition of powers to the Technical Panels. Regardless of other considerations, there is a need for both Monitoring Committee and Technical Panels to be both efficient and effective. Considerations of membership and size are highly relevant in this context as are transparently declared reasons for the particular format chosen.

Additionality

A longstanding bone of contention between Brussels and UK government has been the issue of additionality. There is also a regional versus national dimension to this conflict. Within the English regions in which the authors carried out *ex-ante* assessments of the SPDs there was considerable unease about precisely how much of the promised spend from the Structural Funds would actually represent *net additional resource* to the regions in question. It is important to be clear about the nature of the additionality clause in the Structural Funds regulation.

The Structural Funds regulations state that:

> For each Objective, each Member State now has to 'maintain, in the whole of the territory concerned, its public structural or comparable expenditure at least at the same level as in the previous programming period, taking into

account, however, the macro-economic circumstances in which the funding takes place, as well as a number of specific economic circumstances, namely privatisations, an unusual level of public structural expenditure undertaken in the previous programming period and business cycles in the national economy.' (CEC 1993b, p.25)

The key issue here is how far it is possible to claim that specific circumstances prevailed which make it possible for the authorities to argue that full net additionality cannot be expected. There is a suspicion widely held that in the case of the English regions Structural Funds were being applied on the basis of a proposition not of net additionality above previous levels of resource and activity but on the argument that, under financial stringency, the regions selected for conversion assistance were better off than they would have been without the input of Structural Funds. One of the fringe benefits of the additionality criterion is that to justify spend the UK authorities will need to provide some form of regional accounts for the designated areas.

Although the lack of transparency of the funding process makes quantitative evaluation difficult, many regional bodies believe that a substantial proportion of the *regional* funds have been *captured* by the GOs to support national programmes. These are operated in the designated areas and elsewhere. Shares of funds attributed to the TECs, the SMART and SPUR technology programmes of the DTI, the Further Education Colleges and the residual business development programmes under the new Business Link initiative are considered by many local authorities, for example, to be allocated to national programmes in ways which make regional additionality impossible to guarantee. Indeed, Knowsley Metropolitan Borough Council on Merseyside recently invited the relevant Commissioner, Mrs Monica Wulf-Mathies, to investigate this aspect of the additionality question.

Since the focal point of both the flow of funding and the management of the Structural Funds programmes resides with the GOs in the regions, *de facto* control of the allocation of the resources is assured. Allocations which feed those projects and programmes for which the GOs, in their officially defined role, are the regional managers for the national state are the focus of the greatest contention. Whitehall sees these as *regional* in the sense that they are delivered within regions. Local interests see them as essentially *national* programmes where it is difficult to discern whether their particular region is doing better or worse than others by virtue of the provision of the Structural Funds. While the debates rumble on the projects are being financed, put in to operation and managed under the auspices of the Secretariats and the Monitoring Committees. Only *ex-post* evaluation will be able to give firm answers to these charges of failing to deliver net additional resource or net beneficial outputs to the designated regions.

Programming, appraisal and evaluation

Earlier sections of the chapter indicated how clear differences exist between the UK authorities and the European Commission on the issue of programming. Brussels requires regional plans, while Whitehall expresses no willingness to provide them. Programming in the UK context involves the organization of the bid, spend, accountability process. Throughout the negotiations on the six SPDs there was no concession on this to the requirements of the Structural Funds legislation. The programming documents which emerged and were approved by the granting of CSFs could in no real sense be described as regional plans or regional strategies. All referred to the previously drawn up (with Brussels funding) regional strategies but having made reference to them and drawn some of their broad objectives from them the SPDs move quickly on to specify measures consistent with priorities. Interestingly, these priorities are never themselves prioritized as a plan would seem to require. The commonality in the priorities provides a clear indication that they are not drawn from regionally-based assessments of the particular local demands for reconversion. They are bases on which to draw down spend and account for ERDF and ESF resources. The programming principle is then carefully redefined to meet the UK government's own national agenda for a flexible market driven response to regional need. Local partners are merely the end points of a conveyor belt delivering nationally devised and promoted policies in the regional context.

Appraisal and evaluation is a statutory requirement under Article 26 of the Structural Funds Regulations. It is a joint responsibility of the Member States and the Commission and is to be carried out 'within the framework of the partnership'. The relevant regulation specifies that:

> appraisal and evaluation shall, according to circumstances, be carried out by contrasting the goals with the results obtained where applicable and by reference to macroeconomic and sectoral objectives and indicators based on regional and national statistics yielded by descriptive and analytical studies and to quantitative analyses. (CEC 1993b, p.69)

One of the difficulties which affected all the SPDs with respect to their ability to provide a suitable basis for future evaluation was the failure internally to prioritize interventions against some prior notion of what might *drive* economic development in a particular regional context. This is inevitable in the face of a plan philosophy which had a theory of regional economic development limited largely to the provision of supporting infrastructures, both physical and human, and waiting for market forces to deliver positive outcomes.

The difficulty with this approach from the point of view of appraisal and evaluation is that it denies the plan-makers the opportunity to conduct a prior appraisal which can anticipate the expected impact of intervention and so evaluate outcomes against goals. Expected outputs can be set at the level of individual measures but the overall impact of the programme with regional specification cannot be readily estimated in terms demanded by evaluation. Evaluation under these conditions depends upon measurements of progress against baseline conditions but is hard pressed to discover which interventions made a real difference in driving any positive outcomes.

Thus, while monitoring of the plans will be relatively easily undertaken, evaluation will depend on movements in macro-economic indicators against baselines and not on progress toward projected regional impacts. Overall, the opportunity has been forgone in the latest round of bids for Structural Funds assistance to develop integrated, coherent plans capturing the benefits of some thinking about what – region by region – would provide drivers for change in the direction of required outcomes.

Conclusions

Returning to the issue of contested governance, what has been witnessed in the process of introducing the new post-1993 Structural Funds Regulations into the English regions is a multi-dimensional contest over power, resources and accountability. This is consistent with the *new times* proposition that institutional searching in the post-Fordist transition is leading to a comprehensive renegotiation of issues of governance and a search for new forms of regulation (Peck and Tickell 1994). New discourses give dominance to the primacy of market forces, to the imperative of restoring entrepreneurialism, to the need to be flexible and to the need to defer to business interests and remove the state as far as possible from the sphere of economic life. These discourses in the more extreme forms see the trickle down from economic development as the primary means of achieving social cohesion at a time when concern for the rise of the underclass or the excluded is rising rapidly up the agenda. In the face of these growing concerns with *social*, and from the viewpoint of this chapter, *spatial* polarization different lines are being taken across the spectrum of views from crude neo-Liberalism to tentatively re-emerging neo-Keynesianism (see, for example, Hutton 1995). The search for the **big idea** continues.

What we are seeing in the debates over the application of the Structural Funds to the English regions are *differing emphases* in these constantly evolving debates between the European Union and the UK government and between the regions and the centre. Caricaturing such debates, we can see them in the spatial context as conflicts between the weight given to business localism and the primacy of competition as opposed to cohesion and Euro-regionalism. Of course, strongly overlaid on this is the issue of *subsidiarity* contested at national versus European level and also at regional versus central level. These two polarizing debates form the prime axes of the contested perspectives set out in this chapter. What this chapter has illustrated is that they play themselves out as much locally as they do nationally and in the European domain.

Focusing more closely on the case of the English regions, what can we say we have learned about contested governance and the role of European rather than UK national forces? Perhaps the most powerful point to emerge is that in spite of the key principles of the Structural Funds as enshrined in the legislation, the application of those principles in the English regions seems to have produced an outcome where relatively orthodox accountability approaches have entirely overridden EU predilections for partnership, strategy, plan and evaluation. What has emerged is much more prosaic than the Delors package had in mind for the reconversion of European regions.

What this can tell us, perhaps, is that in the context of the English regions, the contest for a more powerful regional ownership role has been easily overridden by prescriptions for flexible local systems of governance for delivering national policy. Government and the orthodox hierarchy of power in the UK has been able easily to dominate those more open and flexible systems of governance which the national state has sought to create. The very flexibility of these systems, seen as a strength for delivering entrepreneurialism and a drive for the new, is a source of inherent weakness in any contest for power and ownership against the centralized state. The dominance of central government prescription for the English regions seems, in the absence of political change nationally, only too assured.

This unequal power relationship in the emerging form of local governance does not relate solely to that between central government and its own flexible progeny (the TECs, UDCs, Business Links, etc.) but also between the state and its quangos and the new participants in local economic development drawn from the increasingly grey area of civil society. The voluntary sector is perhaps the main standard bearer in this context and perhaps one of the most interesting (and unintended?) consequences of the recent round of institutional searching has been the growing role of this sector in local economic development. Nowhere has this been more marked than on Merseyside where the invitation, however qualified, to participate in the development and implementation of the SPD and in other initiatives such as City Challenge has been gladly seized. As a result, partnership has indeed been broadened in the spirit at least of such notions as a *Citizen's Europe* (European Communities Economic and Social Consultative Assembly 1992). But the foothold remains a precarious one and the experience to date appears to be one of the relatively established groups defending their share of the available funding and less established ones remaining on the outside unsure, and in many cases unable (not least because of the bureaucratic rules of the game) to participate.

The established hierarchy of central government and the quangos oscillating around it eclipse the organic and loosely structured networks that characterize the activities of these voluntary groups. It is all very well then for Eurocrats to make noises about cohesion, about social partners and about excluded groups but it has to be recognized that to include the excluded means the active building of capacity from amongst the excluded, a careful nurturing of the inherent strengths of local civil society. But this is a long-term strategy requiring intervention that does not easily fit the timetabling of SPD programming, sensitively developed, non-traditional output measurements and constant monitoring. Such a strategy, moreover, is difficult to implement in a political and policy context in which established groups and interests are zealously defending their programme delivery. To return to the analogy used earlier in the chapter, some groups cannot elbow their way to the table, they need to be invited and guaranteed a place at it.

Another feature of the debate over the latest round of Structural Funds transfers to the English regions is the *ephemerality* of the contest. The debates addressed in this chapter were on the agenda while the SPDs were being created and while the negotiations were taking place. As soon as the CSF was signed, however, two things happened. The Commission retreated to the edge of the arena (to reappear only at the evaluation stage) and the principle of **take** came to dominate the principle of **partnership** locally. For the moment then, in bidding processes and scoring systems, the sheer weight of the bureaucratic procedure of spending £1.6 billion dominates the agenda on Merseyside – as it can expect to do for the remainder of the programme period.

The most problematic aspect of the governance issue in respect of local economic development which emerged from the Merseyside case in particular takes us back to the heart of the current theoretical debate. What seems also to have been lost in the process of applying the Structural Funds to the English regions is the *pragmatic*, not political, importance of institutional capacity. At the most practical level there is a lack of the sheer capacity to conceive, manage and develop programmes as ambitious as, say, Merseyside's Pathways to Integration programme. This is potentially innovative and ground-breaking but the necessary local capacity to deliver it is largely absent. A process of mutual learning, of discussion, of idea-sharing, of strategy formulation is essential *before* the bid process can even begin to be effective. Across all the programmes there is a need locally to acquire the knowledge skills and to create *new institutional forms* to deliver competitive edge and address social exclusion.

The task is not trivial and it is certainly not one which a drive for bureaucratic effectiveness and value for money is going to address. At the level of *functionality*, therefore, there is a need to build the capacity even to spend the resources effectively for the achievement of the ambitious aims of the SPDs. If differential institutional capacities are a key variable in achieving competitive success in a flexibly-specialized global order, then there is a signal failure in the application of the Structural Funds to the English regions so far to deliver this advantage. The prescriptions of the key principles are beguiling. The outcomes are distressingly orthodox and surely unintended. In this respect the contested governance in the English regions may well play out to deliver rigidity rather than flexibility, hierarchy rather than governance, and bureaucracy rather than institutional effectiveness. Of course, the process is still in motion and change may come, but there is a serious concern that once the bid, spend and account motor starts to run, higher order – and competitively important – drivers for economic and social development will be run over in the process.

As to futures and prescription, at the very least there is a need to address the effectiveness of the concentration of power in the GOs. There is a need to consider institutional structures as a whole. Are British regions (and especially English ones) constitutionally and institutionally handicapped in participating fully in a *Europe of the Regions* (Meegan 1994)? At the very least there need to be regional think-tanks to take a slower, more considered and more strategic view outside the bid process. There is a need to look closely at transparency and additionality in the regional context. There is a need to avoid resources being more subsidy than investment. There is a need seriously to address the claims of private sector interests in some areas that Structural Funds programmes are public sector dominated. At the national level this should feed serious debates about regional governance in the wider political sense. At the European level a plea can be made for a far greater concern with allocating funds only where it can be demonstrated that a prior capacity building exercise has been given time to develop.

In the end, issues of local governance emerge not simply as debates about the democratic deficit and representational politics. They also emerge clearly set within the terms of the hegemonic neo-liberal discourse as providing the necessary *skills* to deliver complex programmes effectively and with value for money.

References

Amin, A. (ed) (1994) *Post-Fordism: A Reader.* Oxford: Basil Blackwell.

Bachtler, J. and Michie, R. (1994) 'Strengthening economic and social cohesion? The revision of the Structural Funds.' *Regional Studies 28*, 8, pp.789–790.

Benko, G. and Dunford, M. (eds) (1991) *Industrial Change and Regional Development: The Transformation of New Industrial Spaces.* London: Belhaven Press.

Child-Hill, R. (1992) 'Japan and the triad: the regional restructuring of the world economy.' Paper presented to the International Sociological Association Conference: *A New Urban and Regional Hierarchy*? University of California, Los Angeles, 23–25 April.

Colchester, N. and Buchan D. (1990) *Europe Relinked: Truths and Illusions on the Way to 1992.* London: Hutchinson.

Commission of the European Communities (CEC) (1993a) 'Local development: economies on human scale.' *Assessment and Outlook Information File.* Brussels: Directorate-General for Regional Policies, Commission of the European Communities.

Commission of the European Communities (CEC) (1993b) *Community Structural Funds, 1994–99: Revised Regulations and Comments.* Brussels: Commission of the European Communities.

Commission of the European Communities (CEC) (1994a) *Growth, Competitiveness, Employment. The Challenges and Ways Forward into the 21st Century*, White Paper. Brussels: Commission of the European Communities.

The authors would like to acknowledge the contribution of John Shutt, Jamie Peck, Gill Bentley, Graham Haughton and Trevor Hart to this chapter. The usual disclosures apply.

Commission of the European Communities (CEC) (1994b) *The Implementation of the Reform of the Structural Funds: Fourth Annual Report.* Brussels: Commission of the European Communities.

Commission of the European Communities (CEC) (1994c) *Community Structural Funds: Guide to the Community Initiatives, 1994–99,* First edition. Brussels: Commission of the European Communities.

Commission of the European Communities (CEC) (1994d) 'Competitiveness and Cohesion: Trends in the Regions.' *Fifth Periodic Report on the Social and Economic Situation and Development of the Regions of the Community.* Brussels: Commission of the European Communities.

Commission of the European Communities (CEC) (1994e) *Europe 2000+: Cooperation for European Territorial Development.* Brussels: Commission of the European Communities.

Commission of the European Communities (CEC) (1994f) *Europe at the Service of Regional Development.* Brussels: Commission of the European Communities.

Commission of the European Communities (CEC) (1994g) *The EC Structural Funds and the Development of Merseyside, 1994–1999: Summary of the Single Planning Document for Merseyside (Objective 1).* Brussels: Directorate General for Regional Policies, Commission of the European Communities.

Commission of the European Communities (CEC) (1994h) *The EC Structural Funds and the Development of the Highlands and Highlands, 1994–1999: Summary of the Single Planning Document for the Highlands and Highlands (Objective 1).* Brussels: Directorate General for Regional Policies, Commission of the European Communities.

Commission of the European Communities (CEC) (1994i) *The EC Structural Funds and the Development of Northern Ireland, 1994–1999: Summary of the Single Planning Document for Northern Ireland (Objective 1).* Brussels: Directorate General for Regional Policies, Commission of the European Communities.

Commission of the European Communities (CEC) (1995) *Merseyside Single Planning Document 1994–1999.* Brussels: Directorate General for Regional Policies, Commission of the European Communities.

Committee of the Regions (1994) 'Birth of the Committee of the Regions: making regional and local voices heard', *Inforegio Fact Sheet.* Brussels: Directorate-General for Regional Policies, Commission of the European Communities.

Cooke, P. and Morgan, K. (1993) 'The network paradigm: new departures in corporate and regional development.' *Environment and Planning D: Society and Space 11,* pp.543–564.

Dunford, M. (1994) 'Divergence, instability and exclusion in Britain and the wider Europe.' Paper presented to the Annual Conference of the Institute of British Geographers, University of Northumbria, Newcastle, 3–6 January.

Dunford, M. and Kafkalas, G. (eds) (1992) *Cities and Regions in the New Europe.* London: Belhaven Press.

Dunford, M. and Perrons, D. (1994) 'Regional inequality, regimes of accumulation and economic development in contemporary Europe.' *Transactions of the Institute of British Geographers 19,* 2, pp.163–182.

European Communities Economic and Social Consultative Assembly (1992) *The Citizen's Europe.* Brussels: European Communities Economic and Social Consultative Committee.

Foster, J. (1995) 'MPs Attack the Powers of Regional "Viceroys".' *Independent on Sunday,* 5 February.

Gertler, M. and Schoenberger, E. (1992) 'Industrial restructuring and continental trade blocks: the European Community and North America.' *Environment and Planning A,* 24, pp.2–10.

Gudgin, G. (1995) Memorandum submitted to House of Commons Trade and Industry Committee on Regional Policy. Appears in Trade and Industry Committee *Fourth Report: Regional Policy*, Volume II Memoranda of Evidence, pp.147–157. London: HMSO.

Hampden-Turner, C. and Trompenaars, F. (1993) *The Seven Cultures of Capitalism: Value Systems for Creating Wealth in the United States, Britain, Japan, Germany, France, Sweden, and the Netherlands.* New York: Doubleday.

Harvey, D. (1989) 'From managerialism to entrepreneurialism: the transformation in urban governance in late capitalism.' *Geografiska Annaler*, 71 B (1), pp.3–17.

Hay, C. (1995) 'Meta-governance after Fordism.' Paper presented to the ESRC-sponsored Seminar Series, *The North in the 1990s: Changing Times, Changing Explanations.* University of Manchester, 4–5 April.

Hirst, and Zeitlin, J. (1991) 'Flexible specialisation versus post-Fordism: theory, evidence and policy implications.' *Economy and Society*, 20, pp.1–56.

Hutton, W. (1995) 'The new Keynesian agenda.' *Employment Policy Institute Economic Report 9*, 3, Employment Policy Institute, April.

Jessop, B. (1992) 'Towards a Schumpeterian Workfare State? Preliminary remarks on post-Fordist political economy.' *Studies in Political Economy*, 40, pp.7–40.

Jessop, B. (1994a) 'Post-Fordism and the State.' In A. Amin (ed) *Post-Fordism: A Reader.* Oxford: Blackwell.

Jessop, B. (1994b) 'Changing forms and functions of the state in an era of globalization and regionalization.' In R. Delorme and F. Dopfer (eds) *The Political Economy of Diversity: Evolutionary Perspectives on Economic Order and Disorder.* London: Edward Elgar, pp.102–125.

Jessop, B. (1995) 'The future of the National state: erosion or reorganisation? General reflections on West Europe.' *Lancaster Working Paper in Political Economy*, 50. Department of Sociology, University of Lancaster.

Lipietz, A. (1992) *Towards a New Economic Order.* London: Verso Publications.

Lloyd, P.E. (1995) Memorandum submitted to House of Commons Trade and Industry Committee on Regional Policy. Appears in Trade and Industry Committee *Fourth Report: Regional Policy*, Volume II Memoranda of Evidence, pp.165–167. London: HMSO.

Lloyd, P.E. and Meegan, R.A. (1994) *Appraisal of the Development Plan for Merseyside – United Kingdom*, CRED Research Unit, Department of Geography, University of Liverpool. In association with M. Garrett (MDS Transmodal), G. Haughton and J. Shutt (Leeds Metropolitan University) and J. Peck (University of Manchester)

Lloyd, P.E., Bentley, G., Haughton, G., Meegan, R.A., Peck, J. and Shutt, J. (1995) *Evaluation of 5 Single Programming Documents for Objective 2 Funding*, CRED Research Unit, Department of Geography, University of Liverpool.

Macleod, G. (1995) 'Regional economic governance in Lowland Scotland: institutions, networks and entrepreneurial logics.' Paper presented to the ESRC-sponsored Seminar Series, *The North in the 1990s: Changing Times, Changing Explanations.* University of Manchester, 4–5 April.

Meegan, R.A. (1994) 'A "Europe of the Regions"? A view from Liverpool on the Atlantic Arc Periphery.' *European Planning Studies 2*, 1, pp.59–80.

Merseyside Business and Manufacturing Challenge Group (1994) *First Things First.* Newsletter of the Merseyside Business and Manufacturing Challenge Group, Liverpool.

Merseyside Task Force (1993) *Merseyside 2000. European Community Draft Objective 1. Regional Conversion Plan for Merseyside.* Liverpool: Merseyside Task Force.

Millan, B. (1990) 'Europe of the Regions.' *Local Work*, 21, Manchester: Centre for Local Economic Strategies.

Morgan, K. (1992) 'Innovating by networking: new models of corporate and regional development.' In M. Dunford and G. Kafkalas (eds) *Cities and Regions in the New Europe: the Global–Local Interplay and Spatial Development Strategies*. London: Belhaven Press.

North West Network (1994) *Building the Pathways to Integration: Approaches to Developing Self-Help for Merseyside Neighbourhoods*. Liverpool: North West Network.

OECD and Commission of the European Communities (1993) 'From global to local: a new perspective on adjustment and reform.' *Innovation and Employment Newsletter 12*, August. Paris: OECD.

Ohmae, K. (1985) *Triad Power: The Coming Shape of Global Competition*. New York: Macmillan.

Peck, J. and Tickell, A. (1994) 'Searching for a new institutional fix: the after-Fordist crisis and the global–local disorder.' In A. Amin (ed) *Post-Fordism: A Reader*. Oxford: Blackwell.

Sassen, S. (1994) *Cities in a World Economy*. California: Pine Forge Press.

Storper, M. and Scott, A. (1992) *Pathways to Industrialization and Regional Development*. London: Routledge.

Trade and Industry Committee (1995a) *Fourth Report: Regional Policy*, Report together with the Proceedings of the Committee. London: HMSO.

Trade and Industry Committee (1995b) *Fourth Report: Regional Policy*, Volume II, Memoranda of Evidence. London: HMSO.

CHAPTER 5

Appraising Europe in the Regions 1994–1999

A Case Study of Recent Experiences in Yorkshire and Humberside, UK

John Shutt

Introduction

Throughout the 1980s and early 1990s, European Community regional assistance has provided a lifeline to many northern UK local authorities and local communities experiencing a financial squeeze and requiring funds for economic conversion and regeneration. At a time when UK urban policy is dwindling in importance and resources have been directed away from local authorities, those selected for European funding have a stream of finance for potential innovation in regional economic development and urban regeneration. For the first time, following the redrawing of the maps of eligible areas in 1993, European Objective 1 status has been granted to Merseyside and Objective 2 status to large parts of North London. In consequence of these trends, European regional policy is becoming increasingly important in the UK's inner city areas, as the purpose of national urban policy has become less certain.

Originally designed as a means of directing resources to the UK, 'so as to help offset its anticipated net budgetary deficit', in the 1970s and 1980s 'the [European Regional Development Fund] ERDF has tended to complement rather than replace national regional policies' (Williams 1994, pp.174–5). In the 1990s this complementarity is increasingly uncertain because the government's urban strategy itself is shrouded in financial uncertainty and lacking in central strategic vision (Robson 1994) and its regional policy has been further weakened and remains confused. Harvey (1994, p.21) refers to the paradox of the Maastrict Treaty: that it increases the temptation of Member States to cut their own regional policy budgets as that of the EC expands. This is also true of urban policy. European regional policy seems to be replacing national urban and regional policy and programmes. Local policy-makers in the regions increasingly focus their attention on Brussels as much as Whitehall, because they feel that Brussels is both more responsive and increasingly in touch with the depth and plethora of problems in Britain's regions and urban areas. Staff of the European Directorate of Regional Policy arguably have a broader appreciation of what successful economic and regional regeneration is and what is required to stimulate regional economies compared to their UK civil servant counterparts. Under successive Conservative administrations, English urban policy has become increasingly targeted on very small urban areas (Enterprise Zones; Urban Development Corporations; City Challenge and now Single Regeneration Bid Areas). English urban policy has lost sense of the broader urban and regional dynamics of local and regional economies. Indeed, Bennington, Geddes and Mair (1992, p.189) go so far as to argue that the new European tier of government is creating 'a new European political arena...calling into question both the traditional hierarchy of tiers of government, and traditional views of the spheres of competence of each tier.'

Whilst UK urban policy resources are being reshaped and reduced, European regional policy has been revised by the EU for the 1994–1999 period. The British government however is now attempting in part to change the delivery mechanisms for European regional policies. In May 1994 it announced that regional priorities and project selection criteria for the Structural Funds will be defined *to favour proposals aimed at improving competitiveness* and that there would be a new Regional Challenge. The President of the Board of Trade, Michael Heseltine, launched the Regional Challenge competition for EU Structural Funds on 8 February 1995.

This chapter identifies the background to the new reforms of the EU's regional policy and examines a case study of Yorkshire and Humberside (see Figure 5.1). It raises a range of outstanding issues which arise in the English regions in the context of *contested governance* between European, national and local governments.

Trends in European Regional Budgets: Background to Current Developments

Following Community enlargement in the mid-1980s the Structural Funds were fundamentally reformed in 1989. The 1989 reforms establish five priority objectives for the Structural Funds designed to take into account the peripheral countries following successive enlargements (Ireland, Italy, the UK, Greece, Spain and Portugal). Objectives 1, 2 and 5b were specifically identified as regional with resources restricted to eligible regions or parts of regions. Objectives 3, 4 and 5a covered the whole of the Community.

The annual budget negotiations during the 1987–1993 period were conducted within a framework regulation (Article 12 (2) of Regulation (EEC) No 2052/88) stipulating that Community appropriation for the Structural Funds was to double in real terms by 1993 compared with 1987. Aid to Objective 1 regions was also designed to double in real terms by 1992 compared with 1987 and the intention

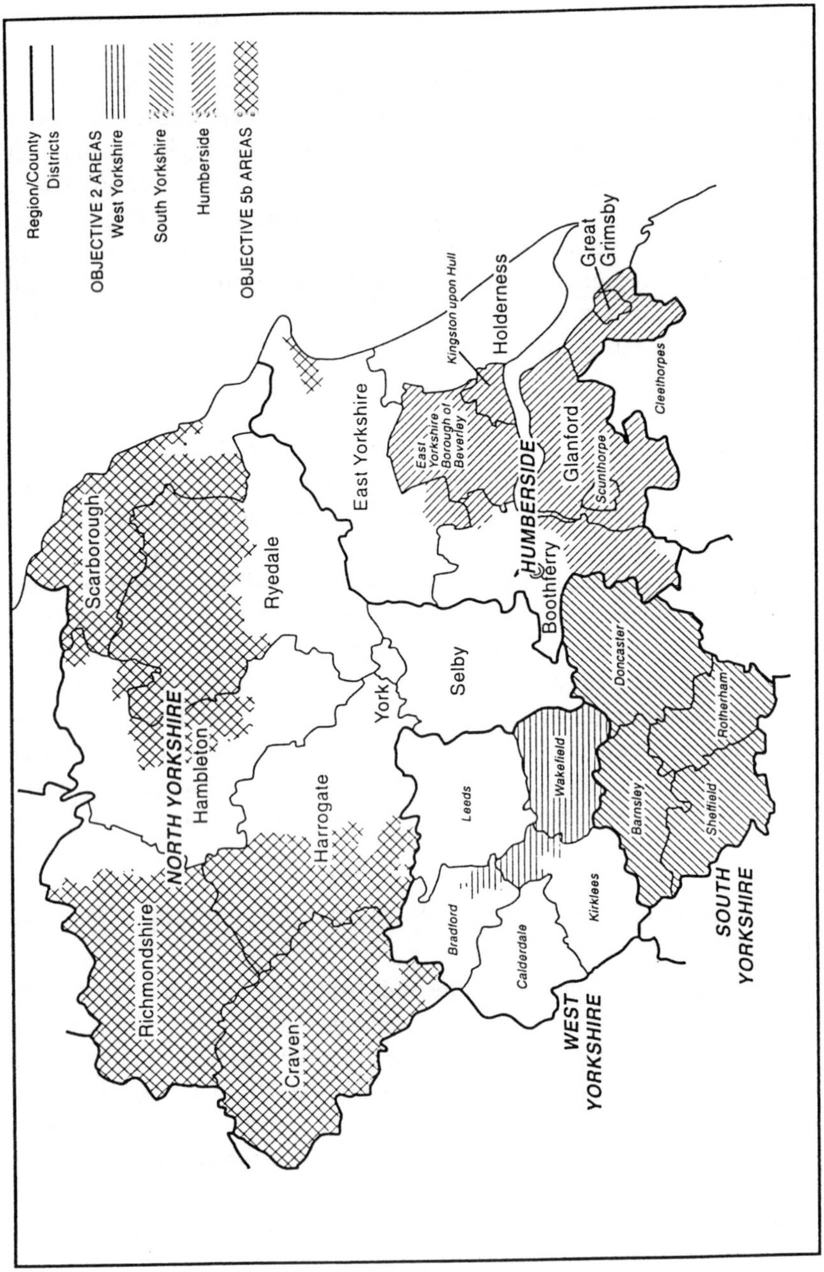

Source: GOYH 1994

Figure 5.1. Map of Yorkshire and Humberside (UK)

was that 80 per cent of ERDF should be devoted to Objective 1 regions. Tables 5.1 and 5.2 reveal that whilst the Structural Funds were doubled throughout the 1989–1992 period Objective 1 regions (excluding the new Länder) obtained some 62 per cent of the Structural Funds budget.

Table 5.1 Proposed and actual execution of commitment appropriations for the Structural Funds as a whole (1988 prices; million ECU)

	1988	*1989*	*1990*	*1991*	*1992*	*1993*
Proposed	7680	8980	10,280	11,580	12,900	14,466
Appropriations in budget	7680	8981	10,280	11,802	13,676	15,072
Final budgets	7939	9367	10,497	12,036	14,018	–
Execution	7877	9280	9845	11,995	13,911	–

Source: CEC (1994a)

Table 5.2 Execution of commitment appropriations under the Structural Funds 1989–1992 (1989 prices; million ECU)

	1989	*1990*	*1991*	*1992*	*Total*	*%*
Objective 1	6137	6352.1	7957.6	8959.4	2906.1	62.3
Objective 2	1060	1325.1	1466.5	1651.8	5503.4	11.7
Objective 3/4	1392	1316.2	1575.8	1867.4	6091.4	12.9
Objective 5 (a)	516	736.3	604	636	2492.3	5.3
Objective 5 (b)	232	194.6	660	795	1881.6	4.0
Not attributable				430.5	430.5	0.9
Innovative measures	330	370.4	367.3	294.2	1361.9	2.9
Total	**9607**	**10,294.7**	**12,631.2**	**14,634.3**	**47,167.2**	**100**
New Länder			831.0	904	1735	

Source: CEC (1994a)

In the 1989–1992 period, Objective 2 eligible areas received 11.7 per cent of the Structural Fund appropriations and in line with the principle of concentration of effort on declining industrial regions, the population achieved by Objective 2 was not to exceed 15 per cent of the Community population.

The 1989 reforms introduced the concepts of concentration of assistance, programming, additionality and partnership into the delivery of the Structural Funds. Throughout the 1989–1993 period, programming, additionality and partnership concepts continued to create problems between the Commission and Member States. Programming was intended to lead to the development of coherent regeneration and conversion programmes with regional development plans followed by Community Support Frameworks (CSFs) and operational programmes developed throughout the plan period. In the UK regional development plans and CSFs were simply a framework for individual EC aid for drawing down projects. European Social Fund (ESF) and ERDF were rarely matched together in coherent regional programmes. Additionality surfaced as a recurring issue as Community aid was continually substituted for national spend. In negotiations on the 1992 RECHAR Community Initiatives Programme the (then) EC Commissioner Millan once again demanded assurances from the UK government that Community Initiative resources identified for the UK would be fully additional. Finally, the social partnerships envisaged in the 1989 Structural Fund reforms between the employers organizations and trade unions did not materialize in the UK (Roberts *et al.* 1993). The report of the Economic and Social Committee of the European Community examined the involvement of the social partners in the period prior to 1993 and points out:

> in some countries involvement of the social partners is significant and systematic. This is the case in Denmark, Germany and to some extent in Italy. In other countries involvement is less pronounced, and at the far end of the spectrum some countries discourage involvement in socio-economic organisations (and in particular have limited the involvement of the trade unions). The country with the greatest formal participation in regional policies is Ireland, which included a social partner in the National Monitoring Committee. In the United Kingdom, the type of partnership established by central government has focused on a network of relations involving the EC, the national and public local authorities and local economic operators. There is thus no real 'social partnership'. (EC Economic and Social Committee 27 January 1994, pp.8–9)

The Delors Package and the 1993 Reforms

The Delors 2 package, approved at the Edinburgh Summit on 11 and 12 of December 1992, provides for a further doubling of the Structural Funds available to the four most peripheral Community countries in the 1994–1999 period. It continues the emphasis on Objective 1 *lagging regions* and creates a major increase in funds devoted to the other objectives, redefines Objectives 3 and 4 and creates a new financial instrument alongside the ERDF, ESF, EAGGF (European Agricultural Guidance and Guarantee Fund) known as FIFG (Financial Instruments for Fisheries Guidance) which will assist in the restructuring of the fisheries sector.

On 20 July 1993, the six revised regulations governing the Community's Structural Funds for the period 1994–1999 were established with a budget of ECU 141 billion for the new six-year period, now one-third of the total Community budget (CEC 1993).

Table 5.3 shows the resources to be committed in the period 1994–1999. Some 70 per cent of Structural Fund expenditure is to be concentrated on Objective 1 regions. The new Cohesion Fund is available only in Spain, Greece, Portugal and Ireland. The new map of eligible areas for each of the three regional Objectives (1, 2 and 5b) has been redrawn. Objective 1 eligible areas now include East Germany (East Berlin and the five Länder), Hainaut (Belgium), Merseyside and the Highlands and Islands (UK), Cantabria (Spain) and Felvoland (Netherlands). The new map of Objective 2 regions created some significant shifts designating six North London Boroughs: Enfield, Hackney, Haringey, Newham, Tower Hamlets and Waltham Forest, as well as Thanet in North Kent and Plymouth. The new map of eligible areas gives the EU a far greater role in national urban policy. This, together with the role of the Cohesion Fund in integrating development between Ireland and the UK, raises key issues for regional development in the period ahead.

Table 5.3 Proposed EC budgets under the Structural Funds 1994–1999

	Structural Funds	*Cohesion Fund*	*Total Structural Funds*	*Objective 1 allocations*
1994	20,135	1750	21,885	13,220
1995	21,480	2000	23,480	14,300
1996	22,740	2230	24,990	15,330
1997	24,026	2500	26,526	16,396
1998	25,690	2530	28,240	17,820
1999	27,400	2600	30,000	19,280

Source: CEC (1994a)

Each region eligible for European financial assistance must bring forward a Single Programming Document (SPD) during the course of negotiations which sets out the principles and provisions governing a programme of Community regional assistance. There must be prior appraisal, monitoring, interim assessment and *ex-post* evaluation of the SPD in each region. The purpose of EU regional aid is to secure a *balanced economic and social development* across Member States. Financial assistance for these eligible areas is meant to reduce disparities between them and the rest of the EU. Most of the money comes as grants from the three separate funds which together are called the Structural Funds: the ESF, the EAGGF and the ERDF.

In England, responsibility for the ESF lies with the Department of Employment, the Ministry of Agriculture, Fisheries and Food has responsibility for the EAGGF, the Department of the Environment (DoE) and the Department of Trade and Industry (DTI) share responsibility for the ERDF, and the day-to-day management from 1 April 1994 is now carried out by the new Integrated Government Offices for the regions (see Chapter 6).

The Commission itself admits that 'compared with the fundamental reform of the Structural Funds in 1988 – the changes now made seem a lot less far reaching. Indeed, the major principles adopted in 1988 of concentration of effort, partnership, programming, additionality are maintained or strengthened' (CEC 1994a, p.7). The changes however *are* far reaching for those new regions in receipt of the Structural Funds and the Cohesion Funds.

The new Objective 3 and Objective 4 also allow for major innovation in ESF. The new Objective 4 provides for ESF 'to facilitate workers' adaptation to industrial changes and to changes in production systems'. However, the UK government has refused to sign up to Objective 4, arguing that this new Objective is too interventionist and that long-term and youth unemployment is more of a priority than retraining existing workers to adapt to new technologies.

The Current Position in the UK

How much money is available?

OBJECTIVE 1

The regions designated under Objective 1, in the 1993 reforms, were required to draw up Regional Conversion Plans for a new six-year programming period: 1994–1999. CSFs were eventually agreed in the UK for Merseyside in July 1994 following a six-month period of negotiation and redrawing of the regional plan submitted by the government to Brussels. A total of £1849m has been committed from the Structural Funds to the three Objective 1 areas for the 1994–1999 period (Table 5.4). Table 5.5 summarizes the choice of priorities approved for the Objective 1 plans for the UK's three eligible regions on 13 July 1994. It is clear at this stage that the Objective 1 priorities contain specific commitments to social regeneration. This encompasses community development and health and education investment. This is not the case with Objective 2 priorities. Table 5.6 summarizes allocations by region for the 1994–1996 period in England and identifies details of monies available for the Objective 5b plans also entering rural areas in decline and in need of assistance.

Table 5.4 Objective 1 SPDs: UK 1994–1999 (MECU = millions of ECU)

SPD	*Total planned investment*		*Contribution from the Structural Funds*	
	(MECU)	*(£m)*	*(MECU)*	*(£m)*
Highlands & Islands	1012	793	311	244
Merseyside	2000	1567	816	639
Northern Ireland	2658	2083	1233	966

Source: Inforegio News (August 1994)

Table 5.5 UK objective 1 regions 1994: the choice of priorities in the SPDs

Merseyside	*Highlands and Islands*	*Northern Ireland*
1. Inward investment and corporate business development	Business development	Economic development and competitiveness
2. Development of indigenous enterprise and local business development	Tourism, heritage, cultural development	Investments in communities and people
3. Knowledge-based industries and advance technologies	Preservation and enhancement of environment	Reducing the effects of peripherality
4. Cultural, media and leisure industries	Primary sector support and related food industries	Development of agriculture, fisheries and the rural economy
5. Action for the People of Merseyside: integration, better housing, community development and a better quality of life	Communications and service networks to support business and community development	Protection and enlargement of the natural and built environment

Source: Lloyd and Meegan (1995)

Table 5.6 ERDF in England (£million) 1994–1996

Region	*Objective 1*	*Objective 2*	*Objective 5b*
North East		239	84
North West		274	
Yorkshire & Humberside		243	
Eastern			46
East Midlands		62	50
West Midlands		287	
London		57	
South East		11	
South West		22	
Merseyside	365		

NB: Converted from ECU at April 1994

The North East Objective 5b monies cover the North East, North West and Yorkshire and Humberside

Source: Department of the Environment (December 1994)

The Objective 1 programmes are extremely ambitious. In the Commission's view, the way for Merseyside to gain success through Objective 1 is to concentrate on a number of key dynamic forces within its economy and society capable as acting as *drivers for change* (see Chapter 6). It is not the intention here to dwell on the Objective 1 process, important though this is for the most depressed areas of the UK.

OBJECTIVE 2

Following the submission of a list of eligible areas for Objectives 2 for all Member States, the Commission formally adopted the list of areas eligible under Objective 2 on 21 January 1994 for the period 1994–1996. With regard to Objective 2, two three-year phases are planned with the possibility of adjusting the eligible areas and the CSFs at the end of the first three years in 1996. In March/April 1994, eleven Objective 2 plans were submitted by the UK central government to Brussels and negotiations on the Objective 2 plans continue on what was undoubtedly a protracted process of appraisal and negotiation (Michie and Bachtler 1994). These negotiations continued throughout September and October 1994 and were concluded in time to achieve *spend* in 1994. Plans for the UK's Objective 5b areas were on a similar trajectory. However, for neither Objective 2 or 5b areas was there the high level of redrafting of the Single Programming Documents which occurred with Merseyside's Objective 1 plan, although the Objective 2 redrafting and negotiation process produced significantly different plans to the first drafts submitted in the spring of 1994. One of the biggest changes to emerge was the renewed emphasis from the Commission on plans which aim to shift the Objective 2 SPD programmes from a regional spend on physical infrastructure to soft infrastructure priorities for small and medium sized enterprises (SMEs) and business development. Support measures have received increasing attention. New European policies and programmes aim to improve the entrepreneurial climate and facilitate the growth and networking of SMEs and this has coincided with the new SPD plan process.

The Community Initiatives

Whilst negotiations on the Objective 2 plans continue, guidelines for the thirteen Community Initiatives were published on 1 June 1994 and Member States had until 1 of November 1994 to put forward applications for operational programmes, global grants, and to negotiate on new areas for inclusion in the initiatives. Some 9 per cent of the commitment of appropriations for the Structural Funds are to be used to finance Community Initiatives – 13.45 billion ECU of which 11.5 billion ECU has been allocated to the thirteen Initiatives so far. Tables 5.7 and 5.8 summarize the Community Initiatives budget for the 1994–1999 period.

Table 5.7 Community Initiatives budget 1994–1999, February 1994 proposal (billion ECU at 1994 prices)

Initiative	*Purpose*	*Total ECU*	*Objective 1*	*UK allocations (MECU)*
INTERREG/REGION	Cross-border cooperation	2.9	2.3	99.4
LEADER	Rural innovations	1.4	0.9	61.0
REGIS	Remote integration	0.6	0.6	–
EMPLOYMENT: (NOW, HORIZON, YOUTH START)	Training innovations	1.4	0.8	146.5
INDUSTRIAL CHANGE:				
ADAPT	Training innovations	1.4	0.4	286.6
RECHAR	Coal mining conversion	0.4	0.1	*
RESIDER	Steel area conversion	0.5	0.1	*
KONVER	Defence diversification	0.5	0.2	*
RETEX	Textiles diversification	0.5	0.4	*
TEXTILES AND CLOTHING IN PORTUGAL	Textile industry modernization	0.4	0.4	–
	SME internationalization			
SMEs		1.0	0.8	61.3
URBAN	Economic/urban regeneration	0.6	0.4	75.6
PESCA	Fishing industry development	0.25	0.1	33.9
RESERVE		1.60	0.8	50.0
TOTAL		**13.4**	**58.3**	*

* Awaiting decision, Newsletter No.7 (August 1994)

Source: Guide to the Community Initiatives 1994–1999, CEC (1994b)

Table 5.8 The Future of the Community Initiatives 1994–1999: The relevance to regional participants

Initiative	
SME/Adapt	These initiatives are not concerned with capital investment but with taking a preventative approach to industrial decline. The emphasis is on the modernization and the internationalization of SMEs, particularly companies with less than 200 employees. The programmes place an emphasis on support for a concentrating know-how, experience exchange and networking. Non-Objective 2 areas can link into the networks. The two initiatives draw heavily on the Delors White Paper on Competitiveness.
RECHAR/RETEX	These include a Transnational element for the first time. The UK government's bid for eligible areas which were lodged with the EC on 1 August 1994 contained a number of new areas which had not been included under RECHAR 1, including Allerton Bywater – Leeds. In contrast, the RETEX 2 area will remain as designated under RETEX 1.
REGIS	This initiative is not applicable in the UK. This programme covers the French overseas territories, the Canaries, the Azores and Madeira.
URBAN	This is an interesting initiative. It follows from the Marseilles–London Urban pilot. The programme places an emphasis on small urban areas. It proposes to encourage an integrated approach to reintegrating the social excluded back into the labour market. It focuses on a limited number of areas affected by social exclusion and economic decline. The priority is on support for urban areas with Objective 1 and 2 eligible areas only.
INTERREG	The designation of eligible areas under this programme has been a big disappointment for the UK. The problems experienced by the North Sea Maritime area were not recognized by the EC. Under the INTERREG 1 programme the only UK eligible area was Kent linked to the Region of Nord Pas de Calais in France, the regions of the entrance and exit of the Channel Tunnel. The new programme has been extended to include East Sussex, Gwynedd, Dyfed, Gibraltar and Northern Ireland (not Belfast).
NOW/YOUTHSTART/ HORIZON	Emphasizes training innovation, support for the training of women, young people aged 16–25, the disabled and disadvantaged. These initiatives draw heavily on the EC White Paper on Social Policy.
LEADER	This initiative attempts to be complementary to actions proposed under the Objective 5b programme. The initiative places an emphasis on innovation, demonstration, structural change in rural areas, transferability of project experience and community involvement.

Source: Colwell (1994)

The Structural Funds in Yorkshire and Humberside 1994–1996

New eligible areas

The Structural Funds and the Community Initiatives have made a major contribution to Yorkshire and Humberside regional development plans since 1989. The 1993 Objective 2 review brought the loss of Objective 2 Status to parts of Bradford TTWA (Travel to Work Area); parts of Grimsby TTWA; Goole and some rural areas in Hull TTWA. Thus Objective 2 assistance for 1994–1996 is now concentrated in three sub-regional areas:

1. South Yorkshire (Sheffield, Rotherham, Barnsley and Doncaster TTWAs)
2. Humberside (Scunthorpe and parts of Grimsby TTWAs, and parts of Doncaster TTWA in Humberside; Hull TTWA excluding Holderness)
3. West Yorkshire (Wakefield, Dewsbury TTWA and parts of Bradford and Kirklees, and Castleford and Pontefract TTWAs).

Since Leeds continued to emerge as the fastest growing regional financial centre, it together with large parts of Bradford failed to qualify for eligibility for Objective 2 status in the 1993 reform.

North Yorkshire contains an Objective 5b area, which is covered by the Northern Upland 5b plan. In contrast to the urban areas of the region, the rural areas are relative newcomers to the EU process and it has recently been argued that the key issues for Objective 5b areas are not at all the same as in Objective 2 areas. Delivery mechanisms are different and in many areas need to be established from scratch and:

> the first key issue for 5b areas was the level of understanding by government departments involved. The Integrated Regional Offices (IROs) did not seem sure how to handle rural areas and the Government has little experience of delivering rural programmes, since they were generally dealt with by other bodies. (Local Government International Bureau 1994 p.49)

It is interesting that the new integrated Government Office for Yorkshire and Humberside administers only the Objective 2 plan. The Objective 5b plans are administered by the Integrated Regional Office for North East England.

Evaluation of Previous Programmes

The revised eligible Objective 2 urban areas are, in fact, closely embedded and integrated into European decision-making processes and have a great deal of experience now of the Structural Funds and Community Initiative Funds since 1989. RECHAR and RESIDER have been particularly important Community Initiatives in the Yorkshire and Humberside context. It is true to say, however, that despite a revived interest in evaluation of EC Structural Funds, there has been a lack of public evaluation and critical reflection within the region in terms of analysing previous achievements and practice and discussing the implications for the new strategy directions.

Within the region only the interim evaluation for the YHSA IDOP[1] and the small RESIDER programme was publicly available at the time that the SPD for Yorkshire and Humberside was submitted to Brussels in April 1994. Subsequently, PIEDA delivered to the Department of the Environment the interim evaluation of the Eastern England CSF programmes (PIEDA 1994).

The Sheffield Business School Interim IDOP and RESIDER programme evaluation study, completed in September 1992, estimated the 1988–1992 programme in South Yorkshire constituted £130 million from the European Commission and £149 million from the UK authorities respectively. 'Associated private investment and loans brought total expenditure to £436m with the eventual creation of 13,000 jobs which will each have cost the Structural Funds some £10,000 on average' (Sheffield Business School 1992, p.8).

The PIEDA report consists of an interim evaluation of five operational programmes within the previous Eastern England CSF. These five programmes are:

1. Bradford Integrated Development Operation, 1988–1992
2. East Midlands Operational Programme, 1990–1992
3. Humberside Operational Programme, 1990–1992
4. Mid-Yorkshire Operational Programme, 1990–1991
5. Uni Fund Operational Programme, 1990–1991 (covering the European Social Fund in the EMROP (East Midlands Regional Operational Programme), HOPI and MYOP areas).

Since Bradford II, the Humberside Operations Programme (HOP II), the mid-Yorkshire Operations Programme (MYOP II), the YHSA II and the RECHAR programmes were only approved at the end of 1993, it has been too early to undertake interim evaluation of these programmes in the region.

The New Integrated Government Offices

On 1 April 1994 the four major territorial departments (Transport, DoE, DTI and Employment) in Yorkshire and Humberside had their regional offices brought together as one integrated Government Office for Yorkshire and Humberside (GOYH).[2] The main responsibility of GOYH is to provide integrated services to a variety of agencies active in the region involved in the delivery of central government programmes. The agencies include local authorities, Training and Enterprise Councils (TECS), Chambers of Commerce, tertiary education institutions and now a new agency initiative, Business Links.

---

1 Yorkshire and Humberside Steel Area (YHSA) Integrated Development Operation Programme (IDOP).

2 For more detail and critical evaluation of the Government Offices see Chapter 6.

GOYH has responsibility for delivering European regional programmes in the region as well as UK government programmes. GOYH has reorganized with the responsibility for ensuring the effective and efficient management of EC programmes in accordance with EC programme guidelines and UK government regional policy guidelines and to ensure that this region receives the maximum benefit from the Structural Funds. The process is typical of that now in train in all of the English regions.

GOYH now has responsibility for delivering the Structural Funds Objective 2 SPD for the region. This was approved in December 1994 and runs for the 1994–1996 period. The SPD has now been published and projects are being considered. The European Fund Secretariat (EFS) invites the submission of new projects. Up to £243 million is to be made available for six priority programme areas.

The EFS is staffed by 21 civil servants mainly from the DTI and DoE with eight secondees from local authorities and TECs. The EFS manages the appraisal and monitoring, budgeting and meeting of deadlines for the programmes for the ERDF and the ESF and the Community Initiatives. On a daily basis the EFS is liaising with customers (known as sponsors or partners) and is assisting them with working up projects and claiming grants.

Table 5.9 Yorkshire and Humberside: Objective 2 priorities 1994–1996 (£million)

Percentage split of resources by priority and fund in terms of £M	*ERDF*	*ESF*	*TOTAL*
1. Action to support SMEs	19.7	20.3	19.8
2. Action to strengthen and diversify mature SMEs	12.4	17.7	13.7
3. Action for knowledge-based industries and technological development	13.2	13.9	13.4
4. Action to attract new industry and services	17.5	12.0	16.1
5. Action to support tourist and cultural industries	18.2	13.9	17.1
6. Targeted action for key deprived areas	18.3	20.3	18.8

Source: GOYH (1994)

The priorities for 1994–1996 summarize the proposed allocation of funding by priority and provide indicative allocations by measure. Table 5.9 shows the final allocation of ERDF and ESF resources by priority. A large proportion of the total has been earmarked for business support measures which are designed to foster, strengthen and encourage the growth of SMEs and to encourage innovation and technological change.

The priorities, target objectives and supporting measures for business support are ambitious and reflect the increasing concern inside the European Commission and the Directorate of Regional Policy to shift expenditure away from physical infrastructure spend to soft infrastructure. This is designed to strengthen the growth of SMEs, and enhance the capacity of the SME sector to assist in job creation. The Delors White Paper *Growth, Competitiveness, Employment* argues forcefully for a European policy which underpins the dynamism of SMEs in order to make the single internal market more effective:

> For many SMEs, completion of the single market means a change in the environment in which they operate, although they do not always see the scope for activity exploiting the new opportunities available because of the lack of a European or international framework for their markets or production processes.
>
> The Community must devise a back-up strategy designed to make it easier for businesses, particularly SMEs, to adapt to the new requirements of competitiveness and thus ensure that economic operators are properly mobilised in support of growth, competitiveness and employment. SMEs play a crucial role in the link between growth and employment. On the usual definition of SMEs (fewer than 500 employees), they provide more than two thirds of Community employment (70.2% of which 29% is accounted for by firms with fewer than 10 employees) and generate more than two thirds of Community turnover (70.3%) and between 65 and 85% of value added in those countries for which data is available. They are considered to be the greatest potential job creators. (CEC 1994c, p.95)

The renewed emphasis of European level on SME policies and support frameworks has been reflected in the new SPD framework for Yorkshire and Humberside. The region has a weak SME sector and the priority actions and measures in the SPD are available to provide business support. The priorities and measures are designed to guide project development bids and spending allocations in the period up to December 1996. Eligible support activities can continue to claim funding up to the deadline of June 1988.

Final confirmation of the Objective 2 plan within the region was released late in 1994. At the time of writing, many agencies within the region have yet to fully absorb the changing nature of the SPD programme, its changing organization, developments within the new GOYH and the full implications of the shift in programme priorities and the measures available to support project bids.

Partnerships, Management and Regional Development Plans

The region is fragmented and whilst having a distinct culture, its traditions of regional cooperation and regional public and private partnership are not as strong as they might be. Nevertheless, the early 1990s have seen renewed partnership building at city, sub-region and regional level. In 1992 the Yorkshire and Humberside Partnership (YHP) was formed by the Trades Union Congress (TUC) and Confederation of British Industry (CBI) in the region, with Yorkshire and

Humberside Regional Association (YHRA) and Yorkshire and Humberside Development Association (YHDA) represented on this new private/public partnership, but not yet the higher education institutions. The TECs and regional government departments are not represented at YHP level, but the Association of Yorkshire and Humberside Chambers of Commerce is. This regional partnership, it is true to say, is at the early stages of formation and will require nurturing. It is not well developed in comparison to similar partnerships in the North West region (see Peck and Tickell 1994). However, it is not yet clear how this emerging partnership will relate to the SPD structuring process, and how such a partnership can be utilized to galvanize regional economic development, if at all.

The local authorities through the YHRA and the YHP produced in 1993 their Yorkshire and Humberside Regional Strategy (YHP 1993). Whilst this strategy document aided the background to the Structural Fund negotiating process, the lack of a coherent framework for regional strategic planning questions the status of such a document in the EU and in the government's regional planning process. Separate to the YHP strategy, the Yorkshire and Humberside office of the Department of the Environment prepared the SPD planning document which provided the basis for negotiating Objective 2 funding across the Yorkshire and Humberside region to the group of diverse and eligible localities.

The role of partnership in CSF delivery at a regional level is critical in the SPD delivery process and in relations between the new GOYH and the Commission. With the development of the TECs and increased accessibilities to Structural Funds by a wider layer of partners, it is clear that the delivery of European Funds is becoming more complex. A CSF regional Monitoring Committee (MC) aids programme delivery and one key issue is the composition of these MCs, with local authorities fearing a loss of control at sub-region and local levels over the European funding process and the private sector feeling it has little role in such processes. The voluntary sector is even further removed from any influencing role.

Within the region, the tradition of privatization and fragmentation are so great that the political leaders and business leaders rarely talk together or with each other. This may change in the late 1990s, spurred on by regionalization of both local government associations and Chambers of Commerce.

Conclusions

The new IROs – at the front line

The common factors behind all the current SPD documents for both Objective 1 and Objective 2 areas is that they reflect current UK government views on regional development, additionality and partnerships, as well as priority allocations for resources. They are guided by the government's views on best allocations for drawing upon European funds. The current Objective 2 negotiations will once again focus on the key issues: additionality, partnership strategy and key projects.

In the search for more effective operation of plans for utilizing the Structural Funds and the Community initiatives, the new Integrated Regional Offices now administer both British urban policy and European regional policy. They are facing some difficult contradictions, recently drawn out by the House of Commons Select Committee on Trade and Industry (1995). Confronted by a UK government hostile to regional long-term planning and to local and regional government they are also required to work with European partners committed to subsidiarity and partnership with regional and local government, and to indicative regional development planning. The European Commission enters the process from a very different perspective to the framework being provided by Whitehall. What can be readily identified in the current conjuncture is the different transition between the broad regional strategies, developed from local government association origins, but often with a great deal of educational, social and private partnership collaboration, for example, the Yorkshire and Humberside Regional Strategy (YHP 1993) and the North West Regional Strategy (NWRA 1993) and the hesitancy of the UK Government, which remains ideologically opposed to deepening Europeanization and to regional planning and regional government. The current SPDs draw on the strategic vision of these regional strategies but do not necessarily contain similar agreed regional objectives and measures. What can also be readily identified is the continued fragmentation of strategy development in different localities within the region.

Regional Challenge

Detailed guidelines for Regional Challenge were published in February 1995. Following the urban policy City Challenge model, Regional Challenge is to be introduced in England and Wales as a competition for money from the ERDF, the largest of the European Structural Funds:

> This is to encourage imaginative value for money proposals, involving significant private sector funding. Subject to the European Commission's agreement to the detailed Community Support Framework, which governs Structural Funds money, the first competitions will be held as soon as practicable. Thereafter, involving total prize money of £150–200m across the eligible English and Welsh areas. Successor competitions will follow three years later. (DTI 1994, p.132)

An agreement on Regional Challenge was included in the Merseyside negotiations, and meetings with the local government associations in July 1994 and the President of the Board of Trade established that Regional Challenge will not involve any redistribution of money. It 'would consist of topslicing within each programme, and money would be allocated within the region...in addition, Regional Challenge projects which were not selected could still receive funding from the standard European Regional Development Fund (ERDF) programmes' (LGIB 1994, p.54).

Regional Challenge raises some interesting questions about the evaluation of Structural Fund projects in the next round and whilst it could aid creativity in local authorities and the voluntary and private sectors, it is also true to say that in its proposed form it has the potential to precipitate regional tensions and create new divisions in English regions which are already too fragmented and inward looking. A successful Regional Challenge would be one that would encourage and foster cooperation and innovation within a region between a range of partners, on key thematic programmes relevant to European integration and the competition they face from outside the region. The current danger is that one part of a region like Yorkshire and Humberside will be placed in competition against other parts of the region, hindering the development of region-wide initiatives. It is also true to say that Regional Challenge will create additional difficulties in a region like Yorkshire and Humberside where large parts of the urban conurbation in West Yorkshire are ineligible for Structural Funds and thus are unable to participate in any significant Regional Challenge which utilizes only European Structural Funds.

As Table 5.10 shows, 12 per cent from most Objective 2 and 5b programmes is being set aside to provide finance for the best ideas for local partnerships to regenerate the region. This means that £23.5 million is available for the Objective 2 areas of South and West Yorkshire and Humberside and a share of £3 million is available in the Objective 5b areas in North Yorkshire from the Northern Uplands Programme. The aims of Regional Challenge are to facilitate local partnerships, to help animate innovative regional development stategies and increase the role of the private sector. Each secretariat is establishing its own timetable for the submission and consideration of Regional Challenge bids according to the needs of the area. In Yorkshire and Humberside bids have to be considered by June 1995 and *winners* will be recommended by Ministers in October 1995. The local agencies groan of *bid fatigue* and local government remains bewildered by the policy mechanisms created by successive rounds of *locality competition* and *partnership* building.

Given the assurances that have been given in the debate on regional strategies, the Regional Challenge topslicing idea now appears primarily as another inadequate response in the UK's urban and regional regeneration game. A much more important issue is whether or not projects can be brought forward in a coherent strategy, by a local government which is financially beleaguered and a TEC movement which is still uncertain with regard to its long-term role in economic and enterprise development, and where the economic regeneration of many urban areas is now so largely dependent upon European regional policy and the European Structural Funds and Initiatives. A rapid contraction of local authority mainstream capital programmes is now being followed by the dismantling of urban policy programmes and this in turn causes major difficulties because urban programme funds have been utilized by local government to provide matching funding to draw down the ERDF and other Structural Funds. The decline in resources available in the new urban policy Single Regeneration Budget (see Chapter 6) is therefore a

Table 5.10 Regional Challenge: 'Prizes' for the 1994–1996 round

SPD area	*Total Structural funds (£m)*	*Regional Challenge 'Prize' Funds (ERDF and ESF) (£m)*
Objective 1 + 2		
Merseyside	816	17.9
North East England	308	23.5
Yorkshire & Humberside	313	23.4
East Midlands	79	6.0
West Midlands	371	28.2
North West	329	23.4
Greater London	74	5.6
Industrial South Wales	188	14.3
Objective 5		
South West	219	7.0
The Marshes	40	1.1
Northern Uplands	108	3.0
Lincolnshire	53	1.7
East Anglia	60	2.0
Rural Wales	184	5.3

Source: Department of Trade and Industry (1994): provisional allocations

cause for concern and will undoubtedly create further uncertainties as we move from the preparation of the CSF to the development of operational programmes. To cap it all the UK has brought another new player on the scene – the 280 Business Link projects currently being established, including some within this region, to examine SME growth and business development partnerships.

As we move into a period when the local government associations are focusing on new ways of 'strengthening European regional policy, including an expansion of funding' leading up to the 1996 intergovernmental conference, reviewing the Treaty of Rome (Gallacher 1994, pp.18–19), attention is increasingly focused on the campaign for a European urban policy (see Stewart 1994; Sampaio 1994). A more positive partnership and framework between Brussels, Whitehall and local government could achieve a great deal over the next three years. Whether or not the new Integrated Regional Offices are allowed by central government to enhance such a partnership and to develop a higher order regional strategy, which will strengthen the delivery of regional policy, remains a crucial question.

Acknowledgement

I am grateful for the comments of Professor Graham Haughton of the School of the Environment, Leeds Metropolitan University on an earlier draft of this chapter.

References

Bennington, J., Geddes, M. and Mair, A. (1992) 'Europe: The New Arena for Local Economic Policy in Europe.' In J. Bennington and M. Geddes (eds) *Restructuring the Local Economy*. Essex: Longman, pp.180–195.

Colwell, A. (1994) *The Future of the Community Initiatives*. Scotland: Central Regional Council.

Commission of the European Communities (CEC) (1993) *Community Structural Funds 1994–1999, Revised Regulations*. Luxembourg: Commission of the European Communities. August.

Commission of the European Communities (CEC) (1994a) *Fourth Annual Report on the Implementation of the Structural Funds 1992*. Luxembourg: Commission of the European Communities.

Commission of the European Communities (CEC) (1st ed) (1994b) *Guide to the Community Initiatives 1994–1999*. Luxembourg: Commission of the European Communities.

Commission of the European Communities (CEC) (1994c) *Growth, Competitiveness and Employment White Paper*. Luxembourg: Commission of the European Communities.

Department of the Environment (DoE) (1994) *The European Regional Development Fund, An Introductory Guide*. London: Department of the Environment.

Department of the Environment (DoE) (1995) *Regional Challenge Bidding Guide*. London: Department of the Environment.

Department of Trade and Industry (DTI) (1994) *Competitiveness Helping Business To Win*. London: HMSO CM 2563.

European and Social Committee of the European Communities (1994) *Initiative Opinion on the Involvement of Social Partners in Community Regional Policy*. Brussels: Commission of the European Communities. 27th January.

Gallacher, J. (1994) 'Deadline 1996.' *Municipal Journal*. Number 33. 19–25 August, pp.18–19.

GOYH (1994) *Yorkshire and Humberside Objective 2 Programme 1994–1996*. Leeds: GOYH. December.

Harvey, A. (1994) 'An Appraisal of the Regional Policy of the EU, 1994–99.' *European Regional Prospects*. European Economic Research and Advisory Consortium (ERECO), abridged version. June, pp.17–21.

House of Commons Trade and Industry Select Committee Proceedings (1995). London: HMSO.

Inforegio (1994) *Structural Funds 1992: An Initial Assessment*. Brussels: Commission of the European Communities.

Local Government International Bureau (1994) *European Information Service Monthly Bulletins*. Issue Number 152. London.

Lloyd, P. and Meegan, R. (1995) 'Contested Governance: European Exposure in the English Regions.' Paper presented to the Regional Studies Conference on *Regional Futures*. Gothenburg, Sweden, 6–9 May.

Michie, R. and Bachtler, J. (1994) 'European Regional Policy News.' *REGIONS: Newsletter of the Regional Studies Association* 192, August, pp.4–6.

NWRA and NWBLT (1993) *Regional Economic Strategy for North West England*. Wigan: North West Regional Association.

Peck, J. and Tickell, A. (1994) 'Too many partners...the future for regeneration partnerships.' *Local Economy* 9, 3, 251–265.

PIEDA (1994) *An Evaluation of the Eastern England CSF.* Report for the Department of the Environment. Manchester.

Roberts, P. *et al.* (1993) *Europe: A Handbook for Local Authorities.* Manchester: Centre for Local Economic Strategies.

Robson, B. (1994) 'Urban Policy at the Crossroads.' *Local Economy.* Volume 9 Number 3. November, pp.216–223.

Sampaio, J. (1994) 'European Urban Policy: the EuroCities view.' *Local Economy.* Volume 9 Number 3. November, pp.287–290.

Sheffield Business School (1992) *Yorkshire and Humberside Steel Area IDO and RESIDER Programmes Evaluation Study.* Sheffield: Sheffield Business School.

Stewart, M. (1994) 'Towards a European Urban Policy.' *Local Economy.* Volume 9 Number 3. November, pp.267–277.

Williams, A.M. (1994) *The European Community.* Oxford: Blackwell.

Yorkshire and Humberside Partnership (YHP) (1993) *Yorkshire and Humberside Regional Strategy: A Partnership for Europe. Yorkshire and Humberside Partnership.* Barnsley: YHRA.

CHAPTER 6

Regional Economic Development and Institutional Mechanisms in Merseyside

Objective 1 Status

Philip Boland

Introduction

In July 1993 the European Council of Ministers awarded Merseyside (see Figure 6.1) Objective 1 Status within the European Community (EC)[1] – 'regions whose development is lagging behind' (MTF 1993, p.vii). This is an excellent policy initiative which can help Merseyside to reverse the enervating cycle of economic, urban and social decline which has afflicted the region during the last 10 to 15 years. In April 1994 the UK government introduced very important alterations to the institutional structures for regional development strategies in England. These are encapsulated in the creation of integrated Government Offices and the Single Regeneration Budget. This chapter aims to discuss the implications of Objective 1 Status and the Government Office for Merseyside, with particular emphasis upon economic development, governance structures and institutional relationships.

The Commission of the European Communities (CEC), or Commission, advocates policies which encourage local authorities to collaborate and devise regional economic development strategies (Martin and Pearce 1993). The UK government, via the Merseyside Task Force (MTF), with the five Merseyside local authorities of Knowsley, Liverpool, Sefton, St Helens and Wirral, and the main public, private and voluntary sector agencies (the Partnership) produced *Merseyside 2000* – a regional conversion plan submitted to the Commission in November 1993 in support of Merseyside's case as an Objective 1 Status region. After more than six months of negotiations at a European level, it was finally approved in the summer of 1994 in the form of a Single Programming Document (SPD). The

1 From November 1993, with the Treaty on European Union, the EC became the European Union (EU). However, this chapter employs the terminology of EC as this is the one that is used by the Commission in respect of Merseyside and Objective 1.

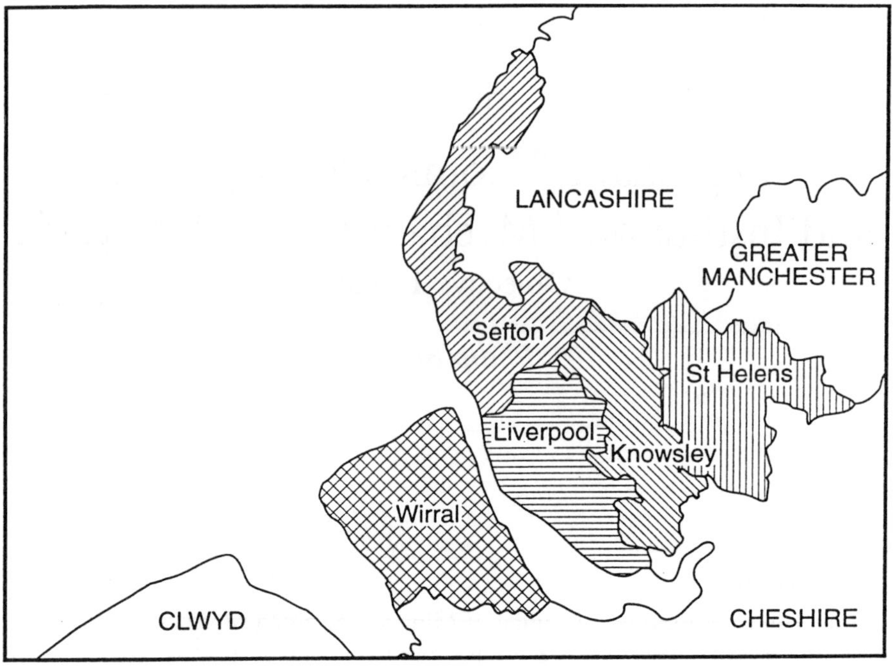

Source: OPCS (1991), Crown Copyright

Figure 6.1 Merseyside in the North West of England, UK

outcome is a strategy centred upon five economic drivers – big companies, small and medium sized enterprises (SMEs), technology transfer, leisure industries and human resources. The details contained in the SPD will be expanded upon later in this chapter.

There seem to be two highly important issues upon which this chapter elucidates. First, the prospects for sustained economic development in Merseyside with the injection of Objective 1 monies. And second, how the changes to the institutional arrangements with regard to Objective 1 and the Government Office for Merseyside are manifesting themselves in the region. In essence, can Merseyside resurrect itself and return from the economic wilderness by developing an economy capable of challenging its competitors in the EC and beyond?

Merseyside: From a Gateway to the World to an Economic Graveyard

Merseyside's numerous problems are well documented and have been dealt with effectively elsewhere (see Meegan 1989, 1990), so only a short recapitulation is required. Merseyside emerged as a vibrant port-based regional economy, the focal point being the port of Liverpool, during the late 19th and early 20th century with the exports of goods such as coal, steel and textiles, and the imports of foods and other commodities from most parts of the world. Other important industrial sectors which provided the backbone of the economy included shipbuilding, coal mining and car production.

However, due to various factors which emerged during the 1970s and 1980s – changes in shipping containerization, greater involvement and integration in Europe, economic recessions and the collapse of traditional industries – Merseyside has endured an acute economic and social malaise. The result has been high levels of unemployment, particularly long-term unemployment, low economic activity rates, low gross domestic product (GDP) per head of population, severe poverty, substantial out-migration, poor educational performances and serious urban and social decay (CEC 1995). The 1980s will doubtlessly be associated with the Toxteth riots and the political hostility between Liverpool City Council and the government – incidents which seem to reveal how intense the situation became on Merseyside, and especially in Liverpool.

Various policy prescriptions were introduced in the 1980s, e.g. Merseyside Development Corporation (MDC),[2] MTF, City Action Team, Enterprise Zone, Inner City Partnership and various local authority strategies. However, it was self-evident that more resources and new policies were necessary if Merseyside was to save itself from terminal decline. Therefore, Merseyside started to engage itself in the process of acquiring EC Structural Funds in the late 1980s.

The Transition from Objective 2 to Objective 1 Status

Merseyside and Objective 2 Status

In 1988 the Merseyside Integrated Development Operation (MIDO) became operational with the declared intention of providing the local authorities with a coordinated approach to EC Structural Funds. MIDO had many different contributors to its agenda, including the regional offices of government, nationalized industries, public utilities, transport organizations, the private sector, including Chambers of Commerce and large firms, voluntary bodies and the five local councils. However, the government was, and still is, the responsible body for the arrangement and sanctioning of the Structural Funds.

Merseyside was awarded Objective 2 Status in 1989 – declining industrial regions – and so began accessing EC Structural Funds. This serves to indicate the severity of Merseyside's plight. There were two phases of Structural Fund support for Merseyside under Objective 2, 1989–1991 and 1992–1993, in the form of regional development projects receiving finance from the European Regional Development Fund (ERDF) and the European Social Fund (ESF). The total amount of EC funding for Objective 2 was some 230 million ECU, using today's prices

2 A central government funded agency, involving the public and private sectors, which is responsible for regenerating the Mersey waterfront and parts of its surrounding area. It is due to end in 1998.

(CEC 1995). What was unusual about the 1989–1993 period was a 'partnership' that was more dominated by the public sector than is the case now under Objective 1 (Kousgaard 1994).

During 1992, the five local authorities formed the Merseyside European Liaison Unit. It was designed to facilitate the coordination of European policy initiatives and strategies, to organize Structural Fund bids, to develop networking at all spatial levels, and to provide council members and officers with information with a European dimension. The Unit remains an integral cog in Merseyside's European wheel under Objective 1.

Changes to the EC Structural Fund regulations

Following the December 1993 Edinburgh Summit the Commission amended the regulations concerning the implementation of Structural Funds for the period 1994–1999. These revisions were inherently linked to the *decentralization* and *simplification* of procedures and the *monitoring* of resource allocations and projects. However, the *guiding principles* of the Structural Funds were not radically altered: concentration, programming, partnership and additionality (CEC 1995). These principles form the foundation upon which Merseyside's Objective 1 programme is erected and so consideration of their importance is essential.

There are two separate aspects to the concentration principle: the concentration of resources in regions which require the highest level of aid (geographical concentration) – within the EC this pertains to the Objective 1 regions and within Merseyside it concerns the most deprived communities; and concentration on projects which deliver the optimum results for the monies applied (CEC 1995). The extent of the social and economic disparities on Merseyside means that the Objective 1 programme includes 'comprehensive packages of economic and social support for specified communities where problems are at their most severe' (CEC 1995, p.18) (see Table 6.1, Driver 5, Measure 1, p.115). Achieving the second element of concentration involves the 'selectivity' of a specified number of priorities, 'targeting' on certain types of activity and the 'visibility' of resource allocations (CEC 1995, p.18).

According to the Commission (1995), programming needs to evolve in a more strategic, integrated and coherent direction. This would involve focusing on explicit strategic objectives and particular socio-economic problems; a higher degree of integration between the different policies through 'synergy' and enhancing the extent to which policies 'reinforce and complement each other' (CEC 1995, p.18). Obviously, these are extremely important building blocks for Merseyside's Objective 1 package (see Chapter 4).

The Commission states that the Objective 1 strategy needs to obtain a 'clear additional impact on the economic and social development of Merseyside', otherwise the monies will have been squandered (CEC 1995, p.19). The resources must not be used to subsidize for current or planned projects which would have gone ahead irrespective of Objective 1. The money has to be additional, and it must be demonstrable that they will raise the 'baseline' of economic activity on Merseyside and deliver 'value-for-money' – the more additionality is achieved the more additional economic activity will be created (CEC 1995, p.19). This issue of additionality remains very controversial and problematic, both in the UK and Merseyside (see Boland, Mannin and Wallace 1995; Chapter 4; Welfare and Beaumont 1993).

The management of the EC Structural Funds is founded upon a 'regional partnership system' (CEC 1995, p.19). This is also the case on Merseyside with a regional partnership of the main actors involved in economic and social development. This can be seen in *Merseyside 2000*, the Monitoring Committee, the Secretariat and the Technical Panels. These issues will be elaborated upon later in this chapter (see also Chapter 4).

Other key factors of direct relevance to Merseyside are prior appraisal and the quantification of objectives (see Chapter 4). The Commission will dispense pecuniary assistance for regional development strategies only when the recipient has evidence of prior appraisal of the 'cost-effectiveness' and 'value-for-money' of their policies (CEC 1995, p.19). Crucial to this is the essentiality that policy objectives are identified and quantified – the rate at which the Structural Funds will increase the resources available, and the 'outputs' derived from current policies already under way in Merseyside, in the form of 'co-financing' (CEC 1995, pp.19–20).

The designation of Objective 1 Status

The EC defines Objective 1 regions as those which have experienced GDP per head of 75 per cent of the EC average for three years. In 1983 Merseyside's GDP per head was 95 per cent of the EC average, but by 1992 it had fallen to 73 per cent – paving the way for the designation of Objective 1 Status, while another powerful reason was the fact that regional unemployment was 70 per cent above the EC average in the early 1990s (CEC 1995).

However, the pursuit of Objective 1 Status for Merseyside received a questionable response in some quarters. The transition from Objective 2 to Objective 1, despite offering the possibility of receiving a substantial increase in EC Structural Funds for Merseyside, was interpreted by some local figures as presenting a distinctly negative image which could conceivably deter potential investors and thereby undermine any progress which may have been secured. This concern was echoed by Bruce Millan,[3] who had ultimate responsibility for the Objective 1 regime within the Commission, when he confessed that when Merseyside was designated an Objective 1 region it was 'in a sense a double-edged sword' – the simple fact that it necessitated such special status 'acknowledges that things have

3 He has since been replaced as European Regional Policy Commissioner by Mrs Monica Wulf-Mathies.

gone badly wrong in the past' which may discourage capital investment (cited in Carvel 1994, p.4). However, he also argued that if the resources are utilized efficiently, then they should 'make a significant impact on the economic and social situation of the region' (cited in Carvel 1994, p.4). The UK government can also be charged with displaying an ambivalent attitude to Merseyside's application for Objective 1 Status, with suggestions that it was politically sensitive for a Conservative government to actively promote a privileged position for Merseyside in the EC. This was extended to include accusations that the government was ashamed of the decline of Merseyside (Carvel 1993).

The final decision by the Council of Ministers was delayed until Summer 1993, when both Merseyside and the Highlands and Islands, Scotland, were confirmed as Objective 1 Status regions and total Structural Fund allocations were finalized. From the Structural Fund pot of 141 billion ECU (approximately £105 billion) for 1994–1999, Merseyside has been granted 816 million ECU (£630 million) over the five-year period, not as much as was initially hoped for. However, it is significantly higher that the £162 million it received during the Objective 2 phase (1989–1993).

The Single Programming Document for Merseyside

Problems with Merseyside 2000

The *Merseyside 2000* document aimed, from 1994 to 1999, 'to reduce economic and social disparities on Merseyside compared with the more prosperous regions in the EC' (MTF 1993, p.vii). This was to be achieved by reducing Merseyside's unemployment level and increasing its GDP towards the EC averages. Merseyside 2000 also boasted a 'very high priority on encouraging substantial private sector investment' (MTF 1993, p.viii). However, Minford and Stoney (1993, p.4) criticized the alleged absence of the private sector from its formulation, and its preoccupation with human resources 'rather than projects aimed at reducing those sub-regional marginal costs that investors evaluate when deciding to invest'. These include transport costs, such as improving the M62 link with Liverpool city centre – improved infrastructure is a key part of the SPD (see Tables 6.1 and 6.3).

Dr Pernille Kousgaard (1994), European Liaison Officer in the Merseyside European Liaison Unit, argued that the Partnership which produced *Merseyside 2000* accepted that the aim was not likely to be satiated by 1999. However, in its defence, at least it was a goal to which all those involved were committed. Both Bruce Millan and Padraig Flynn, the European Social Affairs Commissioner, believe that *Merseyside 2000* was somewhat over-ambitious in its aims and objectives (see Carvel 1994). It was met with a guarded cynicism from the Commission and needed a fundamental revision before the monies were released. Thus *Merseyside 2000* was originally rejected by the Commission because it would 'have involved the disbursement of funds on projects not dissimilar to others that have so far failed to stop the decline' (Fazey 1994a, p.19). It was not until July 1994 that the SPD for Merseyside's Objective 1 package was finally accepted by the Commission (see Chapter 4). The expenditure details of the SPD remained in the domain of the Member State and the Commission.

Aim

The SPD, which is Merseyside's bible in respect of the Objective 1 programme, aims to 'break the cycle of slow growth and even stagnation that has affected the region' (CEC 1995, p.22). To completely close the 'economic gap' between Merseyside and the EC would demand growth in GDP of 5 per cent above the EC average and an increase in employment of 8400 jobs for the next five years (CEC 1995, p.20). However, the SPD acknowledges that these are optimistic targets which will not be reached by 1999, especially given the region's present socio-economic fabric.

Vision

The vision for Merseyside as espoused in the SPD is to: establish Merseyside as a thriving and successful European city with a strong and varied economic base, enhance the skills of the people of Merseyside, stress the importance of Merseyside as a 'gateway' between Europe and the rest of the World, promote the region as a centre of learning, arts and cultural quality and innovation, establish Merseyside as a region with a strong sense of environmentalism and a high quality of life (CEC 1995, p.23). This is a very challenging vision for Merseyside to strive for.

Strategic objectives

The vision is to be realized via seven strategic objectives:

1. **Investing in industry** – maintaining and enhancing the manufacturing sector by supporting investment in the key corporate sector, and helping SMEs expand and become more competitive.
2. **Investing in people** – to improve job prospects in Merseyside, animate enterprise and enhance the capabilities and expertise in the local labour market.
3. **Enhancing technology** – increasing the scope for technology transfer between research and development (R & D) institutions and industry, which will enable R & D projects to reach fruition and become commercially viable.
4. **Pathways to integration** – improving access to employment for those living in Merseyside's most depressed areas.
5. Helping to support Merseyside's role as a principal **gateway** between Europe and the rest of the world.

6. Consolidating Merseyside's already well established **cultural, media** and **tourism** industries.
7. Pursuing sustainable development policies which will provide a **high quality of life**.

The five 'drivers' of economic change

The SPD concedes that the aforementioned strategic objectives are extremely exacting for a regional economy such as Merseyside's, but stresses that they are by no means completely unattainable. To accomplish them demands a concentration on 'key dynamic forces within Merseyside's economy and society' and the provision of 'integrated projects' – the 'drivers of change' (CEC 1995, p.24):

1. **Action for industry: inward investment and key corporate business development** – this involves the preparation, servicing and accessibility of strategic sites for large companies and inward investors, while it also relates to infrastructure expenditure and the marketing of the region.
2. **Action for industry: indigenous enterprise and local business development** – this focuses on encouraging SMEs to grow and expand with financial assistance in the form of training, services and advice via the Training and Enterprise Councils (TECs)[4] and Business Links (a DTI initiative formerly known as One Stop Shops providing advice for new businesses). There is also a Merseyside Special Investment Fund, sponsored by the clearing banks and European monies, with subsidized interest payments for business loans.
3. **Action for industry: knowledge-based industries and advanced technology development** – here the emphasis is on technology transfer between the universities and industry and also a graduate retention programme to encourage graduates to remain in the city.
4. **Action for industry: developing the cultural, media and leisure industries.**
5. **Action for the people of Merseyside: pathways to integration, a better training system, community development and a better quality of life** – this incorporates an extensive programme of training and economic and social support for the region's most acute areas of high unemployment (Fazey 1994b; Carvel 1994).

The precise details of the drivers and their measures are illustrated in Table 6.1.

4 The TECs deliver government training programmes and also seek to stimulate enterprise. There are three TECs on Merseyside: Merseyside TEC covering Knowsley, Liverpool and Sefton; QUALTEC servicing St. Helens; and CEWTEC catering for Wirral.

Table 6.1 The Merseyside Objective 1 Programme: drivers and measures

Driver 1 Action for industry: inward investment and key corporate business development

(i) Quality sites and premises for industrial and commercial investors
(ii) The specific training needs of the key corporate sector: improving business competitiveness
(iii) The Merseyside Image Campaign
(iv) Gateways for industry: developing Merseyside's ports and airport for business needs
(v) Access to key sites for industrial and commercial development
(vi) Managing and recycling industrial waste

Driver 2 Action for industry: indigenous enterprise and local business development

(i) Premises for SMEs
(ii) Incentives for local business development:
- The Merseyside Special Investment Fund
- Assisting with industrial investment plans
- Marketing assistance
- Developing supplier networks
- Industrial quality and design
- Telecommunications links for SMEs
- Energy efficiency and environmental best practice

(iii) Support for the specific training needs of SMEs
(iv) The farming sector and food industries on Merseyside

Driver 3 Action for industry: knowledge-based industries and advanced technology development

(i) Research, innovation and technology development for business needs:
- Merseyside Research, Development and Innovation Strategy
- Assistance with new product and process development
- Support for a commercial application of research
- Help with participation in research programmes
- Incubation centres

(ii) Specific training for new technology skills
(iii) Developing clean technologies and environmental awareness on Merseyside
(iv) Specific training for environmental skills

Table 6.1 The Merseyside Objective 1 Programme: drivers and measures (continued)

Driver 4 Action for industry: developing the cultural, media and leisure industries

(i) The cultural and media industries of Merseyside: development of facilities for investors

(ii) Better quality in the cultural and media industries: specific skills training

(iii) Attracting visitors to Merseyside: help for investment in festivals, events and tourist attractions, and upgrading the standard of accommodation

(iv) Improving quality: upgrading skills in the tourist industry

(v) Protecting and developing the natural and historic built environment

Driver 5 Action for the people of Merseyside: pathways to integration, a better training system, community development and a better quality of life

(i) Pathways to integration: economic and social support for the areas of inner Liverpool, Bootle, Birkenhead, Huyton, Knowsley and Speke/Garston

- *Pathway to education*: school–college link courses; school–industry link courses; awareness of educational opportunities for school leavers
- *Pathway to skills*: basic literacy and numeracy; confidence building; guidance and counselling
- *Pathway to training*: customized training; training for skills in demand in the local labour market; outreach and mobile training facilities; telecommunications for distance learning
- *Pathway to jobs*: work placement schemes; employment subsidies for target groups; community enterprises; targeted business support; childcare and the care of other dependents
- *Better quality of life*: targeted environmental improvements; community facilities; health awareness; tackling crime
- *Community involvement*: a public awareness campaign; setting up and developing the initiatives

(ii) Career development: responding to people's needs for lifetime training in identified growth sectors

(iii) Accompanying measures to improve equal opportunities for men and women in the labour market

(iv) Targeted action to improve access to jobs and training for those with special needs facing exclusion from the labour market

(v) Improved and more flexible education, training and employment services

- Improving the quality of education and training advice
- Improving the quality of the employment services: support for every unemployed person on Merseyside
- Better understanding between training providers and business: closer industry–education links

(vi) Access to work: improving the public transport system

(vii) Better environment: measures to treat derelict and contaminated land

Source: Adapted from CEC (1995)

The Objective 1 strategy is driven by the belief that 'the provision of a trained workforce in the right place and at the right time is at least as important to new or expanding businesses as the right premises, infrastructure and support services' (Carvel 1994, p.5). Padraig Flynn has stated that the underlying theme and overarching focus of the programme is employment creation (see Carvel 1994). In light of these protestations it is necessary to explore the spending proposals which guide Merseyside's Objective 1 package.

Resources

Table 6.2 displays the expenditure plans for Objective 1 during 1994–1999. Total spending is 2000 million ECU – over £1.6 billion (£630 million from Europe, £630 from the UK public sector and £340 from the UK private sector). Total ERDF expenditure amounts to 1244 million ECU (62%), ESF will reach 748 million ECU (37%), while European Agricultural Guidance and Guarantee Fund (EAGGF) spending barely reaches 1 per cent (8 million ECU) – Merseyside being a predominantly urban and industrial region. The ERDF component will provide support for 'productive investment', it will assist in the renovation of the region's infrastructure and help to procure the best conditions for endogenous development and investment, while the ESF element aims to reduce unemployment by creating jobs, enhancing access to employment, improving equal opportunities, and developing the skills base of the local people (GOM 1994, p.7). The EAGGF covers agricultural and rural issues, which are not high on Merseyside's economic development agenda.

Figure 6.2 Actors involved in economic development in Merseyside

Table 6.2 Merseyside Objective 1 Programme 1994–1999 financial table by driver (million ECU)

		Total		*European Community*				*National*	
		Cost	*Public*	*Total*	*ERDF*	*ESF*	*EAGGF*	*Public*	*Private*
Driver 1		**482**	**318**	**186**	**178**	**8**		**132**	**164**
	ERDF	485	302	178	178			124	156
	ESF	24	16	8		8		8	8
Driver 2		**401**	**299**	**149**	**106**	**40**	**3**	**150**	**102**
	ERDF	273	213	106	106			107	60
	ESF	120	80	40		40		40	40
	EAGGF	8	6	3			3	3	2
Driver 3		**172**	**121**	**62**	**42**	**20**		**59**	**51**
	ERDF	124	86	42	42			44	38
	ESF	48	35	20		20		15	13
Driver 4		**146**	**104**	**54**	**38**	**16**		**50**	**42**
	ERDF	98	72	38	38			34	26
	ESF	48	32	16		16		16	16

Table 6.2 Merseyside Objective 1 Programme 1994–1999 financial table by driver (million ECU) (continued)

		Total		*European Community*				*National*	
		Cost	*Public*	*Total*	*ERDF*	*ESF*	*EAGGF*	*Public*	*Private*
Driver 5		**791**	**782**	**361**	**109**	**252**		**421**	**9**
	ERDF	287	278	109	109			169	9
	ESF	504	504	252		252		252	
Technical assistance		**8**	**8**	**4**	**2**	**2**		**4**	
	ERDF	4	4	2	2			2	
	ESF	4	4	2		2		2	
Total		**2000**	**1632**	**816**	**475**	**338**	**3**	**816**	**368**
	ERDF	1244	955	475	475			480	289
	ESF	748	671	338		338		333	77
	EAGGF	8	6	3		3		3	2

Source: Adapted from CEC (1995)

An important feature of the SPD is that there has been a 10 per cent reduction in the amount of resources allocated to the ESF. *Merseyside 2000* had allotted 47 per cent of total expenditure to human resources, whereas in the revised SPD the ESF measures only account for 37 per cent – a noticeable decrease for which the Commission regards itself as the prime motivator (Carvel 1994). However, this remains the largest percentage spent on the ESF in any Objective 1 region. Millan and Flynn defend this decision by citing the scale of Merseyside's unemployment problem, which requires a large proportion of spending to be dedicated to ESF training measures (see Carvel 1994).

The resources flowing from the Objective 1 coffers are dispensed between various bodies, such as the local authorities, the three TECs, the universities and colleges, Merseytravel, English Partnerships,[5] The Mersey Partnership,[6] the MDC, voluntary and non-profit making agencies, while the private sector will be able to benefit from both 'indirect and direct support' (CEC 1995, p.25). These are shown in Figure 6.2 which illustrates the main organizations involved in economic development in Merseyside.

The first round of Objective 1 project funding was announced on 1 November 1994 (see Table 6.3). In total £176 million (£75 million European monies, £75 million from the UK public sector and £26 from the million UK private sector) was allocated to diverse projects which seek to 'transform the area and halt the spread of urban decline' (Hunt 1994a, p.1). The spending was designed to generate 25,000 training places, 3900 new jobs and 341,000 square feet of modern industrial floorspace and 291 acres of land primed for redevelopment (GOM 1994). Some 56 per cent of the grants will be spent on regional development (ERDF), while 44 per cent will be used for social purposes (ESF) – 'a marked shift from government proposals earlier this year which would have used most of the money for social purposes such as training' (Fazey 1994c, p.13) – thereby reiterating the point made earlier that the Commission has engaged itself in a policy of limiting the size of the ESF commitment from Objective 1. Nevertheless, one-third (£30 million) will be 'injected into a training programme to help create a super-skilled workforce' (Hunt 1994a, p.1). The first round of spending has engendered a fierce debate on Merseyside which will be discussed in more detail later in this chapter.

The projects receiving the largest share of the first funding round are those which are aimed at helping firms, particularly SMEs, to start up and become competitive by providing them with the necessary physical and social infrastructure (see Table 6.3). John Stoker, Chair of the Objective 1 Monitoring Committee, has stated that the projects contained in Table 6.3 herald a brighter future for the

---

5 A central government funded agency which works with the private and public sectors to regenerate derelict and contaminated land throughout England.

6 An organization involving the public and private sectors which markets Merseyside to audiences both nationally and internationally, with the avowed aim of attracting inward investment and thereby stimulating economic development.

people of Merseyside because they will serve to create and protect jobs, attract inward investment, improve the skills in the local labour market, enable local companies to expand and strengthen their competitiveness and also enhance the quality of life in the region (see GOM 1994). Bruce Millan endorses Stoker's optimism by contending that these resource allocations will provide the initial stimulus for creating approximately 49,000 jobs on Merseyside between 1994 and 1999 (see GOM 1994).

Table 6.3 The first round of Objective 1 resource allocations (November 1994)[7]

Grant award	*Project*
£19 million	Industrial development and improvement throughout Merseyside, involving expanding industrial estates, reclamation of land, security, landscaping and the local environment
£15.5 million	To assist SMEs via the local TECs and Business Links to promote new local firms and to enable existing companies to expand
£6 million	Improving public transport in the region
£4 million	Improvements of Queen Square area of Liverpool
£3 million	Investment in the Port of Liverpool
£2.5 million	The MDC's renewal of the A565
£2 million	To promote the establishment of partnerships in the most deprived communities in Merseyside
£1.29 million	To local TECs aid the setting up and future success of local SMEs
£1 million	To The Mersey Partnership towards The Merseyside Image Campaign contained in Driver 1
£750,000	Towards the development of an International Business Park in Wirral
£624,000	To Liverpool University's project on laser technology which seeks to improve the international competitiveness of local firms by giving them access to modern technology
£313,000	To a partnership of the two universities and Liverpool Institute of Higher Education to assist 265 graduates in obtaining a year's work with local firms
£237,855	To the Merseyside Innovation Centre as part of the Merseyside Waste Minimisation Demonstrator Programme
£100,000	Towards the creation of Merseyside Special Investment Fund led by Liverpool Chamber of Commerce to provide loans of up to £250,000 to help local investment projects materialize – it is in this sphere that money will be made available for hairdressing and beautician training
£18,000	To Knowsley Council's Vocational Skills Project to help school children between 14 and 16 years of age who play truant to obtain some vocational qualifications

7 This does not include all the projects which were funded, only the main ones which received the largest grants.

Table 6.4 The second round of Objective 1 resource allocations (July 1995)

Grant Award	*Project*
£4 million	Support for Merseyside's TV, media and film industry
£3.7 million	Renovation of Liverpool Royal Infirmary
£1.7 million	Sefton Maritime Development
£1.3 million	Upgrading of business and employment in the Netherton area of Sefton
£972,000	Towards the building of a new Brunswick Station in the South Docks of the Brunswick Business Park
£962,000	Refurbishment of Bootle Strand bus station
£937,000	To the MDC to regenerate Morpeth Dock
£698,000	Regeneration of the Sandhills Business Park West
£645,000	To Moving Image Development Agency to encourage film production in Merseyside
£642,000	To improve and upgrade Southport Pier
£600,000	For a series of tourism initiatives and festivals to attract visitors to Merseyside
£503,000	To the MDC for environmental improvements in the Brunswick Business Park
£439,000	To the MDC to restore listed buildings in Hamilton Square, Wirral
£341,000	Network 2000 – Wirral Metropolitan College for training and equipment in computers and information technology
£329,000	Kirkby Town Centre regeneration
£329,000	To the Unity Theatre in Liverpool
£307,000	Haydock Industrial Estate – to provide a new road and open up new land for development
£241,000	To improve the River Alt
£161,000	Landlife flowers – to provide windflower seeds for garden centres and the reclamation of derelict sites

At the time of writing a second round of grant support from Objective 1 was announced, totalling some £91 million (£35 million European monies and £28 million from the UK public and private sectors) covering 68 projects – the main ones are displayed in Table 6.4. The grant awards are from the ERDF and translate into mainly capital projects. Once again these announcements received unqualified support from both John Stoker and various Government ministers, who envisage them as providing a firm foundation for the continued regeneration of Merseyside and its economy (GoM 1995). At the time of writing it is too early to proffer a firm analysis of this particular round of resource allocations.

Institutional Mechanisms for Regional Development on Merseyside

Implementation arrangements for Objective I

Having examined the economic and social development contents of the SPD, it is necessary to discuss the institutional structures which have been established on Merseyside for Objective 1. A Monitoring Committee (MC) performs the function of regulating the 'implementation' of the SPD (CEC 1995, p.149). Its membership includes the UK government, the Commission, the European Investment Bank, the private sector, TECs, statutory bodies, the voluntary sector, the local authorities and other important regional actors. It normally meets twice a year at the behest of the UK government or the Commission and possesses its own remit and set of rules and regulations. The MC undertakes an annual review of the SPD's progress. However, there has been serious disquiet expressed regarding the absence of the local social partners on the MC (see Conclusions).

In order to assess the quality of the bids requesting Objective 1 support there exist two Technical Panels: one relating to the first four drivers concerned with industrial development and the other focusing on the fifth driver – the people of Merseyside. Membership includes the government, the Commission, the private sector, the local authorities, TECs, voluntary groups and other important organizations. There is a high degree of 'cross membership' and 'close liaison' between the Panels, and the Chairs of both Panels will report frequently to the MC (CEC 1995, p.149). There is a strong contingent representing the private sector, with six members on both Panels selected from large firms and SMEs. The Panels can authorize projects up to 5 million ECU subject to the selection criteria determined by the MC, but all schemes above that ceiling are approved by the MC acting on advice from the Secretariat and the Panels. The selection criteria are a demonstration of the need for Objective funding and how this support will be translated into additional benefits for the Merseyside economy. There is a 'competitive bidding' process for project support from Objective 1 and bids can be placed on a collaborative basis between any of the 'partners' involved in Merseyside (CEC 1995, p.151).

A Secretariat, with secondees from the local authorities, government departments, statutory agencies and the private sector, is located within the Government Office for Merseyside to assist in the 'pro-active development' of Objective 1 and to support the work of the MC and the Panels (CEC 1995, p.150). It reports to the Chair of the MC on its 'technical appraisal' of bids and its 'coordination' of the various components of the programme (CEC 1995, p.150).

The Government Offices and Single Regeneration Budget

Alongside the organizational arrangements which have accompanied Objective 1, the UK government also introduced new institutional mechanisms which have implications for Merseyside and Objective 1 – unified Government Offices (GOs) and the Single Regeneration Budget (SRB). These changes govern the administration of economic and urban development in the English regions. The GOs, which are headed by Senior Regional Directors, became operational in April 1994 with the explicit aim of providing a more integrated institutional structure for the coordination of regional development in England – as they unify the previously separate government regional offices of Environment (DoE), Employment,[8] Transport and Trade and Industry (DTI). The government believed that they would presage a 'shift' in power from the centre to the localities, thereby ensuring that the government became more 'responsive' to local needs and aspirations and enabling the private sector and the local authorities to liaise with one combined office (DoE 1993, p.1). However, on Merseyside this reorganization has led some to term this as a deliberate attempt at 'rationalising Central Government control' (Parry 1993).

There are ten GOs throughout the English regions,[9] and while they are concerned with current regional office main programmes, relating to housing, planning, transport, training and investment in industry, they endeavour to ensure that there is greater synthesis and linkage between them (DoE 1993). The GOs administer the SRB, which has brought the many disparate main programmes together and placed them into one single fund (such as City Challenge,[10] Urban Programme, Urban Development Corporations, TECs, English Partnerships and Regional Enterprise Grants). The government decided that a proportion of the SRB be set aside to fund bids from local partnerships led by local authorities or TECs for area-based initiatives, with competition for resources. Working alongside the GOs are individual Sponsor Ministers who represent the interests of their respective regions on the Ministerial Committee for Economic Development and Regeneration (EDR), which discharges government regeneration policies and decides which bids for SRB support are accepted.

Merseyside has its own Government Office (GOM) whose Senior Regional Director is John Stoker, former Director of the MTF,[11] and its Sponsor Minister is Robin Squire MP, from the Department for Education and Employment. The GOM allocates government monies among the local authorities and other organizations which have a role to perform in economic development in Merseyside, it coordinates bids from the SRB and facilitates the disbursement of Objective 1 funds – as Stoker is also the Chair of the MC and the Secretariat operates from within the GOM. In the first round of SRB bid applications for 1995/6 Merseyside attained a success rate of 61 per cent (second only to Yorkshire and Humberside with 88%), and when compared with an average of 45 per cent for

8 Following the government reshuffle of July 1995, the Department of Employment was merged with Education.

9 In the North East, North West, Yorkshire and Humberside, Merseyside, East Midlands, West Midlands, Eastern, London, South East and South West.

10 A central government funded initiative designed to regenerate inner city areas, involving the public, voluntary and community sectors. There are three on Merseyside: Liverpool, Bootle and Wirral.

11 The MTF and its 'partner' the City Action Team, have been subsumed into the GOM.

the ten GOs (Griffin 1995) this represents a very positive achievement. Of the £139 million on offer for SRB bids (out of a total budget of over £1 billion) Merseyside was granted 7.46 per cent for 1995/6, London was the highest with 26.28 per cent (Griffin 1995), which translates into some £10 million for the regional economy.

Conclusions

Although they are generally pleased with Merseyside's SPD, both Bruce Millan and Padraig Flynn – the European Commissioners responsible for overseeing the approval and passage of Merseyside's Objective 1 programme through the Commission – were prepared to express two basic reservations regarding the *management* of the Objective 1 strategy (Carvel 1994). They attempted to convince the UK government of the value of including the trades unions and the other social partners on the MC, and for the Secretariat to be contracted out under the control of an independent chief executive – as in the Strathclyde Objective 2 and the Highlands and Islands Objective 1 mechanisms (Carvel 1994). However, the government displayed its usual intractability and decided against both these positive suggestions.

Issues such as the social partners' absence from the MC, the bureaucratic nature of the Objective 1 bidding system and the *inadequacy* of the Secretariat have been raised in the House of Commons. Indeed, one local MP teased the Minister of Local Government, Housing and Urban Regeneration, David Curry MP, by reminding him that the European Regional Policy Commissioner, Mrs Monica Wulf-Mathies, stated in November 1994 that the social partners 'should be represented' on the local MC (*Hansard* 1995, p.884). The Minister's response was a promise to initiate a concerted attempt to accelerate the whole process, but it maintains that the procedures for Objective 1 are 'imposed' by the Commission and so it is therefore not in a strong position to streamline them (*Hansard* 1995, p.884).

A heated debate has erupted over the power and privilege which the Senior Regional Directors of the GOs currently enjoy. These government appointed officials have been disparagingly compared to 'district commissioners' of the British Empire, Roman 'pro-consuls', French 'prefects' and 'viceroys' (Foster 1995, p.9). Their control over the spending of the combined GOs and their administration of the SRB have led many observers to question their accountability and discretionary powers (Foster 1995). They are not ultimately responsible to either local government nor MPs, but to Secretaries of State and the EDR. More specifically, one Merseyside MP has alleged that regeneration monies, and resources from Objective 1, have been disbursed by the GOM without a detailed analysis of the requirements of Merseyside economy and that the whole process of grant allocations is excessively secretive, with the Senior Regional Director running the show: 'The system seems to be running secretively, with grants of up to £3.8m awarded without any elected representative considering the application' (Kilfoyle cited in Foster 1995, p.9).

A report by Brian Hogwood, of Strathclyde University, for the Commission for Local Democracy refutes some of the statements propagated by the government on the GOs and the SRB. His fundamental criticism is that local authorities will 'continue to have to deal with a multiplicity of government bodies and government-funded agencies which have a multiplicity of office locations and a multiplicity of boundaries' (cited in Burton 1995, p.1). So it appears that the transfer of power from Whitehall to the regions is not borne out by the evidence. He also argues that agencies *not* functioning through the GOs account for the largest amount of resources which central government allocates for regional/local economic development; that the SRB is 'small scale both in terms of allocation to local authorities and to other bodies operating at a local level' and that it will encounter further reductions in its funding during the next three years (cited in Burton 1995, p.1).

The first round of Objective 1 resource allocations received unfavourable critical comment from some local businessmen and politicians. The main criticism was that the spending plans will result in young unemployed people being trained in Merseyside, who will then leave in search of employment in other parts of the UK, or even the EC, because Merseyside will not be able to offer the jobs that they seek (Hunt 1994b) – since the UK operates within the parameters of the Single European Market. However, it is also true to say that if the Objective 1 programme fulfils its expectations then such a pessimistic scenario will not emerge, as Merseysiders are proud and loyal people and would not leave the area if sufficient jobs were available. The key for the region is to train people in the skills and expertise that are likely to be demanded in the labour market, when job prospects do materialize – the low skill threshold of the local working population has often been cited as a major debilitating force for many years. The Objective 1 strategy should go a long way towards remedying this imbalance between the supply and demand of labour.

Particular criticism was levied at the decision to spend some £1,170,000 of Objective 1 monies, totalling £2.3 million with matching funding, on training unemployed adults in the performing arts and as hairdressers and beauticians. Both John Stoker, as Chair of the MC which drew up the spending plans, and Peter Houghton, of Employment Training on Merseyside, strenuously defended these measures (see Hunt 1994b). Stoker went on to argue that a large proportion of the resources will generate 'direct benefits' to the private sector (cited in Hunt 1994b, p.4). Admittedly, these schemes will not raise regional GDP as they do not directly help the export sector, which would lever in additional capital to finance economic regeneration. A substantial increase in regional GDP is more likely through support for manufacturing and export industries. However, at least they offer the unemployed an opportunity to obtain a skill or trade with which to sell their labour and procure employment, which is the second fundamental tenet of Objective 1.

The award of Objective 1 monies affords Merseyside with a vital opportunity to stimulate economic and social redevelopment. A key factor in the future will be the success of the attempted complementarity, linkage and integration between central government regional and urban policies and the Objective 1 programme. This is a crucial component for the *conversion* of the region – the problems of isolation, parochialism and disunity of purpose were particularly enervating forces which acutely affected Merseyside during the 1980s. The creation of the GOM and the Objective 1 strategy have compelled all those involved in economic development in the region – the Partners – to cooperate with each other, and coordinate their energies, efforts and policies towards achieving the long-term targets of Objective 1.

Objective 1 resources should to be targeted on projects that precisely aim to raise the regional GDP and reduce unemployment on Merseyside. What remains important is that activities are geared towards supplementing and complementing Objective 1. Thus Objective 1 and the GOM, alongside the City Challenges, MDC, the TECs, The Mersey Partnership, English Partnerships, the private sector, the local authorities and other agencies provide the region with an excellent an opportunity to launch itself as a vibrant and successful city region. What is required in Merseyside is a *coherence* and *integration* of policies, energies and resources so that each initiative complements and supports others and thereby creates a comprehensive and sustainable economic and social development strategy which takes Merseyside on a positive and dynamic journey into the year 2000 and beyond.

The Merseyside Objective 1 programme contains some very bold predictions and ambitious targets, from which it will be judged over time. Should these not be met, then Merseyside will leave itself open to allegations of waste and misuse of resources – and there will be plenty of vultures hovering over Merseyside's carcass to gleefully feast upon its remains.

References

Boland, P., Mannin, M. and Wallace, J. (1995) 'Merseyside – Implications of Objective 1 and the Government Office.' *Regional Studies 29,* 7, 698–705.

Burton, M. (1995) 'Research Report Summary' based on the original report: *The Integrated Regional Offices and the Single Regeneration Budget,* by Brian Hogwood. London: Commission for Local Democracy.

Carvel, J. (1993) 'Silence could cost Merseyside millions.' *The Guardian.* February 6th.

Carvel, J. (1994) 'Objective Europe. Two into one will go.' In *Quorum* Issue 1. Liverpool: The Mersey Partnership, pp.4–7.

Commission of the European Communities (CEC) (1995) *Merseyside Single Programming Document 1994–1999.* Brussels: Directorate General for Regional Policies, Commission of the European Communities.

Department of the Environment (DoE) (1993) *Department of the Environment News Release.* London: Department of the Environment. 4 November.

Fazey, I.H. (1994a) 'The double-edged sword.' *Financial Times Survey on Merseyside.* Thursday 14 July, p.19.

Fazey, I.H. (1994b) 'The "drivers" of change.' *Financial Times Survey on Merseyside.* Thursday 14 July, p.21.

Fazey, I.H. (1994c) 'Mersey are to receive aid fund.' *Financial Times,* November 1, p.13.

Foster, J. (1995) 'MPs attack powers of regional "viceroys".' *Independent on Sunday.* 5 February, p.9.

Government Office for Merseyside (GOM) (1994) *Merseyside 2000. £176 Million Objective 1 Package Announced for Merseyside.* Press Release. Liverpool: Government Office for Merseyside.

Government Office for Merseyside (GOM) (1995) *Merseyside 2000 Objective 1. Merseyside 'Premieres' its Latest Objective One Announcement.* Press Release. Liverpool: Government Office for Merseyside.

Griffin, C. (1995) 'Beyond city challenge.' *International Cities Management.* January/February, pp.16–17.

Hansard (1995) *Parliamentary Debates. House of Commons.* Issue No. 1681, Volume 256, No. 71, Column No.884, 15th March. London: HMSO.

Hunt, A. (1994a) 'SPEND, SPEND, SPEND! Revealed: How Mersey will share out Euro millions.' *Liverpool Echo.* Saturday 29 October, pp.1–2.

Hunt, A. (1994b) 'Euro money men hit back.' *Liverpool Echo.* Tuesday 1 November, p.4.

Kousgaard, P. (1994) Merseyside European Liaison Unit Officer, Merseyside European Liaison Unit, Liverpool. Interview 28.1.94.

Martin, S. and Pearce, G. (1993) 'European regional development strategies: Strengthening the meso-government in the UK?.' *Regional Studies* Volume 27, Number 7, pp.681–685.

Meegan, R. (1989) 'Paradise postponed: the growth and decline of Merseyside's outer estates.' In P. Cooke (ed) *Localities. The Changing Face of Urban Britain.* London: Unwin Hyman, pp.198–234.

Meegan, R. (1990) 'Merseyside in crisis and in conflict.' In M. Harloe, C. Pickvance and J. Urry (eds) *Place, Policy and Politics: Do Localities Matter?* London: Unwin Hyman, London, pp.87–107.

Merseyside Task Force (MTF) (1993) *Merseyside 2000. European Community Objective 1. Regional Conversion Plan for Merseyside.* Liverpool: Merseyside Task Force.

Minford and Stoney (1993) 'Objective One Must Be Growth.' *Merseyside Economic and Business Prospect* Volume 8, Number 2. Liverpool: Liverpool Research Group in Macroeconomics, pp.3–6.

Office of Population Censuses and Surveys (OPCS) (1992) *1991 Census County Monitor: Merseyside.* CEN 91 CM 28. London: HMSO. August, p.3.

Parry, D. (1993) Marketing and Information Manager, Economic Initiatives Unit, Liverpool City Council. Interview 26.11.93.

Welfare, D. and Beaumont, K. (1993) 'Additionality: the key to understanding it.' *MR and AMA News,* December, pp.182–183.

CHAPTER 7

The Transfer from a Problem to Powerful Region

The Experience of Wales

Jeremy Alden

The Legacy of the Past

Regional development policies in the UK have traditionally been closely linked to the problem of the depressed areas in its peripheral regions. The Special Areas Act of 1934 was the first official attempt by central government to address the high rates of unemployment in the older industrial areas of the UK, and to influence the spatial distribution of economic activity. Industrial South Wales was one of the first four areas to be designated a Special Area under the 1934 Act.

Wales acquired the label of being a *problem region* of the UK as it experienced the highest rates of unemployment of any region throughout the 1930s (see Table 7.1), with an average rate of some 30 per cent, which was twice the UK rate.

In July 1967, the government published a White Paper on the Welsh economy, *Wales: The Way Ahead* (Welsh office 1967, Cmnd. 3334). It noted that Wales in the 1960s was undergoing a transformation as sweeping and far-reaching in scope, but much faster in pace, than all the changes it underwent during the first Industrial Revolution and up to World War One in 1914. By 1921, some 36.7 per cent of the working population of Wales were employed in either coal mining or metal manufacture, compared to a corresponding figure of 10.2 per cent for England and Wales as a whole. In 1921, there were 250,000 men employed in the coal industry in Wales: in 1995 only one deep coal mine (now in private ownership by former coal miners) remains, employing some 250 men.

The legacy of the past in Wales has led to a situation where the level of economic activity has always been too low to fully utilize the resources available. This has been shown in the relatively high levels of unemployment, low labour activity rates, and low levels of gross domestic product (GDP) per capita, and low personal and household income, compared to the national average.

Table 7.1 Regional unemployment rates in the 1930s (%)

Region	*1929*	*1932*	*1934*	*1938*
London	5.6	13.5	9.2	7.8
South East	5.6	14.3	8.7	7.7
South West	8.1	18.1	13.1	8.1
Midlands	9.3	20.1	12.9	10.0
North West	13.3	25.8	20.8	17.7
North East	13.7	28.5	22.1	12.9
Scotland	12.1	27.7	23.1	16.8
Wales	19.3	36.5	32.3	25.9
N. Ireland	14.8	27.2	23.4	24.4
UK	10.4	22.1	16.7	12.9

Source: Alden and Morgan (1974, Table 2.1 p.16)

This chapter examines the extent to which Wales has made any transition from being a longstanding problem region of both Great Britain and the European Community (EC)[1] to one enjoying greater economic success in the 1990s. The chapter particularly focuses upon trends of convergence and divergence between Wales and other regions on a range of economic indicators covering output, income, productivity, employment, labour force participation and unemployment. These are similar variables to those adopted by the European Commission in its analysis of regional trends, contained in the Fifth Periodic Report, *Competitiveness and Cohesion: trends in the regions* (CEC 1994b).

The Welsh Development Agency (WDA) was established 20 years ago in 1975, and given the task of regenerating the Welsh economy. In January 1995, the WDA published its Corporate Plan for the next three years, and identified its main objective as being to promote the growth of quality jobs and competitive businesses. Its targets for the next three years include creating or safeguarding 31,000 jobs by winning more than £1.6 billion of inward investment. The Corporate Plan was designed to address the main weaknesses in the Welsh economy, which have become known as *the prosperity gap* between Wales and the UK as a whole (the geographical position of Wales as a standard region in the UK is illustrated in Figure 7.1). The main features of this prosperity gap have been identified as GDP and income per head some 15 per cent below the UK average, earnings for both men and women well below the UK average, and unemployment,

1 For purposes of this chapter, the same terminology has been adopted as used in the Fifth Periodic Report, namely references to the European Union (EU) as the political and administrative organization, and the EC as the economic system of regions. This is also the terminology adopted by Bruce Millan, the former Commissioner for Regional Policy in his Introduction to the Fifth Periodic Report.

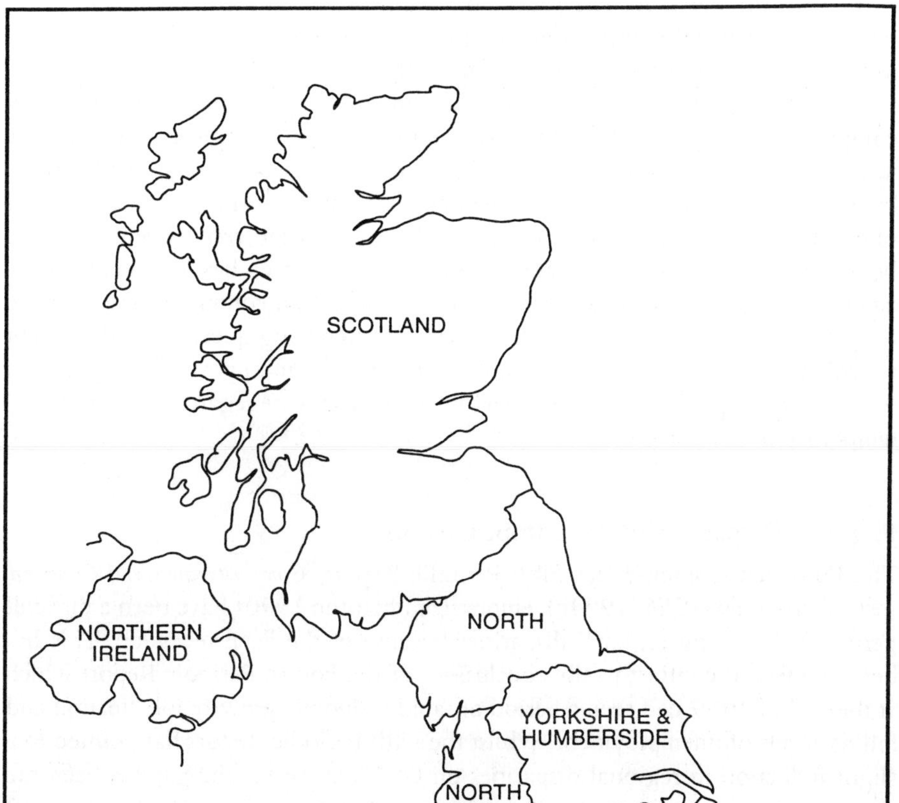

Source: Regional Trends 30 1995

Figure 7.1 Standard regions of the United Kingdom

particularly in the industrial valleys of South Wales and in certain rural areas remaining persistently high, even though the unemployment rate for Wales overall in recent years has closely matched that for the UK.

Indeed, in July 1992, Wales had an unemployment rate of 9.7 per cent compared to 9.8 per cent for the UK, the first time since regional records were kept that Wales's unemployment rate was below the national average. Furthermore, by July 1993, the Welsh unemployment rate not only continued to be below that of the UK as a whole, at 9.9 per cent and 10.2 per cent respectively, but even below that for south-east England at 10.1 per cent, which has long enjoyed the label as being the most prosperous region in the UK in contrast to the problem region label attached to Wales. This raises the interesting question of the extent to which Wales has now made the transfer from problem to powerful region, and whether any improvements which have been made may be regarded as either only temporary or permanent.

Regional Disparities in the European Union

The European Commission's Fifth Periodic Report, *Competitiveness and Cohesion: trends in the regions* (CEC 1994b), emphasized that the 1990s have been a difficult period for reducing regional disparities because of the deep recession. This has been in marked contrast to the conclusions of the Fourth Periodic Report which at the end of 1989 had seen a period of rapid economic growth, job creation and falling levels of unemployment. Whilst the Fifth Periodic Report has pointed to a slight reduction in regional disparities on GDP per capita, the gap between the richest and poorest regions is still considerable. For example, by 1991, the top 10 regions had an average income per head 3 times that of the bottom 10 regions, and 4 times if the new East German Länder were included.

The European Commission's most recent policy document on regional development is *Europe 2000+: Cooperation for European Territorial Development* (CEC 1994a). The document stresses that there is growing acceptance of the need for spatial planning at a European level among Member States, as well as in academic and professional circles. The European Parliament, the Economic and Social Committee, the Consultative Council of Regional and Local Authorities, and most recently the Committee of the Regions, have all emphasized the need for increased cooperation on spatial planning issues.

Europe 2000+ has identified three main objectives of the European Commission's regional development strategy, namely (a) the increased competitiveness of areas in an increasingly competitive global economy, (b) more sustainable economic development, and (c) the reduction of regional disparities and need for greater cohesion. However, there is clearly a tension and contradiction here between *competition* and *cohesion.* Greater competition implies winners and losers. Wales has been seen as a loser in economic development: the problem region of

Britain. The European Commission will become more involved in identifying just where the losers are.

The relative position of Wales within the EC, in terms of GDP per capita, did not improve at all over the 1981–1991 period. In fact, it worsened considerably. As shown in Table 7.2, whilst Wales had a GDP per capita equal to 85 per cent of the EC average (10 countries), this fell to 83 per cent in 1991 (12 countries). The addition of poorer regions in the new member countries of Portugal and Spain, and the addition of the East German Länder, should have led to an improved GDP per capita relative to the EC average in 1991 than 1981. It can also be seen in Table 7.2 that in 1981, out of 54 regions in the EC 10, Wales was ranked 44th, i.e. just out of the poorest 10. Its relative ranking had improved by 1991 in the sense that it achieved a position of 48th out of 68 regions, and one of being just out of the poorest 20 regions. However, the 1991 performance of Wales based on the 1981 regions, i.e. EC of 10 countries, would have placed it in the same ranking as 1981, i.e. 44th out of 54 regions.

Table 7.2 Regional disparities in GDP per capita in EC 1981–1991

EUR 10	*Gross Domestic Product EUR 10 = 100 1981*	*EUR 12*	*Gross Domestic Product EUR 12 = 100 1991*
Belgium	**106**	**Belgium**	**108**
Vlaams gewest/ Region flamande	105	Vlaams Gewest	109
Region bruxelloise/ Brussels gewest	170	Region Wallonne	87
Region wallonne/ Waals gewest	87	Bruxelles-Brussels	171
Denmark	**110**	**Denmark**	**111**
France	**110**	**France**	**115**
Ile-de-France	156	Ile-de-France	172
Bassin parisien	105	Bassin parisien	105
Nord-Pas-de-Calais	97	Nord-Pas-de-Calais	93
Est	108	Est	106
Quest	92	Quest	97
Centre-Est	106	Centre-Est	101
Mediterranee	97	Mediterranee	98

Table 7.2 Regional disparities in GDP per capita in EC 1981–1991 (continued)

EUR 10	*Gross Domestic Product EUR 10 = 100 1981*	*EUR 12*	*Gross Domestic Product EUR 12 = 100 1991*
Germany	**114[1]**	**Germany**	**106[2]**
Scheswig-Holstein	99	Baden-Wurttemberg	130
Hamburg	193	Bayern	127
Neidersachsen	99	Berlin	95
Bremen	149	Brandenburg	36
Nordrhein-Westfalen	112	Bremem	159
Hesson	125	Hamburg	209
Rheinland-Pflaz	102	Hesson	149
Baden-Wurttemberg	119	Mecklenburg-Vorpommem	33
Bayern	109	Neidersachsen	108
Saarland	105	Nordrhein-Westfalin	115
Berlin (West)	131	Rheinland-Pfalz	104
		Saarland	112
		Sachsen	33
		Sachsen-Anhalt	35
		Schleswig-Holstein	102
		Thueringen	30
Greece	**56**	**Greece**	**49**
Voreia Ellada	50	Voreia Ellada	46
Kentriki Ellada	60	Kentriki Ellada	48
Anatolkia kai notia nisiA	44	Nisia Aigaiou, Kriti	44
Ireland	**64**	**Ireland**	**72**
Italy	**89**	**Italy**	**106**
Nord-Ovest	110	Nord-Ovest	122
Lombardia	117	Lombardia	139
Nord Est	95	Nord Est	122
Emilia-Romagna	113	Emilia-Romagna	132
Centro	96	Centro	110
Lazio	91	Lazio	121
Campania	61	Campania	73
Abruzzi-Molise	70	Abruzzi-Molise	91
Sud	60	Sud	70
Sicilia	61	Sicilia	70
Sardgna	64	Sardegna	77

Table 7.2 Regional disparities in GDP per capita in EC 1981–1991 (continued)

EUR 10	*Gross Domestic Product EUR 10 = 100 1981*	*EUR 12*	*Gross Domestic Product EUR 12 = 100 1991*
Luxembourg	**115**	**Luxembourg**	**131**
Netherlands	**104**	**Netherlands**	**104**
Noord-Nederland	142	Noord-Nederland	106
Oost-Nederland	87	Oost-Nederland	91
West-Nederland	111	West-Nederland	111
Zuid-Nederland	89	Zuid-Nederland	100
		Portugal	**60**
		Continente	60
		Acores	–
		Madeira	–
		Spain	**80**
		Noroeste	66
		Noreste	92
		Madrid	100
		Centro	65
		Este	92
		Sur	64
		Canarias	79
United Kingdom	**92**	**United Kingdom**	**98**
North	89	North	86
Yorkshire and Humberside	84	Yorkshire and Humberside	88
East Midlands	87	East Midlands	94
East Anglia	86	East Anglia	99
South East	107	South East	117
South West	87	South West	94
West Midlands	81	West Midlands	89
North West	89	North West	90
Wales	85	Wales	83
Scotland	93	Scotland	94
Northern Ireland	72	Northern Ireland	74

Source: *Regional Trends* (1985, Table 13.1; 1994, Table 2.1)

[1] Excludes the new German Länder in former East Germany

[2] Includes the new German Länder in former East Germany

NB: GDP per capita converted to purchasing power standards

It is also the case that Wales was one of the only two regions in Britain (the other being the North) not to improve its relative position within the EC in terms of GDP per capita between 1981 and 1991. This situation is illustrated in Table 7.3. The low level of GDP per capita in Portugal, some of the Spanish regions, and all five of the new East German Länder, should have resulted in an improved relative position for all British regions.

Indeed, within the UK, Northern Ireland improved its relative position, although its actual value remained lower than that of Wales. In contrast to Wales, Scotland continued to have a GDP per capita ten percentage points above that of Wales and close to the EC average.

Table 7.3 Ranking of UK regions within EU in 1981 and 1991: EUR = 100

	1981 (EUR of 10)	*1991 (EUR of 12*)*
UK	92	98
North	89	86
Yorkshire & Humberside	84	88
East Midlands	87	94
East Anglia	86	99
South East	107	117
South West	87	94
West Midlands	81	89
North West	89	90
Wales	85	83
Scotland	93	94
Northern Ireland	72	74
Points difference between South East and Wales	22	34

* includes the new German Länder in former East Germany
Source: Compiled from Table 7.2

The EC regional GDP per capita, shown in Tables 7.2 and 7.3, also point to a trend of divergence within the UK over the 1981–1991 period. The disparity between the richest and poorest regions in Britain, i.e. South East and Wales, in 1981 was 22 index points (i.e. Wales 85 per cent and South East 107 per cent of EC average) but increased to 34 index points by 1991 (i.e. Wales 83 per cent and South East 117 per cent of EC average).

The main regional trends in population and the labour force, output, employment and unemployment within the EC have been illustrated and discussed in the Fifth Periodic Report of the European Commission. In particular, since the mid-1980s, the EC has not succeeded in creating sufficient jobs to prevent unemployment from rising steadily. From 1973 to 1985, unemployment in the

EC increased annually from an average of 2.6 per cent to 10.8 per cent. Although the economic recovery in the second half of the 1980s led to a fall in unemployment, the rate was still 8.3 per cent in 1990 when the recovery ended. The rise in unemployment by some 3 million between 1991 and 1993 pushed unemployment rates up to 10.9 per cent by the end of 1993, thereby completely offsetting the progress of the second half of the 1980s.

However, as far as Wales is concerned, as already mentioned, its unemployment position improved relative to both the UK and the EC as a whole. Table 7.4 shows that whilst Wales had an overall unemployment rate considerably higher than both the UK and EC 12 in the second half of the 1980s, there has been a marked improvement in the 1990s. Indeed, by 1993 the overall EC harmonized unemployment rate for Wales at 9.7 per cent was below that of both the UK at 10.3 per cent and EC 12 at 10.4 per cent. It can be noted that male rates in Wales and the UK are well above the EC average, whilst the reverse is true for female rates.

The extent to which this improved relative performance on unemployment by Wales is due to growth in the Welsh economy and job creation, rather than a worsening situation facing other regions in Britain, particularly the South East, is examined more fully in the following section of this chapter.

Table 7.4 EC harmonized unemployment rates[a] as at April

	1986	*1987*	*1988*	*1989*	*1990*	*1991*	*1992*	*1993*
Wales								
Male	14.7	13.6	11.3	8.9	8.3	10.8	11.8	12.0
Female	12.2	11.6	9.8	7.8	6.8	7.2	6.6	6.6
Persons	13.7	12.8	10.7	8.5	7.6	9.3	9.6	9.7
UK								
Male	11.9	11.4	9.1	7.5	7.2	9.7	11.6	12.2
Female	10.9	10.4	8.5	7.0	6.6	7.6	7.5	7.8
Persons	11.5	11.0	8.9	7.3	6.9	8.8	9.9	10.3
Eur 12[b]								
Male	9.4	8.8	8.1	7.2	6.5	7.1	7.9	9.2
Female	12.8	13.0	12.7	11.8	10.7	10.7	11.4	12.2
Persons	10.7	10.5	9.9	9.0	8.2	8.6	9.3	10.4

[a] International definition of unemployment expressed as a percentage of the workforce
[b] Average of the twelve member states of the European Community
Source: *Welsh Economic Trends* (1994, Number 15)

The Fifth Periodic Report (CEC 1994b) discussed the extent to which the disparities between the regions reflect their different underlying circumstances, which are a combination of historical patterns of development and capacity to adapt to the rapidly-changing world of the late twentieth century. This is certainly the position facing Wales. The Fifth Periodic Report identified some of the factors which lie behind the regional disparities in income per head. These include levels of education and training of the labour force; research and technological development activity; labour force participation rates; new investment, particularly in transport, energy and telecommunications; foreign direct investment linked to creation of the Single Market; and productivity/unit labour cost levels which are critical for the competitiveness and adaptability of regional economic structures.

The Welsh Prosperity Gap

A number of reports have suggested that during the recent recession of the 1990s, Wales has fared better than other industrial areas of the UK. The European Commission reports, *Portrait of the Regions* (Eurostat 1993a) and Regions Statistical Yearbook (Eurostat 1993b) both noted that although for at least the past 20 years Wales' GDP per capita has been the lowest in Britain, and well below the EC average, the region's economy has improved in a number of ways following a period of rapid and extensive industrial restructuring. Recent improvements in communications and other infrastructure, financial support from both the EC Structural Funds and British government's urban and regional policies, together with proactive economic development policies being pursued by local and regional development agencies, have meant that Wales has attracted a high level of inward investment, especially by foreign manufacturers.

The Regional Economic Prospects forecasts to the year 2005, prepared by organizations such as Cambridge Econometrics (1994), have provided evidence that the Welsh economy is showing signs of sustained economic recovery. Both short and medium-term indicators suggest that it is Welsh manufacturing, characterized by high productivity and low unit labour costs, that will consolidate regional economic growth. Whilst there is a widespread recognition that Welsh GDP per capita will grow faster than the average UK levels, and that unemployment levels now match those of the UK nationally, there remains a concern for the disparities in earnings, personal incomes and labour-force participation rates between Wales and the UK, and for disparities between areas within Wales over unemployment rates, particularly for men.

Gross Domestic Product measures

As Dunford (1993) has illustrated in his article on regional disparities in the EC, regional GDP per capita is the most common indicator of regional inequality and provides a relief map of economic development. There are wide variations in GDP

Table 7.5 Gross Domestic Product per capita 1983–1993 (factor cost: current prices)

Region	*1983*	*1984*	*1985*	*1986*	*1987*	*1988*	*1989*	*1990*	*1991*	*1992*	*1993*
United Kingdom	100.0	100.0	100.0	100.0	100.0	100.0	100.0	100.0	100.0	100.0	100.0
North	93.2	91.9	92.5	89.9	90.7	89.0	89.6	88.1	89.6	90.0	89.4
Yorkshire & Humberside	93.5	92.9	93.7	94.0	92.9	91.3	91.3	90.8	91.8	90.8	91.2
East Midlands	96.9	98.4	98.3	97.1	97.1	96.2	96.8	95.9	96.8	96.4	95.8
East Anglia	97.5	102.4	100.6	101.1	99.6	99.8	100.9	101.3	100.1	101.9	101.7
South East	115.7	115.5	115.7	116.7	117.4	118.4	118.6	118.5	117.3	116.7	116.0
Greater London	124.2	122.9	124.2	125.7	127.2	126.8	126.7	126.5	126.3	125.4	124.7
Rest of South East	110.1	110.7	110.1	110.8	110.0	113.0	113.5	113.4	111.6	111.4	110.5
South West	94.8	94.7	94.3	94.7	94.6	94.3	94.2	94.6	94.5	95.2	96.6
West Midlands	90.3	91.2	92.2	91.6	91.6	92.5	92.0	92.9	92.5	93.2	93.1
North West	94.3	93.9	93.5	93.1	92.2	92.1	91.3	90.6	90.2	90.0	90.8
England	101.9	102.0	102.1	102.2	102.3	102.3	102.4	102.2	101.9	101.8	101.7
Wales	85.2	84.4	82.4	83.8	84.8	86.4	85.1	84.6	85.0	83.4	84.7
Scotland	97.4	96.3	96.2	94.8	94.5	93.2	93.3	95.0	96.6	98.6	98.4
Northern Ireland	78.7	79.2	78.5	78.5	76.4	76.1	76.6	77.5	81.5	81.4	81.9

Source: *Economic Trends* (1994, Number 494)

per capita between the UK regions, as shown in Table 7.5. The latest estimates for 1993 show that Welsh GDP per capita is some 15 per cent below that of the UK average, and a little lower than that of ten years ago. Wales clearly continues to have the lowest GDP per capita of any region in Britain, and is being caught up by Northern Ireland which has steadily improved its economic performance and relative position over the past decade.

Wales has been seeking to address its poor performance on GDP in recent years, and particularly to focus on raising the level of value-added in the manufacturing sector and improving the quality of jobs in a parallel attempt to raise the level of earnings and personal incomes. One of the most hopeful signs of an improvement in Welsh GDP performance has been the rate of increase in nominal GDP in recent years. As shown in Table 7.6, nominal GDP at factor cost increased by 7.1 per cent in Wales between 1992 and 1993, well above the UK average rate of 5.8 per cent, and the third highest regional growth rate in the UK (outperformed only marginally by the South West at 7.2 per cent and Northern Ireland at 7.3 per cent). However, this performance will have to be maintained in the future if Wales is to break through the elusive 90 per cent of the UK average GDP per capita barrier by the end of this decade.

Table 7.6 Growth in nominal GDP (factor cost: current prices) 1992–93 for UK regions

Region	*1992 (£million)*	*1993 (£million)*	*% change 1992–93*
UK	516,027	546,120	5.8
North	24,508	25,640	4.6
Yorkshire & Humberside	39,937	42,287	5.9
East Midlands	34,430	36,190	5.1
East Anglia	18,702	19,699	5.3
South East	181,539	190,622	5.0
Greater London	76,125	79,926	5.0
Rest of South East	105,415	110,696	5.0
South West	39,724	42,598	7.2
West Midlands	43,227	45,533	5.3
North West	50,628	53,832	6.3
England	432,696	456,401	5.5
Wales	21,247	22,761	7.1
Scotland	44,304	46,614	5.2
Northern Ireland	11,515	12,360	7.3
UK excluding Continental Shelf	509,762	538,135	5.6

Source: Economic Trends (1994, Number 494)

Table 7.7 illustrates the good performance in recent years of GDP growth for Wales, particularly since the mid-1980s when Wales emerged from the recession of earlier years. Table 7.7 shows that during the 1986–90 period Wales had the fastest growth of GDP of any UK region, and forecasts for the 1990s suggest that this performance will continue.

Table 7.7 GDP growth for UK region: actual and expected 1980–1999

	Annual average GDP growth (% change)							*GDP per head*
Region	*1980–89*	*1986–90*	*1993*	*1994*	*1995*	*1996*	*1995–99*	*1993*
United Kingdom	1.8	2.4	0.8	3.3	2.9	2.8	2.4	89
Yorkshire & Humberside	2.1	3.2	2.2	3.4	3.1	2.9	2.7	91
East Midlands	2.9	3.9	1.3	3.6	3.4	3.2	2.8	96
East Anglia	4.1	4.2	1.2	3.8	3.7	3.6	3.0	102
South East	2.4	3.9	1.2	3.4	2.9	2.8	2.4	116
Greater London	1.4	3.4	1.2	3.1	2.8	2.6	2.2	125
Rest of South East	3.2	4.2	1.2	3.5	3.0	2.9	2.5	111
South West	3.3	3.8	3.2	3.7	3.5	3.4	2.9	97
West Midlands	1.8	3.7	1.3	3.6	3.3	3.2	2.6	93
North West	1.4	2.9	2.4	3.4	3.1	2.9	2.5	91
Wales	2.8	4.4	3.3	3.8	3.4	3.3	3.0	85
Scotland	1.9	2.7	1.4	3.2	3.0	2.7	2.4	98
Northern Ireland	2.5	2.7	3.2	3.0	2.6	2.3	2.2	82
UK excluding Continental Shelf	2.3	3.5	1.7	3.4	3.1	3.0	2.6	–
UK Total	2.4	3.3	2.1	4.0	3.1	3.0	2.6	100

Source: National Westminster Bank (1995)

Provisional 1993 estimates of manufacturing GDP showed that manufacturers experienced the highest regional growth rate in the UK. Table 7.8 illustrates that manufacturing GDP increased by 11.6 per cent between 1992 and 1993, almost twice the UK average of 6.0 per cent. Whilst manufacturing GDP as a percentage of total GDP for Wales fell from 29.5 per cent in 1990 to 25.6 per cent in 1992, it recovered to 26.7 per cent in 1993. Table 7.8 also shows that Wales is one of only five regions in the UK which had 25 per cent or more of its total GDP in the manufacturing sector.

Table 7.8 Gross Domestic Product in Manufacturing sector and growth 1992–93

Region	*Manufacturing GDP as % of total GDP 1993*	*Manufacturing GDP growth 1992–93*
North	28.9	3.9
Yorkshire & Humberside	26.1	6.9
East Midlands	29.2	5.4
East Anglia	21.9	7.7
South East	15.9	3.4
Greater London	13.2	6.1
Rest of South East	17.9	5.2
South West	19.1	7.5
West Midlands	29.0	3.8
North West	28.3	7.3
England	21.9	5.8
Wales	26.7	11.6
Scotland	20.3	3.8
Northern Ireland	19.2	8.2
United Kingdom	21.7	6.0

Source: *Economic Trends* (1994, Number 494)

The Fifth Periodic Report (CEC 1994b) identified productivity and unit labour cost levels as important factors in regional competitiveness. This view is supported by the literature on the regional distribution of foreign manufacturing investment in the UK (Hill and Munday 1994). High productivity, combined with low wage growth, has generated very competitive manufacturing unit labour costs for a number of regions in Britain. The 1993 figures, shown in Table 7.9, suggest that unit labour costs in Wales are nearly 9 per cent below the Great Britain average. Further consideration needs to be given to the situation where, as the regional earnings gap is reduced, then so too will be regional competitiveness for the low earnings regions. However, it must be stressed that the key to sustained economic development lies with high rates of productivity rather than low labour costs *per se*.

Foreign direct investment

The Fifth Periodic Report (CEC 1994b) has emphasized the extent to which the creation of the Single Market has favoured EC regions as a whole as a location for new investment. This has led to a large gross inflow of foreign direct investment (FDI) into the EC from third countries, estimated at nearly 120 billion ECU between 1986 and 1991. When combined with the flows between Member States, some 150 billion ECU between 1986 and 1991, FDI represents a significant source of potential investment for the EC's weaker regions and, except in the case of Greece, has outstripped the transfers from the Structural Funds. In the weaker Member States, the flows from their EC partners are the most important, whereas the UK is a major recipient of FDI from third countries. Indeed, Chapter 5 of the Fifth Periodic Report (CEC 1994b) illustrates that the UK is the major destination for FDI flows into the EC, accounting, between 1986 and 1991, for some 45 per cent of the total.

Table 7.9 Regional unit labour costs in Manufacturing for 1992 and 1993

Region	*Manufacturing GDP per head*		*Weekly manual F/T Manufacturing Earnings*		*Unit costs*	
	1992	*1993*	*1992*	*1993*	*1992*	*1993*
North	114.82	126.44	100.44	99.84	87.47	78.97
Yorks. & Humberside	92.04	90.33	98.17	98.25	106.65	108.76
East Midlands	92.23	86.29	95.53	103.58	111.78	
East Anglia	100.10	96.94	100.36	98.79	100.34	101.91
South East	105.70	106.85	107.06	107.09	101.29	100.23
South West	96.21	94.49	93.82	96.14	97.51	101.75
West Midlands	91.69	88.40	96.69	97.00	105.45	109.73
North West	102.01	109.54	98.09	98.79	96.15	90.19
England	99.76	99.50	100.32	100.58	100.56	101.10
Wales	101.16	103.59	94.62	94.70	93.53	91.42
Scotland	101.84	103.24	100.08	97.62	98.27	94.56
Great Britain	100.00	100.00	100.00	100.00	100.00	100.00

Source: *Regional Trends* (1993, Number 28; 1994, Number 29), *New Earnings Survey* (1992, 1993), *Economic Trends* (1994, December)

In terms of the relative regional performance on FDI in Britain, Wales has been most successful. Hill and Munday (1994) have shown that although Wales is small in respect of its share of UK employment (it comprised 4.7 per cent of the UK labour force in 1991), it has consistently attracted a high share of new foreign projects and jobs. Table 7.10 provides a regional league table of inward investment success in terms of projects and new jobs attracted. Whilst Wales had 18 foreign companies employing some 14,000 people in the early 1950s, by 1993 there were 278 foreign manufacturing companies employing 68,000 people, accounting for 28 per cent of Welsh manufacturing employment.

Table 7.10 Regional Performance Index on FDI, 1982–1992

Region	*Average 1982–92 Project Index**	*Average 1982–92 New Jobs Index**
Wales	3.82	3.71
North	2.03	2.68
Scotland	1.77	2.33
West Midlands	1.65	1.48
North West	1.10	0.72
Yorkshire & Humberside	0.71	0.69
East Midlands	0.65	0.66
South West	0.42	0.56
South East	0.41	0.30

* Both regional shares of new projects and associated jobs are divided by regional shares of employment to provide a relative regional performance index. A value higher than one indicates the attraction of a share of projects greater than its equivalent employment share.
Source: Hill and Munday (1994, Table 3.8, p.43)

FDI in Wales has historically been dominated by North American firms. Table 7.11 shows that in 1993 US multinationals accounted for some 36 per cent of the total number of foreign manufacturing units, and 46 per cent of foreign manufacturing employment. However, the 1980s saw a marked increase in the number of investments from both the EC and Japan, again illustrated in Table 7.11.

Table 7.11 Employment in Wales in overseas-owned manufacturing plants, by country of ownership (1993)

Country of Ownership	*No. of plants*	*No. of companies*	*Employment (thousands)*	*Employment as % of total in overseas-owned plants*
USA	125	104	31.3	46.0
Japan	34	24	11.2	16.5
EC (excl. UK)	106	90	14.5	21.3
Other European	39	33	5.1	7.5
Other	44	27	5.9	8.7
Total Overseas	348	278	68.0	100.0

Source: *Welsh Economic Trends* (1994, Number 15, Table 86, p.66)

However, a note of caution needs to be given here. There will undoubtedly be greater global competition for FDI in the future than in the past as noted in a recent United Nations World Investment Report (1994). Both the European Commission and the development agencies in the UK may be too optimistic of their abilities to attract further large volumes of FDI. Both South East Asia and Eastern Europe will become more attractive locations for FDI in the future. Within the UK we are likely to see much greater competition between areas for FDI, and regions able to identify only a small number of strategic FDI sites.

Productivity and unit labour costs

As Hill and Munday (1994) have shown, traditionally, relatively low wage regions have been associated with relatively low labour productivity. Table 7.12 shows that the successful regions in Britain on FDI have been those in which productivity growth has interacted with relatively low earnings to push unit labour costs well below the UK average.

Table 7.12 Productivity and unit labour costs in Manufacturing 1979–1993 (UK=100)

Region	*Productivity*			*Unit labour costs*[a] *(GDP/person)*			
	1979	*1986*	*1991*	*1979*	*1986*	*1991*	*1993*[b]
North	101.3	103.9	115.3	101.6	107.5	97.8	78.9
Yorkshire & Humberside	93.1	96.7	93.5	102.1	103.6	94.8	108.8
East Midlands	92.3	90.9	92.6	103.4	104.2	102.3	111.8
East Anglia	104.4	102.5	103.3	95.3	95.0	100.6	101.9
South East	110.4	105.0	103.9	95.4	95.5	99.3	100.2
South West	100.4	96.7	90.8	100.6	111.5	109.4	101.8
West Midlands	90.4	91.3	93.7	106.3	100.4	103.4	109.7
North West	103.3	105.0	106.2	92.0	97.2	96.2	90.2
Wales	89.9	112.6	110.2	113.9	96.1	91.7	91.4
Scotland	100.4	99.8	99.7	98.3	102.2	99.4	94.6
Northern Ireland	81.4	84.0	83.5	109.7	104.9	106.3	–

[a] Unit labour cost is defined as average manufacturing earnings divided by average manufacturing GDP per person employed

[b] See Table 7.9

Source: Hill and Munday (1994, Table 4.8, p.77)

With the exception of the South East, the regions which have had least relative success in attracting inward investment projects and jobs have been those that experienced high unit labour costs. Table 7.9 has already shown that unit labour costs in Wales in 1993 were nearly 9 per cent below the Great Britain average. The regions with the highest relative success in attracting FDI (i.e. Wales, the North and Scotland) have had relative earnings well below the UK average. Of the regions with lowest unit labour costs, Wales and the North have had most relative success in attracting inward investment in recent years.

The prosperity gap between Wales and the UK focuses particularly on the level of GDP per capita, total personal income per capita, personal disposable income per capita, and consumer expenditure per head. Table 7.13 shows the Wales–UK gap on these key variables. Whilst income per head in Wales remains some 15 per cent below the UK average, the gap on consumer expenditure is less than 10 per cent and matches more closely the position of many other regions in the UK.

Table 7.13 Measures of regional income per capita 1992 (£)

Region	*GDP per capita*	*Total personal income per head*	*Personal disposable income per head*	*Consumer expenditure per head*
United Kingdom	100.0	100.0	100.0	100.0
North	91.2	90.6	93.3	88.3
Yorkshire & Humberside	92.3	93.2	94.8	90.6
East Midlands	95.5	94.3	94.3	93.3
East Anglia	102.2	100.4	100.5	102.6
South East	115.9	114.9	112.2	115.5
Greater London	123.4	122.0	121.1	120.9
Rest of South East	111.1	110.4	106.5	112.0
South West	94.7	95.2	95.1	102.4
West Midlands	92.8	93.1	93.3	91.2
North West	90.5	93.3	94.7	94.3
England	101.6	101.6	101.1	102.0
Wales	86.1	84.1	85.4	91.1
Scotland	98.3	99.1	101.0	90.4
Northern Ireland	82.0	84.1	89.6	85.4

Source: Regional Trends (1994, Number 29, Tables 12.1, 12.5, 12.6, 12.7)

Table 7.14 shows that the level of average gross weekly earnings of full-time employees in Wales in 1993 was 11 per cent less than the average for Great Britain as a whole. Overall, wages in Wales in 1993 were lower than in any other region of Great Britain. Moreover, and more worrying, since 1983 the average for all employees has declined, relative to the rest of Great Britain, from 94 per cent to 89 per cent of the national figure. Over the same period, earnings in South East England moved from 10 to 15 per cent per cent above that average. Table 7.15 shows that males and women manual workers in Wales received earnings close to the Great Britain average in 1994 at 97 per cent and 96.6 per cent respectively. However, both males and females in Wales had lower weekly earnings in 1994 in terms of percentage of the Great Britain average than was the case in 1983. Whilst there was a small improvement in the earnings position of males in Wales between 1993 and 1994, the relatively low levels of earnings for males and females in Wales remains one of the most important aspects of the prosperity gap.

Table 7.14 Average weekly earnings of full-time employees by region* 1983–1993

Region	*1983*		*1991*		*1992*		*1993*	
	£ per week	*% of GB*	*£ per week*	*% of GB*	*£ per week*	*% of GB*	*£ per week*	*% of GB*
North	141.0	95.1	258.0	90.6	282.3	92.7	288.6	91.1
Yorkshire & Humberside	141.4	95.3	257.9	90.6	277.3	91.0	287.4	90.7
East Midlands	137.6	92.8	261.3	91.8	276.1	90.6	285.7	90.2
East Anglia	141.3	95.3	268.9	94.5	288.4	94.7	292.2	92.2
South East	162.9	109.8	326.7	114.8	348.7	114.4	365.5	115.3
South West	139.6	94.1	265.6	93.3	283.1	92.9	298.4	94.2
West Midlands	138.1	93.1	261.1	91.7	279.9	91.9	291.9	92.1
North West	141.0	95.1	267.1	93.8	285.6	93.7	298.8	94.3
England	149.0	100.5	288.3	101.3	308.1	101.1	320.9	101.3
Wales	140.0	94.4	252.2	88.6	270.9	88.9	281.2	88.7
Scotland	145.2	97.9	265.3	93.2	286.8	94.1	296.8	93.7
Great Britain	148.3	100.0	284.7	110.0	304.7	100.0	316.9	100.0

* In April, employees on adult rates whose pay for the survey period was not affected by absence

Source: *New Earnings Survey* and *Welsh Economic Trends* (1994, Number 15)

Some reference must be made here to the wide intra-regional disparities in prosperity within Wales. Table 7.16 shows the extent of these disparities in terms of GDP per capita, household income per capita, and household disposable income

Table 7.15 Average gross weekly earnings of full-time males and females,* Wales and GB 1983–1994

	1983		*1991*		*1992*		*1993*		*1994*	
Full-time	*Wales (£)*	*% of GB*	*Wales (£)*	*% of GB*	*Wales (£)*	*% of GB*	*Wales (£)*	*% of GB*	*Wales (£)*	*% of GB*
Manual males	140.2	97.6	239.3	94.5	254.3	94.8	258.6	94.3	272.3	97.0
Non-manual males	180.2	92.5	328.8	87.5	351.8	87.9	364.1	87.1	375.1	87.7
All males	156.3	93.3	280.1	87.8	299.2	88.0	308.3	87.2	320.9	88.6
Manual females	88.8	101.0	153.3	96.3	161.7	95.1	172.5	97.4	175.7	96.6
Non-manual females	109.4	95.0	212.8	89.9	235.4	91.8	247.6	92.1	257.4	92.5
All females	104.4	96.0	199.1	89.5	218.7	90.7	231.6	91.7	239.0	91.3

* In April, employees on adult rates whose pay for the survey period was not affected by absence

Source: *New Earnings Survey* and *Welsh Economic Trends* (1994, Number 15) per capita. Mid Glamorgan scores the poorest of all counties in the UK on each of these criteria. The extent of the differentials on GDP per capita between the counties of Wales matches very closely the extent of the differentials between the UK regions on GDP per capita.

Table 7.16 Intra-regional disparities in prosperity on GDP and income per capita within Wales: 1991 (UK=100; £ capita)

	GDP/capita	*Household income per capita capita*	*Household disposable income per*
Wales	85.1	88.1	91.2
Clwyd	92.5	88.7	91.0
Dyfed	75.5	89.2	92.0
Gwent	85.9	87.4	91.2
Gwynedd	76.4	90.8	95.8
Mid Glamorgan	69.4	78.9	80.7
Powys	N/A	N/A	N/A
South Glamorgan	110.9	95.0	97.7
West Glamorgan	88.3	90.7	94.6

Source: Regional Trends (1994, Number 29, Table 14.4)

Employment and labour force participation

The prosperity gap between Wales and the UK is largely due to the relatively low level of earnings and low participation rates in the labour force. Both male and female activity rates in Wales are the lowest in Great Britain, as illustrated in Table 7.17. Male rates fell by 4.3 percentage points to 69 per cent between 1981 and 1991, and a further decline to 67.7 per cent is forecast by 2001. Female rates rose by 5.9 percentage points to 48.1 per cent in the ten years to 1991, and a further increase to 50.8 per cent is expected by 2001. These trends will see Wales' activity rates move from 91.6 per cent of the UK average for females in 1991 to 92.5 per cent in 2001, but virtually no change for males, with figures of 93.4 per cent and 93.2 per cent respectively over the 1991–2001 period.

The claim that the Welsh economy has fared better than that of many other regions in recent years is supported by the level of employment maintained. Table 7.18 shows that between June 1990 and September 1994 there was very little fall in the number of employees in employment in Wales, and the Welsh economy performed much better than the UK economy as a whole and than many other regions. Wales experienced some growth in employment between 1992 and 1994, as shown in Table 7.18.

Table 7.17 Regional activity rates*: 1981–2001 (%)

Region	*Male*			*Female*		
	1981	*1991*	*2001*	*1981*	*1991*	*2001*
United Kingdom	76.5	73.8	72.6	47.5	52.5	54.9
North	76.9	70.1	68.7	46.3	49.7	51.7
Yorkshire & Humberside	76.6	73.3	72.1	47.7	51.4	53.9
East Midlands	77.8	75.3	74.2	48.4	53.8	55.8
East Anglia	73.8	72.6	71.8	46.3	53.4	55.6
South East	77.3	75.7	75.0	48.8	54.7	57.6
Greater London	77.6	74.4	74.7	50.1	53.9	57.9
Rest of South East	77.2	76.5	75.2	47.9	55.3	57.4
South West	72.2	71.9	71.0	44.0	32.2	54.7
West Midlands	78.0	75.7	73.8	48.8	52.7	54.5
North West	77.0	74.3	73.2	47.9	53.1	55.5
England	76.7	74.3	73.2	47.9	53.1	55.5
Wales	73.3	69.0	67.7	42.2	48.1	50.8
Scotland	76.9	72.6	70.9	47.4	51.2	52.6
Northern Ireland	76.5	71.3	70.7	43.5	47.4	49.4

* Percentage of the home population aged 16 or over who are in the civilian labour force. GB labour force definitions for 1981, ILO definitions for 1991 and 2001

Source: *Regional Trends* (1994, Number 29, Table 5.13)

Table 7.18 Level of regional employment 1990–1994: employees in employment (June 1990=100)

Region	*June 1992*	*June 1993*	*June 1194*	*September 1994*
United Kingdom	94.8	94.4	94.2	94.6
North	98.0	97.3	97.4	97.4
Yorkshire & Humberside	95.8	95.4	95.1	95.3
East Midlands	96.0	95.8	96.1	97.0
East Anglia	96.3	97.3	98.3	99.6
Greater London	90.3	89.0	89.2	89.8
Rest of South East	92.9	92.0	91.7	91.4
South West	94.6	95.4	96.1	96.8
West Midlands	94.0	93.2	92.1	93.2
North West	95.6	95.3	93.8	94.5
Wales	95.8	97.0	97.5	98.0
Scotland	100.5	101.2	101.2	101.2
Northern Ireland	101.0	101.6	102.5	102.9

Source: *Economic Trends* (1994, Number 494)

The relatively good performance of the Welsh economy in recent years, due in part to real improvements made in Wales, and in part to the recession having had greater effect on some other regions, has led to a position where Wales can no longer be regarded as one of the UK's high unemployment regions. Whilst the rate of unemployment has been a key indicator of Wales being labelled as a problem region from the 1930s through to the 1990s, this is no longer the case. Table 7.19 shows that since 1992 the unemployment rate for Wales has matched that for the UK as a whole very closely, and has been lower than that facing many other regions. As Barnes (1992) has observed, it remains to be seen whether or not the new regional pattern of unemployment is only temporary or is evidence of a more permanent change. For the months of April, May and June 1995, for example, the seasonally adjusted rate of unemployment in Wales, at 8.3 per cent, matched exactly that for the UK as a whole.

Table 7.19 Regional unemployment rates* 1989–1994 (seasonally adjusted)

Region	*1989*	*1990*	*1991*	*1992*	*1993*	*1994*	
						June	*Nov*
United Kingdom	6.3	5.8	8.1	9.8	10.3	9.4	8.8
North	9.9	8.7	10.3	11.3	12.1	11.3	11.0
Yorkshire & Humberside	7.4	6.7	8.7	10.0	10.3	9.6	9.1
East Midlands	5.4	5.1	7.3	9.1	9.5	8.8	8.3
East Anglia	3.5	3.7	5.9	7.8	8.4	11.5	6.7
Greater London	5.1	5.0	8.1	10.6	11.5	10.8	10.3
Rest of South East	2.9	3.1	6.0	8.3	9.0	7.9	7.1
South West	4.5	4.4	7.1	9.4	9.8	8.5	7.8
West Midlands	6.5	5.8	8.5	10.6	11.0	9.6	8.9
North West	8.5	7.7	9.4	10.8	10.8	9.7	9.0
Wales	7.3	6.7	8.9	10.0	10.3	9.6	8.8
Scotland	9.3	8.1	8.6	9.4	9.6	9.2	8.7
Northern Ireland	14.3	13.0	13.3	14.0	13.8	13.2	12.5

* Unemployment claimant count as a percentage of total workforce
Source: *Economic Trends* (1994, Number 494)

Both the UK government and European Commission have included long-term unemployment as a measure of regional prosperity. Long-term unemployment is defined as those unemployed over 12 months expressed as a percentage of the workforce. Table 7.20 shows that between 1985 and 1990, long-term unemployment in Wales fell from 6.2 per cent to 1.9 per cent of the workforce, the same rate as for the UK as a whole. The rate of improvement over this period was considerably higher for Wales than for the UK. Although the rate climbed back to average 3.7 per cent in 1993, over the whole period 1985–1994 the Wales rate has converged to stand 0.2 points below the national average. This is another indication of the improved performance of unemployment in Wales relative to the UK as a whole.

Table 7.20 Long-term unemployment in Wales and the UK 1985–1994 (annual average)

Year	*Unemployed over 12 months*			
	Wales		*United Kingdom*	
	Number	*Rate*[a]	*Number*	*Rate*[a]
1985	75,998	6.2	1,332,260	4.8
1986	75,446	6.1	1,354,252	4.8
1987	65,423	5.3	1,260,030	4.5
1988	50,128	4.0	990,889	3.5
1989	34,740	2.7	713,354	2.5
1990	24,374	1.9	534,680	1.9
1991	27,159	2.2	581,527	2.0
1992	39,997	3.1	862,173	3.0
1993	46,389	3.7	1,064,384	3.8
1994[b]	41,031	3.2	956,475	3.4

[a] Expressed as a percentage of the workforce
[b] October 1994

Source: Employment Department, *Welsh Economic Trends* (1994, Number 15), *Economic Trends* (1994, Number 494)

Finally in this section on the regional prosperity gap, some reference must be made to intra-regional disparities in unemployment rates. While this chapter has highlighted the marked improvement of the unemployment position facing Wales as a whole, to an extent that on unemployment grounds it can no longer be identified as a *regional problem*, significant variations continue to exist between localities within Wales. Table 7.21 shows that in January 1995 the rate of unemployment in Wales varied from 14.0 per cent for the Aberdare travel-to-work area to 3.4 per cent for Newtown travel-to-work area, i.e. a ratio of more than 4:1 between the highest and lowest unemployment rate areas. Table 7.21 also illustrates the extent to which the unemployment problem facing Wales continues to be male dominated. However, of the 34 travel-to-work areas in Wales as at January 1995, 16, i.e. nearly half, had an unemployment rate below that of the UK average, and 24 had a rate either below or within 1.0 percentage point of the UK average.

Table 7.21 Unemployment rate* disparities in Wales as at January 1995 by travel-to-work area

Travel-to-work area	*Male rate %*	*Female rate %*	*Total rate %*
Aberdare	20.7	5.9	14.0
Aberystwyth	8.4	4.4	6.6
Bangor & Caernarfon	14.9	5.6	10.8
Blaenau, Gwent & Abergavenny	14.6	5.0	10.3
Brecon	7.4	4.1	6.0
Bridgend	12.4	4.5	8.9
Cardiff	13.2	4.2	9.1
Cardigan	9.4	7.0	8.6
Carmarthen	6.9	2.8	5.1
Conwy & Colwyn	13.2	5.2	9.5
Denbigh	8.4	4.4	6.8
Dolgellau & Barmouth	12.8	6.5	10.1
Fishguard	9.4	5.7	8.2
Haverfordwest	16.2	5.6	11.4
Holyhead	16.2	8.9	13.7
Lampeter & Aberaeron	10.3	5.3	8.3
Llandeilo	5.6	5.0	5.4
Llandrindod Wells	6.7	5.3	6.1
Llanelli	12.8	5.9	9.9
Machynlleth	10.2	6.5	8.6
Merthyr & Rhymney	17.4	5.4	12.1
Monmouth	10.8	4.5	7.9
Neath & Port Talbot	12.1	4.6	9.2
Newport	12.2	5.3	9.3
Newtown	4.6	1.9	3.4
Pontypool & Cwmbran	11.7	4.3	8.5
Pontypridd & Rhondda	14.2	4.2	9.7
Porthmadoc & Ffestiniog	13.2	8.0	11.1
Pwllheli	13.7	9.3	12.0
Shotton, Flint & Rhyl	9.6	4.2	7.4
South Pembrokeshire	18.3	8.9	14.4
Swansea	13.5	3.8	9.0
Welshpool	5.1	4.0	4.6
Wrexham	10.9	4.2	8.0
Wales (unadjusted)	12.6	4.7	9.2
UK (unadjusted)	12.0	4.8	8.9

* Unemployment claimant count as a percentage of the total workforce. The figures are all on an unadjusted basis.

Source: Employment Department Group (1995)

European Union and UK Regional Aid to Wales

The Fifth Periodic Report (CEC 1994b) noted the contribution which both FDI and transfers from the Structural Funds can make as a significant source of investment for the EC's weaker regions. The successful performance of Wales in attracting FDI has already been covered in this chapter. Wales has also benefited from the EC Structural Funds, in addition to transfers from UK urban and regional policies.

Table 7.22 shows that Wales has been a major beneficiary of EC Structural Funds, with both European Regional Development Fund (ERDF) and European Social Fund (ESF) each contributing some £60 million in 1993. However, it should be noted that the £120 million paid to Wales in 1993 via ERDF and ESF was exceeded by the £169 million paid via the European Agricultural Guidance and Guarantee Fund (EAGGF), which provides support to farmers in Wales under

Table 7.22 European Union financial transfers to Wales (£million)

Year	*European Regional Development Fund to Objectives 2 and 5(b) programmes and Rechar*	*European Social Fund payments*[a]	*European Agricultural Guidance Fund*[b]	*Other EU initiatives*[c]	*European Agricultural Guarantee Fund*[b]
1980	21.5	–	5.8	–	4.4
1981	25.8	–	7.0	–	11.6
1982	46.7	–	6.0	–	8.6
1983	48.7	–	10.6	–	19.8
1984	63.0	–	10.1	–	25.0
1985	54.9	–	9.3	–	26.9
1986	49.7	–	8.3	–	41.5
1987	57.8	–	8.6	–	24.8
1988	63.3	–	9.5	–	40.2
1989	38.8	–	9.2	–	36.2
1990	27.4	10.1	9.8	Nil	57.9
1991	89.0	28.5	10.6	2.3	88.9
1992	54.9	29.1	9.2	0.1	106.9
1993	61.9	58.2	8.9	2.5	159.6

[a] Before 1990 all applications handled directly by the European Commission and information not held centrally in UK

[b] Data is for financial years: e.g. 1980 = 1980/81, 1981 = 1981/82, etc

[c] These include, for example, LEADER, STRIDE, RETEX, KONVER and Conservation of European Cities

Source: Welsh Office (1995)

various initiatives. However, it should be noted that the EAGGF, which comprises the major share of this funding, is basically a price support mechanism. The smaller share accounted for by the Guidance Fund does have a particular focus on regional investment and development. Together they represent a substantial financial transfer to Wales. Total EC Structural Funds payments to Wales in 1993 were £289 million. These sums were matched by nearly £143 million of regional aid expenditure by the UK government, as illustrated in Table 7.23. If urban regeneration expenditure is also added to that of regional policy expenditure, then nearly another £100 million of aid was injected into the Welsh economy in 1993/94 (comprising £61.8 million under the Strategic Development Scheme/Urban Programme, £9.9 million under the Urban Development Grant, and £26.7 million capital expenditure on its urban development programme by the WDA). The contribution of urban regeneration expenditure to regional and local economic development has been emphasized by Alden and Romaya (1994).

These three expenditure programmes, namely the EC Structural Funds, UK Regional Policy expenditure, and Urban Regeneration expenditure, are therefore injecting additional investment expenditure into Wales in excess of £530 million per annum. They represent an important source of investment which both supplements and levers other sources of private and public expenditure.

Summary and Conclusions

The Welsh economy of the 1990s has been transformed from that of earlier decades after several periods of rapid industrial restructuring. Wales has fought hard to make the transition from being one of the UK's, and the EC's, problem regions to being one of its more successful and economically powerful ones. This chapter has shown that Wales has made considerable progress in achieving greater convergence with national performance in terms of trends in unemployment, employment, growth of real GDP and manufacturing GDP, productivity and unit labour costs, FDI, and labour force participation rates. However, a prosperity gap remains in the mid-1990s between Wales and the UK nationally. This gap is primarily reflected in trends of divergence in terms of GDP per capita, personal disposable income, household income, and weekly earnings. Wales seems unable to break through the elusive 90 per cent of UK average GDP per capita. Persistent disparities also exist between areas within Wales in terms of unemployment rates, output and income levels.

Despite the many achievements of recent years, the prosperity gap between Wales and the UK as a whole remains significant. All the agencies in Wales with a responsibility for promoting economic development in the Principality must seek to maintain, and improve on, the progress achieved in recent years. Reducing the prosperity gap further for Wales will require the continued attraction of quality inward investment, enhancing the competitiveness and structure of the Welsh economy as local companies will increasingly have to compete in a global economy,

Table 7.23 Regional policy expenditure in Wales, 1984/85–1996/97 (£million)

Scheme	*1984/85*	*1985/86*	*1986/87*	*1987/88*	*1988/89*	*1989/90*	*1990/91*	*1991/92*	*1992/93*	*1993/94*	*1994/95*	*1995/96*	*1996/97*
RSA Projects	13.8	19.4	26.0	23.2	35.1	34.9	30.5	55.0	58.8	50.8	51.8	59.3	65.0
RSA Exch Risk	4.9	3.8	5.9	6.0	2.8	5.3	4.1	3.5	5.5	6.6	5.1	2.7	2.7
REG [a]					0.2	0.9	1.5	1.4	1.1	1.6	1.7	2.7	2.7
RDG I & II [b]	31.3	81.9	85.2	47.5	55.1	27.5	21.7	14.2	5.5	4.8	0.8	2.4	2.4
WDA [c]	32.1	30.3	31.7	52.3	61.9	69.8	81.2	87.2	78.4	69.5	59.1	69.1	69.1
DBRW [c]	5.4	4.7	7.9	6.9	8.7	9.6	10.3	11.5	13.2	13.9	14.4	9.9	9.9
Total	**87.5**	**140.1**	**156.7**	**135.9**	**163.8**	**148.0**	**149.3**	**172.8**	**162.5**	**147.2**	**132.9**	**146.2**	**142.8**

[a] Regional Enterprise Grants began on 1 April 1988

[b] Regional Development Grant II began on 29 November 1984. Figures include expenditure by DTI in Wales prior to responsibility being transferred to the Welsh Office in November 1984

[c] Expenditure includes all grant in aid activities

NB: 1994/95 onwards are estimates by Welsh Office

Source: Welsh Office (1995)

focus particular attention on high value-added economic activities which will raise GDP per capita levels, and promote the growth of quality jobs which pay earnings levels closer to the national average. Competition between cities and regions in the European and global economy will become increasingly intense in the years ahead, and there are bound to be winners and losers in terms of economically successful regions. Wales is in a transitional period, seeking to break free from the legacy of its past and its label as a problem or unsuccessful region. Much has been achieved, but much remains to be done.

References

Alden, J. and Morgan, R. (1974) *Regional Planning: A Comprehensive View.* Leonard Hill Books. Kingswood House, Heath and Reach, near Leighton Buzzard, Bedfordshire.

Alden, J. and Romaya, S. (1994) 'The challenge of urban regeneration in Wales.' *Town Planning Review 65*, 4, pp.435–461.

Barnes, C. (1992) 'The end of the North–South fivide?' *The Planner* 2 October 1992, pp.12–14.

Cambridge Econometrics (1994) *Regional Economic Prospects: Analysis and Forecasts to the Year 2005 for the Standard Planning Regions of the UK* July 1994.

Central Statistical Office (1985) *Regional Trends* Number 20. London: HMSO.

Central Statistical Office (1993) *Regional Trends* Number 28. London: HMSO.

Central Statistical Office (1994a) *Economic Trends* Number 494, December 1994. London: HMSO.

Central Statistical Office (1994b) *Regional Trends* Number 29, 1994 Edition. London: HMSO.

Central Statistical Office (1995a) *Regional Trends* Number 30. London: HMSO.

Central Statistical Office (1995b) *Economic Trends, Annual Supplement* 1995 Edition. London: HMSO.

Commission of the European Communities (1994a) *Europe 2000+: Cooperation for European Territorial Development.* Luxembourg: Commission of the European Communities.

Commission of the European Communities (1994b) 'Competitiveness and cohesion: trends in the regions.' *Fifth Periodic Report on the Social and Economic Situation and Development of the Regions in the Community.* Luxembourg: Commission of the European Communities.

Dunford, M. (1993) 'Regional disparities in the European community: evidence from the REGIO databank.' *Regional Studies 27*, 8, pp.727–743.

Employment Department Group (1994) *New Earnings Survey 1994, Part E, Analyses by Region.* Department of Employment, HMSO.

Employment Department Group (1995) *Employment Gazette*, February 1995, HMSO.

Eurostat (1993a) *Portrait of the Regions* Vol. 2. Luxembourg: Directorate General for Regional Policy: Commission of the European Communities.

Eurostat (1993b) *Regions Statistical Yearbook.* Luxembourg: Directorate General for Regional Policy: Commission of the European Communities.

Hill, S. and Munday, M. (1994) *The Regional Distribution of Foreign Manufacturing Investment in the UK.* The Macmillan Press Ltd, Basingstoke, UK.

National Westminster Bank (1995) *Economic and Financial Outlook.* Market Intelligence Department. London: National Westminster Bank. February.

United Nations Conference on Trade and Development (1994) *World Investment Report.* New York and Geneva: United Nations.

Welsh Development Agency (1995) 'Working for Wales.' *WDA Three Year Corporate Plan.* Cardiff: WDA.

Welsh Office (1967) *Wales: The Way Ahead,* Cmnd. 3334, July 1967. London: HMSO.

Welsh Office (1994) *Welsh Economic Trends,* 1994 Edition. Welsh Office: Cardiff.

Welsh Office (1995) Information supplied by European Division of Welsh Office, Cardiff.

CHAPTER 8

Local Development Theory and Practice

Recent Experience in Ireland

James Walsh

Introduction

Over recent years there has been a recognition in Ireland (see Figure 8.1), as in many other countries, of the role of local development initiatives. The rationale for such initiatives is not always clearly articulated. For some, local initiatives are seen as little more than a scaling down of interventions that were previously organized from the top by centralized policy-making units, and delivered through sectoral agencies with little emphasis on coordination or integration. An alternative approach is to view local development strategies as a radical response that seeks to achieve new objectives in relation to the development process by focusing on concepts such as multi-dimensionality, integration, coordination, subsidiarity and sustainability. In other words, local development is not only about changing the scale at which interventions are made – it is also about finding new approaches to facilitating a broader concept of development. This chapter commences with an outline of the components of a local development theory which will be used as a *yardstick* in the remainder of the chapter for evaluating the outcomes from recent initiatives on local development in Ireland.

Theory of Local Development

Much of the recent literature on local development is guided by the perspective that development is a multi-dimensional process through which society seeks to achieve a variety of goals. Kulkarni and Rajan (1991, p.102) define development as 'an organised and articulated effort of a community to empower itself in the context and conditions of its collective existence'. It involves social, economic and political processes through which a society attempts to achieve a range of objectives. These may include economic, social, cultural, political and environmental objectives which at times are likely to be in conflict. Therefore, part of the

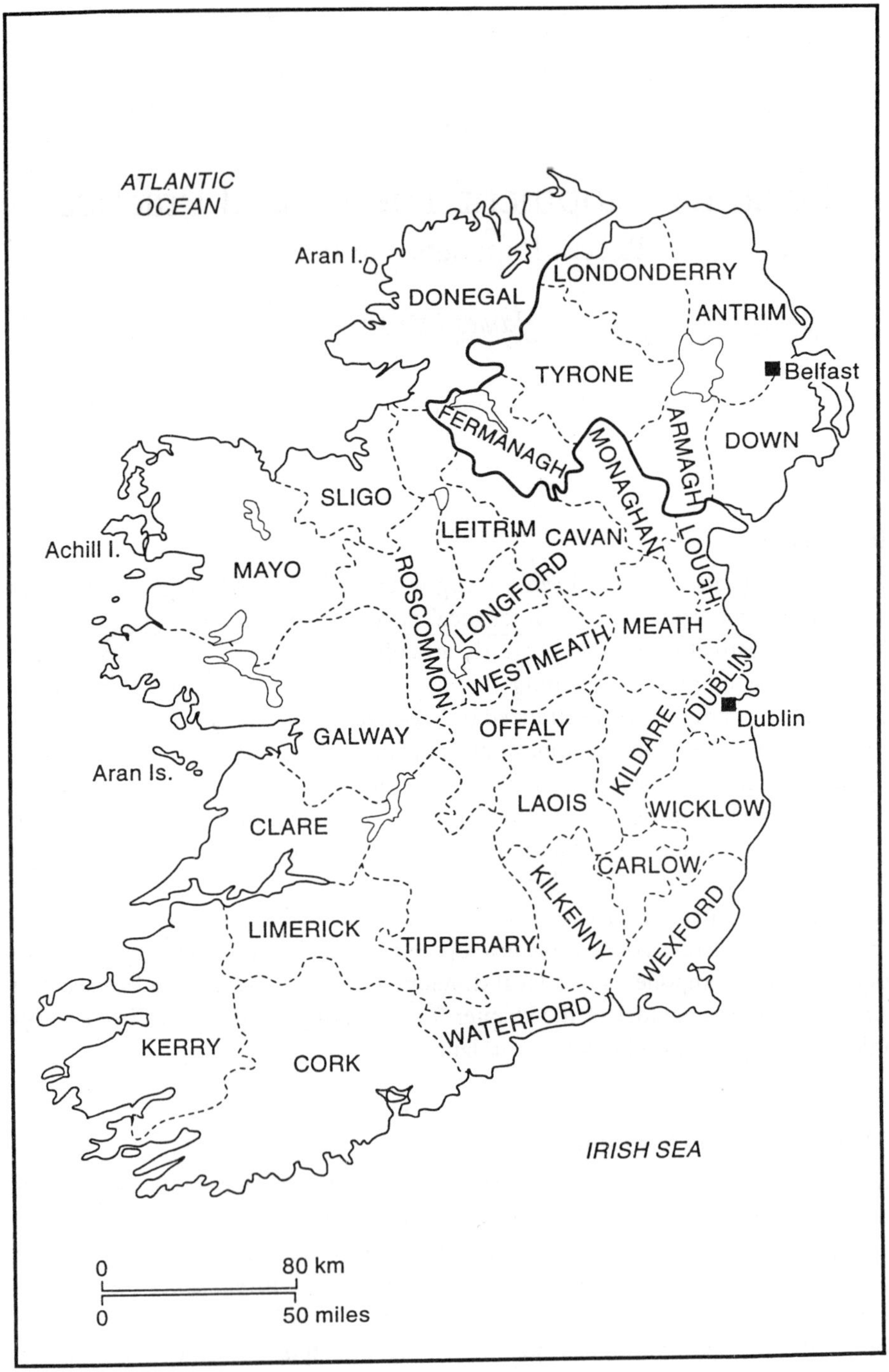

Source: *Whitaker's Almanack* 1995, p.913

Figure 8.1 The Counties of Ireland

development process is to establish procedures for reducing and ameliorating potential conflicts.

Several local development models have been proposed in Ireland and elsewhere. From a review of the literature in this area one can identify a number of common features that can be combined to suggest an outline theory of local development (for a comprehensive review see Kearney, Boyle and Walsh 1995, especially chapter 3). First, it is necessary to ask what are the specific rationales for local development. The answer to this question will lead to consideration of such basic issues as how to *organize* the preparation and implementation of a local development initiative, what is an appropriate *methodology* for planning local development, and what are the *processes* that are central to successful implementation of local plans.

Three different but interrelated rationales can be suggested for local development initiatives. These are (a) to overcome market failures, (b) to improve local capacity, and (c) to facilitate empowerment. Local capacity building is a critical objective as it enables local communities to become empowered (Friedmann 1992) which in turn helps to overcome some instances of market failure (Michaelson 1979). The three rationales broadly relate to different types of objectives, e.g. economic, social and political. In order to achieve these objectives it is necessary to adopt several basic principles which can be conveniently categorized under three headings: partnership structures for subsidiarity as an organizing model; strategic planning as a methodology; and animation, facilitation and capacity building as processes for implementation.

The main features of each of these principles is summarized briefly as follows. There seems to be widespread acceptance of the proposition that policy formulation and implementation in the area of local development should be guided by the principle of subsidiarity. This requires the establishment of *partnership structures* that allow for devolution of authority and delegation of responsibility to the lowest level, but which at the same time ensure that the public interest of society as a whole is protected. Responsibility must be matched with accountability. The partnership model attempts to give explicit recognition to the fact that different sets of actors – statutory bodies, the private sector and community/voluntary agencies – each have a role in the local development process. The involvement of statutory bodies, most of which are organized along sectoral lines from the top, is crucial to the forging of productive relationships between the centre and the local level. The partnership should be involved at all stages in the preparation and implementation of the local action plan – essentially they should view their role as *owners* of the plan.

However, a distinction has to be made between the establishment of a broadly based partnership and its transformation into a dynamic entity through a partnering process. The partnering process implies a commitment to working towards common objectives; a high level of mutual trust; a willingness to cooperate, share responsibility and accept accountability; and where necessary to alter the prevailing institutional structures. This requires that each partner accepts agreed objectives based on negotiation between partners coming from different perspectives (e.g. private sector business interests versus community social objectives). This aspect of partnership is much more challenging for all participants and likely to require fundamental changes in attitudes and priorities. Consequently, it is important to view this dimension of local development as one that will require a lengthy learning curve, which may be shortened by appropriate interventions under a strategic approach to local planning.

The main requirements of a *strategic approach to planning* are that it must be:

1. unified in the sense of tying all the components together
2. comprehensive in relation to all sectors
3. focused on target groups and areas
4. innovative rather than imitative
5. integrated so that all parts of the plan are compatible with each other.

Following O'Cinneide and Keane (1990) a typical strategic planning model involves a number of stages that include:

1. preparation of an agreed framework as to how the planning is to be undertaken
2. a Strengths, Weaknesses, Opportunities and Threats (SWOT) analysis
3. assessment of what types of interventions already exist, and where are the gaps
4. preparation of alternative scenarios
5. selection of preferred scenario and prioritization of actions
6. on-going monitoring and periodic evaluations.

A number of positive aspects of this model have been noted by O'Cinneide and Keane (1990). First, it allows for widespread community participation in the planning process and helps to overcome the sense of powerlessness and apathy. Second, it facilitates the achievement of a consensus which will greatly enhance the prospect of the plan proposals being supported rather than being opposed by local interests. However, it must be noted that there are considerable variations between communities in their levels of preparedness to participate in this type of process. The risk is that the planning process may be hijacked by some well organized interests while others are effectively excluded from participation (Amdam 1992). Another possibility is that the planning process becomes 'consultant driven' in which case the local community have difficulty in developing a sense of ownership of the plan. This is particularly likely to happen when several local action groups (LAGs) are simultaneously preparing plans, and some consultants may be assisting a number of LAGs. These potential problems can be avoided to some extent if the local LAG establishes a partnership structure at an early stage, and if it engages in a process that explicitly involves animation and capacity building.

The processes that help to distinguish recent local development initiatives are usually referred to as *animation, facilitation* and *capacity building*. These processes are central to the objective of empowering communities that in many cases have become dependent and apathetic (Kulkarni and Rajan 1991).

The role of animation is to improve the effectiveness of the human resource factor in local development. It is usually initiated through an intensive process of community consultation which is aimed at maximizing the extent of local involvement. There are several ways of increasing the level of local participation: e.g. through public meetings, adult education and training courses, personal contacts, local surveys, use of public media, dissemination of information through libraries, exhibitions, fairs, etc. The relative importance of each of these methods varies at different stages in the development process. Public meetings aimed at information dissemination and a preliminary SWOT analysis can be very important in the initial stages whereas training programmes (e.g. community leadership and business skills) become more important at a later stage. Essentially, the nature of the animation process can be expected to become more focused and specialized as groups progress along a development path. Apart from being of benefit to the local community the animation process also provides an opportunity for the animators to listen to the needs and views of the community, which they can subsequently incorporate into the local action plan. Animation is an ongoing process, though it is likely to be most intensively undertaken in the early stages of a programme (Moseley and Cherrett 1993).

Facilitation is a more personalized form of animation involving intensive contacts between project promoters and the animation or project development officers of the local partnership. Its objective is to assist project promoters in the preparation of their proposals so that they have a good chance of being approved by the partnership board. Facilitation essentially attempts to overcome the problems associated with the perceived bureaucracy of larger and remoter agencies. It also tends to dramatically reduce the level of rejection of project applications which can be psychologically very important for communities that have become alienated from the national institutions.

Capacity building is a gradual and complex process aimed at upgrading the local physical and human resource bases. The concept as used here relates to the capacity of the entire local population as distinct from that of individuals – in this sense it can be considered as being about the provision of public goods. It can be achieved by making provision for skills improvement, encouraging new forms of organization, and stimulating new types of linkages between groups and public agencies. While much of the activity that is typically described as capacity building is concerned with training it can also cover activities such as resource audits, mentor services, formation of marketing cooperatives, provision of specialist hardware to guarantee the quality of products, etc.

A strategy for improving local capacity has been developed through the European Union (EU) sponsored Local Employment Development Action Programme (LEDA) which relies on the existence of some hardware and software components along with facilitators who can initiate a strategic development programme that can be implemented in a number of stages (Martinos 1989). Three non-discrete stages in the local development process can be identified.

The first is concerned with acquiring the 'know-how of development'. This is usually a preparatory phase during which the pre-conditions for development are put in place. These include provision of information, promotion of demonstration projects, and recruitment of consultancy and training services. The emphasis is very much on learning how to take actions that will lead to wealth creation and employment. By the end of the first phase there should be in place some local leaders and structures to carry forward the process, an animation and capacity building programme, and a small number of demonstration projects.

In the second stage the emphasis moves on to using the knowledge and experience that have already been acquired so as to encourage a more spontaneous flow of projects. A number of supports may be required at this stage which can range from financial aid packages, provision of workspace, upgrading of management skills, and investment in marketing strategies. The third and final stage may only be arrived at after ten years, by which time there is a sufficient critical mass of projects and other activities being promoted spontaneously and there is also an experienced local support structure in place (Bennett and Krebs 1991).

Recent Local Development Initiatives in Ireland

For most of the period from the mid-1970s to the late 1980s the regional and local dimensions of development were largely neglected while governments sought to tackle macro-economic problems related to fiscal imbalances and rising unemployment (Walsh 1992). However, the situation has changed radically over recent years so that there are now a plethora of agencies involved in local development. Furthermore, the role of local initiatives has been given greater official status through the inclusion of an 'Operational Programme on Local Urban and Rural Development' (Government of Ireland 1995) in the EU Community Support Framework (CSF) for Ireland covering the period 1994–1999 (CEC 1994). The Operational Programme is a response to a commitment to local development in the government's National Development Plan 1994–1999 (Government of Ireland 1993). The inclusion of a structured local development programme in the National Development Plan was a major innovation in national planning which reflected an appreciation gained by the policy-makers from the pilot programmes of the potential which could be harnessed through a combination of bottom-up and top-down strategies. It was also an important political response to demands from local and regional interests that the spirit of partnership as envisaged in the 1988 reform of the EU Structural Funds was not being fully addressed in Ireland

(Walsh 1993). This section provides a summary of four recent initiatives that have been piloted at several locations throughout the state in order to demonstrate the variety of models that have been employed.

Pilot area programme for Integrated Rural Development (IRD) (1988–1990)

The first attempt to apply the principles of integrated rural development in a systematic way was through a pilot programme administered by the Department of Agriculture and Food during 1988–1990. The general objective of the programme was to improve employment opportunities, earning potential, quality of life and sense of community identity among people in rural areas. The emphasis was on encouraging viable private and community sector enterprises based on the full utilization of the abilities and talents of local people.

The programme was put into operation on a pilot basis in twelve sub-county areas, each of which had between 6000 and 15,000 inhabitants. A rural development coordinator was appointed to each area. Their role was to stimulate, assist and facilitate the initiatives of members of the local community – they were not intended to be leaders or initiators. As animators the first task of each coordinator was to organize a 'core group' of local leaders. Each core group had responsibility for deciding on local development priorities and ensuring their implementation. As there was no special fund for the programme, apart from a small amount for technical assistance, the core groups and the animators took on a brokerage role in their approach to the mainstream funding sources. Another important feature of the programme was an emphasis on shared learning through workshops and other forms of networking.

An assessment of the programme identified a number of positive outcomes that are relevant to the local development process (O'Malley 1992). The programme did facilitate the development of almost 400 projects. Of particular importance was the observation that many of the projects required a coordination or linking up of individuals. This was especially the case in relation to tourism projects. Thus the programme was able to demonstrate the benefits of an integrated approach. A structured approach to networking between groups was also found to be very beneficial in relation to sharing of experiences as it enabled groups to learn from one another.

The small size of each of the areas and the selection of the core group members (most of whom were already involved in local development) contributed to a strong sense of identity between the groups and the larger communities which in turn helped the groups in their efforts to promote an integrated approach. The programme also demonstrated the significance of the brokerage role which a local development group can perform on behalf of project promoters. There were differences between the groups in relation to their ability to generate projects. The groups could be classified according to their stage of development. For some who were at the pre-development stage the main requirement was animation and capacity building. For others more emphasis was placed on facilitation. Finally, the assessment concluded that while the programme helped to stimulate and encourage initiatives from the local communities the process was not spontaneous. The programme had to work through a focused, directed and quite conscious process which relied heavily on systematic central guidance and a considerable amount of local voluntary input.

The EU LEADER Initiative 1991–1994

Following the success of the Pilot IRD programme the government indicated that it intended to extend the bottom-up integrated approach in a nation-wide programme. While this particular aspiration was not achieved, the locally-based integrated approach was given a new lease of life under the EU LEADER (*Liaisons entre actions de developpement de l'economie rurale*) Initiative for the period 1991–1994. The objective of the Initiative was to find innovative solutions which will serve as a model for all rural areas and ensure maximum integration between sectoral measures. The concept underlying the Initiative reflected the new thinking on rural development that was contained in the European Commission's own document on *The Future of Rural Society* which had been published in 1988.

The Department of Agriculture, Food and Forestry (DAFF) was the intermediary body with responsibility for the implementation of the Initiative in the Republic of Ireland. Following the publication of the Initiative in March 1991 the DAFF invited local groups to prepare and submit integrated business plans for their areas. After consideration of the submissions 16 groups were selected for inclusion in the Initiative – in practice there were 17 groups as one of the original sixteen split into two separate entities.

The 17 local groups represented almost half of the population residing outside the main urban areas. There was a high level of variation between groups in relation to population and size of area served (e.g. one group served a population of 9250 while another catered for 126,000). Six of the areas had populations of less than 50,000 while five had more than 90,000. The population densities in the areas ranged from 10 to 39 persons per square kilometre, with four having densities less than 20 and only five where the densities exceeded 30. There was also a wide range of unemployment levels from 13 to 33 per cent. The groups also differed in relation to their prior experience of implementing integrated strategies – two-thirds had already participated in the pilot IRD programme or some other initiatives aimed at promoting an integrated approach to local development. By contrast, some of the other groups came together specifically for the purpose of securing LEADER funds – some of these had a strong enterprise orientation but they were generally inexperienced in relation to the role of animation and capacity building activities. The total budget for the Initiative was 70 million Irish Punts, of which 35 million were provided by both the EU and the Irish government.

The implementation of the Initiative in Ireland has been evaluated by Kearney *et al.* (1994). Much of the evaluation focused on the processes involved. In general terms the evaluation was very positive, claiming that there had been a considerable degree of success in relation to the achievement of the objectives set for the Initiative. However, there was a lot of variation between the groups in the manner in which they implemented the Initiative. A number of lessons can be drawn from the diversity of experiences.

For the intermediary body the Initiative represented a significant break with traditional practice in that it allowed for local groups to devise their own plans, and also it provided for a transfer of public funds to local partnership companies. These aspects of the Initiative required the DAFF to accept the principle of subsidiarity. While there appears to have been a genuine commitment to the principle, the level of central support for such an innovative measure was weak. Only a few civil servants were assigned to the programme, and furthermore, they were not provided with any special training on the nature of the processes involved in local development. Consequently, there was a considerable amount of learning by doing in relation to the implementation of the Initiative.

While each local group was required to establish a legal entity, such as a limited company to manage the Initiative in the local context, they were allowed a considerable amount of discretion in relation to the composition of the boards. All of the boards claimed to be based on a partnership model. However, the boards varied considerably in terms of size and representativeness of different interests. In terms of size they ranged from 5 to 21 members with an average of 14. The smaller boards tended to provide inadequate representation (in some cases none at all) for community interests, while some of the larger boards were dominated by the community sector. Neither extreme is desirable as it tends to unduly influence the orientation and effectiveness of the board as a strategic decision-making entity.

The boards, for the most part, included representatives of the local community (voluntary organizations), the local business sector, the statutory bodies and government agencies such as the local authorities, FAS (the National Training Authority), Teagasc (the National Institute for Agricultural Research and Training), Forbairt (the national agency for supporting indigenous industry) and Coillte (the national agency for developing forestry). One of the successes of the partnership approach was the linkages established between the statutory agencies and local community-based development associations and the local private sector. A number of joint ventures arose out of the linkages forged between the local communities and the public agencies. What was most significant about these initiatives was that, in most cases, it was the LEADER group rather than the agencies that provided the catalyst for ensuring that the events actually happened. Some of the most successful actions by the groups arose out of adopting a brokerage role in relation to existing agencies – in this way they were able to ensure that LEADER funded actions were complementary (actions that are not duplicating those covered by other programmes) to the measures funded by the more heavily resourced Operational Programmes.

While partnership has been central to the operation of the Initiative in most areas, it is important to note that there were some difficulties. One arose from the level of local discretion in the composition of the boards – as indicated above in some instances this resulted in situations where the pattern of representation was unbalanced. A second problem was the lack of commitment of some of the statutory bodies to a partnering process. Essentially, in some cases the LEADER groups were perceived as a threat – this situation arose mainly due to a lack of clarity and understanding in relation to issues of complementarity and additionality. The fundamental criticism here was that the groups and government agencies did not always see their role as providing some new or innovative response which would be additional to what was already there – instead they interpreted *additional* as more of the same. However, the more experienced groups that have worked in harmony with statutory agencies for a number of years have demonstrated that there can be mutual benefits from a serious commitment to a partnership process. Another feature of the partnership model is that it relies on a very high level of voluntary commitment, especially by representatives of the local community.

The extent of the geographical areas represented by some of the groups presented some logistical difficulties which in turn influenced the effectiveness of the partnership approach. Where the groups were catering for extensive areas they should have established area-based sub-committees in order to ensure that all parts of the group's area were treated equally. In practice this did not always happen, with the result that the activities of the group tended to be confined to certain areas, which were usually in close proximity to where the group had its offices. However, some groups tried to overcome problems associated with the size or shape of their area by establishing local offices which were connected to the central office via modern information technology.

A second aspect of the LEADER Initiative that merits some attention was quality of the business plans prepared by the groups. A review of the business plans suggests that the concept and methodology of strategic planning was poorly understood in most cases. This was partly due to inexperience, but the planning process itself was in most cases severely hampered by a lack of baseline data which hindered the undertaking of a comprehensive SWOT analysis. At the beginning of the programme a number of the groups clearly had little appreciation of the role of animation and capacity building functions. Consequently, the substance of many of the business plans consisted of little more than lists of potential projects. The concepts of innovation and integration were generally not well understood, and neither was there much awareness of the potential problems associated with deadweight (supporting projects that would have gone ahead anyway) and displacement (providing support for projects that may force others out of business).

The hasty preparation of many of the business plans relying on traditional methodologies of planning for people instead of planning by the local community, with assistance from consultants, was not conducive to giving the boards any sense of *ownership* of the plans. In reality, many of the original business plans were subsequently of limited assistance to the groups, particularly as many of the potential projects in the business plans were never developed. The main lesson from this experience is that the group business plan should focus mostly on specific actions to implement a strategy aimed at achieving particular objectives. If an appropriate support structure is established it is likely that the projects will follow more or less spontaneously.

The third dimension of the LEADER Initiative that requires discussion is the emphasis placed on animation and capacity building. This was probably the strongest attribute of the Initiative which resulted in a very positive new type of relationship between the LEADER group officers and the population which they served. Most groups engaged in some level of animation and capacity building, though in many cases it was not seen as a specialist task. In the first year of the programme some groups did not engage professional animators because of difficulties in raising matching funds, though the requirements in this area were later relaxed. In a few instances the LEADER boards failed to appreciate the role of animators – this happened mostly in those groups which had no prior experience in local development. In fact these groups could be described as local top-down agencies.

The animation and facilitation work undertaken by LEADER personnel was generally highly praised. Its *open-door, easily accessible* and *informal* aspect has been frequently contrasted with the more bureaucratic and compartmentalized approach of the longer established agencies. A wide range of activities were undertaken under the general heading of capacity building. These included training courses in business planning, community leadership, niche marketing of local food products, heritage management, women in rural development, horse breeding and shellfish cultivation. Other types of capacity building included formation of producer/marketing groups, preparation of local resource audits and sectoral/area strategies, and the establishment of local advisory/mentoring panels.

In addition to its support for the local development process LEADER also provided financial assistance to eligible projects in rural tourism, small enterprises including crafts, and projects that involved innovative uses of natural resources. By the end of 1993 the total number of projects that had been approved was over 2350, and by a year later the total exceeded 3100. By far the most popular types of projects were in the area of rural tourism. These included accommodation, golf/pitch and putt courses, water sports, heritage centres, equestrian centres, cultural activities, open farms, and amenity improvements such as mountain parks, bog trails and long distance walking routes.

Finally, the evaluation established that most groups had only a very limited understanding of how the concepts of innovation and integration might be operationalized, of the significance of deadweight and displacement (particularly in relation to projects outside the LEADER areas), and that most project promoters were primarily interested in the financial support they could obtain from the groups. Also, many of the private beneficiaries from LEADER were already quite well off, though in terms of employment it was encouraging to discover that almost 50 per cent of those who obtained full-time employment were previously unemployed.

In summary, the evaluation of the Initiative in Ireland concluded that it had attained a considerable degree of success in relation to the achievement of its objectives, the enormous commitment of board members and local communities, the positive and constructive relationship between the groups and the DAFF, and the support and participation of government agencies and the local authorities. While the level of financial resources available to the Initiative was very small by comparison with mainstream programmes for rural development, it afforded the first opportunity for most groups to examine the potential of their own areas, and to cooperate and coordinate their activities in devising and implementing an innovative local development strategy for the betterment of their communities. The merits of the model underlying LEADER have been endorsed in a recent report from the National Economic and Social Council (1994) on *New Approaches to Rural Development.*

Area-based partnership responses to long-term unemployment

In 1990 the National Economic and Social Council published its *Strategy for the Nineties* in which it identified the tackling of long-term unemployment as a prime objective for government policy. It saw a special role for a localized area-based response (ABR). It claimed that:

> intensive programmes in small areas containing elements of housing and environmental improvement as well as retraining and employment schemes, and 'outreach' health and educational projects, can have an impact over and above the separate effects of individual programmes. Furthermore, the more closely involved are local communities in planning and delivery of area-based projects, the more they will reflect local needs and priorities. (NESC 1990, p.74)

In 1991 12 areas, 8 urban and 4 rural, were selected by the government as pilot projects for an ABR to long-term unemployment. The areas were selected on the basis of three criteria: geographical spread, the extent of unemployment and long-term unemployment, and the existence of structures and activities on which the initiative could build. The objectives of the ABR programme are:

1. to improve the personal skills and attributes of people who are long-term unemployed or those at risk of becoming unemployed
2. to promote attitudinal changes needed to enable individuals to generate enterprise

3. to promote local economic projects and initiatives which will sustain confidence and investment.

The implementation of the initiative is based on the principles of partnership, local area focus, community participation and integration of actions. In order to achieve its objectives Area Partnership Companies (APCs) were established in each area. Each partnership consists of a board of approximately 18 members – 6 representing relevant government agencies, 6 to represent the social partners (i.e. trade unions, employers and farmers), and 6 representatives of the local community. The partnership model was justified on the grounds that it was necessary to achieve a local consensus on the optimum use of resources, and also as a means of creating a new sense of community identity. The operating arrangements for the partnerships were drawn up by a National Coordinating Team (NCT) comprising seconded staff nominated by the public sector agencies, the employers' organizations and the trade unions. In October 1992 the NCT was transferred from the Department of An Taoiseach (the Prime Minister) to a new intermediary body, Area Development Management (ADM) Ltd. The partnerships are financed through a Global Grant from the EU plus funding from the government and private sources within the partnerships.

The pilot phase of the ABR programme has been evaluated by Craig and McKeown (1994). They concluded that a considerable degree of progress had been made in relation to the achievement of the programme objectives. The partnership organizational model was found to be particularly effective. At the local level it has provided an opportunity for the local communities to engage directly with the statutory agencies. The inclusion of private sector representatives on the boards has helped to alter some of the bureaucratic procedures associated with public agencies. The existence of a formal link between the local development bodies, the partnerships and central policy-making through the National Coordinating Team was vital to the success of the programme. In addition to the role of the partnership model another important factor in the success of the programme was the requirement that each group prepare an integrated area action plan.

While the assessment was generally positive it also noted a number of limitations. In relation to the partnerships the main problems derive from the national system of centralized and compartmentalized decision-making. This has tended to result in a situation where some of the statutory delivery agencies have adopted a defensive position. The evaluation claimed that some of the key agencies had failed to deliver on any aspect of the initiative. The evaluation concluded that training for participation should be undertaken by the partners to enable them to develop a genuine partnership process.

At the local level difficulties were experienced in relation to the ability of community representatives to participate fully in the partnerships. The problems in this area arose from the inexperience of some community representatives, and the lack of resources available to this sector. The resources that are available are often short-term, insecure and inadequate. In these circumstances it is difficult for community representatives to sustain participation in partnership activity over a long period. An additional problem for some of the partnerships was a high level of intra-community rivalry and competition for scarce resources – this was due in part to practices that developed prior to the ABR initiative when resources for community development were even more scarce.

There was some concern over the composition of the partnership boards. The tri-partite structure with equal representation for all sectors was essentially imposed from outside the local areas. No account was taken of differences between areas, nor did there appear to be any detailed consideration of the contribution expected from each board representative. It was generally felt that the boards were too large and that perhaps 12 to 15 rather than 18 members would be more appropriate. It was also felt that there should be more local discretion in relation to the board composition.

The partnerships adopted a variety of ways of working towards the objectives. These varied from a delivery approach where the partnership started providing services that previously were not available in the area (e.g. a revolving fund), to an *agency* approach where the partnerships adopted a secondary role in relation to delivery and placed more emphasis on development of programmes to respond to local needs. Partnership resources were allocated to other organizations to implement the programmes. Finally, some partnerships began to reduce their delivery and agency roles, and instead concentrate on a *brokerage* approach where the main emphasis is on strengthening the support infrastructure through the medium of the partnership.

The area action plans were considered to be a key component in the success of the programme. However, there were also some difficulties in this area. One was the novelty of applying a strategic approach – many of the participants in the partnerships were inexperienced in relation to this methodology. In some cases the plans were prepared in haste in order to meet submission deadlines – this resulted in some plans being written very much to a standard formula by external consultants. The groups did not have sufficient time to participate sufficiently in the preparation of the plans and to give due consideration to prioritization of actions. The result was that some of the plans were over-ambitious relative to the experience and resources available to the groups, who were also unable to identify the possibilities for integration.

Finally, there was concern over the limitations of an area-based approach. The main problem here was related to targeting those for whom the programme was intended. The geographical distribution of the target group (the long-term unemployed and those at risk of becoming unemployed) does not always conform to a neat pattern.

County Enterprise Boards

The final initiative in local development that is considered here is a programme to assist small and medium sized enterprises (SMEs) through 35 County Enterprise Boards (CEBs). The CEBs are organized according to the partnership model with representatives of the public agencies concerned with enterprise development, the private sector, community interests, and elected members of the local authority. The Executive Manager of the local authority is also a member. These partnerships are unique in that they include some democratically elected local councillors – this is a significant inclusion in that it provides for democratic accountability. Of course, some view it as a potentially dangerous development opening up opportunities for local councillors to influence the allocation of resources in a manner that would be to their advantage. The reality is that the elected members are a minority on the CEB and are therefore unlikely to be able to unduly influence its actions, even if they wished to do so.

According to the Department of Enterprise and Employment the objective of the CEBs is to encourage local initiative by a greater devolution of functions, which will empower local communities to obtain local funding to develop their own areas. More specifically each CEB is required to focus, develop and support local entrepreneurship and enterprise within the framework of a coherent, integrated County Enterprise Action Plan so as to build a local economy of real strength and permanence which will provide jobs and wealth sufficient to its needs.

The activities of the CEBs are targeted at SMEs, of less than ten employees, through a series of measures that include:

1. preparation of County Enterprise Action Plans
2. promotion of enterprise culture
3. business information/advice, counselling and mentoring support
4. financial assistance
5. management development.

The funding for the County Enterprise Boards is provided under the Operational Programme for Local Urban and Rural Development which is part of the EU CSF for Ireland up to 1999. The most important element is the preparation of the County Enterprise Action Plan. Most of the CEBs have now completed their plans. The planning process was initially intended to be undertaken largely by the CEB itself. This proved impossible in most cases. Most CEBs have relied on external consultants. A number of the plans are weak in terms of analysis of the local economy (frequently due to data deficiencies). The major difficulties in identifying appropriate strategies were related to how general strategies could be adapted to the local circumstances. A further difficulty that has arisen relates to the operation of the CEBs, particularly their relationship to larger enterprise support agencies which in some cases have seen the CEBs as a threat to their position.

Most of the action plans include a wide range of proposals such as the following: one-stop-shops to coordinate the supply of information to SMEs; a schools-based programme to encourage an enterprise culture among young people; seed capital and small loans; incubator units and enterprise centres in places where there is already in existence a small business development association; finance for feasibility studies; establishment of advisory and mentoring panels; special management development training for new entrepreneurs – for a more thorough elaboration see Boyle and Walsh (1995).

Conclusions

There are a number of general conclusions that can be drawn from the recent initiatives on local economic development in Ireland. All of the evaluations that have been considered have demonstrated that locally focused, area-based integrated strategies can make a significant positive contribution to the economic and social well-being of many individuals and their communities. The level of experience with structured approaches to local development by actors at both local and central levels is still quite limited. Much can be learned from the pilot initiatives of recent years. More emphasis has to be placed on understanding the processes of local development and on education and training of activists in local development. Such training is required for individuals at both the local and central levels so as to facilitate more cooperation and to bring about a change of attitude that will lead to a greater emphasis on soft support measures instead of the more traditional reliance on financial grants and physical infrastructure. Tri-partite partnerships representing local voluntary interests, the private business sector, and the statutory agencies provide a basis for innovative responses to local problems, particularly if the partnerships adopt a brokerage approach in their relationships with existing agencies. The optimal size of partnership boards seems to be about 12 to 15 members. Boards need to be supported by sub-board level structures.

The transformation of partnerships as organizational models into dynamic entities that are capable of taking innovative initiatives requires a commitment to developing the partnering process. This is a gradual and complex process that requires careful and sensitive nurturing and support. The roles of the Chairperson of the board and the Chief Executive are crucial in this respect. The extent of centralization in the Irish administrative system is a constraining factor on the development of effective and dynamic partnerships. While several of the local partnerships have demonstrated that they can be very effective in addressing problems that were previously neglected or inadequately addressed by the larger agencies, there is still an element of distrust, and in some cases antagonism, among some personnel in the longer established agencies towards the recently established partnerships. The reasons for this situation are due in part to a tradition where the bulk of public finances have been controlled by central authorities, and also the threat to existing power structures posed by the partnerships.

Another issue is that in some areas a degree of tension has developed between the democratically elected members of the local authority and the local partnership boards. One of the issues that has encouraged such tensions is what is perceived to be an absence of democratic accountability in the partnerships. The underfunding of local authorities for many years which has left them almost powerless in the area of local development is probably also a contributory factor to the antagonistic relationship between local authority members and partnership boards in many areas. Much of the success of the partnerships has been due to an enormous voluntary contribution of time and effort by representatives of local communities. Given the long-term nature of the local development process it is essential to ensure that the voluntary members of boards and sub-committees are not over-burdened and that due recognition is given to their contribution. Partnerships should include provision for rotation of membership after a fixed period in order to reduce the burden that is frequently carried by a few and also to safeguard against the emergence of local cliques which could serve to frustrate the ideal of partnership.

All commentators on local development in Ireland are agreed on the need for carefully prepared strategic action plans. However, in practice the quality of many of the action plans does not reflect a systematic application of the principles of strategic planning. This has been partly due to defects in local data. However, it is probably also due to more fundamental problems such as a tendency to rely on private consultants who may not have been trained in planning for integrated multi-dimensional programmes that are intended to be innovative and complementary to existing plans. Local planning has in many cases been undertaken with great haste so as to meet submission deadlines for the different programmes. In effect much of the local planning is funds driven and led by consultants who may at times be assisting more than one group. There have been very few instances where local groups have prepared medium to long-term strategies which were flexible enough to be capable of adaptation to the guidelines for various funding initiatives as they became available. This type of planning has only been undertaken by very experienced groups. And finally, it is essential that regular monitoring and evaluation is undertaken. This type of activity should be built into the work programme of each partnership from the beginning as it can provide a most valuable means of self learning. Internal evaluations need to be complemented by external independent assessments which can be more objective and more critical. Additionally, the latter type of evaluation can usually provide a basis for a comparative assessment. Given that much of the effort of local development groups is directed towards the facilitation of a process it is important that evaluations consider both qualitative and quantitative indicators of performance.

The neglect of local development for many years has now been replaced by an almost unbridled enthusiasm which is reflected in a plethora of local agencies implementing a number of initiatives that share a number of common objectives. Under the Operational Programme for Local Urban and Rural Development, funding is provided for the 35 County Enterprise Boards and 36 Area Partnership

Companies to implement integrated programmes in Designated Disadvantaged Areas (essentially an extension of the ABR programme). Also, 33 local groups covering the State of Ireland, with the exception of the main cities, will receive funding under the EU LEADER 2 Initiative. In many areas all three initiatives will be operating. Under this arrangement there is considerable scope for duplication of effort, and rivalry between local agencies. The situation is not helped by the fact that each initiative is under the responsibility of a different government department and that there is not a strong mechanism for a central level of coordination. At county level the government proposes to establish non-executive County Strategy Teams that will seek to coordinate and rationalize the local development process within each county. To date very little progress has been made in this respect as many of the local partnerships do not appear to be interested in local cooperation – in fact in a number of areas there is a high level of mutual distrust between the partnerships.

Finally, there is a need for a realistic assessment of how much can be achieved through local initiatives. The overall outcome will most likely remain quite small and relatively marginal when set against the outcomes from the mainstream programmes. There is a risk that an uncoordinated approach to local development via a plethora of partnerships will be considered by policy-makers and the political system as an adequate response to demands for a spatial/regional perspective in development planning. The partnerships provide an effective low-level tier in a spatial planning system. They need to be coordinated horizontally at both the local and central levels. They also need to be coordinated vertically into a regional level tier which should in turn be linked to central level government departments and public agencies. Without such vertical and horizontal coordination the full potential of the recent experience gained from local initiatives will not be fully realized.

References

Amdam, J. (1992) 'Local, planning and mobilization: experiences from the Norwegian fringe.' In M. Tykkylainen (ed) *Development Issues and Strategies in the New Europe.* Aldershot: Avebury.

Bennett, R.J. and Krebs, G. (1991) *Local Economic Development: Public Private Partnership Initiatives in Britain and Germany.* London: Belhaven Press.

Boyle, G. and Walsh, J. (1995) *Kildare County Enterprise Board, Enterprise Action Plan 1995–1997.* Centre for Local and Regional Development, Maynooth University.

Commission of the European Communities (CEC) (1994) *IRELAND Community Support Framework 1994–1999.* Brussels: Commission of the European Communities.

Craig, S. and McKeown, K. (1994) *Progress Through Partnership.* Dublin: Combat Poverty Agency.

Friedmann, J. (1992) *Empowerment – the Politics of Alternative Development.* Cambridge: Blackwell Publishers.

Government of Ireland (1993) *IRELAND National Development Plan 1994–1999.* Dublin: Government Publications Office.

Government of Ireland (1995) *Operational Programme for Local Urban and Rural Development 1994–1999.* Dublin: Government Publications Office.

Kearney, B., Boyle, G. and Walsh, J. (1995) *EU LEADER 1 Initiative in Ireland: Evaluation and Recommendations.* Dublin: Stationery Office.

Kulkarni, G. and Rajan, R.S. (1991) 'Perceptions of development as empowerment.' In M. O'Cinneide and S. Grimes (eds) *Planning and Development of Marginal Areas.* Centre for Development Studies, UCG, Galway.

Martinos, H. (1989) *The Management of Local Employment Development Strategies.* Report for LEDA Programme, LRDP Consultants: London.

Michaelson, S. (1979) 'Community-based economic development in urban areas.' In B. Chinitz (ed) *Central City Economic Development.* New York: Abt Books.

Moseley, M.J. and Cherrett, T. (1993) *Involving People in Local Development.* LEADER Dossiers, AEIDL, Brussels.

National Economic and Social Council (1990) *A Strategy for the Nineties: Economic Stability and Structural Change.* Dublin: Government Publications.

National Economic and Social Council (1994) *New Approaches to Rural Development.* Dublin: Government Publications.

O'Cinneide, M. and Keane, M.J. (1990) 'Applying strategic planning to local economic development: the case of Connemara Gaeltacht, Ireland.' *Town Planning Review 61*, 4, pp.475–86.

O'Malley, E. (1992) *The Pilot Programme for Integrated Rural Development 1988–1990.* Paper No. 27, Broadsheet Series, ESRI, Dublin.

Walsh, J.A. (1992) 'The Republic of Ireland.' In P. Townroe and R. Martin (eds) *Regional Development in the 1990s: the British Isles in Transition.* London: Jessica Kingsley Publishers, pp.127–135.

Walsh, J.A. (1993) 'Regional development in Ireland under the Community Support Framework: review and prospects.' In H. Van der Kamp (ed) *EC Funds for Ireland: Getting it Right.* Dublin: Regional Studies Association (Irish Branch), pp.55–74.

Whitaker's Almanack (1995) London: J. Whitaker & Sons, p.913.

CHAPTER 9

Spatial Planning in Flanders
Looking for Strengths and Weaknesses Through its Regional Approach

Rik Houthaeve

Introduction

This chapter focuses on recent developments and perspectives of regional planning in Flanders, Belgium (see Figure 9.1). More specifically it will examine the problem of the unfolding of spatial planning on a regional level in general and will discuss the challenge of territorial integration. The case of regional planning in Flanders is understood as spatial planning on a regional level (strategic planning).

The momentum of this discussion is the project of the Flemish government on the redefinition of the spatial planning system. Since 1992 a process has been under way towards the formulation of a planning strategy for the Flemish region and the establishment of a new planning law in which a planning hierarchy will be set on three levels providing structure plans for: the 'region', the 5 'provinces' and the 306 'communes'.[1] In the end the structure plans and implementation plans have to replace the existing zoning plans at the level of the sub-region (known as the 'sector plans'). These sector plans are the core of the current planning system according to the Law on Town and Country Planning (29 of March 1962).

The objective of the actual project, and therefore the main focus of this chapter, is the elaboration of a structure plan for the whole of Flanders, a political strategy formulated by a central government. This structure plan was approved by the Flemish government in March 1995 as a guidance document that will set the framework for the revision of strategic planning and land use management in Flanders. But, as the new planning law is not yet approved by the Flemish

1 The objectives of the structure plans will be executed through implementation plans, programmes and projects (for instance for zoning, development, management of urban and rural areas). The structure plans will have obligatory force towards the actions of regional, provincial and local governments; the statutory power towards individuals will be set in the implementation plans.

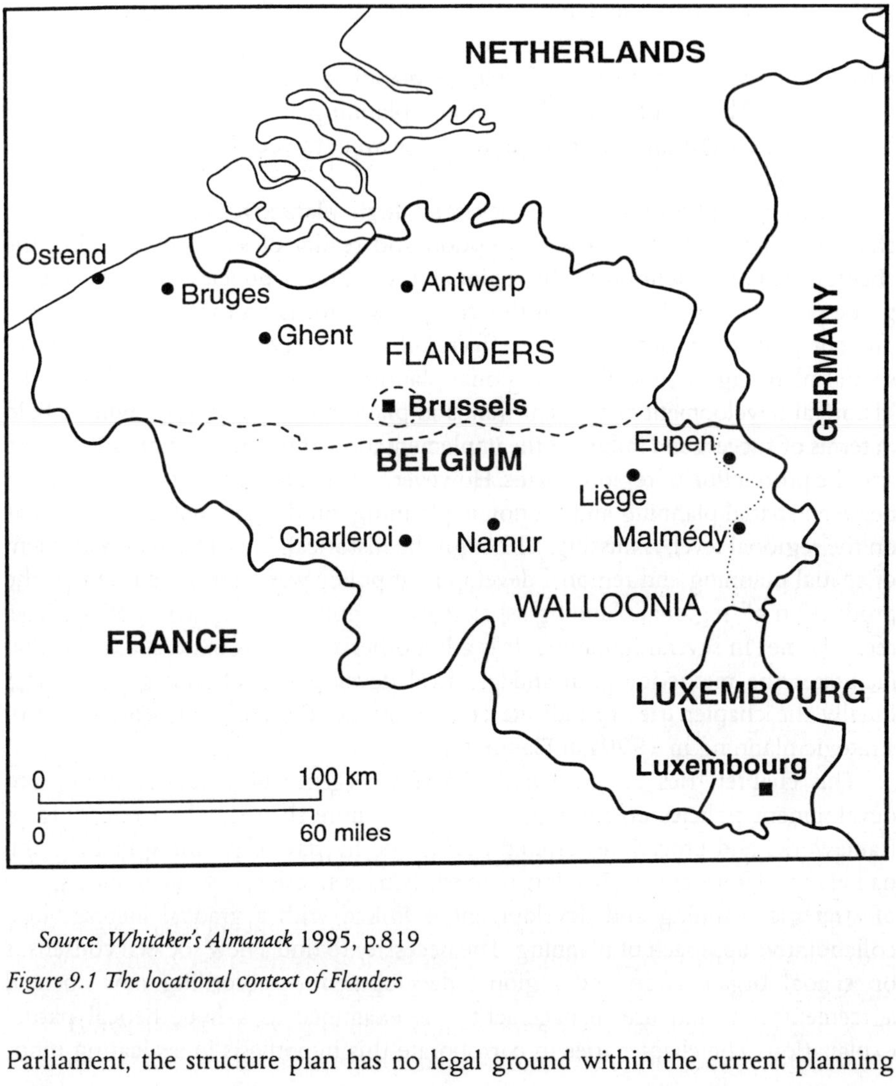

Source: *Whitaker's Almanack* 1995, p.819
Figure 9.1 The locational context of Flanders

Parliament, the structure plan has no legal ground within the current planning system.

The chapter will describe and explain the nature and context of both planning policies, first the elaboration of the current planning system in the 1960s and 1970s and second the actual spatial policy. Briefly it describes the dilution of strategic planning during the 1970s and the re-emergence of strategic planning in the 1990s. It tries to deduce transitions in planning thought and planning practice through the examination of the unfolding of spatial planning on a regional level at these different periods and within the socio-political context of these moments. In the 1980s the establishment of the Flemish government during the devolution process of the former unified state of Belgium,[2] and the gain of competence on spatial and regional planning by the Flemish region, and the increasing pressure to change the existing statutory land use plans (the sector plans) have facilitated the production of strategic planning and frameworks for development policy. This chapter describes relevant planning initiatives at the level of the Flemish region and the sub-regional level that were the outcome of this evolution and context.

Spatial planning on a regional level, strategic planning, is the subject of the chapter, but to cope with the conception and reality of strategic planning the chapter shifts its attention to the regional development policies for these appropriate periods. The discussion in this chapter will focus on these regional development policies in order to trace effects on the conception and elaboration of spatial planning in general and regional planning in particular. To deal with the historical development and recent trends in planning this discussion will be held in terms of success and failure of the implementation of the spatial planning system and the production of regional plans. However, a firm integration and coordination between spatial planning and economic planning, on the national level as well as on the regional level, is missing. Although the historical, interrelated development of spatial planning and regional development policy was merely a burden on the production of 'regional planning', spatial and regional development policies have recently met in several initiatives. It is a hypothesis that this trend is a factor that facilitates the methodological and practical development of strategic planning. Finally the chapter tries to indicate and to explain the relative re-emergence of strategic planning in 1990s in Flanders.

This chapter tries to understand the re-emergence of spatial planning and development policies on the regional level as more than simply a rereading of frameworks and procedures offered during the heyday of planning in Belgium, namely the 1960s and 1970s. It tries to explain, as an aside, that the re-emergence of strategic planning and development is linked with a gradual increase in a collaborative approach of planning. The necessity to find a new societal consensus on spatial organization and regional development – according new societal agreements on land use management – is examined as a hypothetical partial explanation. The chapter tries to corroborate this hypothesis in evaluating inno-

2 In the 1980s the former centrally organized state of Belgium evolved towards a federally organized state with three regions: Flanders (the Dutch-speaking part in the north), Wallonia (the French-speaking part in the south) and Brussels (the capital region between it). The word 'regional' can be part of some confusion in this Flemish application. 'Flemish region' is used regarding the meaning above. The reformulation of regional economic development policies is using more and more the notion of 'sub-regions'. Some of them can be compared with the areas of the sub-regional sector plan. The term 'regional' is used by the author to describe the spatial entities with a regional level of scale situated between the local level and the level of the Flemish region. The territory involved in the term 'regional' can be linked with the notion from the sub-regional (according to the sector plans) to the regional (in the notion of the regional studies and never operationalized regional plan in the 1960s).

vations in recent plan-making in Flanders in respect of the examination of planning as democratic decision-making. This view includes a sociocratic approach of planning that includes a collaboration of divers actors in the field and a communicative and argumentative approach of the planning process. This framework is understood through the reading of literature on planning theory provided mainly by Faludi (1987), Friedmann (1987, 1989 and 1993) and Healey (1993, 1994). Faludi and van der Valk (1994) on the concept of Dutch planning doctrine and the work of Zonneveld (1991) on the communicative function of explicit concepts of spatial organization offers a framework for comparative evaluation. The comments of Albrechts (1993, 1994) on the project of the Flemish structure plan and the interpretations of Roberts (1994) who has discussed the substantial principles of regional planning, for instance regarding the work of Friedmann and Weaver (1979), offers a final examination on the role of planning.

The chapter concludes with some hypotheses on the reformulation of spatial planning in general and on a regional level in particular regarding the conditions and opportunities to work out planning frameworks which incorporate territorial integration and sociocratic decision-making.

The Current Spatial Planning System in Flanders

The conception of the post-war planning system

In the post-war period a process was started to create a planning system in Belgium. The present planning system is largely founded upon legislation passed at the end of the Second World War. A special decree of 17 November 1944, taken by the acting government at the end of the war was confirmed by a Special Legislation of 2 December 1946. The essential mechanism of planning is basically permits for land-parcelling and building, granted in accordance to the general plans for a whole municipality and special plans for part of a municipality; plans which had to be approved by central government. Only a limited number of municipality authorities have made special plans for part of their areas, for purposes such as zones for industrial development, play and recreation areas or social housing projects; very few local authorities have made a general plan for their municipality. The need for greater intervention in local planning was generally acknowledged by central government at that time. This was a basis of the definitive Law of 29 March 1962 on Town and Country Planning (Zoning and Planning Act). This reorganization of land use planning and urban design confirmed a highly centralized legislation. In addition to the existing local planning level, the 1962 Law provided the elaboration of sub-regional and regional plans (Anselin 1984, Boes 1992, Laconte 1992).

The objective of the Law of 1962 was the provision of a system of hierarchical statutory plans on regional, sub-regional and local levels. The intention was that the regional plan should become the instrument of strategic planning. It should set the main signposts for the structural development of the territory. In addition the sub-regional plans should emphasize the outlines of land use management within the structural framework for spatial organization and development designed in the regional plans. Finally at the local level detailed zoning should have been worked out.

The elaboration of the post-war planning system started, parallel with the parliamentary preparations for the planning law, in the 1950s. In the period 1956–1966 twenty regional studies were commissioned by the central (Belgian) government. The outcome of these studies, known as 'directory plans', was a series of proposals for strategic spatial organization and regional development.

These regional studies, worked out in 20 regions, were of great influence for the concepts of regional planning but they did not result in regional plans. The discussions and conflicts between the two Belgian communities (the Flemish and the French-speaking community) were amongst other reasons why no agreement could be set to define the 'regions'. The choice between five large 'economic regions' and three 'regions' could not be determined. National planning and the regional plans were never operationalized. A later section in this chapter (Elements of the Socio-economic, Cultural and Political Context and its Implications for Strategic Planning) tries to explain this failure.

According to the intentions of the legislative work, as observed by Saey (1988) in the parliamentary preparations of the Organic Law of 1962, the aim was to renew the old economic machinery. In this period of rapid economic growth, authorities were frequently confronted with the need to allocate industrial sites. Concepts of regional development were advocated and there was a general understanding that Belgium must not lag behind other industrialized countries in adopting some machinery for planning (Anselin 1984). The tools for that purpose were a better allocation of enterprises and the construction of an efficient traffic network. Spatial planning was seen as an instrument that was usable to aim for a more 'rational' and 'efficient' spatial organization to reach goals of economic expansion and growth of welfare.

The choice for a pragmatic physical planning

By 1966 the politicians in charge chose a pragmatic approach to cope with the different spatial claims. At that time the urgent need for land use management became clear. Because, through a rather permissive spatial policy and contemporary individualism, the situation in Flanders resulted in a process of a spatial anarchy and consequently a continuous deterioration of the environment, an incredible expansion of building activity across the country, an increasing ribbon development, unplanned industrialization and a general fragmentation of green and agricultural areas (Albrechts 1992; De Decker *et al.* 1987). A later section in this chapter (Elements of the Socio-economic, Cultural and Political Context and its Implications for Strategic Planning) examines the underlying socio-cultural reasons for this attitude. As the discussion on the regional planning could not be determined at the appropriate time, the attention of the leading politicians and public officials has shifted from the regional to the sub-regional level and the issue of land use management has replaced the unfinished proposals for strategic planning. In order to organize the spatial zoning the elaboration of the sector plans was the result.[3]

The preparation of these plans was given to private consultancies and academic departments outside the government administration – this is a rather constant theme in Flanders' planning practice. However the influence of the regional studies and the directory plans were important. Anselin (1984) indicates the awareness at that time that spatial planning and land-use policies are necessarily the result of far-sighted discussion and democratic decisions. In a reflection on the process of these regional studies, he has mentioned that at that time the public response to planning has progressed in two ways. At a professional level people in related professions acquired an appreciation of planning, and educational provisions for planning qualifications increased. Among members of the general public, concern about the need for a better living environment increased. Anselin sees this partly as a consequence of the activities of the regional studies project groups, who collected a great deal of information and held discussion sessions with all kinds of organizations, including local authorities and groups of individual citizens. But in reaction to this a number of local politicians realized that democratic planning could stop easy land speculation, at the level of the cabinet of the responsible minister one feared that planning would erode their centralized power (Anselin 1984). Consequently the final version of the sector plans were drawn by officials in central government.

In Flanders the last of these sector plans were approved at the end of the 1970s and gained an obligatory force for governments and a statutory power for the citizens. A unique situation was established: the sector plans were characterized by an approach of separation of activities by assignment of mono-functional areas with a cadastral precision. They were worked out and approved by government on the national level with a main objective, characterized by Saey (1988) for functional coordination of spatial claims and to resolve social conflicts on these claims. The plans can therefore be seen as an arbitration agreement between pressure groups, officials and politicians at all levels of government.

With the disappearance of the regional plan the structural guidelines for development coherence within and between the marked sub-regions diluted too (Lagrou 1983), as was the case with the discourse on comprehensive strategic planning at the regional level. The initial plan options of these land-use plans, such as a stringent containment of urban sprawl, crumbled at the moment of their final approval. The results are land-use plans with a consolidation of the existing

3 'Gewewstplannen', 'Plan secteurs' for territories which one can compare with an 'arrondissement'. Only for a procedural objective in the approval process of these sub-regional plans for the 'regions' were defined according to the administrative boundaries of the 'provinces'.

situation and development, with vast residential areas (in which building facilities exceed the needs). For many years the very detailed determination of the land-use was a heavy burden on the further planning not only at the regional but also at the local level.

Looking back at the establishment of the planning system in Belgium and the elaboration of planning practice, with the sector plans as the central instrument, the lack of a real planning tradition on the regional level has to be criticized. A second criticism is concerned with the approach of spatial planning as the physical planning of a space as an autonomous object.

The Regional Development Policy and its Influence in Strategic Planning

In the middle of the 1950s a programme of regional development was instituted in Belgium to deal with 'backward' regions. This policy was formalized in the General and Specific Expansion Legislation (1959). In comparison with other Western European countries these establishments came rather late. In the early post-war period, as the industrial capacities and infrastructural potentials of Belgium were not so badly damaged, the economic life could be restarted almost immediately (Albrechts 1992). The slowing down of economic growth during the 1950s, and for example the decline of the coal-mining in Wallonia, stimulated this legislation (Gay 1989).

The policy objectives were a more balanced economic and social development and welfare and consequently a better dispersion of the allocation of the production structure. For that purpose 'development areas' were determined. The programmes of economic incentives concerned with these areas provided on the one hand subsidies to support the investments of private enterprises and on the other hand support by the national government for the construction of infrastructural accessibility, the development of 'industrial estates' or the implementation of a 'reconversion' programme for declining regional industrial structure. The legislation of 1959 also gave the power to public authorities to encourage firms to move into 'development areas', which were defined by reference to unemployment, trends of economic decline, out-migration and commuting.

In 1966 special measures to revitalize the local economies of coal-mining and textile-producing areas reinforced these policies. And in 1970 new criteria were introduced, together with the recognition of the political necessity of balancing assistance between Flanders and Wallonia, a set of very extensive 'development areas' were marked, to include one-third of the country (Gay 1989). According to Albrechts (1992) the pressure of trade unions in demanding more substantive structural changes, as the programmes of regional economic development and national economic planning were rather hesitant during the 1960s, was important. These developments resulted in the Framework Law of 15 July 1970 concerning the organization of economic planning and decentralization. Its announced purpose was to secure through a general economic policy a maximal and balanced economic expansion and continuous social improvement together with a fair division of the advantages of growth and cultural development of the Belgian people nationally and regionally (Albrechts 1992). This Law is also a clear step in the devolution process of Belgium.

Within the framework of this Law on Economic Planning and Decentralization (1970) a National Planning Bureau and consultative Regional Economic Councils were made operational. The former had the task of elaborating the National Five Year Plan; the latter could give recommendations on regional economic matters. They were described by Gay (1989) as an indicative planning with something of a regional dimension. The plans for 1971–1975 and 1976–1980 gave very little space to regional matters and the regions (for instance the Flemish region) were simply recognized as areas in which nationally defined policies for economic sectors would be implemented. None of these Five Year Plans were ever finally approved. Nevertheless they were an important step in the decentralization process of planning competence. During the 1980s, with the formal devolution process of Belgium, competence on certain matters such as spatial planning and regional economic policy was withdrawn from the national level and allocated to the level of the Flemish Region. The emergence of more liberal principals in the 1980s finalized the suspension of these types of national economic planning.

The framework of the Law on Economic Planning and Decentralization (1970) established also Regional Development Authorities in each Flemish province, with specific tasks and modes of operation. These Authorities had a more active role in the elaboration of an economic policy for a maximization of economic development. As Albrechts (1992) indicates, these Regional Development Authorities have played a major role in producing studies on the socio-economic needs of the area, formulated proposals and promoted economic activity, spatial planning, improvements in the social and economic infrastructure as well as undertaken concrete action to facilitate or expand private and public investment (e.g. expropriating land, buying and selling premises, providing infrastructure, etc.). Some Regional Development Authorities, such as the one in the province of West Flanders, have played a major role in interfering in the process of spatial planning and development.

The ideas of regional planning and balanced development, as they were developed in the policies and programmes described above, has been of great importance for the planners who were working, in the 1950s and 1960s, on the establishment of the spatial planning system in general and on the regional studies in particular. Spatial planning was seen as an instrument that was usable to aim for a more rational and efficient spatial organization of the production structure in order to reach the goals of an interregional balanced economic expansion and growth of welfare. This expressed a conceptual link between spatial planning thought on regional levels and the classical concept of regional development as it was also observed by Saey (1988) in the parliamentary preparations of the Law of 1962 on Town and Country Planning. The aim was to renew the old economic machinery; the tools for that purpose were a better allocation of enterprises and the construction of an efficient traffic network.

The idea of a comprehensive link between spatial and economic development was present in the regional studies and reflections on regional development at that time, although Albrechts (1992) remarked the little influence of, for example, the growth-pole theory (Perroux) in these studies. It was in the 1970s that this theory became a dominant concept in a scientific report on spatial planning on a regional level. This report commissioned by the former National Commission for Spatial Planning (1979, Nationale Commissie voor de Ruimtelijke Ordening) can be seen as a final stage of the specific period in thought, but not in practice, on regional and spatial planning in Belgium. This was an approach out of a more functional vision of space. The original regional studies, worked out in the 1950s and 1960s were orientated by a conception of regions in a more classical geographical way.

A common criticism of the conception and implementation of spatial and regional-economic planning is their reduction to planning of separated objects. Spatial policy and the policy on regional economic development were in fact elaborated as separated activities. Although the spatial planning system provided in regional plans was seen as regional structure plans, the elaboration of a hierarchical system of plans resulted on the supra-local level only in pragmatic zoning. The sector plans were essentially aimed at a functional coordination and facilitation of spatial claims. Additionally the regional economic development policies, programmed since the 1950s, merely saw spatial planning as an instrument for a more rational – efficient – spatial organization, in reaching goals for economic development and growth of welfare. In that perspective the sector plans offered tools for a broader allocation of economic activities. Strategic planning was incriminated as merely a functional coordination of space; the sector plans were tools for economic development, for instance the design of industrial zoning.

Elements of the Socio-economic, Cultural and Political Context and its Implications for Strategic Planning

The political, economic and cultural differences between the two Belgian communities resulted in inadequacy to cope with economic and geographical realities, for instance as mentioned above the determination of 'regions'. This was, according to Gay (1989), one of the greatest weaknesses in Belgium's complex and administrative framework. The historic socio-economic differences between the northern and southern part of Belgium, as Mandel (1963, quoted in Massey 1978) and Albrechts and Swyngedouw (1989) have remarked, resulted in divergent political strategies towards the formulation of economic (development) policies and according to the concepts for national and regional planning. Gay (1989) has explained this reality in a clear way as he mentioned the difficulties in devising a regional policy that was other than 'a costly compromise acquired at State's expense'.

Nevertheless these policies produced a relative success as within the framework of the Expansion Legislation of July 1959. The regional policies indeed have achieved a measure of success, for instance in the establishment of numerous industrial estates. In Flanders the industrial estates (developed and equipped by the state, port authorities, agencies for regional development, special inter-communales and private firms) have allowed the region to catch up its rather slow rate of early industrialization. Investments by foreign capital during the 1960s were to a large extent located in the northern part of Belgium (Gay 1989). The internationalization of capital brought the traditional Wallonian industry to a deep crisis. This development deepened the socio-economic differences between the northern and southern part of the country and was expressed in the confrontation during the 1960s between two geographically separate communities who have advocated in general total different models of social organisation (Albrechts and Swyngedouw 1989). These developments had the effect of slowing down the further determination during the 1960s of regional planning in general and the determination of regions as the object of these policies in particular, but it eventually has facilitated the process towards devolution.

Also some other dimensions of the Belgian socio-cultural context can be characterized as an even greater burden on the development of planning practice. De Decker *et al.* (1987) quoted Strauven (1980) to indicate the contemporary individualism, leading to spatial anarchy, which was instrumented especially after the Second World War. This process has its foundations in the constitution, which was one of the most liberal in 19th century Europe. The central idea was the development of a situation in which the individual full of initiative could ameliorate and extend his position in the social hierarchy. The almost unbounded right of economic initiative and property took an exceptional place in it, because parcelling out and building would remain throughout recent history mainly a private matter. As De Decker further explains, the specific attitude towards the urban and industrial evolution of Belgium since the 19th century has been rather anti-urban. To stop the migration of the labour force towards the main urban-industrial centres specific policies were designed. For instance, the introduction since 1869 of the social commutation ticket for employees. This commutation ticket has thoroughly changed the regional outlook of Flanders. The consequences were that labourers continued living in the countryside and that the extension of vast labour working-class quarters – and the rise and growth of an urban working class – was slowed down. In the period between the two world wars a specific public housing corporation (NMKL) was established to operate in the countryside. They constructed mainly single houses with gardens in neighbourhood units inspired by the ideas of Ebenezer Howard. The aim of this activity was also to stop the migration to the cities. After the Second World War, increasing unemployment, amongst other reasons, caused the government to set up a policy to stimulate the building of houses. The De Taeye Law (May 1948) stimulated, by a premium system, the acquisition of property. Private and public housing were mainly situated in the urban fringe and in the countryside, as land was relatively cheap. Suburbanization became the main problem of spatial organization and an important issue for planners.

But, as mentioned above, the sector plans became a part of the problem rather than solving it. In the procedure of approval of the sector plans the public inquiry at the local level, the engagement of many local politicians and the lobby work of real estate groups influenced the detailed zoning plans. These changes were ad hoc and mostly not carried out within a more integrative structural approach in spatial planning. As a result, one of the main goals of the sector plans, initially formulated by the planning experts, namely the containment of urban sprawl, was eroded. This process is a clear example of how the idea of planning was challenged and tackled by populist clientelism. Spatial planning and land use management in Flanders is characterized by a tradition of liberal principles to the allocation of housing and economic activities, in which the importance of property rights is a main factor. A wide dispersion of settlement and laissez-faire attitude towards the idea of physical planning were the results.

Countering the Planning System: The Concept of Structure Planning

During and after the establishment of the sector plans planners and decision-makers criticized the planning method and its factual implementation. The criticism resulted in the formulation of a planning method called 'structure planning' in the mid-1970s (Vermeersch 1975). The context of this counter methodology was on the one hand the overall change in planning thought towards a more process-oriented planning; this evolution was not passed by the Flemish planning community at that time. Also, the central issue in the 1970s regarding the role of planners as interveners in social reality had an effect on the way planning thought and practice were seen in Flanders.

Structure planning as a method of planning has been used on the local level in Flanders since its definition by Vermeersch (1975). Structure planning presents itself as a comprehensive, continuous, cyclic, participation-oriented and action-oriented planning process. The characteristic orientation of structure planning is process orientation and its purpose is a voluntary perspective. This method allowed planners to see planning as an instrument that belongs to a concrete context of society and that carries in it such context. Most of all they had an implicit aim to change the long-term developments of society with a specific strategic approach in the short term.

The process-orientated approach made it possible to deal with various uncertainties regarding the object of planning at the appropriate time. The scope for flexibility in regard to the substantive aspect was ensured. This formulation was a reaction against an 'end-state approach' (blueprint approach) of zoning plans at the local and sub-regional level. Because of its procedural conception – a step-by-step process from the normative to the strategic and the operational level

– this process allows the interference of citizen participation in the explicit moments of the planning process. Consequently the aim was to open the decision-making in current planning practice. The inquiry applied in the current planning system, for instance in the elaboration of the sector plans, only allowed a possibility of interference at the end of the procedure. On the one hand this way of interference only led to protest and conflict and not to a full participatory engagement. On the other hand the disclosure of decision-making also led to parallel, hidden, circuits of decision-making.

Structure planning, as a method of planning, dealt with substantial and procedural aspects of planning. The reason of its existence as a counter-planning is to be found in the context of that time: process- and participatory-oriented planning. The substantial object of the planning process was to recognize the structure itself of the spatial environment of the planning subject and to render an explicit vision of its future development, as a structural framework offering suggestions and directions to public decision-making. Most of all the method of structure planning became the moral property of community groups who countered the exclusive rights of authorities to regulate the communal environment.

But in all these years the structure planning did not find a judicial ground. Implementation of tasks set up in the structure planning were only possible by a parallel implementation procedure with the existing documents in the current planning system. This can be considered as a weakness of the instrument, as pragmatic decision-makers can only with great difficulties be convinced of the relevance of this structural learning approach in their incremental day-to-day practice. But on the other hand this can mean a strength as the informality of the process creates a freedom of choice. This can lead to more creativity in the planning and design process.

Until the early 1990s, with one exceptional case, structure planning remained a planning process used on the local level. Nevertheless it can be seen as an important learning process for planners, decision-makers and people involved in the process. Even if the structure planning process was not implemented directly in a statutory plan or in concrete actions of planning authorities, the learning process was necessary for a valuable politicization of the planning discussion. The implications of participatory involvement in the process were especially important. For professional planners and members of local planning agencies it was a learning process by which they became more involved in the planning discussions in their community on the one hand, while gaining expertise in a more structural way of thinking about the future spatial development in their community.

The Planning System Under Pressure

The general thought in the 1980s, defended by planning professionals, academics and many politicians, saw planning as an instrument and thereby not as a strategy to intervene in the process of social and economic development (Albrechts 1994).

This thesis is based on a view of limited state intervention, in contrast with the models of planning and development strategies formulated in the 1960s and 1970s. This assumption and its circumstantial effect on the development of planning thought and planning practice in Flanders underlines the remark that there is in Flanders no tradition for planning (Allaert 1994).

Once beyond the planning horizon (1980) of the sector plans, a tendency due to economic dynamics (the need for relocation of industrial plants, changes in the distribution and logistic system) and changed public opinion (for instance on environmental issues) undermined the statutory position of the sector plans. The strategy of local governments and sectorial lobby groups towards fragmented one-issue inspired revisions of the sub-regional sector plans was undoubtedly a reason. The ambition of these revisions was, for instance, the expansion of zoning areas for economic activities which were often contested/tackled in the public forum by community/environmental groups. Besides, during the 1980s the planning practice and the general acceptance towards planning slowed down. Initiatives concerning land use management were often decided ad hoc. This situation resulted partly in an immobility in the decision-making process or in contested decisions. Both eroded the legitimacy of planning while they created an atmosphere of uncertainty and indistinctiveness. The more general context of planning in Flanders, mentioned above, has increased this condition.

To conquer this situation of immobility in planning and decision-making, answers were formulated in the late 1980s, for instance a more sectorial approach by interest groups, regional Chambers of Commerce and Industry, Regional Development Authorities, inter-communales for regional development. The cases of the regional Chambers of Commerce and Industry who launched Strategic Plans, for example in the regions of Kortrijk, Oostende and Gent, are characteristic, beneath the strategic plans for regional development formulated by the public Regional Development Authorities, for instance in the provinces of Western Flanders and Limburg. All of these plans came out of a process of collaboration of privileged actors (for instance captains of industry, leading politicians, scientific experts), and an orientation towards the development of 'endogenous potentials' and were characterized by an action-oriented entrepreneurial approach. The key issue was 'getting things done'.

The discourse on interregional competition, ascribed to scale enlargement of socio-economic processes and the growing exchangeability of places, is a hypothesis used to explain the broader perspective and momentum of the formulations of these regional strategies and visions. The constant issue in these strategies is the enforcement of the economic and spatial (locational) strengths of the region. The plan implementation deduced from that purpose the functional adaptation of the regional space and advocates consequently for the availability of instruments of spatial planning.

The content of these plans is referring to a comprehensive multi-issued view on development and spatial organization, but the purpose is mainly economic, the statutory position is no more than informal, the targets are sectorial and the actors involved in the collaboration are chosen on a rather selective base. However, these facts erode their claim as a 'regional vision' and undermine their legitimacy in planning. Nevertheless, the inductive capacity in pointing out the agenda for 'regional discussion' is important.

These developments, mentioned above, partially led to the re-emergence of the need for an integrative strategic framework to deal with the problems of spatial organization and regional development. This evolution led finally on the on hand towards strategic planning initiatives at regional level and on the other hand to the reformulation of the idea of a 'structure plan for Flanders', as a more integrative answer by the planners' community.

By the early 1980s, very soon after the approval of the last sub-regional zoning plan, the search for a conceptual coherence in spatial planning and development in Flanders was reformulated and conceptually linked with an overall structure plan for the Flemish region as a whole. The facilitation of this new development was partially the gain of an exclusive responsibility on spatial planning by the Flemish region.

The professional and academic experts formulated an answer to the frictions between the planning system and the factual development based on the idea of the elaboration of a comprehensive integrative vision on the spatial structure and development of Flanders: the Structure Plan for Flanders. This project of the experts was sometimes supported by individual politicians or enlightened ministers responsible for spatial planning. But the effective elaboration of the plan became a rather mythical concept during the 1980s. Only in the 1990s did it become a political factor. A later section in this chapter (The Project of the Structure Plan for Flanders) examines the outlines of this project and its perspectives for the development of planning thought and planning practice in Flanders.

The Re-orientation of Regional Policy and its Implications for Strategic Planning

In the late 1980s a discussion on the relevance of an additional Flemish regional programme took place. There was a general feeling in leading socio-economic consultative committees that the Flemish reconversion and expansion policy focused at that time towards the coal basin of Limburg ('Kempense Steenkoolmijnen') could be widened to more areas in Flanders. A monitoring of the socio-economic situation of the (sub-)regions in Flanders was executed by the Socio-Economic Council of Flanders (Sociaal Economische Raad Van Vlaanderen 1994). Both discussions and evaluations resulted in a general understanding that there were, beneath the problem areas recognized by the European Commission, still some smaller sub-regions that could be given special attention towards their development. The outcome was that eight sub-regions were marked and named according to the programme as 'Impulse Regions'. These rural and urban sub-regions were selected according to socio-economic criteria. For each region a 'regional manager' was selected with a budget to create and implement projects over a period of three years (1991–1994).

The programme is specifically economically oriented and the link, integration, with spatial planning on the regional level is not obvious. The instruments of planning were important to illustrate the degrees of freedom in project implementation (infrastructure, industrial estates). Nevertheless some interesting observations, usual for the further outline of a regional approach in planning can be made.

An evaluation by Van den Stockt and Van den Bergh (1993) has showed that the small base of the chosen selection criteria was hardly able to establish significant 'regions'. The Impulse Regions were often found to be too small to carry the proposed projects. The effectiveness of the classical reconversion approach and the creation of direct employment seems to be rather low, while the effective use of new industrial estates will be probably most of all due to relocation of existing enterprises. This still reflects the traditional policy of regional incentives, mainly geographically differentiated towards industrial investments (Cabus 1995).

Another often-heard criticism during the first year of the programme was the lack of coherence between various projects, such as infrastructural (the development of industrial estates and improvement of accessibility) and even tourism projects in more rural areas. The large variety of possible projects also has showed the complexity of territorial potentials, often a critical condition that generates conflicts in spatial claims. The need for the integration of different projects within the programmes and common problem-solving came in a more explicit way on the agenda.

As the programme broadens the regional agenda, two major shifts in the 'Impulse Region Programme' became evident. The first concerns the organizational approach itself – the shift from project-based to a more comprehensive approach. The second considers a conceptual change in the targets of regional development in general.

To resolve the incoherence problems in the project-oriented approach it was decided to work out a regional vision in collaboration with the regional committee (in which regional politicians, trade unions and the business community were involved). A learning process on regional thought was activated within these consultative committees, the forming of a social network and inter-municipality cooperation was encouraged and a more comprehensive way of thinking about the region was induced. Partnerships between local and regional authorities and (inter)national authorities became the rule (Cabus 1995). The process of regional networking and preliminary comprehensive thinking can be considered as important innovations in regional development practice. From a purely regional economic approach greater attention was paid to non-economic factors important for regional development, such as territorial and environmental quality.

One of the results of this conceptual shift is the actual possibility, offered and encouraged by the Flemish government, for regional socio-economic and political actors to organize their region within so-called regional platforms. This illustrates the broadened perspective of the new regional policy. Partnerships between public and private actors and between local and central authorities, who meet at a regional level, became a more common rule.

The second, conceptual, shift concerns the formulation of the targets of regional development in Flanders. Cabus (1993) has stressed the relativity of a regional policy within Flanders in relation to a policy to support backward regions. In this perspective the performance of the urban network, with a high degree of functional penetration in the Flemish region, is becoming an important issue in spatial economic development thought. A discussion on the goals of regional development and the use of financial means as incentives towards so-called backward regions was initiated. The Flemish government formulated a policy to use their scarce development resources to hold and reinforce the strong competitive position of the best performing localities (spaces) in the spatial (urban-economic) structure of Flanders. This strategy was further worked out by the Socio-Economic Council of Flanders in advice on regional development, mainly in preparation for the revision of the regions which could benefit from European Structural Funds. This new concept on regional development is inspired by the ambition of an efficiently run regional development policy, of which the targets for regional planning are the organization of an efficient and balanced urban network (Momper (CEMAT) 1992). In this perspective the strong regions became the subject of regional policy. As a consequence the attention towards backward regions is passed on to the European level.

The Project of the Structure Plan for Flanders

The Structure Plan, prepared by a team of experts, chosen outside the administration, is now approved by the Flemish government as a guidance for the partial revisions of the current sector plans. But the Structure Plan for Flanders still has no legal foundation and is therefore no formal part of the planning system.

One of the fundamental failures of the ambition that planners had in mind for the sector plans, namely the containment of urban sprawl, was pointed out above. This aim was hardly reached, but the same normative goals are still present in the notion of sustainable spatial development, used as a basic idea for the Flemish Structure Plan. Albrechts (1994), one of the two senior academics leading the project team for the Flemish Structure Plan, describes this new Structure Plan for Flanders as a vehicle for introducing structural change in the field of spatial planning. The structural reorientation of the policies of the last decade, which resulted in an increasing decline of the environment, had a major impact on the functioning of society as a whole and on spatial planning in particular. From that experience Albrechts (1994) was aware of the failures of planning in the 1970s and 1980s, and described the planning as rather naive, utopian and unsuccessful.

The innovations in Flemish strategic planning practice in the project of the Structure Plan for Flanders can be evaluated through a substantial and a procedural element.[4] The latter refers to the concepts of spatial organization that were introduced; the former refers to the cooperative decision-making model that was established at a central level.

Firstly the containment goal is now projected in a concept as the enforcement of city regions, bounding of growth towards urbanized areas, and deconcentrated bundling (clustering). The whole of these spatial concepts is formulated in a central metaphor: Flanders, Urban and Open (Albrechts and Vermeersch 1994). The most relevant concept is the deconcentrated bundling of economic urban activities. The principal objective of this spatial concept is the enforcement of a well organized urban system with an explicit hierarchical structure and a finely-woven pattern throughout the containment of its growth.

The target of the spatial policy follows the spatial concept on regional development, as described above. Both policies meet with a mutual perception of spatial organisation and preferential treatment of the locations of the urban network, and consequently a stringent policy of growth allocation.

Second, to tackle issues related to action orientation and the building of public support necessary to implement the plan, a cooperative model was constructed for the process of the Structure Plan (Albrechts 1994). The basic structure of the cooperative model consists of three groups of actors – the government, the planners and the organized population – and is based on the initial ideas of the structure planning. On the other hand the challenge of the cooperation in the structure plan was to integrate the various sectorial departments. The outcome of the technical integration of the sectorial policies was discussed in a steering committee in which the three groups of actors regularly met. The ultimate goal in working in this way with sectors is to reach a collective (spatial) agreement through bargaining and lobbying and to ratify this agreement formally. Transferring the method of structure planning, designed to the scope of local practice, towards large-scale application in the project of the structure plan, clearly shows its general inappropriateness as well as the lack of consensus in the cooperation model between the different participants. Coordinating the different agencies towards a common strategy according to the substantial reference of the project, namely the sustainable spatial development, emphasized more a closed bargaining between interest groups. Cabus (1994) has mentioned that there was never a real commitment of various sectorial partners to collaborate and Saey (1994) has concluded that this will lead to a parallel, hidden, circuit of decision-making.

4 According to Faludi (1987), in planning methodology the distinction can also be made between a more decision-centred and object-centred approach. The concept behind structure planning can be seen as dealing with both these approaches.

A Changing Context and Content for Planning

In the 1970s several experiences with structure planning gradually emphasized the inclusion of public participation in planning. Although this evolution slowed during the 1980s, the involvement of different public and private actors in the planning process has steadily grown. The involvement of private groups in urban and regional planning referring to city and regional marketing process principles characterized planning thought and practice in the late 1980s (Allaert and Tydgat 1994). The activity of private groups in formulating regional strategies, as above mentioned, is another clear element of this evolution. The inclusion of public and private participation in planning illustrates the trend towards a gradual enlargement of the community involved in planning (such as the public, social organizations, public and private institutions, various groups of professionals, etc.). This collaboration within the planning process became gradually a main characteristic for feasible and efficient planning.

The return of substantive issues is undoubtedly another important evolution in planning thought and planning practice. The integrative approach of planning, a key element of the discipline, refers to the need for a substantial frame of reference (Albrechts 1993). The design-oriented turn in Western urban planning and development during the 1980s, and the few experiences with this method in Flemish cities, is a modest example of this turn. Far more important in the development of planning thought is the attention towards 'substantial planning concepts' (concepts on spatial organization and development) in Dutch strategic planning practice in the late 1980s and their communicative function in the decision-making process (Zonneveld 1991). The emergence of the theme of sustainable development in general and the relation to sustainable spatial development (Blowers 1993, Roberts 1994) also emphasizes the need for innovative concepts of spatial organization. Consequently the focus has shifted towards the professional task in the formulation of qualitative substantial planning frameworks that deals with the optimization of economic, ecological, social and spatial environmental issues in a regional dimension (Allaert 1993). Following Allaert, the key element from a methodological point of view is the definition of 'territorial quality' and the operationlization of this concept within the planning and decision-making process.

Roberts (1994) has traced the origins of regional planning to its environmental concerns, linked with principles of resource management and a comprehensive planning approach (for instance river basin regions – see the case of the Tennessee Valley Authority) and with concepts of territorial integration (put forward by Friedmann and Weaver (1979)) emphasizing balanced development between natural and socio-economic systems within a territory. Roberts argues that the principles for sustainable development are basically linked with regional planning as the sustainable planning of regions (characterized in their Fordist modes of spatial organization by a neglect of the environmental consequences of production). Roberts (1994) situates the roots for a strategy for a sustainable regional planning, and the objective of a sustainable spatial organization, within a post-Fordist mode of regulation that tackles both ecological and economic problems. Roberts (1994) assumes the creation of consensus to ensure the implementation of agreed objectives. This 'strategic vision approach' includes in his vision cooperation in the formulation and generation of the planning process as a whole.

Friedmann (1993) has remarked that, in linking knowledge to action, the planner should work normatively, innovatively, politically and transactively. Regarding the objectives of regional planning, as Roberts has put forward, and following Friedmann (1989), planning that seeks to improve the quality of the environment for the whole population is seen to become increasingly politicized. This concept of planning is in the interest of those planners who felt responsible for potential future developments in society. The normative approach, expressed by Friedmann, implies the formulation of qualitative substantial answers on spatial and social organization and development, as Albrechts (1994) is aware regarding the planning process of the Flemish structure plan. This, rather voluntary, orientation is according to Brooks (1988) the essence of planning: to visualize the ideal future community and to work towards its realization.

Following Faludi (1987) planning methods are ways to structure a necessary dialogue between planners and outside actors in finding correct answers to the planning situation. This view entails, says Faludi, an argumentative approach. This methodological approach in planning should reduce the danger of decision-making, as experts only arrogate it to themselves, described as technocracy. Planning was associated with technical and bureaucratic disclosures of the debate and the dominant position of scientific rationalism. Faludi encourages a way of planning that opens this debate.

This view accords with the idea of planning linked with the concepts of democracy and progress that centres on the challenge to find ways in which citizens can act together in managing their collective concerns with respect to sharing space and time (Friedmann 1987, quoted in Healey 1993). A focus for a further alternative conception of planning purposes and practices is the exploration of the communicative dimensions of collectively debating and deciding on matters of collective concern. This idea is put forward by Healey (1993) as she discusses the work of Forrester (1989) and the conditions of communicative rationality following the work of Habermas. This process is, according to Dryzek (1993), linked with participatory and discursive democracy. Healey (1993) is convinced that Habermas' communicative rationality offers a way forward through a different conception of human living in shared space and time and reasoning formed within inter-subjective communication, as is required in finding agreements on how to address our collective concerns. Nevertheless, an important problem, in a communicative turn in decision-making, rests with the conditions of consensus formation and the unequal position of the actors involved.

The communicative turn in planning thought is going beyond the classic idea that the central resource of reasoning is obtained from scientific knowledge and rational procedures. Additionally the conceptions of democratic acting become far more important. Healey (1993) emphasizes in this perspective the collective and interactive process of addressing and working out planning concerns. In that respect planning through debate, as she advocates in this model, is based on a positive and active collaborative approach. Faludi and Korthals Altes (1994) see communicative planning as a more sociocratic approach that pays attention to the views of others, in contrast with a technocratic approach that assumes a strong role for authorities in safeguarding the public interest.

The role for planners becomes less central; their function and the communicative potentials of the plan are therefore to encourage and to steer public debate and decision-making. Strong communicative concepts of spatial organization (according to Zonneveld 1991) are in that respect a vehicle for opening the debate on planning, enlarging the community involved in planning and finally a firm consensus building.

Conditions and Opportunities for Strategic Planning in Flanders

The regional level as momentum for further experience

This chapter has argued that there was no real tradition in spatial planning at the regional level in Flanders. Even the sector plans were in fact the product of centralized planning. This tradition is still working through in the conception of the new planning system on the level of the Flemish region. Now the centralized idea of steering the spatial development is inspired by the normative aspirations of containment and allocation of growth. The project of the structure plan originally intended to assign new locations and contingents for housing and economic activities by a quota system. These goals are believed to be attainable only by a tight centrally organized locational assignment and planning control.

The subsidiarity between planning policy at the central (the Flemish region), the intermediate (regional) and the local level is narrowed towards a concept in which the lower levels are mainly seen as an executive department. The intermediate level is seen as a passing through level in this top-down process. A preliminary evaluation of this new organization of planning is that it is at least reasoned with a mechanistic thought.

This last remark opens a discussion on what can be seen as a nonchalant approach of the 'regional' factor in planning. This chapter has observed a movement of regional mobilization in strategy and policy-making characterized by an implicit but greater collaborative approach.

A most interesting case of a recent planning process at a regional level – that expresses in a more explicit way this regional momentum to deal with spatial problems – can be observed in the region of Kortrijk. This case, relatively independent from the project of the structure plan for Flanders, includes also some elements of planning innovation through debate and structuring regional dialogue. Following a forgotten article in the 1962 Law, twelve communities are working together to formulate a common strategic vision and zoning plan for their region (GAPAK) in order to remove the friction between the existing sector plans and socio-economical development. A collaborative model, partially inspired on the cooperative models of structure planning, with relevant society groups, governmental institutions of different levels and politicians, supported by a communicative strategy, was started in 1993, and is in that respect a unique example in Flanders.

Substantial and democratic legitimacy of planning

On social and democratic grounds the relevance of a regional approach can be indicated. The centrally organized plan-making procedures in the current planning system, its rather technocratic planning approach in the past and its rather mechanistic model for the regulation of the interaction between different planning levels, and even the relative weakness of the cooperative model set up for the guidance of the planning process of the Flemish Structure Plan, advocates the necessity of the enforcement of the regional (inter-local) interplay and a collaborative approach in planning.

Even the entrepreneurial strategic plans, although they had a selective network and reductionist purpose, are an appeal to review planning practice towards a regional entity and to involve a multiple field (network of actors). The territorial-oriented approaches of central government in various experiences, although they are most of all sectorial, express the need to broaden the regional discussion.

The experiences of the regionally organized community work, the more collaborative approach of plan preparation by the inter-communale society in Kortrijk, even the bargaining process of socio-economic partners in the entrepreneurial approach of 'strategic visions' and the emergence of partnerships in regional development, illustrate the importance of the intermediate level between central and local governments.

Territorial and contextual notions of planning at regional levels

A key issues regarding actual planning practice and thought is to find firm grounds to link the collaborative turn in planning with the substantial turn in plan-making. For that case the regional level can offer a valuable condition. The complexity of the supra- and juxtaposition of spatial processes results in a more fragmented organized space. These fragments are the results of a particular integration of a historical (cultural and physical) spatial structure and more recent restructuring processes. In abstraction these spatial entities (regional spaces) are the framework of a low dynamic spatial structure and a higher dynamic process. The former can refer to a cultural-historical landscape structure or its physical ecological foundation. The latter refers to a functional structuring process, for instance the (poly)nodal urban organization, or changes in the inter-locational interdependency relations. This notion refers to the layers of development in the rewriting-reproduction-process of the social-regional space, which reflects the interaction of general processes with specific regional contingencies (Massey 1984, quoted in Johnston, Hauer and Hoekveld 1990). As the spatial planning process expresses various regional spatial entities (of various scales) the task is to look for spatial scale suitable for a practical social mobilization regarding a relevant spatial structuring process.

The thoughts above open also a reflection on some transcendent moments of (regional) planning. The notion 'transcendent moment' refers to the inductive capacity of planning to lead community debate on planning issues and therefore to deliver substantial criteria to define planning problems (socio-economic, environmental, welfare distribution, etc.). The task is to construct frameworks to structure debate in giving directions to look for solutions. In that perspective planning can be seen as an activity that reaches for community debate and consensus on its future spatial and social organization, that stimulates a common definition of the planning concerns. This reflects a 'collaborative turn' in plan-making. The importance is that this seeks the enlargement of the community involved in the planning debate (Healey 1993) and addresses a more connective approach that situates planning within an environment populated by many actors (Mastop 1989). Briefly, it is an appeal for a more sociocratic approach to planning.

As regional development policy is also gradually going beyond the traditional concept of a central government policy to channel resources to regions in order to correct the economic imbalance between one region and another and some integrative experiences at a regional level were observed, the need for a more collaborative approach in dealing with territorial integration is obvious.

Territorial integration and the planning debate

What about the role of planners and the role of the plan in this context and content? One of the basic tasks of the profession is the interdisciplinary and integrative approach and the capacity to visualize the perspective on the likely – sustainable – evolution of spatial organization. For this the planning language includes a specific communication medium: plans, such as structure plans. This condition of planning stresses the quality of the plan as communication medium. The plan should be seen in the perspective of the professional tasks of the planner mentioned above. The skills of planning have to be adapted to induce a public engagement in sharing strategic regional visions. The role of the planner is to structure the social debate about sustainable futures, and not to impose their vision of the future. Hall (1992) even makes more restrictions. Planning he says – and in that case the plan – should not claim what is good for the people, but on the contrary it should provide a resource for democratic and public decision-making. The plan as a basic instrument needs to induce mobilization of the public interest. The method of the plan should therefore be explorative and instructive.

Observations on the factual development of planning processes in the field, the organization and reformulation of regional and spatial policies of the Flemish government, the upgrading of the efficiency of regional networks of actors involved in planning, the communicative approach in the public debate in some areas show a way to a gradual enlargement of the planning community. This stresses the regional factor in policy-making. This chapter has indicated some of the substantial and social, democratic grounds for strategic planning out of the evolution of planning thought in general and planning practice in Flanders in particular. It is in that perspective, within the specific context and content of Flanders and the actual momentum of current policies and social demands, that the exploration above of the previous and actual strategic planning processes and regional development policies and economic strategies should be situated. Regarding the momentum at the regional level, the collaborative and communicative experiences have the opportunity to broaden the public discussion on planning and give direction and strength to a process that seeks a common, agreed definition of the planning situation.

References

Albrechts, L. (1992) 'Changing aspects of Belgian public planning.' In A. Dutt and F. Costa (eds) *Perspectives on Planning and Urban Development in Belgium.* Dordrecht/ Boston/London: Kluwer Academic Publishers. pp.27–42.

Albrechts, L. (1993) 'Rereading the sixties: reconsidering planning as a vehicle for structural change.' Paper for the 7th Aesop Congress Lodz, July 14–17, 1993, 19.

Albrechts, L. (1994) 'Making (national) planning work'. Paper for the 8th AESOP Congress Istanbul, August 24–27th 1994, 14.

Albrechts, L. and Swyngedouw, E. (1989) 'Regionale planning en ontwikkeling: exponenten van maatschappelijke ontwikkeling.' In Ruimtelijke Planning, Afl. 23, II.A.2.b, 40.

Albrechts, L. en Vermeersch, Ch. (1994) Ruimtelijk Structuurplan Vlaanderen. Gewenste Ruimtelijke Structuur, AROHM, Brussel.

Allaert, G. (1993) 'New approaches in environmental planning and management in Belgium: the case of the Scheldt region.' Paper presented at the European congress of the Regional Science Association, Moscow 24–27 August 1993.

Allaert, G. (1994) 'Ghent: the western node of the metropolitan network of Flanders.' In P. Kooij, and P. Pellenbarg (eds) *Regional Capitals. Past, Present, Prospects,* Van Gorcum, Assen. pp.19–35.

Allaert, G. and Tydgat, T. (1994) *Regiomarketing en regiomanagement, naar een toepassing in de ruimtelijke planning.* Gent: Academia Press.

Anselin, M. (1984) 'Belgium.' In R.H. Williams *Planning in Europe. Urban and Regional Planning in the E.E.C.* London: George Allen & Unwin. pp.63–72.

Blowers, A. (ed) (1993) 'Planning for a sustainable environment.' *A report by the Town and Country Planning Association.* London: Earthscan Publications Ltd.

Boes, M. (1992) 'Procedures for planning in the Flemish Region.' In A. Dutt and F. Costa (eds) *Perspectives on Planning and Urban Development in Belgium.* Dordrecht/Boston/ London: Kluwer Academic Publishers. pp.61–69.

Brooks, M. (1988) 'Four critical junctures in the history of the urban planning profession.' In *A.P.A. Journal 54*, 2, 241–248.

Cabus, P. (1993) 'Dossier Impulsgebieden.' In L. Goossens (ed) *Ruimtelijke Planning*. pp.1–33.

Cabus, P. (1994) 'Het Voorontwerp Ruimtelijk Structuurplan Vlaanderen van 28 maart 1994.' In *Planologisch Nieuws*, jg. 14, nr. 2, 102–110.

Cabus, P. (1995) 'Recente ontwikkelingen bij de invulling van het streekbeleid: Een aanzet tot positionering van het Vlaamse streekbeleid.' In *Planologisch Nieuws 15*, nr. 3.

De Decker, P., Lammens, E., Van Der Sluys, P., Van Der Vliet, L. and Van Severen, P. (1987) 'Flanders' urbanity – an outline.' In *Planning Outlook 30*, 2, 91–98.

Dryzek, J. (1993) 'Policy analysis and planning: from science to argument.' In F. Fischer and F. Forester (eds) *The Argumentative Turn in Policy Analysis and Planning*. University College London, 213–32.

Faludi, A. (1987) *A Decision-centred View of Environmental Planning*. Oxford: Pergamon Press.

Faludi, A. and Korthals Altes, W. (1994) 'Evaluating communicative planning: a revised design for performance research.' In *European Planning Studies 2*, nr 4, 403–418.

Faludi, A. and van der Valk, A. (1994) *Rule and order. Dutch planning doctrine in the Twentieth Century*. Dordrecht, Kluwer Academic Publishers.

Friedmann, J. (1987) *Planning in the Public Domain: From Knowledge to Action*. Princeton, NJ: Princeton University press.

Friedmann, J. (1989) 'Planning politics and the environment.' *A.P.A. Journal 55*, 3, 334–38.

Friedmann, J. (1993) 'Towards a non euclidian mode of planning.' *A.P.A. Journal 59*, nr; 4, 482–85.

Friedmann, J. and Weaver, C. (1979) *Territory and Function: The Evolution of Regional Planning*. Berkeley and Los Angeles, CA: University of California Press.

Gay, F.J. (1989) 'Benelux.' In H.D. Clout (ed) *Regional Development in Western Europe*. London: David Fulton Publishers.

Hall, P. (1992) *Urban and Regional Planning*. London: Routledge.

Healey, P. (1993) 'Planning through debate: the communicative turn in planning theory.' In F. Fischer and F. Forester (eds) *The Argumentative Turn in Policy Analysis and Planning*. University College London. pp.233–53.

Healey, P. (1994) 'The argumentative turn in planning theory and its implications for spatial strategy formation.' Paper presented to the Conference *Are Local Strategies Possible – Planning Theory and Social Theory in the Face of Sustainable Development Problematique*. Tampere University of Technology, USA, September 22–25.

Johnston, R.J., Hauer, J. and Hoekveld, G.A. (1990) *Regional Geography – Current Developments and Future Prospects*. London and New York: Routledge.

Laconte, P. (1992) 'The administrative structure of planning in Belgium.' In A. Dutt and F. Costa (eds) *Perspectives on Planning and Urban Development in Belgium*. Dordrecht/ Boston/London: Kluwer Academic Publishers. pp.43–59.

Lagrou, E. (1983) 'De gewestplannen 1962–1980: de gemiste kans.' In *Ruimtelijke Planning*, Afl. 8, II.A.2.b., 84.

Massey, D. (1978), 'Survey: regionalism – some current issues.' In *Capital and Class*, 6, 106–25.

Mastop, J.M. (1989) 'The case of provincial structure planning.' In A. Faludi (ed) *Keeping the Netherlands in Shape (Special Issue): Built Environment*, 15, 49–56.

Momper, N. (CEMAT) (1992) *European Regional Planning Strategy*. Strasbourg: Council of Europe.

Roberts, P. (1994) 'Sustainable regional planning.' In *Regional Studies 28*, 8, 781–787.

Saey, P. (1988) De eerste generatie projecten van ruimtelijke ordening op macro-niveau in Vlaanderen, Publikaties van het Seminarie voor Menselijke en Ekonomische Geografie Universiteit Gent, nr. 17.

Saey, P. (1994) 'Kan het ruimtelijk structuurplan Vlaanderen gerealiseerd worden?' In *Planologisch nieuws*, jg. 14, nr. 2, 90–101.

Sociaal Economische Raad Van Vlaanderen (1994), Rapport 1994 m.b.t. de regionale ontwikkeling.

Strauven, F. (1980) 'Hoe België zijn huidige aanblik kreeg.' *Wonen-Ta/BK, 12*, 7–20.

Van den Stockt, W. and Van den Bergh, M. (1993) Evaluatie van het produkt en het proces van het 'Impulsgebiedenbeleid 1991–1994'.

Vermeersch, Ch. (1975) De structuurplanning als type ruimtelijke planning, een geldig alternatief?, in Stero, nr. 10, 24–34.

Whitaker's Almanack (1995) London: J. Whitaker & Sons, p.819.

Zonneveld, W. (1991) Conceptvorming in de Ruimtelijke Planning. Patronen en processen, Planologisch en Demografisch Instituut, Universiteit van Amsterdam, Amsterdam.

CHAPTER 10

Competitiveness, Innovation and Technical Change from a Nordic Perspective

A New Tool for Regional Economic Development

Roland N-G Gustafsson

Introduction

This chapter provides a private sector approach to regional economic development within the context of heightened international competition. It focuses upon the Scandinavian countries of Norway, Sweden, Denmark and Finland – all of whom except Norway are members of the European Union (EU). The essence of this chapter discusses the increasing importance of technical change and innovation for firms who are active in a highly competitive European, and indeed global, market. The issues of competitiveness, innovation and technical change are the key concepts which are continually uttered and espoused by the European Commission with regard to regional development, and they provided the cornerstone for the Commission's Fifth Periodic Report (1994) entitled *Competitiveness and Cohesion: Trends in the Regions* (see Chapter 1).

The Nordic Economies

Historically speaking, the Nordic area as a whole has experienced fast economic growth. In the 1950s, Sweden was among the richest nations in the industrial world, but since then the other Nordic countries have caught up. Measured in terms of gross domestic product (GDP) per capita, Norway has in fact surpassed Sweden, and Finland overtook Denmark during the 1980s. All the Nordic countries must be regarded as open economies, Norway being the most open and, at the same time, with the thinnest and most vulnerable export base. Norway stands out as the Nordic country with the most concentrated export pattern, relying on fewer products and fewer markets than any of the others. By international standards, the Nordic countries are geographically rather specialized in their exports. All the

Nordic countries count the United Kingdom and Germany among their most important trading partners. The EU, as a whole, is certainly the most important export market for Nordic firms. The share of the EU in total Nordic exports is more than 50 per cent, ranging from about 45 per cent in Finland to over 60 per cent in Norway. In addition inter-Nordic trade is of great importance: more than 20 per cent of the total exports of each country ends up in the Nordic region.

The manufacturing industries in the four Nordic countries exhibit quite different corporate structures. The huge Swedish corporations are much larger than the large companies in the other Nordic countries. On average, the Swedish manufacturing companies employ more than twice the average number of employees in the largest Finnish, Danish and Norwegian companies. The production of large Swedish companies is more internationally oriented than that of large Danish, Finnish and Norwegian companies. Half the number of employees in these Swedish companies is in their foreign subsidiaries. In large Danish corporations foreign subsidiaries account for a quarter of the corporate personnel, in Norwegian corporations one-fifth, and in Finnish companies one-sixth. These large companies operate in the other Nordic countries through subsidiaries. The Finnish and Norwegian companies are relatively the most Nordic, having more than a third of their foreign operations in another Nordic country. The large Swedish companies are the least Nordic in this respect, reflecting the world-wide base of their business. However, in absolute terms, this group of Swedish companies has more people employed in the Nordic countries than the groups of large Danish, Finnish or Norwegian companies.

Ownership of these largest manufacturers in the Nordic countries is predominantly domestic. The relative importance of large companies in the domestic economies of the Nordic countries is also shown in the export figures. In Finland and Sweden the 10 largest export companies account up for one-third or more of exports. In Denmark export concentration in this respect is much lower, probably well below 20 per cent. While manufacturing companies dominate exports in these three countries, petroleum production puts oil companies at the top of the Norwegian list, and even causes a higher concentration ratio for Norway than for the other three countries. However, while a few large domestic companies dominate international sales and operations of Swedish, Finnish and Norwegian manufacturing, a large set of fairly small companies are responsible for Danish exports.

The future of the Nordic economies as advanced welfare states rests with their capacity to remain a competitive base for the production of products and services for international markets. Although one can see a stronger interdependence of manufacturing and services, manufacturing will continue to play a vital leadership role for the other industrial sectors. The importance of the manufacturing sector will not diminish in a foreseeable future.

The Nordic economies, and Sweden's in particular, seem to be developing in two directions. Many of the 50 largest industrial groups, which represent the

Table 10.1 The top 50 industries in Norden

Name of industrial sector		Sweden	Empl	Turnover		Norway	Empl	Turnover		Finland	Empl	Turnover		Denmark	Empl	Turnover	Number of Empl	Turnover MSEK
Manufacturing	1	ABB	215154	157993														
	2	Volvo	68797	83185														
	3	Electrolux	150900	82434														
	20	Saab-Scania	29388	29035														
	21	SKF	49305	27930														
	22	Terta Pak	13172	27000														
	25	Trelleborg	21939	25601														
	34	Sandvik	25781	18256														
	35	Alfa Laval	20809	17881														
	41	Atlas Copco	21507	15915														
	44	ASEA	18066	15445														
	50	Saab-Automobile	13626	14697					42	Valmet	17646	15685					666090	531057
Conglomeraos	7	KF	33760	59225	8	Norsk Hydro	33042	57816	15	Repola	33987	36374	46	Östasiatiska Komp.	15888	15383		
	14	Procordia	47500	37033					23	Eka-Koncernen	22566	26572						
	26	Nordstjernan	23178	23158														
	45	Bilspeditionen	10341	15432													220262	270993
Petroleum					5	Sstatoil	13222	68611	4	Neste	11278	72343					24500	140954
Wholesale	32	Ikea	18612	41921					9	Kesko	8111	47374						
	11	ICA	16850	19400					38	SOK	6786	16357					50359	125052
Pulp/Paper	6	Stora	69691	62369					27	Kymmene	17567	21041						
	19	SCA	30139	31366														
	33	MoDo	12961	18463													130358	133239
Electronics	10	Ericsson	66138	46400					16	Nokia	37336	34336					103474	80736

Table 10.1 The top 50 industries in Norden (continued)

Name of industrial sector		*Sweden*	*Empl*	*Turnover*		*Norway*	*Empl*	*Turnover*		*Finland*	*Empl*	*Turnover*		*Denmark*	*Empl*	*Turnover*	*Number of Empl*	*Turnover MSEK*
Trading	13	Axel Johnson	17908	37210													17908	37210
Construction	12	Skanska	31746	37216													31746	37216
Transportation	17	SAS	40830	31883	17	SAS								17 SAS				
	30	SJ	35017	20152													75847	52035
Service	18	Televerket	47971	31415														
	29	Posten	57372	20553													1053431	51968
Chemical	24	Nobel Industrier	26654	26399						36 Kemira	15256	17661					41910	44060
Retailing	48	Systembolaget	2704	15351										28 FDB	14405	20836	17109	36157
Mining	43	SSAB	12014	15619						37 Outokumpu	18819	17511					30833	33130
Power	31	Vattenfall	10100	19462													10100	19462
Shipping														39 Tank-og Ruteskibe		16152	0	16152
Others	40	Esselte	175541	16050													17554	16050
Total			1277484	1141449			46264	126427			189352	305254			30293	52341	1543393	1625471

Source: Gustafsson (1992)

backbone of the Nordic economy, are internationalizing at a fast rate, growing more rapidly abroad than at home (see Table 10.1). The major part of their turnover is generated outside Norden.[1] As their employment-base is growing faster abroad than at home they will transform more and more into an *offshore* economy, developing under the conditions of global competition. On the other hand, the non-trade and public sectors represent an *onshore* economy, which runs the danger of developing at a slower rate and with lower productivity.

In respect of *techno-globalization*, the Nordic research and development (R&D) resources totalled US$10 billion in 1987. However, this should be compared with the total R&D costs in the world which are estimated at US$200 billion. The Nordic resources as a whole amount to some 190 thousand scientists and qualified engineers. Government support accounts for about 40 per cent of the total R&D expenditure. Sweden accounts for just over half of the total government support in the Nordic countries, but the proportion fell during the 1980s. Denmark's and Finland's shares have increased whereas Norway's remain more or less unchanged. In Sweden some 3 per cent of gross national product (GNP) is invested in R&D. The main part of governmental R&D support is given to the academic institutions (0.7 per cent of GNP). Compared with the support to academic R&D, the investment in cooperative R&D is at a modest level, i.e. around 300 million Swedish Krona per year.

The regional division of Norden has been brought in line with EU nomenclature for territorial units for statistics on the so-called NUTS II level. In a borderless economy, the units that make sense are the *natural economic zones* – regions that are large enough to provide an attractive market for leading consumer products but small enough for their citizens to share economic and consumer interests. These regions are illustrated in Figure 10.1.

Techno-Globalism and the International Dimension

One of the major challenges facing industrialized countries at the present time as regards science and technology is to maintain and develop a comprehensive network of links to be able to follow up world-wide what is being done in these areas. This is particularly true for the smaller Nordic countries. When it comes to basic research, these connections determine the extent of one's awareness of the rapid advances which are occurring in so many areas that no one country can cover them all. In respect of applied research and development, knowledge of trends abroad will ensure wiser choices at national level and prevent costly duplication.

The phenomenon of *techno-globalism* is evident in the financial market, which now operates on full information around the clock around the world. It is also, however, increasingly apparent in the industrial goods market, where R&D, sources and production are spreading around the world. Furthermore, the establishment

1 A term used to denote the combination of Norway, Sweden, Denmark and Finland.

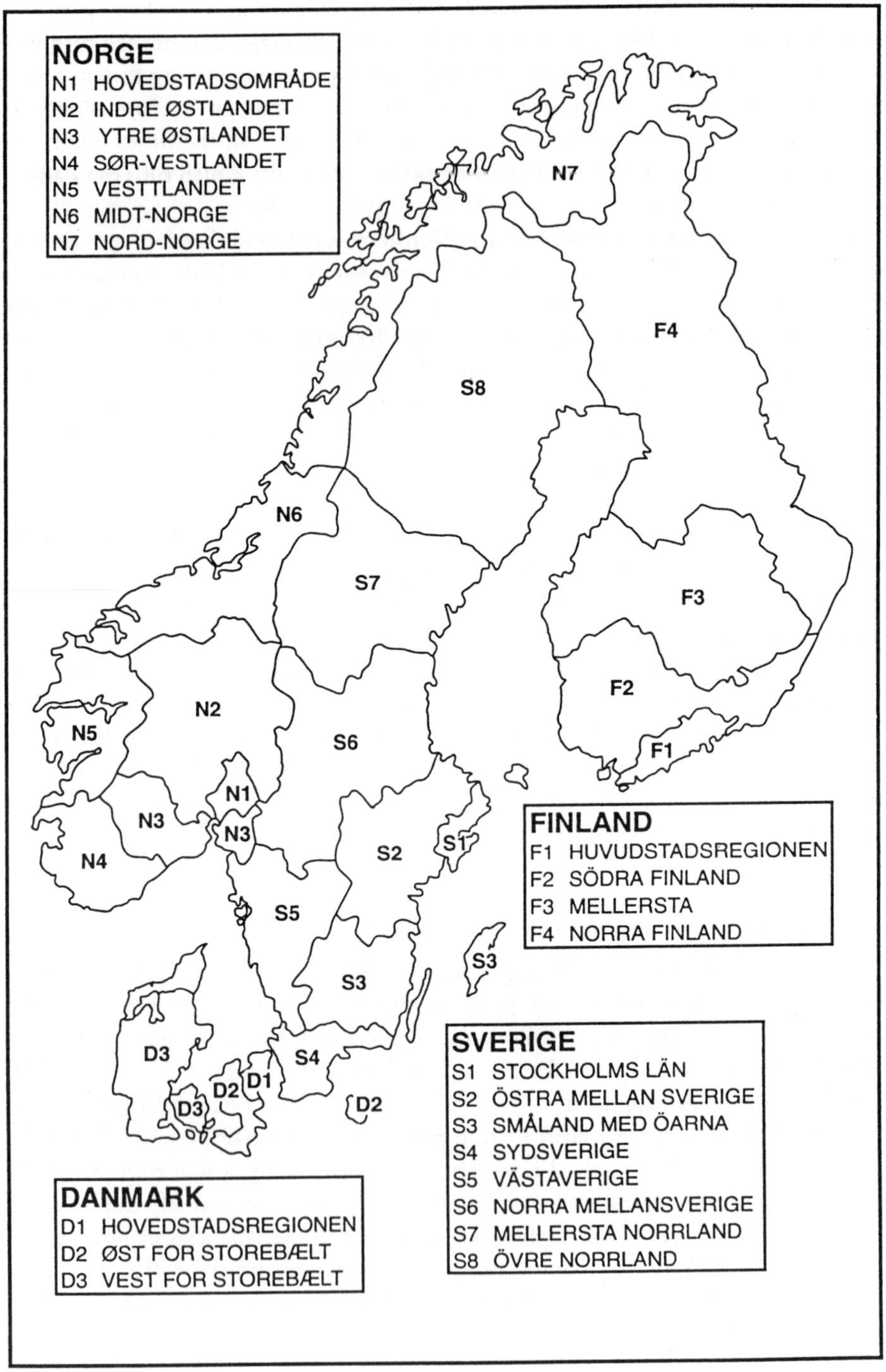

Source: Gustafsson 1991

Figure 10.1 Regional division of the nordic countries (NUT II level) of international networks is a vital factor in the establishment of national networks. The latter cannot be fully effective without the former; for example, industry will reap maximum benefit from the national basic research effort, when this effort provides a window into the international scientific world. Another facet of this globalization is the increasing cooperation between firms at the global level. In a number of instances such cooperation is taking place between competing firms. Such *strategic alliances* appear as a delicate mix of cooperation and competition, closely linked to the emergence of globally networked organizations. These may take the form of cooperative agreements in R&D and production, in cross-licensing and in cross-share holdings. Moreover, enterprises are tending to evolve from the traditional multinational firm, rooted with its headquarters in one nation, and to become more transnational, operating at a global level, but at the same time emphasizing decentralization. This explains the increasingly popular concept of the *global firm* with its own culture and clearly defined global strategy. Its identity and strategy may become largely independent of its country of origin as it becomes a *network firm.*

An alternative route for a smaller single firm, operating at the national level and perhaps without all the relevant technological knowledge, and not wishing tread the path of merger or acquisition, is to seek collaboration or alliances at the international level, thereby spreading the risks involved as well. The globalization of the goods market is also reinforced by the shortening of the product cycle. This requires firms that wish to remain successful to have access to the world market rapidly in order to realize the considerable investments required by the development of the highly sophisticated systems that make access to a global operative environment possible. For all these reasons *techno-globalization* is an essential dimension in the overall picture of Nordic science and technology policies. In exploiting this dimension, small but highly developed countries can achieve great leverage in various areas, such as basic research, industrial development and technology.

It is widely accepted that restructuring a national economy requires technological change. Recently, industrial R&D has been identified as one important source of technological change. However, there is little solid quantitative evidence linking industrial R&D with economic restructuring. For many companies investment in R&D, training, and streamlined organization have been larger than investments in tools, machinery, and buildings. Evidently, Japanese companies are now investing more in R&D than in plant and equipment. When R&D expenses are greater than capital investment in many companies, it is necessary to rethink what manufacturing companies are. The corporate archetype is changing from a production-intensive organization to a knowledge-intensive organization.

One force behind this development is that factory robots and other forms of soft automation have been installed, reducing industry's need for capital expenditure sharply. Such flexible machinery is merely reprogrammed, rather than replaced, when a factory is being switched over to making a new product. The change-over is completed in hours instead of weeks, and the cost of doing so is marginal. Retaining flexibility has become a strategy in itself. Another reason which will also jeopardize the Nordic manufacturing industry is the struggle for higher value markets. To survive, many manufacturing companies have to abandon much of their old core business and hasten where possible into higher value markets. In this process, they have to add all kinds of high-tech components and/or services to their products.

The traditional archetype of a manufacturing company is an organization which produces high quality products at the lowest possible cost, using the most advanced equipment. However, for Japanese manufacturing companies, it has been seen that the total capital investment became less than the total R&D expenditure during the 1980s and in 1987 they spent on average 26 per cent more on R&D than on plant and equipment. This leads more or less to a redefinition of the manufacturing company. The manufacturing company is traditionally a site for production, and in the economist's terms therefore a production function: capital plus labour equals output. But in many Japanese manufacturing companies, R&D investments surpassed capital investment, so the corporation shifts from being a place for production to being a place for generation of knowledge and production.

There is a remarkable structural difference in R&D/capital ratio between the Japanese manufacturing industry (over 100 per cent) and the Nordic manufacturing industry. The available data shows that in Sweden the R&D/capital ratio is in the 50–60 per cent range, while in Norway it varies between 30 and 45 per cent and in Denmark the level was between 25 and 30 per cent during the 1980s.

Technological Changes and Productivity

Technological change in its development and application is, fundamentally a social process, and should be viewed not in static but in dynamic terms. That it is a social process is demonstrated by the useful distinction between pervasive technologies, such as information technology, which have an impact throughout the economic system, and others whose impact is principally on particular firms or individual sectors. In distinguishing between these types of innovations, it is essential to begin by recognizing that there are some innovations which have very widespread effects and may change the whole quality of life, but whose quantitative economic effects are so small that they have no perceptible influence on the behaviour of economic aggregates. An example is *genetic fingerprinting* – a new advance in bio-technology that could be of great importance in medicine. It could have major implications for medical prognosis and life insurance, which will raise questions of medical and social ethics.The innovation has already been introduced and has many potential uses. However, even if genetic fingerprinting comes into widespread use, its economic significance will be very slight – thus it has little or no effect on output or employment. A second distinction is between innovations that find applications in only one sector and those that effect many or all sectors of the economy. Again, an example will be helpful. The Pilkington *float-glass* process introduced in the 1960s was certainly of enormous economic importance for the glass industry, as it was licensed to nearly every major glass manufacturer in the world in the following years. However, it has few applications outside the glass industry and its macro-economic significance is therefore relatively small. If this is compared with the electronic computer, which has found applications in every single sector of the economy without exception, the distinction becomes clear. Computers are now used in every industry and service, but they are also used in all the main functions such as administration, production, design, marketing and research. The following will serve as a clarification and a taxonomy of technological changes, distinguishing a generic technology from a single discrete innovation.

Incremental innovations occur all the time throughout the economic system, albeit at varying rates in different sectors of the economy. Their cumulative effects are very important for long-term productivity growth and for quality improvements since they affect only existing series of products, services and processes. The important point is that, although they are of great economic importance, they do not raise any major problems of structural adjustment because they do not require entirely new skills or types of capital equipment; instead they call for improvement in the use of already existing resources. On the other hand, radical innovations are non-continuous events and cannot emerge simply from the improvement of existing products and processes. Nuclear power did not derive from oil- or coal-fired power stations, nor did genetic fingerprinting from existing techniques of fingerprinting. A radical innovation raises problems of structural change, since it requires new types of capital equipment and/or new skills to produce or supply the new product or service.

Generic technologies or *new technology systems* are concepts of *constellations* of innovations that are technically and economically interrelated. Obvious examples are the innovation *cluster* of synthetic materials and petrochemicals. Contemporary examples are the ranges of composite materials and seed and plant varieties based on genetic engineering. Here the important point is that when a number of radical innovations are clustered together, they may generate more severe problems of structural adjustment since they can give rise to the growth of entirely new branches of the economy, as well as to the displacement of older ones. For example, the growth of synthetic materials had important consequences for other materials – such as jute or cotton – and on the supply for industries – such as the packaging, construction, textile, electrical and automotive industries. New inputs, equipment, technical standards, skills and products were required.

Some generic technologies or *new technology systems* have such a wide range of applications that they affect the conditions of production and distribution in all or almost all sectors of the economy, i.e. pervasive generic technology. Electric power is an example of pervasive technology. It made possible the mechanization of most manufacturing processes and through its application in railway systems etc. completely changed distribution systems, transport costs and economies of scale for many services as well as for manufacturing. Today's most pervasive technology is information technology, defined as a combination of radical innovations based primarily on computers, micro-electronics and telecommunications. The common denominator for these generic technologies is that they have the most pervasive effect on the economy, since they have great implications for investments, employment and structural change.

For a technology to have pervasive economic effects and substantial employment implications it must:

1. generate a wide range of new products and/or services
2. have applications in many sectors of the economy
3. reduce costs and improve the performance of existing processes, products and systems.

The importance of the productivity dividend

The principal economic goal of a nation is to produce a high and rising standard of living for its citizens. The ability to do so depends on the productivity with which a nation's resources (labour and capital) are employed. Real productivity is the value of the output (adjusted for inflation) by a unit of labour or capital. It depends on both the quality and features of products (which determine the prices they can command) and the efficiency with which they are produced. Productivity is the prime determinator in the long run of a nation's standard of living, for it is the prime generator of national per capita income. The productivity of human resources determines wages, while the productivity with which capital is employed determines the return it earns for its holders. High productivity not only supports high levels of income but also allows citizens the option of choosing more leisure instead of long working hours. It also creates the national income that is taxed to pay for public services, which again improves the standard of living. A nation's firms must relentlessly improve productivity in existing industries by raising product quality, adding desirable features, improving product technology, or boosting production efficiency.

A nation's firms must also develop the capabilities required to compete in more sophisticated segments of industry, where productivity is generally higher. At the same time, an upgrading economy is one which is able to compete successfully in entirely new and sophisticated markets. It must be remembered that at the margin, the productivity of resources deployed in all industries is equalized by market forces. Crucial to national economic prosperity, however, is achieving an equilibrium in which the resulting average productivity of resources is as high as possible. This depends on raising the quality of factors and increasing the level of technology, broadly defined, with which factors are utilized. The opportunities to do so vary by industry and industrial segments of industry, and the productivity differences between firms in given industries and segments can also be substantial because of differences in skill and technology. Clearly, the capacity to improve productivity in all major sectors of an economy, not just manufacturing, is important to economic prosperity and regional development. International trade and foreign investment constitute both an opportunity to boost the level of national productivity and a threat to increasing or even maintaining it. International trade allows a nation to raise its productivity by eliminating the need to produce all goods and services within the nation itself – thereby facilitating regional development.

A nation can thereby specialize in those industries and segments in which its firms are relatively more productive and import those products and services where its firms are less productive than foreign rivals, thus raising the average productivity level in the economy. Imports, therefore, as well as exports are integral to productivity growth. Historically, rising output in the industrialized regions has gone hand in hand with rising employment and the growth of labour productivity, the latter attributable in large measure to technological change. Rates of unemployment tend to be high in periods of low productivity growth, such as the inter-war years and the 1970s, and low in periods of high productivity growth, such as the 1950s and 1960s. The productivity growth made possible by technological change is in the nature of a dividend, which can increase both profit and labour incomes. In the latter case, it can be distributed in the form of better wages, hours and working conditions. In other words, improvements in labour productivity permit sustained improvements in wages and working conditions as well as improvements in the quality of life.

New technologies and society

It is now apparent that technological change is closely associated with not only economic but also a complex interaction of social, legal and cultural changes. Transformation in society and technology are, at the same time, cause and effect. The way in which societies adapt to these transformations is no more systematic than the technical system is static. In this sense, technology can be defined as a social process which, by meeting real or imagined needs, changes those needs, just as it is changed by them. A good example of the complexity of this social interplay is telecommunication, where computers, television, telephony and new materials combine to multiply the audio-visual resources available for information, management, leisure and education. The telecommunication business represents one of the healthiest and most active high-tech sectors which cut across national markets. The fact is that technical innovations cannot be widely applied without the requisite socio-institutional infrastructure. The success of the motor car depended not only on new, modern manufacturing methods but also on the establishment of a network of petrol stations and garages, new roads and motorways. Television required not only the installation of a network of transmitters and relay stations but also the creation of programmes, and here the financing methods used –

combining resources from public and private institutions – were themselves a social innovation.

The Total Business System

In looking upon an industrial organization as a socio-economic microsystem which must learn from its environment how to survive, then the variations in the speed of learning produce the competitive conditions that shape the character of success. The company has then to focus on the time-based interdependencies between its organizational resources and its environment, and on the role of strategy in creating these links not passively, but well in advance. This is how an organization's strategy comes about and how it evolves. This dynamic lock-in with its environment – how an organization gradually grows and declines through its search for a competitive advantage – is the basic hypothesis for strategic management and how managers must constantly link their organization's unique resources and core capabilities to different types of strategies across time.

A company's sustained profitability is based on the interrelationships that gradually develop, between its customers, its competitors, and the environment. Sophisticated strategic control and leadership are required to maintain coherence and growth in companies with diverse resources. Processes must be well in hand yet evolutionary in nature, recognizing the steady process by which companies seek out new sources for advantages and bring about strategic renewal. Corporate leadership plays a particularly strong role in bridging differences in decision-making styles, reconciling control systems, and accommodating diverse payback criteria. However, strategic planning and strategic control based on financial criteria and analysis alone, although helpful, is not enough to guarantee that the organization will succeed in its aims. The quality of a decision rests on the ability to construct a simplified mental model of the real-life situation. It is essential that the model includes the most important phenomena and their relationships in order to describe the connection between cause and effect in all the most important parts of the company.

Industrial survival and sustainability

Much of the competitive pressure that an industrial organization faces can be traced to the degree of sustainability of its products. Thinking in these terms, an organization's strategy represents the search for the ways by which organizational capabilities are strengthened and animated. When anticipating a product's sustainability, it is very helpful in predicting competitors' reactions to first-mover advantage – to assess how fast an organization must manoeuvre *vis-à-vis* a range of competitive conditions. For instance, the stronger and more vigorous the effect of isolating mechanisms, the slower competitors will be able to duplicate a company's product advantage. As a product's isolating resources are stripped away, time moves faster. And the organization will experience a time-based competitive pressure to become more severe, often pronounced in short product cycle times, rapid price reductions, stiff cost reduction targets, eroding profit margins, etc.

The following three-fold classification illustrates the broad scope of time-based resource imitation patterns:

1. **Slow-cycle resources** Products and services in this category reflect resource positions that are strongly shielded from competitive pressures. The core capabilities behind these products and services include patent and geography, and they can also include complex buyer/supplier relationships and highly durable brand names.
2. **Standard-cycle resources** Products and services in this class are typically standardized for high volume production, e.g. automobiles, appliances and fast food. Companies within these industries face higher resource-imitation pressures. These organizations tend to be mass-market- and market-share-oriented, process-focused and multinational or global.
3. **Fast-cycle resources** Organizations in this category face the highest resource-imitation pressures. These products are *idea-driven*, that is, based on a concept, technology, or idea alone, detached from other effective isolating mechanisms. One measure of sustainability used in the analysis is the *economic half-life* of a product (defined as the rate of product profit margin erosion without re-investment). With little effective shielding from imitation, the economic half-life of this class of products is typically in the order of two years or even less. To maintain dynamic resource control, these organizations must master competitive routines currently associated with quick time-to-market, *fast-cycle* business.

A company's core capabilities do not always fall into one class or another. They are obviously being constantly refined and adapted, and some capabilities are more important than others. On a case-by-case basis, sustainability of advantage also results from the effect of industrial structure and leadership as well as change and uncertainty. Also, large complex global companies often compete across resource classes.

As the complexity in the economic, technological and the political environment increases, industrial leaders must devote more attention to definition and improvement of the few critical business processes that determine success or failure in each sub-system of their own organization. Shifts in the characteristic rate at which an industry's products are imitated reflect a change in the rate of change of decision-making needs. Such shifts precede a new category of market, bring in unfamiliar management pressures, and reflect a fundamentally altered way of doing things. These shifts can be difficult to predict and tough to adjust to. However, as sustainable resource analysis uses rates of change as benchmarks for competition, many such frame-breaking changes do not have to be unpredictable – early warnings of frame-braking change can be made by monitoring changes in sustainability.

The main benefit of this approach is to make strategy actionable – across products, organizations and industries. Since time is the common denominator, managers must be ready to create change – innovate new products and new processes and access new markets. Success comes by changing the rules of the game so completely that rivals are relegated to playing catch-up. Strategy – the search for advantage – becomes the means for guiding this socio-economic system called an industrial organization towards sustained growth and profitability.

The total business system and total productivity approach

The *total business system* aims to describe the connection between cause and effect in all the most important parts of the company, and consists of four components:

1. **The Pre-production system** acts as the framework for the implementation of all the measures devised by the company to ensure its survival and long-term profitability.
2. **The Industrial system** very high standards of efficiency are demanded in the industrial system. In production everything must harmonize. It is here that workers and machines bring into being what the designer has created and what a customer expects.
3. **The Commercial system** requires that the company's earning capacity is guaranteed for both the short- and the long-term.
4. **The Support system** in their capacity as specialists, the various staff provide support for all the operative sections of the company.

The total business system is designed to visualize the interdependencies between the company (including its sub-systems) and the environment.

An industrial company must be both productive in its use of existing resources and knowledge, and capable of technological innovation. Yet it is difficult and possibly counter-productive to both. The relationship between productivity and technology is far from straightforward. Long-term productivity growth requires more than just more of the same output from the same inputs. It requires changing the nature of the output, through product innovation, and this, in turn, is likely to cause shifts in market demand. It also requires changes in the inputs and manufacturing processes. A company that is highly efficient in producing an obsolete product may find itself out of business despite its high productivity. On the other hand, the changes in products and processes that are essential to remain competitive in a global market are usually both risky and expensive. The investment needed for such innovation will reduce immediate financial returns to the business, and the disruption of production that is caused by such changes can have a severe impact on productivity.

To be able to manage the uneasy alliance between productivity and technology, it appears to be essential to look upon the *total productivity approach* as an integrated part of the company's strategy and tactics. Total productivity includes both effectiveness and efficiency where several areas are of the strategic kind. Total productivity is achieved by efficient strategic management and development. This will identify and decide upon the risks and positions the company is to take in order to reach its major long-term objectives. It is important to establish that it is from the total productivity that a company prospers. A company may temporarily make large profits because of favourable market conditions, despite poor internal efficiency. Conversely, it may achieve good results because internal efficiency temporarily cancels out poor market adaptation. Taken together, this forms a measure of the company's capacity for survival and sustained profitability.

A New Tool for Regional Economic Development

The competitiveness of a company depends not only on its own competitive strength but also on the interaction of its capabilities with the capabilities of the external environment in which it operates. It is a well known fact that both the cultural legacy and government policy affect the competitiveness of a company. Fundamental to competitiveness is innovation: the search, development and adoption of new products and processes. Innovation stems from the interaction between capabilities within the company and industry and the company's external environment, an omnibus term which comprises the soft infrastructure (government policy, education, macro-policy, trade policy, investment policy, capital market regulation, etc.), together with the traditional tangible infrastructure and the market behavioral phenomena such as the taste and attitudes of consumers. In comparison with an industrial organization described as a socio-economic system, where its success is measured by sustained profitability and growth, it is possible to describe the external environment as a socio-political macro-system defined as an economic region. Regional attractiveness could then be measured by its time-based productivity and sustained development.

Competition among companies (micro-systems) is also competition among regions (macro-systems), and the slow process of convergence will produce serious discord (system friction along the way) – a globalizing world has low tolerance for system divergence. It has been argued extensively that the measures currently seeking to encourage greater competition across Europe will lead to greater efficiency in the allocation of goods and services and, hopefully, a higher level of economic activity in the EU. The removal of barriers to trade and the encouragement given to the free movement of capital and labour offer a potential for great benefits to all the members of the Single European Market (SEM). However, what is also equally clear is that the infusion of competitive power associated with greater liberalization will mean that some companies in some industries, in certain regions, will no longer be so competitive and will be forced to rationalize or close down. While, over the longer term, capital and labour will find new uses, in the interim these resources may not be properly utilized. To bring about a convergence between regions in respect of these economic disparities which exist within the EU, the European Commission has sanctioned a large expansion in the level of resources devoted to assisting the process of structural reform across the Member States.

Regional competitive positioning

In this section, some of the most affluent EU regions are examined in terms of their current level of GDP per capita together with their research and technology development (RTD) potential, all important factors within the total dynamics of regional development. This regional competitive positioning within the EU is shown in Figure 10.2. With regard to the method for assessing regional positioning, this has traditionally concentrated on nations as the unit of analysis. Little work has been done at the regional level in the past. As it is now available for the first time, it must be used with care. Its purpose is to condense a variety of factors so as to facilitate assimilation of the overall situation in a region. However, when a region receives a low rating on this basis, the various factors which make up the measure should be examined to see which factors contribute to this low positioning and which, in fact, may indicate some regional strengths. Only in this way can a balanced assessment of regional positioning be ensured.

RTD covers a wide spectrum. In fact it is a somewhat unsatisfactory abbreviation for the full complex of **means** (research and technology) and **ends** (innovation) which together constitute a technical capacity in the fullest sense of the word. RTD, therefore, as used here, covers the full spectrum from the generation of knowledge to application. RTD mechanisms are the operational tools for the stimulation and development of all elements of the spectrum, and consequently include a large number of individual mechanisms. The role of RTD in fuelling economic growth is not disputed, even if its influence is complex and difficult to quantify exactly. RTD describes a web of activities related to the generation, acquisition, transfer and use of technology. It includes research, development, demonstration, technology transfer and technical innovation. It covers the spectrum of knowledge generation as well as application. RTD-intensive industries are innovative, produce several new products and have higher levels of productivity, expand their employment base more rapidly and are ultimately more competitive than traditional and low technology businesses. The dynamics of this process will vary between regions. The technology acquisition behaviour of local enterprises, their sources of supply and modes of access to technology will reflect the unique RTD environment of the region. The economic performance of a region indicates, therefore, whether its enterprises are technologically innovative and dynamic, or technologically backward and in decline. Programmes and mechanisms seek to

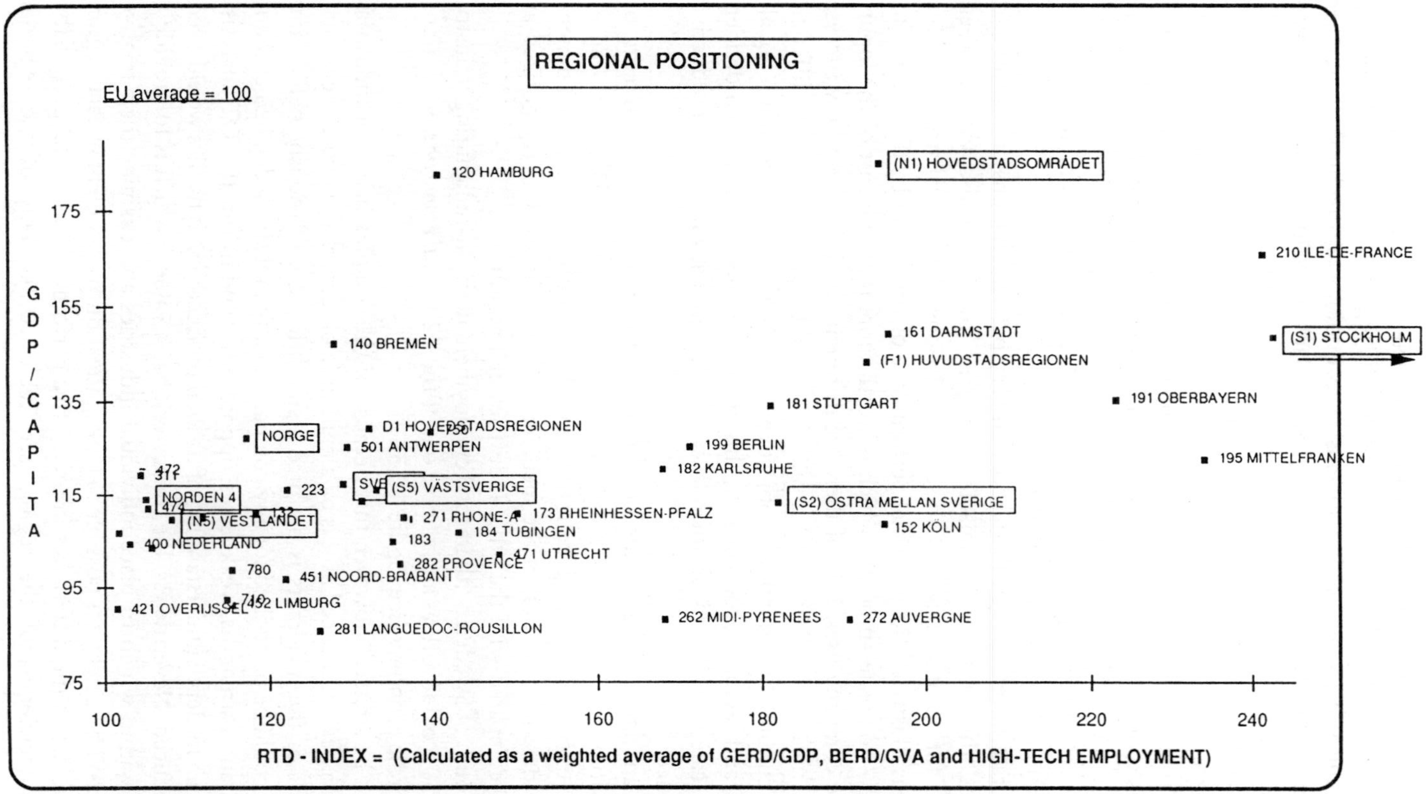

Source: Gustafsson 1991

Figure 10.2 Regional competitive positioning

foster an awareness of technological progress and to encourage manufacturers and industry generally to modernize and upgrade their level of technology.

The insufficient esteem of RTD in the Nordic regions as a whole is gradually reducing the effectiveness of investments in technology and technology transfer mechanisms. The need for cooperation is particularly acute in small countries such as the Nordic nations. Individual Scandinavian countries as a basis for RTD activities and a domestic market are becoming less attractive as the level of risk and the pace of RTD expenditures increases – for a product to be profitable, higher volumes/revenues are required. Thus an innovation must reach the international markets as soon as possible. The survival and future profitability of industry in the context of the SEM will depend heavily on the screening, identification and evaluation of technological needs and the definition of future international business and technological requirements.

If the rate of technological advance can vary between nations, industries and enterprises, then it seems reasonable to suggest that it can also vary between regions, if for no other reason than spatial variations in industrial structure. This chapter has illustrated the industrial performance of companies by their ability to add value – to create an output which is worth more than the cost of the inputs which the company uses. Even if there are different opinions about how success should be measured and how added value is created by different firms or different business culture the underlying objective of adding value is common to all industrial and regional economies. In this analysis, industries have been divided into four categories based on their level of internationalization and productive performance.

Thus, an industry in quadrant 3 of Figure 10.3 is performing well in terms of productivity in the absence of a significant level of internationalization. And in respect of expected techno-globalization and the intensified international dimension of industrial activities, in the medium term, this industry is categorized as *developing* compared with the other industries in a region.

The South of Sweden, with its total employment in the manufacturing industry of 113,550, could work as an example out of the 22 *natural economic zones* regions in the Nordic economy (see Figure 10.3).

It must be stressed, however, that because of the complex nature of industrial competitiveness, influenced as it is by a multitude of factors, the two-dimensional framework of the quadrants is perforce a simplification. Obviously, before any measures could be prescribed for any company in any industry, a detailed account of a company's strengths, weaknesses, opportunities and threats (SWOT analysis) as well as an in-depth understanding of its total productivity dynamics would need to be produced. Nevertheless, the framework has a value – which is to provide a structure within which to place individual industries and examine their relative potential. With its help it is possible to look at the industrial content in each region in order to assess the differences in productive performance as a vital part of the overall attractiveness of the region (see Table 10.2). Many of the regional

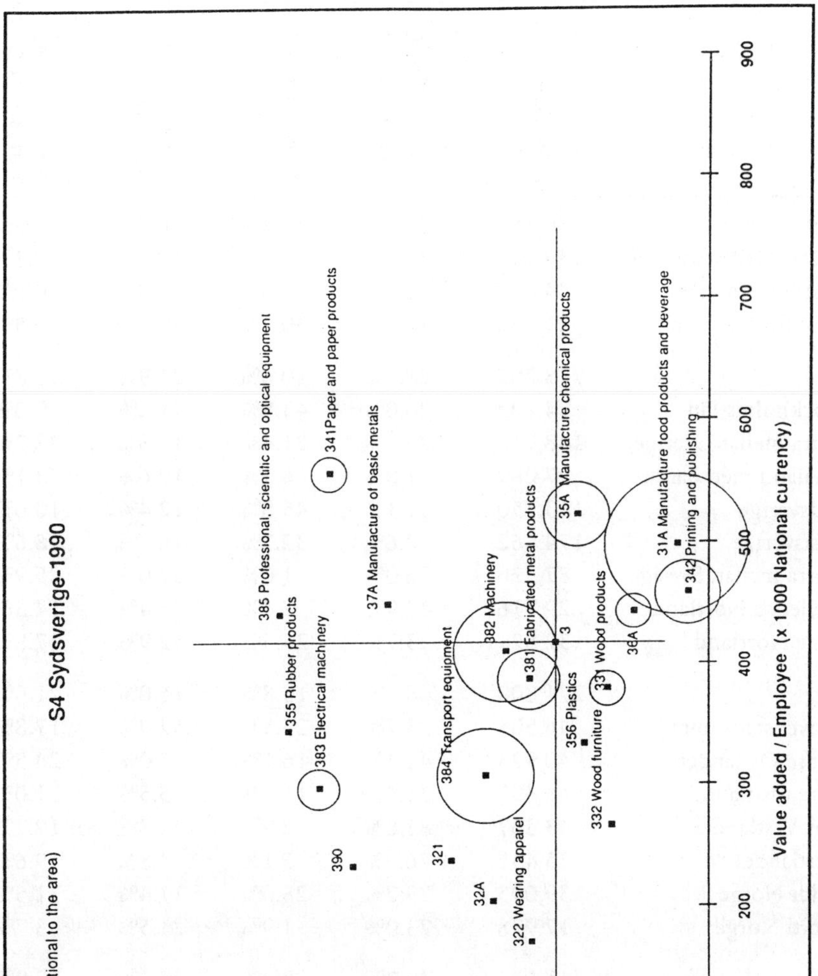

Source: *Gustafsson 1993*

Figure 10.3 Regional industrial performance – South of Sweden

Table 10.2 Regional variations in industrial employment, internationalization and productive performance

Norden 4	*Employment*	*1) Internationally less favourable*	*2) Internationally vulnerable*	*3) Internationally developing*	*4) Internationally more favourable*
Danmark	504,363	25.3%	36.3%	26.2%	12.2%
(D1) Hovedstadsregionen	139,140	33.5%	34.1%	18.1%	14.3%
(D2) Ost for Storebælt	44,067	22.5%	21.8%	45.0%	10.6%
(D3) Vest for Storebælt	321,156	22.2%	39.2%	27.1%	11.5%
Sverige	778,207	28.6%	30.6%	21.9%	18.8%
(S1) Stockholms län	94,122	26.0%	43.8%	21.2%	9.0%
(S2) Östra mellan Sverige	148,913	26.7%	21.4%	19.3%	32.7%
(S3) Småland med öarna	97,089	41.0%	6.3%	19.6%	33.1%
(S4) Sydsverige	113,550	31.1%	45.8%	12.4%	10.6%
(S5) Västsverige	174,662	32.6%	32.7%	16.2%	18.6%
(S6) Norra mellan Sverige	87,326	36.0%	1.0%	37.0%	25.9%
(S7) Mellersta Norrland	29,716	47.9%	2.4%	35.4%	14.3%
(S8) Övre Norrland	32,829	3.7%	25.5%	52.9%	17.8%
Norge	271,800	48.6%	13.8%	16.0%	21.6%
(N1) Hovedstadsområde	46,508	3.7%	25.5%	52.9%	17.8%
(N2) Indre Ostlandet	40,923	44.4%	16.1%	15.0%	24.5%
(N3) Ytre Osttlandet	48,497	51.6%	11.9%	5.5%	31.0%
(N4) Sor Vestlandet	43,367	81.6%	2.9%	2.8%	12.7%
(N5) Vestlandet	35,432	76.5%	2.1%	1.8%	19.6%
(N6) Midt Norge	39,095	29.2%	28.0%	11.4%	31.5%
(N7) Nord Norge	17,978	73.0%	1.9%	21.5%	3.7%
Finland	418,506	29.7%	28.3%	25.1%	16.9%
(F1) Huvudstadsregionen	102,610	32.5%	36.3%	21.0%	10.2%
(f2) Södra Finland	189,734	24.3%	29.6%	28.2%	17.9%
(F3) Mellersta Finland	82,491	36.0%	27.4%	18.4%	18.2%
(F4) Norra Finland	43,671	34.6%	6.1%	33.8%	25.5%
Norden 4	1,972,876	30.8%	29.3%	22.9%	17.1%

Source Gustafsson (1993)

(2) Internationally vulnerable	**(4) Internationally more favourable**
(1) Internationally less favourable	**(3) Internationally developing**

differences are probably linked to industrial tradition in the region and a number of other factors, such as the process of developing skills. There is also the influence of innovation, stemming from the interaction between capabilities within the company and the industry and the company's external environment, to be taken into account – all of which are subject to intriguing variations between regions and nations.

The essential point of this kind of economic analysis is to build intuition. If the informed readers feel that they have gained a significantly greater insight into an important problem, then it is an insight whose major content is often that of providing a language to discuss that problem – in this case the problem of assessing the differences in industrial productive performance as a vital part of the overall attractiveness of a region and regional development.

References

Gustafsson, R. N.-G. (1991) *Norden and the Nordic Regions at a Glance.* Gothenburg: Ergoma AB. May.

Gustafsson, R. N.-G. (1992) *The Top 50 Industries in Norden.* Gothenburg: Ergoma AB. April.

Gustafsson, R. N.-G. (1993) *Industrial Revitalization and Productivity in a Nordic Perspective.* Gothenburg: Ergoma AB. February.

CHAPTER 11

European Integration and Development of the Finnish Regions

Hannu Tervo

Introduction

Finland, together with Sweden and Austria, joined the European Union (EU) on 1 January 1995. This means closer links with Western Europe. Apart from its political implications, the integration process also implies economic changes in both the country as a whole and its regions. In the referendum on the accession of Finland to the EU a majority of 57 per cent of the voters were in favour of membership while a minority of 43 per cent were against (Statistics Finland 1995). From a regional point of view, a striking result was that most of the Finnish municipalities – 328 of the 455 municipalities – voted No to joining the EU (Figure 11.1).[1] The vision of the new Europe as a *Europe of Regions* seems to meet with little favour in the Finnish regions (see Figure 11.1).

The less prosperous rural regions in the northern and eastern parts of Finland were all against membership, while the southern regions, and urban centres on the whole, were for membership. In fact, the less prosperous the region the higher was its opposition. When the sub-regions are divided into five equal-sized categories according to their gross domestic product (GDP) per capita in 1990, the percentage of No votes were, respectively from the poorest region to the richest region: 63 per cent, 61 per cent, 49 per cent, 44 per cent and 35 per cent. A simple correlation coefficient between regional gross domestic product per capita and the share of No votes was as high as -0.74.

1 The share of No votes was also greater at sub-region level – 52 of the 88 sub-regions were against membership. Only at province level was a majority of regions – 11 out of 19 provinces – in favour of membership.

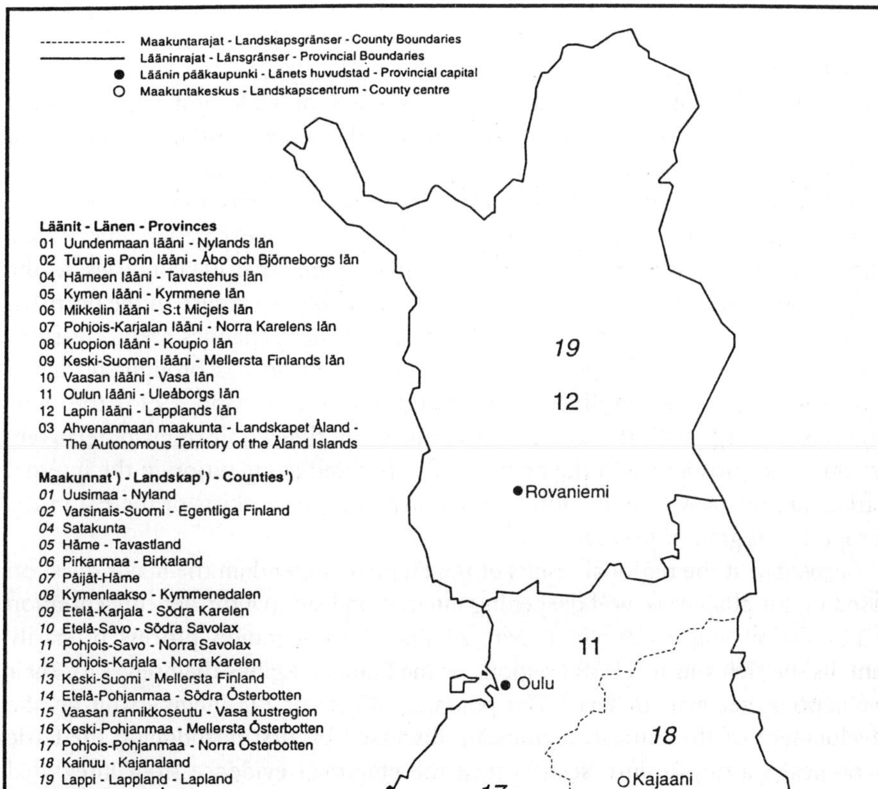

Source: Statistical Yearbook of Finland 1994, p.32

Figure 11.1 Provinces and counties in Finland

The question as to whether increased European economic integration will increase or decrease regional inequalities has given rise to a lively debate.[2] Some argue that the process of European integration will largely benefit more advanced core regions because of, for example, economies of scale and agglomeration economies, large markets and human capital. On the contrary, others maintain that peripheral areas will benefit from lower labour costs, inflows of capital, improved transportation and communications, access to greater markets, etc.

Finland, together with Sweden, forms the northernmost geographical zone within the EU, and is in many respects dissimilar to the other EU countries. As the integration process strengthens, changes will inevitably occur also in the northern regions of the EU, even though the directions of these changes are not easy to foresee. From the Nordic perspective, the new situation has brought up many important issues (see Eskelinen 1992; Lundqvist and Persson 1994) the most important being: will the Nordic economies on the whole remain relatively dynamic and prosperous in the new era of intensified competition in the internal market, and what will be the role of the northernmost outskirts of the EU in the European integration process?

Seen against the regional results of the Finnish referendum the major question posed in this chapter is: will deepening integration lead to a further concentration of population and economic activity so that the integration process primarily benefits the rich and successful regions, as the Finnish regions themselves (or their populations) seem to believe? The potential effects of EU membership on the development of the Finnish regions are discussed by first introducing the basic theoretical starting points, seen against the empirical evidence from integrated areas, and then outlining the current situation of Finnish regional development from the perspective of the European integration process.

Regional Implications of the Integration Process

Neoclassical theories, related to the idea of equilibrium, predict regional specialization and (long-term) convergent growth. The neoclassical growth theory emphasizes that automatic forces lead to regional convergence over time in an integrated area. The neoclassical trade theory rests on the principle of comparative advantage: every region will produce a higher valued output as each region specializes in the production of those goods which it can produce comparatively cheaply. A corollary of this theory, the factor price equalization theorem, even predicts that free trade equalizes regional factor prices in the absence of factor migration.

On the other hand, the traditional centre–periphery models and their variants, related to the idea of disequilibrium, predict divergence of interregional growth and concentration to the detriment of lagging regions. Theorizing of this type may

2 See, for example, the special issue of *Regional Studies*, 1992 Number 4: '1992 and Regional Development'; or Dunford (1994).

have different starting points, such as the processes of circular and cumulative causation and growth pole dynamics; or agglomeration and external economies, transportation costs and regional accessibility; or simply the principle of absolute advantage instead of comparative advantage. Recently, the development of mainstream economics has also lent some support to the traditional centre–periphery models of regional economics (see Krugman 1991). Economies of scale and imperfect competition play a crucial role in new models of international trade. Endogenous growth theory has also rediscovered the importance of cumulative causation.

Accordingly, different starting points produce different results on the direction of regional growth: in the neoclassical world regional growth is well-balanced, while the centre–periphery-type models predict unequal growth. Given this, predicting the effects of European integration on the development of the Finnish regions is a very uncertain task. This is even more uncertain when remembering that European integration is essentially a dynamic process. None of the existing theories of development and inequality offer clear directions for evaluating the dynamics that will be set in motion by a rapid process of integration (Roura and Suárez-Villa 1993, p.372).

One way to evaluate the possible effects of integration on Finnish regional development is to base the appraisal on the experiences of other countries. The empirical evidence is, however, also more or less vague. Recent European and United States experiences do not give a clear-cut picture about regional development lines in an integrated area. As far as Europe is concerned, empirical studies in particular seem to have given support for both regional convergence and divergence (e.g. Armstrong 1994; Barro and Sala-i-Martin 1991; Dunford 1994; Monnesland 1995; Roura and Suárez-Villa 1993). The European Commission's Fifth Periodic Report (CEC 1994) on regional trends demonstrates that within the general trend of slow economic convergence there have been Member States and regions showing significant improvement, while certain others have experienced a relative decline.

Actually, more recent research has suggested that assumptions of both regional convergence and agglomeration are too simplistic and that the economic patterns lead to a complex web or mosaic of regions (e.g. Bachtler, Clement and Raines 1993; Illeris 1993; Peschel 1992; Roura and Suárez Villa 1993). Different growth processes do not exclude each other. Rather, they may occur simultaneously. As well as there being no particular reason to expect the benefits of the EU integration to fall evenly across all regions, neither is there any obvious reason to believe them to agglomerate exclusively in favour of the already strong core-regions. Thus the regional picture is likely to be complicated without clear overall tendencies.

Accordingly, seen from the viewpoint of the regions of such individual member states as Finland, the mosaic model implies – optimistically, as the advocates of the core–periphery models might say – that the possibilities are at least partly open. And what is still more important from the standpoint of the peripheries, the model implies that the peripheral regions are not automatically losers, despite their locational disadvantages and difficulties in benefiting from a large scale economy. In the process of development towards a *Europe of Regions*, local economic development will, more and more, depend on local conditions and activity. Of course, the successful regions are presumed to have the necessary qualifications through which the opportunities provided by European integration can be exploited (see Peschel 1992, pp.389–90). On the other hand, EU regional policies are aimed at helping the disadvantaged regions, but, given the scale of the regional disparities which exist in Europe and the limited resources available for these policies – the Commission's total budget remains below 1.5 per cent of the EU's GDP – EU intervention has been argued as having more to do with crisis management than genuine convergence (Martin and Pearce 1995).

In principle, an integrated market will provide peripheral regions with market potential due to the lifting of trade barriers, technology potential due to imitation possibilities, capital due to capital movements and improvement in infrastructure resulting from regional policies (Camagni 1992). Peripheral regions can exploit these assets provided they can show some favourable conditions. In the case of the Objective 1 regions, Camagni (1992, p.364) has shown these conditions to be:

1. the presence of some basic preconditions in terms of infrastructure endowment and human capital which enhance both the attractiveness for external capital and the competitiveness of local firms
2. the presence of an export base capable of benefiting from the widening of potential markets
3. the presence of production specificities or *vocations* developed historically on the basis of localized know-how or a localized natural/environmental resource, which grant a competitive advantage beyond low labour cost
4. the presence of entrepreneurship capable of exploiting all these local assets and the opportunities provided by European integration.

As the core-regions are more likely to be characterized by these favourable features, the tendency towards concentration remains, but this does not exclude the possibilities of other, perhaps more peripheral, regions possessing some of these favourable conditions.

With so many factors underlying regional development processes the lines of development may be very complicated. The integration process makes it even more difficult to forecast where and to what extent growth or decline will take place. Accordingly, it is easy to agree with Roura and Suárez-Villa (1993, p.370), who pointed out that 'economic integration may...introduce much uncertainty in the future dynamics of interregional disparities, with some regions advancing while others experience greater hardship'.

Potential Regional Effects of EU Membership in Finland

Regional development in Finland

From the European standpoint, Finland lies on the periphery and is characterized by a cold climate, large area, low population density and a scattered pattern of settlement. Forests cover a large part of Finland. Finland together with the Nordic countries may even be called the 'outer periphery', the 'inner periphery' being countries such as Ireland and Scotland (Bachtler *et al.* 1993, p.92; Dawson 1993, pp.14–16).

Finland's post-war economy has been marked by vigorous economic expansion accompanied by rapid structural change. Only a few decades ago, the Finnish economy was based almost entirely on the production of primary goods. Finland arrived late on the industrial scene and continued its industrialization process into the 1970s, when many other countries had already started to decline. However, in contrast to the evolution experienced elsewhere, Finland's employment structure shifted directly from one dominated by primary occupations to one in which the tertiary sector became the largest, the structure now bearing many similarities to that in the EU. Of the total employed labour force of 2.5 million persons in 1990, 8 per cent were engaged in primary production, 31 per cent in manufacturing and construction and 61 per cent in services. Industry is mainly concentrated in the processing of natural resources.

As well as in the other Nordic countries, there is a North–South divide between poor and rich regions in Finland, though the gap is relatively narrow despite the harsh climatic conditions of the North, partly because of the scale of public sector employment and regional transfers. Most people live in the South. The public sector is an important employer in the most sparsely populated areas, where local authorities provide a wide range of services. Despite their peripherality, Finnish regions have been comparatively prosperous as measured by their level of income. Historically, unemployment has been lower and labour force participation higher in Finland than in the EU. The 1990s, however, have seen a relatively sharp fall in GDP per capita associated with a dramatic rise in unemployment. This is due to the economic crisis into which Finland has drifted. There are many reasons for this severe recession, the collapse of exports to the former Soviet Union being a major external factor behind this development. Unemployment has traditionally been higher in the northern and eastern regions of Finland. The prosperous industrial parts of the South have previously been relatively immune from job losses, but they also now appear to be suffering badly, even though significant regional unemployment rate differentials still remain (Pehkonen and Tervo 1995; Tervo 1994).

Integration and regional development

The impacts of economic integration are conventionally divided into static and dynamic effects. The static effects follow from the improved allocation of available resources within given production possibilities due to changes in the relative prices of goods and factors. Dynamic repercussions are more important and they involve long-run changes in the national product due to a number of dynamic processes, such as stronger competition, accelerated technological progress and the exploitation of economies of scale. On a regional basis, the favoured approach is a static analysis based on the classification of sensitive and non-sensitive industries (see Halvorsen 1993; Steinle 1992). In this structural approach, it is often simply assumed that regions with an above-average share of sensitive sectors will meet with changes in the integration process and, thus, the likely losers and winners of integration will be found among these regions.

As a mechanistic approach, such an analysis may be criticized from many viewpoints (see Peschel 1992). The major critique, however, follows from the tendency for various dynamic integration effects to dominate. Those regions which are able to exploit the long-run opportunities produced by European integration will be the likely winners in the integration process as their share of investment increases and as labour migration to these regions accelerates. Peschel (1992) has recommended a *growth-trend approach* in regional integration analysis. As she claims, the most promising way to assess the regional impacts of integration is to analyse recent trends in regional economic development and to try to answer the question whether these trends will be strengthened or broken by the on-going integration process (Peschel 1992, p.389).

Next, the regional effects of EU membership are roughly appraised from both the static and dynamic viewpoints (see Tervo, Niittykangas and Nenonen 1994). The important question of the potential regional repercussions following from the changes taking place in the Finnish agricultural sector will not be treated in great depth here (see Malinen, Häkkilä and Jussila 1993; Tervo *et al.* 1994). However, it is noticeable that with EU membership Finland has transited from an era of national agricultural policy to that of the Common Agricultural Policy (CAP), which has radically changed the circumstances in which agriculture is carried on in Finland. The less favourable climatic and other physical production conditions are permanent hindrances which make it difficult for the northern agriculture to compete with other EU regions. Membership has forced Finland to remove its strict border protection of basic foodstuffs, and adopt a more market-oriented price and trade system in line with the CAP and the competition policy of the EU, which has led to a marked reduction in producer prices. Since agriculture continues to have a very important role in many Finnish rural areas – e.g. in the provinces of Etelä-Savo, Pohjois-Karjala and Etelä-Pohjanmaa its share of employment is over 20 per cent – its future will, more or less, also dictate the future development of these areas. In the short run, the negative effects will be mitigated, or prevented, by the significant agricultural and regional support handed out by both the EU and the Finnish government. In the long run, however, the destinies of peripheral agricultural regions are more open.

The regional analysis of this chapter relates to the *static* changes in manufacturing, and is based on a list of sensitive manufacturing industries constructed in Finland by Kajaste (1990), who used a common EU list of sensitive sectors as a starting point (Buigues and Ilzkovitz 1988). Kajaste (1990) also used several indicators in assessing the competitive performance of the sensitive group. With the help of this analysis, the industries were divided into those with a strong competitive performance and those with a weak competitive performance. Non-sensitive industries belong either to the *closed* or *open* sector. The open sector includes those industries which are already fully exposed to international competition, the most important being the forest industry. The closed sector comprises those industries which are naturally or otherwise sheltered so that the integration will not remarkably change their competitive position. In the regional analysis, both the provinces (19) and sub-regions (88) were used as regional units.

The regional distributions at province level are shown in Table 11.1. As this table shows, some of the provinces, like Kymenlaakso and Etelä-Karjala, are already rather open, while there are also provinces in which manufacturing has been more sheltered. The regions also seem to confront the *static* integration impacts in rather different ways. A high degree of sensitivity can be found from the provinces of Varsinais-Suomi and Pohjois-Pohjanmaa, where the employment shares of the sensitive sectors were 55 per cent in each, while the provinces of Ahvenanmaa and Etelä-Karjala show a low degree of sensitivity – 16 per cent and 19 per cent, respectively. The regional distribution of the *weak* sensitive sectors varied from 0 per cent to 15 per cent, while that of the *strong* sensitive sectors varied from 11 per cent to 45 per cent. At sub-region level, the distributions are even wider (not shown here): in some sub-regions over half of the manufacturing jobs are located in those sectors where competitive performance is assessed to be good, while there are other sub-regions which do not have a single job in these sectors. Thus, the pressures to adapt to the new circumstances created by European integration seem to differ rather among the Finnish regions. The tendency towards a mosaic regional structure may strengthen if one region prospers and its neighbouring region does not.

Further analysis, however, explicitly confirms the view that there is no systematic tendency for regions of a certain type – like the core regions – to do well and regions of another type to do badly. This is indicated by the correlations which were calculated between the variables describing the sensitivity of the sub-regions and the variables measuring wealth, development and unemployment in these regions (see Table 11.2). None of the correlations shown in the table is statistically significant. The zero correlations suggest that the rapid growth of rich regions is by no means the inevitable result of the European integration process. Like regions in general, some of these strong regions may succeed and others may not. In light of this analysis the effects of European integration on the prevailing regional trends thus seem to be minor.[3]

Table 11.1 Regional distributions in the sensitivity of manufacturing industries at province level

Province	*Share of employment (%)*			
	Open sector	*Closed sector*	*Sensitive sector*	*(strong + weak)*
Uusimaa	23	36	41	(26+15)
Varsinais-Suomi	18	27	55	(45+10)
Satakumta	38	25	37	(26+11)
Häme	28	43	30	(25+5)
Pirkanmaa	42	24	33	(22+11)
Päijät-Häme	26	44	30	(24+6)
Kymenlaakso	56	23	22	(18+4)
Etelä-Karjala	49	32	19	(14+5)
Etelä-Savo	20	54	27	(20+7)
Pohjois-Savo	26	36	38	(33+5)
Pohjois-Karjala	31	44	25	(22+3)
Keski-Suomi	33	35	32	(27+5)
Etelä-Pohjanmaa	20	53	27	(25+5)
Vaasanrannikkoseutu	29	26	45	(40+5)
Keski-Pohjanmaa	31	30	40	(23+17)
Pohjois-Pohjanmaa	12	32	55	(41+14)
Kainuu	30	36	34	(34+0)
Lappi	44	24	32	(28+4)
Ahvenanmaa	39	45	16	(11+5+
Finland	29	33	38	(28+10)

Source: Statistics Finland (1991), *Manufacturing* (special output)

3 It is interesting to discover the existence of a slight negative correlation (-0.22) between the sensitivity of the regions and their share of No votes in the referendum, indicating that the populations of the *sensitive* regions were slightly more in favour of EU membership than those of other regions.

Table 11.2 Correlations between three main economic indicators and the sensitivity of the manufacturing sector among the sub-regions

Sensitivity indicator	*GDP per capita 1990*	*Growth rate 1990*	*Unemployment rate 1991*
Share of sensitive sectors	0.16	0.18	0.02
Share of sensitive sectors with strong competitive performance	0.09	0.12	0.04
Share of sensitive sectors with weak competitive performance	0.13	0.13	-0.04

Source: Statistics Finland (1993), *Manufacturing, Regional database of Statistics Finland*

Regional trends have been towards centralization in Finland. Table 11.3 reveals how regional GDP per capita depend on the degree of urbanization of these regions. Previously rich regions – such as the province of Uusimaa which contains the Helsinki area – have grown rapidly. Within the provinces, the more prosperous centres have grown faster than the other regions. It is interesting to note in this context that many of the slow growth regions voted No in the referendum. The correlation coefficient between the share of No votes and the regional growth was also statistically significant (-0.26).

Table 11.3 Growth and GDP per capita among Finnish regions according to their degree of urbanization

Degree of urbanization	*Population growth 1980–1991 (%)*	*GDP per capita 1990 (Fmk)*
Low	-2.4	64,000
Average	1.6	75,500
High	6.8	101,200

NB: Sub-regions have been divided into three equal-sized groups according to their degree of urbanization

Source: *Statistics Finland* (1993), *Regional database of Statistics Finland*

Apart from a high degree of urbanization, those sub-regions which grew rapidly during 1980–1991 are characterized by the following features (the correlation coefficients are presented in parentheses):

1. large population (0.30)
2. high density of population (0.33)
3. short distance to the centre of the province (-0.26)

4. high per capita GDP (0.37)
5. low unemployment level (-0.24)
6. low share of primary production (-0.48) and a high share of service sector (0.51)
7. high share of qualified people (0.61)
8. low share of local government workers (-0.28).

The correlations were all statistically significant.

These findings would suggest that *strong* regions have grown rapidly in Finland. As it seems probable that the European integration process strengthens the trend towards centralization, the fear of those living in the stagnating regions seems to be, at least partly, justified. The findings may also be seen as well in line with Illeris' (1993) inductive theory of regional development by which he accounted for the mosaic-type regional development pattern in Western Europe. In this theory, he stressed the importance of local conditions such as the availability of people with adequate skills and sufficiently high population densities, both of which seem to characterize the sub-regions which have experienced growth in Finland during the last few years.

As the relatively small coefficients in many cases indicate, the interdependencies shown by the correlations are not very strong. Accordingly, the pattern of development is not unambiguous so that, in spite of the overall tendency to centralization, a mosaic-type development is likely simultaneously to occur. The simple core–periphery structure tends to loosen if *new* regions with favourable local conditions and goal-directed action succeed in exploiting the opportunities created by the European integration process.

Conclusions

This chapter has discussed the effects of European integration on regional development in the case of Finland – a country which joined the EU in 1995. It is widely believed that the process of European integration will largely benefit more advanced regions because of their agglomeration economies, large markets and human capital. This also appears to be the belief among Finns so far as the regional voting results of the referendum are to be believed. Regional trends have been towards centralization in Finland. In this light, it seems probable that these trends will continue and even strengthen due to the integration process.

Economic integration may, however, affect regional development in several ways so that the assessment of the effects *ex ante* is a very uncertain task. In general, the dynamics of the regional structure are rigid, which means that changes will not occur instantly. Because of this *geographical continuity*, the regional structure is multi-layered: at any given moment one can see traces of the lines and modes of production of preceding periods. To generalize, it might be said that there are three different Finlands: a dispersed rural Finland of declining economic and industrial importance, an older industrial Finland based on raw materials such as wood pulp and paper, and a contemporary high technology Finland with a strong service and communications sector heavily based in the south and west. One might say that, due to the European integration process, rural Finland is in difficulties, forest-based industrial Finland is not faced by great changes and contemporary high-technology Finland will meet with new opportunities.

Developments will not, of course, be as straightforward as stated above. The analysis would also suggest that different growth processes may occur simultaneously. The European integration process may create new possibilities for all regions provided they are able and willing to utilize them so that the process, at least potentially, can also level out regional disparities. The most crucial factor is how well a region can adapt to the new situation and how competitive it is under changing – and perhaps even turbulent – circumstances. In this sense, every region is more and more the architect of its own fortune.

References

Armstrong, H. (1994) *Convergence versus divergence in the European Union regional growth process, 1950–1990.* Paper for the 34th European Congress of the Regional Science Association, 23–26 August 1994, Groningen: Netherlands.

Bachtler, J., Clement, K. and Raines, P. (1993) 'European integration and foreign investment: the regional implications.' In L. Lundqvist and L.O. Persson (eds) *Visions and Strategies in European Integration. A North European Perspective.* Berlin: Springer-Verlag, pp.81–96.

Barro, R. and Sala-i-Martin, X. (1991) 'Convergence across states and regions.' *Brookings Papers on Economic Activity 1,* pp.107–182.

Buigues, P. and Ilzkovitz, F. (1988) *The Sectoral Impact of the Internal Market.* Directorate General for Economic and Financial Affairs, Document II/335/88-EN. Brussels: Commission of the European Communities.

Camagni, R.P. (1992) 'Development scenarios and policy guidelines for the lagging regions in the 1990s.' *Regional Studies 26,* 4, pp.361–74.

Commission of the European Communities (1994) 'Competitiveness and cohesion: trends in the regions.' *Fifth periodic report on the social and economic situation and development of the regions in the Community,* Luxembourg: Commission of the European Communities.

Dawson, A.H. (1993) *A Geography of European Integration.* London and New York: Belhaven Press.

Dunford, M. (1994) 'Winners and losers: the new map of economic inequality in the European Union.' *European Urban and Regional Studies 1,* pp.95–114.

Eskelinen, H. (1992) *The Nordic Model of Regional Policies in the 1990s Crisis: Collapse or Reorientation.* Paper for the Symposium on European Integration and Regional Policy, 22–23 May 1992, Galway: Ireland.

Halvorsen, K. (1993) 'European integration and the effects on regional development in Norway,' In L. Lundqvist and L.O. Persson (eds) *Visions and Strategies in European Integration. A North European Perspective.* Berlin: Springer-Verlag, pp. 61–78.

Illeris, S. (1993) 'Regional development in Western Europe: a mosaic model.' In L. Lundqvist and L.O. Persson (eds) *Visions and Strategies in European Integration. A North European Perspective.* Berlin: Springer-Verlag, pp.32–50.

Kajaste, I. (1990) *The Impact of 1992 on Finnish Industry*. Ministry of Finance, Economics Department, Discussion Paper 28. Finland.

Krugman, P. (1991) *Geography and Trade*. Cambridge, Massachusetts: Massachusetts Institute of Technology.

Lundqvist, L. and Persson, L.E. (1994) 'Northern perspectives on European integration – an introduction.' In L. Lundqvist and L.O. Persson (eds) *Northern Perspectives on European Integration*, NordREFO 1994:1, Stockholm: Sweden, pp.9–24.

Malinen, P., Häkkilä, J. and Jussila, H. (1993) *Finland's National Rural Policy Facing the Challenge of European Integration*. Research Institute of Northern Finland, University of Oulu, Research Reports 114, Oulu: Finland.

Martin, S. and Pearce, G. (1995) *Economic convergence or crisis management: European regional assistance in the UK*. Paper presented to the Regional Studies Association Conference, 'Regional Futures: Past, Present, East and West', May 1995, Gothenburg, Sweden.

Monnesland, J. (1995) 'Regional redistribution in Western Europe.' Paper presented to the Regional Studies Association Conference, 'Regional Futures: Past, Present, East and West', May 1995, Gothenburg: Sweden.

Pehkonen J. and Tervo H. (1995) *Persistence and Turnover in Regional Unemployment Disparities*. University of Jyväskylä, School of Business and Economics, Working Paper 154, Jyväskylä: Finland.

Peschel, K. (1992) 'European integration and regional development in Northern Europe.' *Regional Studies 26*, 4, pp.387–397.

Roura, J.R.C and Suárez-Villa, L. (1993) 'Regional economic integration and the evolution of disparities.' *Papers in Regional Science 72*, pp.369–388.

Statistical Yearbook of Finland (1994) Tilastokeskus Statistikentralen/Helsinki: Statistics Finland, p.32.

Statistics Finland (1991) *Database of Manufacturing Statistics*. Helsinki: Finland.

Statistics Finland (1993) *Manufacturing, Regional database of Statistics Finland*. Helsinki: Finland.

Statistics Finland (1995) *Finland's EU referendum, Population Statistics: Elections 1995:2*. Helsinki: Finland.

Steinle, W.J. (1992) 'Regional competitiveness and the Single Market.' *Regional Studies 26*, 4, pp.307–318.

Tervo, H. (1994) *Changing Regional Unemployment Differentials in Finland?*. Paper for the 34th European Congress of the Regional Science Association, 23–26 August 1994, Groningen: Netherlands.

Tervo, H., Niittykangas, H. and Nenonen, T. (1994) *EL ja Suomen aluekehitys* (The European Union and regional development in Finland), Jyväskylän yliopisto Keski-Suomen taloudellinen tutkimuskeskus julkaisuja 128, Jyväskylä: Finland.

CHAPTER 12

Regional Planning in Brandenburg

Putting Traditional Approaches to the Test

Wilhelm Benfer

Introduction

The State of Brandenburg represents one of five states that together make up what was the German Democratic Republic (GDR) (see Figure 12.1). It is five years since its people demanded and accomplished the abolishment of an entire state that was based on a very extensive system of government planning and control. Since unification in 1990, far-reaching attempts have been made to gradually transform the East German society in all its segments and dimensions with the objective to *westernize* its structure and functioning. With respect to Brandenburg, this process of adaptation has recently also extended into the field of regional planning. During the first half of 1994, the establishment of regional planning authorities in all parts of Brandenburg was completed. These authorities have been charged with the task of formulating regional development plans as a means of improving the living conditions of their inhabitants.

In this context, the chapter will first engage in some theoretical perspectives, naming some of the basic assumptions that underlie the pursuit of regional planning. This review will reveal that regional planning represents a very elaborate form of state activity demanding far-reaching powers to influence the course of regional development. It will then turn to a description of the current position of regional planning in the State of Brandenburg. It will be demonstrated that the way regional planning has been introduced in Brandenburg is a reflection of a rational and traditional approach to spatial planning on the regional level within the framework of national, state, and local plan formulation and implementation. The application of such an approach which developed over several decades in what was West Germany faces many challenges in the country's New Länder. The confrontation of these challenges with the expectations and assumptions that characterize the rational and traditional model of regional planning at work in Brandenburg casts serious doubt over the appropriateness of the approach to

Source: Statistisches Jahrbuch (1994) *für die Bundesrepulik Deutschland*

Figure 12.1 Brandenburg and the regions of Germany

regional planning chosen by the state government. The final part of the chapter, therefore, will elaborate and evaluate some of the critical issues that can be foreseen in the continued pursuit of this planning model. In doing so, some new elements of a revised strategy to effectively influence the process of regional development are introduced. They represent a necessary rejection of rational planning theory as a guiding principle for regional planning and a move toward a more pragmatic pursuit of regional management.

Theoretical Reflections on Regional Planning

One of the relatively few things that planners will agree on – regardless of either their specific field of work or their place of work – is the virtual impossibility of defining the nature and content of spatial planning. It is suggested that regional planning in Germany does not present an exception to this rather generalized observation. In the absence of an unequivocal definition it is not surprising that there exist various and significantly differing opinions about the historical origin of regional planning in this part of Europe. To some, regional planning is understood as one element in the puzzle of supra-local, state planning. Consequently, the origin of such activity in Germany is being traced back to the times of the Merowinger, i.e. dating from the fifth century AD onwards, when institutions of secular power were selectively placed at certain locations within the territory of the potentates (see Franz 1960).

Others argue that regional planning is the result of efforts to combine local development plans of neighbouring communities. From their point of view, regional planning in Germany began its life with the formation of planning compacts, such as the compact for Greater Berlin (established in 1910) and others that were mainly set up during the 1920s (see Brentano 1978). These compacts emerged as a result of the on-going process of industrialization. This process fostered the awareness that an approach to spatial planning was needed which focused its attention, first, on areas larger than that of a single community, and, second, on a comprehensive treatment of the many facets characterizing the developing centre–periphery phenomenon instead of the pursuit of single-issue planning which had existed before.

According to a third, rather formalized, line of thought, regional planning as an institutionalized form of public policy began after the passage of the Federal Regional Policy Act in 1965. This act opened the way for state governments to establish organizations charged solely and explicitly with the task of regional planning.

Irrespective of these differences, regional planning is usually understood as a form of supra-local and comprehensive spatial planning. In that sense, regional planning is supposed to, on the one hand, coordinate the different and at times conflicting spatial demands that exist within a given entity, and, on the other, to bring about a development that corresponds with objectives defined beforehand. In other words, regional planning as state activity serves as a means to influence the distribution of spatial resources in such a way that certain pre-set development goals will be achieved. Furthermore, regional planning is to integrate the various development objectives and activities of the plethora of groups and individuals that participate in the spatial development process.

In order to effectively perform these functions regional planning has to be capable of (Benz 1982):

1. selectively devising and applying policy instruments amidst a political environment that principally prefers equality and equal treatment over favouritism and discrimination
2. securing a status quo where necessary by fighting off development pressures which would be counter-productive in achieving pre-defined development goals
3. initiating activities, inducing investments, and activating resources which may promote or even secure a development process toward a given set of objectives
4. intervening in existing spatial structures and development processes where necessary in order to redirect them toward the desired development goals
5. coordinating national and local development goals
6. mediating the different interests of the various localities which together make up a region
7. coordinating the many policies and programmes of groups and organizations which do not have a specific spatial component.

This basic theoretical introduction to regional planning illustrates the complexity of this field of public policy. To successfully plan the course of spatial development at the regional level a wide array of conditions has to be met. The following part of the chapter illustrates to what extent the groundwork has been laid for the adoption and implementation of regional planning in one of Germany's New Länder: Brandenburg.

The Current State of Regional Planning in the State of Brandenburg

The institution of regional planning in post-war Germany reflects the general understanding of this government function as reviewed above. The institutions which were set up before and after the passage of the 1965 Raumordnungsgesetz (Regional Policy Act) were primarily charged with the task of mediating between any kind and form of supra-local planning committed to the promotion of equal living conditions in all parts of the country, and the demands of the individual communities trying to secure as big a slice of the overall development cake as possible.

When the Federal and Democratic Republics of Germany became united in 1990, the structure of public governance as it had developed in the western part of the country was adopted in its entirety by the eastern part of country. In this context, is not surprising that in order to harmonize the two planning systems the forms and functions of spatial planning as they had evolved in the Federal Republic became the standard model for the institutionalization of local, regional, and state-wide planning in the New Länder, i.e. the old GDR.

Before regional planning was institutionalized in Brandenburg, in 1991 the State government passed the 'Preliminary Act for the Establishment of State-Wide Planning and a State Development Programme' (Vorschaltgesetz zum Landesplanungsgesetz und Landesentwicklungsprogramm des Landes Brandenburg). Without being able to pass a law which would deal with the subject of state-wide spatial planning in a comprehensive way as soon as the other states in eastern Germany, the State Government of Brandenburg intended to formulate a set of rough guidelines for the development of its territory. In the absence of any regional planning, this preliminary act was to present local communities with goals and objectives to which they would have to adhere in order to get approval for their land-use plans.

On this basis, another law which marks the official beginning of regional planning in the State of Brandenburg was passed in 1993. The Act for the Establishment of Regional Planning and Soft-Coal Planning and the Redevelopment of Old Coal Areas (Gesetz zur Einführung der Regionalplanung und der Braunkohlen- und Sanierungsplanung im Land Brandenburg, RegBkPlG) divided the State into *five planning regions* varying in size from 4519 to 7180 square kilometres, in population from about 310,000 to 720,000 inhabitants (LUA 1994). In addition, the law defined an organizational structure which was to be adopted in all regional planning entities, the tasks and issues to be taken up by the planning agencies, the features of the regional plan, and the procedures which have to be followed en route to the formal passage of such a regional plan. These elements as defined in the RegBkPlG are reviewed below.

Regional Planning – A Definition By Law

In its introductory paragraph, the law stipulates that regional planning is to be understood as the 'supra-local and comprehensive state-wide planning in the spatial context of a region' by which 'the natural and economic bases and conditions for human existence should be secured and developed' (Paragraph 1, RegBkPlG).

As has been argued above, such a far-reaching definition of regional planning and its functions is typical for its implementation in Germany. It rests on the assumption that a single agency is capable of coordinating all those forces that impact upon the process of spatial development in a region and of manipulating them towards the achievement of certain development goals. These forces comprise all those institutions in the public sector that pursue a comprehensive planning approach, other public sector agencies which are involved in sectoral planning, quasi-governmental organizations which are also engaged in sectoral planning, and an almost indefinite number of private sector actors that influence the process of spatial development through their investment decisions.

Organizational structure and funding of regional planning

Within the German system of governance, regional planning can be placed either in the realm of state or local government. In the absence of any federal regulations prescribing a certain format in which regional planning has to be pursued, the forms and organizational structure of regional planning varies from state to state. The State government of Brandenburg decided on a somewhat peculiar institutional model. Five regional planning associations were set up whose members are the counties that belong to respective planning areas. Given the relatively large size of the Brandenburg counties it only takes between two and four of them to make up a regional planning association. Although delegating regional planning, in principle, is a function of local government, the state government provides all the funding necessary for setting up the planning agencies and their day-to-day work.

Each regional planning association follows the same organizational layout, with an administrative arm, the *regional planning unit*, and a political body, the *regional planning council*. The former elaborates the *regional development plan* while the latter is responsible for making all those decisions that are necessary to ratify the plan. The council is comprised of up to forty members who are to be nominated and elected by the respective county councils. The political parties are represented in the regional planning council by the same ratios as in the county councils. The regional planning council elects an executive board of up to seven of its members who are then responsible for running the association in between the general meetings of the council.

The regional planning agenda

As pointed out above, the basic task of the regional planning associations is to produce a development plan for the region. The law which established regional planning in the State of Brandenburg also specifies the content of such planning documents. It stipulates that planning principles and objectives should be formulated with regard to the following areas:

- population and the labour market
- settlement pattern
- housing and transportation
- commerce
- technical infrastructure
- social and cultural infrastructure, historic preservation
- tourism and leisure

- agriculture and forestry
- landscape preservation and protection, open space development
- water resources
- waste disposal and contaminated land
- emission control
- soft coal mining
- energy and heat supply
- protection of raw materials
- military defence and civilian use of military premises (conversion).

In light of the complexity of the above issues, the regional planning associations are free to produce plans that cover only a selection of issues or focus on parts of the entire region. The latter option was included in the regional planning legislation in view of the particular layout of the planning regions. With the State of Brandenburg forming a ring around Berlin, each of the five regions was to have a common border with the nation's capital in the middle as well as a share of the rural, often underdeveloped, hinterland. In order to avoid all attention being be focused upon the growth and development within the Greater Berlin area, the five regions in Brandenburg were established as a means of hopefully shifting some of that growth away from Berlin to those outward places that are in urgent need of economic development. Without such a perspective, it was feared, these areas would continue to suffer from depopulation and impoverishment.

For all of the above substantive aspects of the development plan, principles and objectives must be formulated which are sought to influence and shape the development process of the region. The regional planning associations are, however, not entirely free to determine the actual content of such principles and objectives. They are bound, instead, by those planning goals which were formulated by the Federal and State governments. In most cases, these goals are more general in nature, and rather unspecific with regard to specific locations or even plots of land. In this context, regional planning is responsible for defining these planning goals in more concrete terms so that they can be used by local communities as guidance for their land-use planning activities.

The planning goals which were defined by higher levels of government, i.e. State and National Ministries, are not the only aspects which have to be taken into account in the formulation of regional development strategies. Reflecting the general nature of spatial planning in Germany with a combination of top-down and bottom-up approaches, the process of formulating regional planning principles and objectives also has to take into consideration the demands and challenges that are put forth by local authorities and other institutions, public or private, which pursue strategies that impact upon the regional development process.

Soon after the regional planning associations had come into existence in the summer of 1994, they all decided individually to immediately focus on the existing and future settlement structure within their regions. These activities seek to adopt and implement the central place theory which has been a basic tool of supra-local planning for many decades (for the theoretical base see Christaller 1933). The State government had, in the meantime, worked out a draft plan of the central places of the higher order leaving it to the regional planning associations to supplement this network of cities by the central places of the lower order. Communities of this kind are expected to function as places where certain public and private goods and services – especially those that are demanded daily, e.g. school education, groceries, local government and administration and basic medical facilities – are located and offered.

Whereas the completion of the network of central places by the regional planning associations was mandated by State government, the five planning units subsequently chose different paths toward the formulation of the overall regional development plan. While one planning association picked transportation as the next issue to tackle, others decided to expand the central places study and include those communities which have the potential to serve as regionally important locations for housing, business, agriculture or tourism. Again others devoted their attention to the issues of mining, the protection of raw materials, and landscape preservation. This variety of strategies is a clear reflection of the fact that the regional planning associations see themselves as institutions of local government.

Procedures

Whatever planning documents the regional planning associations are involved in they all need the official approval of the State government, i.e. the Ministry of the Environment, Nature Preservation and Regional Policy. Yet, before a plan is submitted for approval, a wide range of institutions, public and private, have to be given the opportunity to state their views and concerns regarding any detail of the planning document. This kind of participation must be done at a very early stage in the formulation of the plan and, again, after the completion of the draft version. Although the number of those institutions which have to be given a chance to participate varies from region to region (reasons are, for example, the different number of local communities and counties), it never constitutes less than several hundreds of participants. After all stated views and concerns have been considered by the regional planning unit, the regional planning association has to formally adopt it. Adding the time needed by the State Ministry to evaluate the document, it becomes obvious that the entire process of regional plan-making takes an extraordinarily long time.

In light of the development pressures that exist in some parts of the regions (especially in those close to Berlin) and the dire need to spare the rural parts of the State of Brandenburg from depopulation, such a timescale appears too long. If regional planning is restricted to the ways and means that are set forth in the respective state law, it is doubtful whether spatial planning on the regional level can succeed. Unfortunately, the systemic characteristics of the approach to regional planning chosen by the State government of Brandenburg are not the only challenges with which development planning within the State's regions has to cope.

Challenges to Regional Planning in Brandenburg

The relatively short period of time in which regional planning has now been operating in the State of Brandenburg has nevertheless been long enough to demonstrate the many difficulties that have to be faced daily. The following selection reviews four of the difficulties which represent serious challenges to the pursuit of regional planning and threaten its chances of successful impact upon the process of spatial development.

The challenge of adopting regional planning in an area where state planning was only recently dismissed

When the wall came down in November 1989 and the two Germanies were united, politically, socially and economically, in October 1990, a state had been abandoned which had been grounded to a large extent on the principle of state planning. Based on the goals and objectives formulated in five-year plans, a vast array of specific development targets were derived for just about every possible aspect of public life, i.e. the production of goods and services in its widest sense. On all but the lowest level of state authority that were involved in this planning process, special agencies were responsible for the spatial ramifications and organization of this tremendous effort to plan a society. Quite fittingly, this approach to spatial policy was described as follows:

> Planning of the location of the production forces as the core of social development, i.e. placement of investments grounded on the principles of spatial proportionality based upon a territorial balance of infrastructure facilities, employees, investments, housing construction etc. aimed at a spatial structure in accordance with the demands of the spatial specification of the laws of social development. (Werner 1981, translated by the author)

When the people of the GDR demanded that their party leadership should tear down the wall and, subsequently, take all necessary steps towards unification with the Federal Republic of Germany (FRG), it also meant a rejection of a system of near total state authority. In its place, a new social market economic order was established which took hold of all spheres of life, private and public. In many ways, this radical change was sold by the new political leadership as a move toward individual freedom and self-determination.

It has become obvious that the overall development during the last five years has swung too far in the opposite direction. The unification with the FRG prompted an understanding of the new order that resented, to a large degree, all state authority. The case of spatial planning very aptly illustrates this point. Many local communities in the New Länder tried to locate as much of the desired growth within their own boundaries. These efforts resulted in a zoning practice that attempted to develop vastly oversized plots of land especially for commercial and industrial use. The State of Brandenburg, which forms a ring around the separate City State of Berlin, represents a good example of these misguided hopes and strategies of local politicians. Attempts by state or regional planning agencies to limit the extent of excessive local zoning were met with harsh criticism by local governments. This criticism can, in most cases, be reduced to the core argument that within the German system of spatial planning local governments are granted the sovereignty over the formulation of local development plans. The notion that local self-determination has to be exercised within the boundaries set by Federal and State laws is thus rejected.

In the State of Brandenburg, such sentiment among local politicians presents an added difficulty for the agencies responsible for regional planning. As pointed out earlier, these agencies were set up by law as institutions of local government, with counties representing the members of the regional planning associations. In this capacity, regional planning authorities are in the delicate position of being entrusted with representing the interests of localities toward State government, on the one hand, as well as specifying the particular goals and objectives set by State authorities to control local development, on the other.

The challenge of pursuing regional planning amidst an almost unparalleled process of industrial decline and transformation

When the political, social, and economic unification of the two Germanies had been completed in October 1990, the economy of the New Länder was ill prepared to successfully take part in the up to then unknown world of market economics. Because of their past, businesses in the former GDR neither had a clear idea of the forces that determine a market economic order nor of the rules of the game which must be mastered in order to survive in the market place. It goes way beyond the scope of this chapter to present an overview of the difficulties that entrepreneurs faced, and still face, in former East Germany. Undoubtedly, however, the following three aspects accounted in large part for the dramatic downturn of the economy in the former East Germany.

First, practically from one day to the next, goods that were produced in the East had to compete with those made in West Germany in a market place in which design and marketing determine to a large extent the success or failure of a product. Both of these critical factors had formerly played almost no part in the Socialist East German economy. Second, in 1990 the East German parliament decided to set up a trust company that was to take ownership of all (roughly 12,000) formerly state-owned businesses and privatize them subsequently. The process of selling off these people's assets (Volkseigentum) did not only take a long time (it still is not quite completed at the time of writing), it also favoured the acquisition of companies by businesses from West Germany or elsewhere in the Western world. Usually, only Western investors could provide the capital necessary for the restructuring of the old businesses in order to make them competitive. In many cases, unfortunately, these attempts failed; some intentionally, some just did not have a chance. Third, the one competitive advantage that the formerly state-owned businesses in the New Länder could have brought to bear, was lost almost as soon as it was needed. Over the four decades since the Second World War, trade relations had developed between the GDR and the other member countries of the Socialist block, most important among them the Soviet Union. With its disintegration and the political liberalization all over the Eastern world, the old order faded. Goods and services produced in East Germany had to be bought using the hard Deutschmark, usually making them too expensive for the former trading partners further east. The resulting dramatic decline and transformation of the former East German economy will now be briefly discussed. The facts and figures mentioned refer, unless stated otherwise, to the State of Brandenburg.

Since the GDR economy had to place more importance on the provision of sufficient jobs for the population (unemployment did not exist officially) than on productivity and efficiency, the unification prompted a massive wave of unemployment. Starting from practically zero in 1989, the number of unemployed people soared to a monthly average of 182,000 in 1992 representing an unemployment rate of about 15 per cent (Ministerium für Arbeit, Soziales, Gesundheit und Frauen 1993). Since then unemployment has slightly but steadily diminished with roughly 158,000 people without jobs equalling 13.7 per cent in May 1995 (Ministerium für Arbeit, Soziales, Gesundheit und Frauen 1995). In some places, especially around the State of Berlin, the negative trends of the past concerning the scale of unemployment have shown a reversal possibly indicating that the worst is over for the respective labour markets. Unfortunately, this may not be true for the outer areas of the State of Brandenburg where unemployment levels of around 20 per cent and above can still be found. Generally, however, it should not be overlooked that present unemployment rates are still well above the national average as well as the average unemployment rate for the New Länder.

Apart from the labour market, it has also been the industrial structure that underwent a dramatic process of change (for the following numbers see Landesamt für Datenverarbeitung und Statistik Brandenburg 1994). The agricultural sector, with its central place in East German ideology and economics, employed about 14 per cent of the total workforce of Brandenburg in 1989. It took only four years for this figure to shrink to just over 5 per cent. Measured in absolute numbers this decline is even more dramatic: from almost 210,000 in 1989 to merely 54,000 people working in agriculture in 1993. The employment in the secondary sector has followed a similar pattern. While manufacturing accounted for about 28 per cent, i.e. 430,000 employees of total employment in 1989, this percentage decreased to 15 per cent in 1993. Again, only the absolute numbers of employees fully reflect the real extent of the industrial transformation that has taken place in

Brandenburg. In 1989, the manufacturing industries employed about 430,000 people. Four years later, only 151,000 jobs were left in the remaining manufacturing businesses. By comparison, the tertiary sector has done slightly better: its share of Brandenburg's total employment increased from 21 per cent in 1989 to almost 35 per cent in 1993 as a result of a workforce that expanded from about 320,000 in 1989 to roughly 350,000 people in 1993. This fact is, however, not surprising given the heavy emphasis of the GDR economy on the production of agricultural and industrial goods.

These dramatic changes of the industrial structure in the State of Brandenburg and elsewhere in the New Länder have been described in the literature as a process of deindustrialization of Eastern German regions (BfLR 1994). In fact, the changes reviewed above indicate the transition from an industrial to a post-industrial economic order which currently characterizes most Western economies. However, despite this apparent similarity in the economic development process in Western and Eastern Germany one tremendous difference exists, namely that the former had several decades to undergo and adjust to such changes whereas the economies of the five New Länder, by contrast, have to go through the transformation toward a service economy within a matter of a few years. Assuming that the Brandenburg economy will eventually, in its industrial structure, become similar to that of Western Germany the above developments also suggest that the restructuring of the State's economy is far from over yet. The fact that the productivity in many industries in the New Länder is still only at about two-thirds of the respective levels in the western part of the country may serve as an indication for how long this process of industrial change will still take.

The challenge of regional planning based on a rational model that may very well not be applicable

The brief description of the system of regional planning as it was put into place in the State of Brandenburg illustrates an approach which is derived to a large extent from planning theory. Regional planning is the lowest form of supra-local planning specifying the goals and objectives of state-wide planning and, on this basis, coordinating local land-use development. In order to ensure that people in all parts of a country enjoy a similar quality of life, regional planning must be comprehensive in its scope and be able to manipulate the course of spatial development as it unfolds.

The environment in which regional planning is to function in the State of Brandenburg (as in other states of the New Länder), however, tells a very different story. Many, if not most, of the preconditions that have to be given for a successful regional planning strategy do not exist.

When the parliament of Brandenburg passed the legislation establishing regional planning three years after the State itself had come into existence, no state-wide development planning in document form existed. Apart from a few principles that were to serve as the basis of such plans (see Vorschaltgesetz 1991), work had just begun on a development plan defining central locations of the higher order affecting about forty cities in the State (see Landesentwicklungsplan I 1994). In this case, regional planning was supposed to further specify the goals and objectives of state-wide planning which were only beginning to be defined themselves.

The unification of the two Germanies meant the repeal of all GDR planning legislation and the sudden adoption of a comprehensive and elaborated system of spatial planning as it had developed in West Germany over four decades. As can easily be imagined, the completion of all the statutory steps in the procedure toward passing a local land-use plan under these circumstances takes considerable time and effort. Yet investors urged to build houses, develop industrial sites, or improve infrastructure facilities as quickly as possible. As a consequence, local communities generally were under considerable pressure to move ahead with the formulation of local land-use plans as fast as they possibly could. Regional planning, thus, started to effectively operate four years after local plans had begun to emerge. This delay prevented local land-use planning from being set in the framework of meaningful supra-local guidelines. This dilemma will have serious implications for the future pursuit of regional planning in that it will have very few opportunities to be proactive in its character toward local land-use planning. Instead, it will have to deal with the consequences of a spatial development process which was largely left to happenstance and, therefore, often capricious in nature.

Further impairing the effectiveness of the regional planning associations is the inadequate staffing of their planning units. Given the shortage of personnel, it will take quite some time before the five regional planning agencies will have formulated any set of regional development plans that reflect the comprehensive nature of the agencies' tasks. In order to avoid the obvious delay in establishing an effective regional planning strategy caused by such an approach, the regional planning associations could pursue alternative courses of action. However, as pointed out earlier, their budgets are entirely financed by State government under the condition that they produce a regional development plan; any other activity would require funding by the members of the associations themselves. Given the dire and worsening state of county finances, especially in the New Länder, it is unlikely that the regional planning associations will deviate from the task they are charged with, i.e. a very traditional pursuit of planning regional development.

The challenge of regional planning amidst great development pressures exerted from outside the region

The final challenge which should be mentioned in the context of this chapter is related to the geographical context in which the State of Brandenburg is set. The pursuit of regional planning in most, if not all, of the State's planning regions is heavily influenced by two factors that are located outside the State. First, three of the five regions border Poland. Second, the State of Berlin as the single most important growth pole in this eastern part of Germany lies in the middle of the State of Brandenburg.

Poland represents a spatial entity that offers obvious and considerable competitive advantages for investors. This fact is playing an increasingly important role as the negotiations for Poland's admission to the European Union (EU) advance, steadily removing various obstacles for cross-border trading. With the capital of Germany being only about 60 kilometres away from the Polish border, the lower wages, the less complicated administrative procedures for developing an industrial or commercial location etc. in Poland are making investments across that border instead of in Brandenburg increasingly attractive. This does not only concern businesses from outside the eastern part of Germany which are attracted to the nation's developing capital, but also those enterprises that are still located in Berlin but have to move outward because of the booming property market and its tremendous price increases for industrial and commercial properties. As a result, the primary task of regional planning, i.e. to secure and develop the economic bases and conditions for human existence, becomes more difficult to fulfil.

The same applies to the State of Berlin and its implications for the process of spatial development in Brandenburg. Berlin, with a population of roughly 3.5 million and an area of 883 square kilometres, represents an economy that is very different from that of the State of Brandenburg where about 2.5 million people are dispersed over 29,500 square kilometres of space. Especially since the national parliament decided to move the capital from Bonn to Berlin, the latter has become a prime target for national as well as international investments. Since unification, Berlin has become the workplace for many people from Brandenburg. According to a recent report (Schuldt 1995), nearly one-tenth of the workforce of the State of Brandenburg is employed by a company located in Berlin. The rate of the reverse job-migration, i.e. from Berlin into Brandenburg, measures only about 30 per cent of the number of employees travelling into Berlin for work.

The attractiveness of Berlin led early population forecasts, which were made soon after unification, to predict a gain of about one million people for the city by the year 2010. These overly optimistic expectations have, in the meantime, become more moderate. The 1994 master plan for the city's development, for instance, was formulated based upon the assumption that the City of Berlin will experience a net population growth of 300,000 up to the year 2010. Undoubtedly, though, Berlin will for quite some time to come attract and accommodate much of the overall economic growth in this eastern part of Germany. While many jobs will go to Berlin, the State of Brandenburg is likely to become more and more the place where people will live and not work thereby avoiding the high living costs in the nation's capital. In addition, the high population density within Berlin's borders makes Brandenburg the preferred place where Berliners enjoy spending their leisure time. If in fact these trends materialize on an even bigger scale in the future, the disadvantages for Brandenburg of having Berlin in the middle of its territory will outweigh its positive side-effects. It remains to be seen to what extent this outlook will have to be corrected if the people of both States confirm the recent parliamentary decision to create the new State of Berlin-Brandenburg possibly by the end of this decade.

From Regional Planning to Management – New Directions for Regional Planning

The challenges reviewed above clearly cast great doubt over the pursuit of regional planning in the form it is supposed to be undertaken. Many of the preconditions which must be given to make a traditional approach to regional planning work successfully do not exist. In addition, the force of external factors is of such a magnitude that they too seriously jeopardize the chances of regional planning effectively achieving its goal, i.e. improving the social, natural and economic living conditions of the region's inhabitants. While it seems comparatively easy to arrive at such a conclusion, it is considerably more difficult to outline out the contours of new regional planning. However, the following elements of such a modified planning strategy can be identified.

Despite the many problems associated with a traditional approach as reviewed above, it nevertheless should be part of any attempts to plan regional development. Although it will take a considerable length of time, regional planning as it has begun to evolve in Brandenburg will eventually cover the entire region with a comprehensive set of development objectives. These objectives represent a necessary framework in which all spatial development initiatives should be pursued. The current focus of the regional planning agencies on defining the network of central places provides a suitable example for illustrating this point. This relatively old tool of regional planning clearly provides a first, yet important, element in structuring a spatial settlement structure. Through the application of this tool those communities are identified that will perform a vital function in securing a comparable quality in the supply of basic public services throughout the region.

As a second element of regional management, the current organizational structure set up for the pursuit of regional planning in Brandenburg needs to be modified. In order to at least have the chance to impact upon the course of spatial development, regional management agencies should be set in place that are also involved in, if not responsible for, the coordination of regional and other forms of state assistance. Such participation in the process of directly pursuing specific development measures represents a prerequisite for ensuring that the provision of development assistance does not run counter to basic regional development goals. This kind of financial responsibility granted to regional institutions, however, may at best represent the realistic, not the desired, role which regional management agencies should assume in this respect. To fully guarantee that regional assistance is given in correspondence with the goals and objectives that exist for a region these agencies should, in fact, themselves be in charge of administering the provision of grants, loans and other forms of assistance. However, getting State

Ministries to let regional institutions coordinate their development assistance schemes should prove to be difficult enough to achieve; having them transfer sizeable amounts of money out of their pockets into those of regional management agencies remains a doubtful possibility for the foreseeable future. In any case, those State Ministries that provide substantial amounts of regional assistance should reformulate their policy guidelines so that the implementation of assistance schemes takes into consideration the goals and objectives that exist for individual places.

In addition, the current regional planning agencies should be expanded and changed into institutions whose tasks go beyond the somewhat narrow pursuit of traditional regional planning, i.e. formulating a plan. As a first step, the economic development offices and companies which usually are part of county administrations, or are in county ownership, would have to be integrated into the newly set-up regional management agencies. Through this organizational change it would become possible to have the economic development activities performed by the counties based upon the existing regional development goals.

Furthermore, the regional planning associations are currently bound by law to produce a planning document as opposed to pursuing other activities toward improving the living conditions throughout their regions. As pointed out earlier, this process is, and will continue to be, time-consuming to an extent that seriously limits the effectiveness of regional planning. This narrow definition of the task has to be abandoned allowing the agencies responsible for regional management to be involved in the pursuit of individual projects which are able to provide a stimulus for the development of a region. Although such a claim appears reasonable it also has the potential for provoking widespread resentment. Local communities, for instance, could feel that their self-rule and determination were being undermined by such activities of regional institutions. Given the fact, however, that in general local communities are increasingly less able to finance their own development measures, it may not altogether be unrealistic to hope that they would agree with such an expanded scope of activities performed by regional management agencies.

The above elements of a regional management strategy which in part would supersede the present system of regional planning are derived from an analysis of the status quo in the State of Brandenburg. If one turns to the literature on regional planning and regional development it can be observed that a great deal of the recently published material reflect a similar need for a new form of regional planning (with regard to Germany see, for instance, ARL 1991, 1994, 1995; Fürst 1990, 1993; Kistenmacher, Geyer and Hartmann 1994). In many cases, the authors develop their arguments for a modification of regional planning based on an analysis of thirty or more years of planning practice at the regional level in West Germany. The scope of changes that are proposed varies considerably.

One set of propositions turns to the traditional instrument of regional planning, i.e. the regional development plan itself. It has become a widely accepted notion that the formulation of such a planning document takes a long time. In Western Germany, the majority of current regional development plans represent updated versions of earlier documents. Given the many particulars of the procedures which have to be followed for revising a regional development plan after it has been in operation for ten or more years, the length of time needed for the completion of this process results in a diminishing ability of regional planning to proactively define the framework for future spatial development.

Within the context of the New Länder, the case of Brandenburg shows that the same argument applies to the first generation of regional plans that are currently in the making. It has been suggested, therefore, that regional planning agencies should focus their attention on the formulation of lean regional plans. Instead of considering a wide array of substantive policy areas, it is proposed that such modified plans concentrate on a definition of the network of central places, a determination of regionally significant locations for future residential and industrial development, a description of the transportation infrastructure needed to support the desired settlement structure, and a delineation of those areas where the preservation of open space should assume the highest priority.

Other suggestions for modifying regional planning in Germany stress the need for effective programmes for action. While traditional regional plans contain a variety of goals and objectives for the development of the region, they generally tend to neglect the issue and importance of what exactly should be done toward achieving the stated goals. In order to effectively influence the course of spatial development regional planning agencies should formulate such action programmes which include details of concrete activities and ways for their implementation.

In this context, it becomes obvious that the agencies responsible for regional planning would have to give up their traditional role working more or less removed from the actual spatial development process. Proposing specific development projects and activities requires regional planning to cooperate much more intensively with other actors who play a significant role in the development of localities and regions. The planning agencies would have to assume a moderating as well as a mediating role among the different interest groups and actors primarily engaged in the implementation of development measures. The pursuit of such measures, especially but not limited to the area of economic development, could in fact be declared the task of specific agencies set up at the regional level. Suggestions have been made for institutions of this sort which would, for example, be responsible for the development and marketing of old industrial sites within a region, or for setting up and administering a regional network of nature preserves etc.

The search for new approaches to regional planning and policy-making has also taken hold of the federal level of government in Germany. In 1994, the Federal Ministry responsible for regional policy decided not to issue yet another report with potentially rather vague policy objectives and guidelines but instead to stage a so-called regional conference. Incidentally, the conference took place in the Brandenburg city of Eberswalde. It was the intention of the organizers to provide a forum for a number of different institutions and interest groups of the region – private as well as public – to analyse the problems that are associated with the difficult and sensitive relations between the States of Berlin and Brandenburg. In addition, it was hoped that this exchange of views and concerns would also result in jointly formulating strategies for the solution of such problems. Based on a preliminary evaluation of the outcomes of this conference, the Federal Ministry has since declared its commitment to a continuation of such meetings thereby making regional conferences a new instrument in its tool box for promoting regional development.

This chapter has illustrated the many problems associated with the implementation of a traditional approach to regional planning in one of the five New Länder in Germany. The particular circumstances under which this approach has been pursued pose serious questions with regard to the applicability and adequacy of a form of regional planning that is largely based on rational planning theory. Brandenburg with its only five-year history as a separate state within the FRG provides a good testing ground in this context, revealing strengths as well as weaknesses of the traditional approach chosen for planning regional development.

In light of the ongoing changes, if not transformations, of Eastern European societies, e.g. Poland, the Czech Republic, Hungary (see Chapter 13), etc., the question arises whether the experiences currently being made with establishing regional planning in Brandenburg could be used or transferred to those countries. In some respect, they also continue to undergo dramatic changes in their internal political, social and economic fabric. Further research is needed to deal with this kind of question. Assuming that regional planning represents an activity that should be carried out in every nation, a case study like the above may provide some guidance especially for countries in Eastern Europe that intend to join the EU. Any efforts to westernize there systems of spatial planning at the regional level should focus on the strengths and avoid the weaknesses of a traditional model of regional planning that appears as no longer adequate for effectively dealing with the many challenges that face today's regions.

References

Akademie für Raumordnung und Landesplanung (ARL) (1991) Perspektiven der kommunalen Zusammenarbeit in Niedersachsen. Hannover: Akademie für Raumordnung und Landesplanung.

Akademie für Raumordnung und Landesplanung (ARL) (1994) Aktuelle Fragen der Landesentwicklung in Nordrhein-Westfalen. Forschungs- und Sitzungsberichte der Akademie für Raumordnung und Landesplanung, No. 194. Hannover: Akademie für Raumordnung und Landesplanung.

Akademie für Raumordnung und Landesplanung (ARL) (1995) Zukunftsaufgabe Regionalplanung. Forschungs- und Sitzungsberichte der Akademie für Raumordnung und Landesplanung, No. 200. Hannover: Akademie für Raumordnung und Landesplanung.

Benz, A. (1982) Regionalplanung in der Bundesrepublik Deutschland – Eine empirische Untersuchung zur Organisation und Problemlösungsfähigkeit. Beiträge zum Siedlungs- und Wohnungswesen und zur Raumplanung, No. 80. Münster: Selbstverlag des Instituts für Siedlungs- und Wohnungswesen und des Zentralinstituts für Raumplanung der Universität Münster.

Brentano, I. (1978) Verfassungs- und raumordnungsrechtliche Probleme der Regionalplanung. Beiträge zum Siedlungs- und Wohnungswesen und zur Raumplanung, No. 47. Münster: Selbstverlag des Instituts für Siedlungs- und Wohnungswesen und des Zentralinstituts für Raumplanung der Universität Münster.

Bundesforschungsanstalt für Landeskunde und Raumordnung (BfLR) (1994) 'Deindustrialisierung ostdeutscher Regionen – eine bittere Realität!' BfLR- Mitteilungen 3 (June 1994): 1–3.

Christaller, W. (1933) Die zentralen Orte in Süddeutschland. Eine ökonomisch- geographische Untersuchung über die Gesetzmäßigkeit der Verbreitung und Entwicklung der Siedlungen mit städtischen Funktionen. Jena.

Franz, G. (1960) 'Raumplanung im Historischen Geschehen.' In Raumforschung – 25 Jahre Raumforschung in Deutschland, ed. Akademie für Raumforschung und Landesplanung. Bremen: Walter Dorn Verlag.

Fürst, D. (1990) Regionalplanung der 90er Jahre. Forschungs- und Sitzungsberichte der Akademie für Raumforschung und Landesplanung, no. 186. Hannover: Akademie für Raumforschung und Landesplanung.

Fürst, D. (1993) 'Von der Regionalplanung zum Regionalmanagement?' Die öffentliche Verwaltung 13 (July 1993).

Gesetz zur Einführung der Regionalplanung und der Braunkohlen- und Sanierungsplanung im Land Brandenburg (1993) State of Brandenburg, GVBl, p.170.

Kistenmacher, H., Geyer, Th. and Hartmann, P. (1994) Regionalisierung in der kommunalen Wirtschaftsförderung. Cologne: Deutscher Gemeindeverlag.

Landesamt für Datenverarbeitung und Statistik Brandenburg (1994) Statistisches Jahrbuch 1994. Potsdam: Landesamt für Datenverarbeitung und Statistik Brandenburg.

Landesentwicklungsplan I – Zentralörtliche Gliederung. Draft (1994) Potsdam: Ministerium für Umwelt, Naturschutz und Raumordnung.

Landesumweltamt des Landes Brandenburg (LUA) (1994) Brandenburg regional '93. Potsdam: Landesumweltamt.

Ministerium für Arbeit, Soziales, Gesundheit und Frauen (1993) Arbeitsmarktbericht für das Land Brandenburg. Potsdam: Ministerium für Arbeit, Soziales, Gesundheit und Frauen.

Ministerium für Arbeit, Soziales, Gesundheit und Frauen (1995) Arbeitsmarktbericht für Mai 1995. Potsdam: Ministerium für Arbeit, Soziales, Gesundheit und Frauen.

Schuldt, K. (1995) Aktuelle Tendenzen der Arbeitspendelwanderung im Land Brandenburg. Landesagentur für Struktur und Arbeit, Study No. 24. Kleinmachnow: Landesagentur für Struktur und Arbeit.

Statistisches Jahrbuch (1994) für die Bundesrepublik Deutschland Statistisches Bundesamt, Wiesbaden.

Vorschaltgesetz zum Landesplanungsgesetz und Landesentwicklungsprogramm des Landes Brandenburg (1991) State of Brandenburg, GVBl, p.616.

Werner, F. (1981) 'Deutsche Demokratische Republik.' In Daten zur Raumplanung, Part B, ed. Akademie für Raumforschung und Landesplanung. Hannover, Akademie für Raumforschung und Landesplanung.

CHAPTER 13

Regional Policy Development in Central and Eastern Europe

Ruth Downes

Introduction

This chapter aims to provide an overview of the main trends in regional socio-economic disparities and regional policy responses which have emerged in Central and East European (CEE) countries since the start of the political and economic transformation process. The focus of the analysis is on the so-called Visegrad countries (Poland, Hungary, the Czech Republic and Slovakia), with particular attention paid to Hungary (see Figure 13.1), although many of the points are applicable to all the countries of the region, as well as to some extent to the successor states of the former Soviet Union.

The chapter first examines the reasons why the regional dimension is an issue at all in the CEE countries and the nature of emerging regional disparities. It then focuses on the present regional policy response and illustrates some of the main trends using Hungary, where the response has been the most advanced, as a case study. Finally, future problems and issues relating to the development of this are highlighted.

Why is the Regional Dimension an Issue in CEE Countries?

Emergence of regional socio-economic disparities

The reform task being undertaken by the CEE countries, and the former Soviet Union, is virtually unprecedented. The need to construct a new political and economic system in the ruins of a completely different one has never before been undertaken on this scale. Experience or models which could be used as a guideline are therefore missing. In addition, numerous factors (both external and internal) influence the progress of transition in the individual countries in both a positive

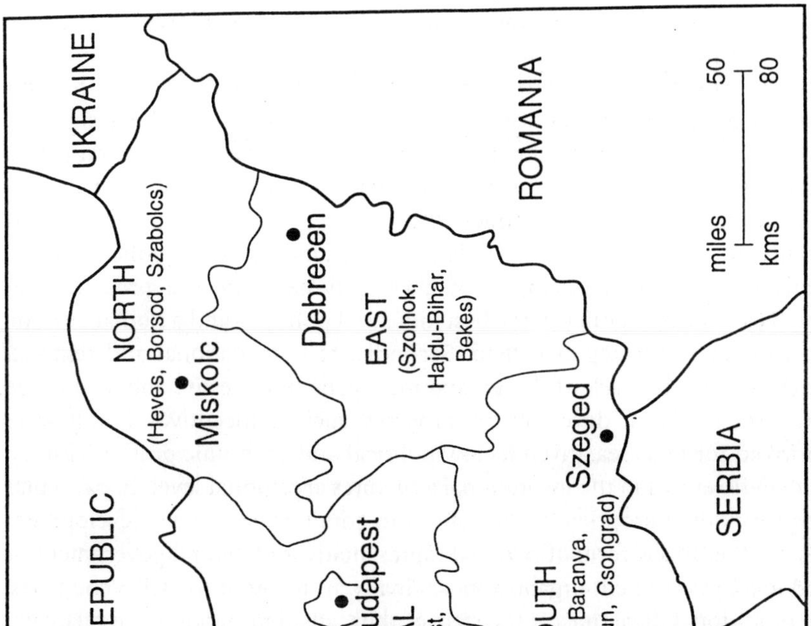

Source: European Marketing Data and Statistics 1993, *28th Edition, p.98*

Figure 13.1 Regions of Hungary

and negative way. Some of these have been anticipated and addressed, while others are unexpected or completely outwith the control of the transition countries.

Given this background, it is perhaps surprising that regional questions should be raised at all in the transition countries. The nature and severity of the economic decline and the enormity of the reform task could suggest that addressing regional ramifications is perhaps rather unimportant.

Certainly, priority was given to *national* rather than regional economic reforms at the start of the process of political and economic liberalisation. The design and implementation of regional development strategies or policies was constrained by several factors. Firstly, regional or spatial problems were considered of secondary importance to national economic policy issues and regional development was left substantially to market forces. In Poland, for example, some policy-makers, particularly in the industrial field, adopted a highly neo-Liberal approach under the motto 'No industrial policy in the best industrial policy' – and a similar attitude was also evident in the regional field. Secondly, at both national and regional levels, there was both a lack of design and management expertise and a shortage of government funds for development measures, such as incentives. Funds were not prioritized for this area, given its low political and economic profile. Thirdly, there were deficiencies in the institutional structures at regional level. In particular there was a lack of appropriate organizations to administer regional development measures – either in the form of regional representatives of central government or enhanced local government organizations. Finally, in many of the CEE countries, the scale of regional disparities at the start of the transition period were relatively minor due to the reallocation and subsidy system under the Communist regime.

However, as economic reform has continued, its spatial ramifications have become increasingly clear, thus forcing the issue of a regional policy response onto the political agenda. Regional disparities have emerged in individual countries, as well as for the CEE region as a whole. There has clearly been a differentiated impact of economic change on individual regions – from relatively positive and balanced transformation in so-called *innovative* and *adaptive regions* to *crisis* regions where the mechanisms for permanent restructuring are either absent or failing to function effectively (Gorzelak 1993a; Gorzelak and Kuklinski 1993).

The reasons for certain regions becoming innovative while others move towards crisis are rooted to a great extent in the nature and structure of the region itself. A number of factors affect the ability of individual regions to adapt to new economic conditions. These include:

1. the regions economic structure, including the level and sophistication of labour force skills and the quality of fixed assets
2. the level of socio-economic development, including employment opportunities and socio-cultural factors such as entrepreneurship

3. geographical and economic peripherality, such as the proximity to urban centres, national and international transport infrastructure and sources of capital and innovation.

The interplay of these, and other, factors have led to the emergence of two main areas of regional socio-economic disparity, both in individual countries and for the Visegrad region as a whole.

First, there are *core–periphery* contrasts, where the cores comprise the capital cities and main diversified towns (including Poznan, Wroclaw, Krakow, Gdansk, Veszprem and Kosice) which appear to have been less vulnerable to the difficulties and costs of economic transformation. The position of such centres as the foci of economic, social, cultural, political and administrative activity is related both to historical factors and the centralist policies of the Communist regime.

New trends which have developed as part of the transition to market economies are also serving in many cases to reinforce the pattern of core–periphery disparities. This is particularly true for the process of new firm formation and patterns of foreign investment. The process of *new firm formation*, for example, has been highly dynamic in the Visegrad countries, and particularly in Poland. However, most activity in this area has been concentrated in capital cities where the advantages of a large population base, the greater availability of financial and consultative support networks, good infrastructure, etc., all serve to facilitate the setting-up of new firms. In addition, the diversified urban centres have disproportionate concentrations (in relation to population) of new enterprises resulting from the privatization process. The second trend, the inflow of *foreign investment*, is also focused principally on the capital cities. In terms of joint ventures, for example, between 50 and 75 per cent of the total are concentrated in Prague, Budapest and Bratislava. However, the focus of investment activity on the capital cities does vary by investor country – 87 per cent of French investment in Poland, for example, is in Warsaw while there is some involvement of German capital in all 49 Polish *voivod*ships (Szlachta 1995).

The second characteristic of emerging spatial patterns is *West–East* disparities, with higher levels of economic development, better growth rates, lower unemployment, and more intensive commercial links in the western areas of individual countries and the CEE region as a whole. Following the dismantling of border controls, regions close to Western Europe have been able to reverse some former problems such as low population density, out-migration and poor infrastructure provision. Considerable stimuli for economic development have diffused from Western Europe, their impact decreasing with geographical distance from the border. Foreign investment, much of which is aimed at western export markets, also favours those east Europe locations geographically closer to western neighbours.

In addition to the regional development problems of peripherality, eastern border locations and distance from urban centres, crisis and problem regions also suffer from several other, often overlapping, sets of difficulties:

1. sectoral crises of heavy industry in mono-activity regions in sectors such as coal and iron ore mining, heavy metal production and armaments, with the danger of high unemployment and few diversification prospects (e.g. Kladno, Ostrava, Pribram and Vsetin in the Czech Republic; Katowice, Lodz and Walbrzych in Poland; Baranya and northern Nograd in Hungary)
2. agricultural underdevelopment (e.g. Szabolcs–Szatmar–Bereg, Borsod–Abauj–Zemplen in Hungary; Suwalki, Ciechanow and Ostroleka in Poland)
3. underdeveloped physical infrastructure (e.g. Szabolcs–Szatmar–Bereg in Hungary; north-east Poland; eastern Slovakia);
4. environmental degradation (e.g. the cola basin of north-western Bohemia in the Czech Republic; Upper Silesia and the Legnica copper mining area in Poland)
5. demographic pressures, such as an ageing population or one-sided sex structure (e.g. Borsod–Abauj–Zemplen in Hungary) or the potential ethnic tension stemming from the occupancy of major ethnic groups (e.g. Romany and Slovaks in Hungary and the Czech Republic; Hungarians in Slovakia).

Current Regional Policy Responses

To what extent, then, has there now been a positive policy response to the clearly serious regional socio-economic disparities which have emerged over the last five years? Is the issue now being given a higher profile in the governments of CEE countries? If so, what is the rationale for the development of a more active regional policy – is regional policy designed to be an instrument for achieving social equality or promoting national economic efficiency?

There has clearly been an increase in focus on regional development issues, particularly in the Visegrad countries. The first rationale for this is economic. In general terms, the better the economic standing of the country, and the more successful the economic reforms, the better the framework conditions for the design and implementation of regional policy. As the turning-point in economic decline is reached and growth starts to appear in key sectors, greater attention can be focused on the more specific ramifications of macro-economic reform, such as its spatial consequences. Increasing political reorientation away from the mentality of central planning and regional development on the basis of sectoral priorities can further reinforce the awareness of regional issues.

Regional policy itself can also be implemented with the goal of increasing economic efficiency, as is the case in the Czech Republic (Kern 1994). If the rationale for regional policy is economic, this policy area is clearly important even in the period of economic difficulty and not a luxury to be enjoyed once the country is on a firmer economic footing. It is also recognized that regional disparities are likely to widen under a market economic system and this could jeopardize the long-term success of national policies. Regional policy represents one method of combating in advance this potential danger to national economic efficiency and security.

The second rationale for the increasing interest in regional policy issues is political. This is linked to the compelling argument that, where very significant regional disparities are developing, regional policy is necessary on social equity grounds. At its most extreme, it could be argued that spatial disparities were an important contributory factor in the break-up of the former Czechoslovakia, Yugoslavia and the Soviet Union. However, even within a unified country, the emergence of sharp disparities could lead to serious social unrest in the more backward regions – with corresponding negative consequences in many spheres. This is perhaps most true in the Russian Federation, where the risk of the exploitation of regional disparities by political extremists in particularly high. This causes Artobolevskiy (1994) to argue that regional policy is vital in order for Russia to prevent further *disintegration*. However, it is interesting to note that although a Regional Strategy was drafted in Russia in 1994, and the awareness of this policy area is increasing, the debate currently remains centred in this country on predominantly ethnic issues.

A third rationale for the development of a regional policy in the CEE countries is the influence of international organizations, and particularly the European Union (EU). The EU has raised the profile of regional policy in the CEE countries through its political involvement and the implementation of EU aid programmes, some of which have a direct regional development component, e.g. PHARE. The EU units are often active in advising a government of possible future directions in the formulation of an effective regional policy. The EU also has a more indirect influence in this area, particularly in those countries furthest down the path to accession (and therefore also those countries which are most economically advanced). These countries are already making efforts to adapt their institutions, structures and policies to EU requirements. The potential vital future role of EU Structural Fund support is effectual in bringing the issue of formulating suitable regional policy structures and instruments into focus. This role of the EU in increasing the profile of regional policy and development at the national level is not isolated to the transition countries, but has also recently been seen in the other new Member States, e.g. Austria.

The importance of the issue of regional policy development has therefore been highlighted through the emergence of regional socio-economic disparities, the economic and political dangers of continuing regional divergence, particularly in regions of greatest economic crisis, and the influence of international organizations. However, practical steps in the formulation of regional policy have still been slow to emerge. They have, to date, included the following areas:

1. The establishment of government departments or ministries at national level with responsibility for regional development, e.g. the Ministry for Environment and Regional Policy in Hungary. This has been quite a

common step, and has even occurred in countries such as Russia with the creation of the Ministry for National Relations and Regional Policy in 1994.

2. Development agencies have been set up to support restructuring. In the Visegrad countries these have been created both through the top-down establishment of networks (e.g. over 50 regional development agencies in Poland), or through bottom-up local economic initiatives.
3. Assisted areas have been defined, partly with a range of economic criteria (as in Hungary) but more commonly on the basis of very high unemployment or severe environmental degradation.
4. Financial incentives are being created, such as the Regional Development Fund in Hungary. In Poland, a range of special employment or environmental measures (including tax and depreciation allowances, infrastructure grants) are being applied in crisis regions, although these are offered under the employment and environmental, rather than regional, policy.

The Case of Hungary

Economic reform and the emergence of regional disparities

Hungary has the longest experience of market-related reforms among CEE countries. Early reforms in the 1960s focused initially only on agriculture and peripheral areas, but the move away from central planning has accelerated since 1987 with greater encouragement for entrepreneurship and private enterprise.

Economic reform has progressed rapidly since the end of the 1980s. The recession now appears to have bottomed out – inflation has been reduced to an annual rate of around 20 per cent, industrial production increased in the first eight months of 1994 by 8.4 per cent, and a significant amount of foreign investment has flowed into the country (estimated at $7 billion over the period 1989–93). The orientation of trade has shifted significantly towards Western countries, and towards the EU in particular. Despite these successes, several major difficulties still confront the process of economic transition in Hungary. The country faces critical budgetary and foreign debt problems, with negative ramifications for financing agreements by international organizations such as the International Monetary Fund (IMF). Hungary is dependent to a great extent on foreign trade and currently has a foreign trade deficit of around $3 billion. Unemployment, although declining slightly during 1994, is still over 10 per cent and represents both an economic and a social problem. And the rise to power in May 1994 of former Communists under the premiership of Gyula Horn slowed the process of privatization and damaged business confidence in the country.

The new government has launched a medium-term economic programme for 1995–97, envisaging the completion of major structural adjustments by the end of that period. The main aspects of this programme include:

1. Reducing annual consumption levels at a rate less than the rise in production. This is hoped to reverse the trend of recent years where the share of consumption in gross domestic product (GDP) has risen relative to investment.
2. The continuation of a similar fiscal policy. The deficit is expected to decline from nearly 8 per cent of GDP in 1994 to around 6 per cent in 1995, principally through increased privatization revenue, and then be reduced further to around 3 per cent of GDP by 1997.
3. To aim at a growth in exports of at least 8 per cent more than corresponding growth in imports. A fall in import duties (within the range permitted by GATT regulations) would help considerably in this regard.
4. A continuation of social policy in the short-term, with potential future reforms schemes for pensions and health care to help alleviate pressures on the budget.

At the regional level, all parts of Hungary have been affected by economic restructuring. However, the two principal areas of regional disparity which have already been mentioned – core–periphery and West–East – are clearly distinguishable. Firstly, the core regions comprise the capital city Budapest and, to a lesser extent, major diversified towns such as Veszprem which are the recognized leaders of economic transformation. The position of such centres as the predominant concentrations of economic, social, cultural, political, administrative and intellectual activity is generally related to historical factors, and furthered by the centralist policies under Communist regimes. Second, higher levels of economic development, better growth rates, lower unemployment, and more intensive business contacts are evident in the western parts of the country. Following political and economic liberalization, regions close to the border with Western Europe have been able to reverse some former problems such as low population density, out-migration, poor housing and infrastructure. Conversely, eastern and north-eastern counties are experiencing particular development difficulties, ranging from severe industrial decline and the problems of mono-industrial towns in the Borsod region to very underdeveloped rural areas in Szabolcs.

Regional policy response

A distinct regional policy can be identified from the early 1970s in Hungary. The government decrees of the time resulted in regional development planning and the incorporation of regional priorities into the redistribution of financial resources. For example, a regional objective was to promote the development of medium and small towns and villages within the national settlement hierarchy, particularly in rural and backward areas.

This cannot, however, be construed as regional policy. The central control of regional development was divided along sectoral lines, and these objectives were superior to regional concerns in government policies. Centralized control was not able to counterbalance the increasingly wide regional disparities across the country. In addition, the dominance of large companies in the economy meant that it was very difficult to guarantee that a particular subsidy would help to stimulate an individual regional economy.

In 1985, a parliamentary decree raised the profile of regional policy in Hungary. It defined the long-term tasks of regional policy, demanding a higher priority for the development of backward areas and a quicker reduction of unjustifiable regional disparities in living conditions. The programme was not, however, able to achieve any significant results. The financial resources were insufficient for the realization of the required tasks, and the institutional system was inadequate. In particular, sectoral priorities continued to take precedence.

Institutional issues

Following the economic and political liberalization at the end of the 1980s, regional policy again crept up the political agenda. One of the most significant ramifications of this was the creation, in 1990, of a new Ministry of Environment and Regional Policy (MERP). The Decree on the competence of the new Ministry specified its role to:

> manage, organize and control the drafting and realization of development projects of backward areas, crisis regions, high-priority recreation areas, border regions, and other relevant problem regions and the utilization of financial resources allocated for these projects.

Although the creation of the MERP was clearly a positive step, the position of the new Ministry has remained relatively weak in the government. The main conflict of competence is apparent with the Ministry of the Interior, formerly in charge of spatial issues and still competent for settlement development. However, a large number of other Ministries also claim to have regional development responsibilities, including the Ministries of Finance, Industry and Commerce, Labour, Transport and Telecommunications, and Public Welfare. There is little or no coordination between the activities of the individual ministries, and no clear leadership or overall strategy to guide otherwise ad hoc initiatives.

The clear allocation of ministerial responsibility for regional policy is necessary within the Hungarian government, as well as greater integration between the activities with a spatial dimension undertaken by individual Ministries. Reconciling this institutional confusion at national level will require choosing between policy integration, whereby each Ministry is required to draft policies that take account of regional objectives, and policy coordination, a less rigid approach whereby fora or mechanisms are created for government departments to coordinate the implementation of their policies.

At the *regional* level, there are also key institutional issues which have arisen in relation to regional development. Perhaps one of the most important developments in this regard was the local government reform at the start of the 1990s. This reform created over 3000 independent autonomous municipal authorities, with no legislation aimed at forming associations or cooperation between them – a far greater number than is required for local government administration and service organization. The highly fragmented nature of the system also means that it is more difficult for towns to play an integrative and functional role in local and regional development. Basic services have inevitably become the most pressing development priorities for the municipal authorities, especially the particular problems of tiny villages (water supply, elementary school rooms, roads, etc.).

These characteristics of the new local government system strongly influence central regional policy. The new, disintegrated structure defines central development priorities and the scope of regional policy. The autonomous operation of a large number of small local governments has made the formulation of an overall regional strategy/concept highly problematic. In addition, as many of the local governments are based only on settlements, the power of the Ministry of the Interior is further strengthened through its competence for settlement development, thus making cooperation between ministries at national level even more difficult. The steps of the government in 1993 have endeavoured to encourage the association and cooperation of municipal governments, especially through the mechanisms for the determination of development support eligibility. At the same time, however, the operational financing is still encouraging autarky, isolation and separation.

An issue which further compounds this problem is the lack of a strong intermediate administrative level, which could provide a regional overview of development needs and an appropriate forum for the implementation of suitable measures (either formulated at this level or decentralized from central government). The county governments formerly fulfilled this role, but their position was seriously weakened during the early 1990s, and they have been left as subsidiary administrative units, fulfilling tasks which the local authorities are not able, or are unwilling, to perform. Although the counties legally still have a role in regional development (e.g. relating to land use and regional development), they receive little support from either central or local governments. There is some indication that the counties have been more involved in the formulation of county programmes over the past year, although they still remain little more than convenient administrative units for the implementation of central government regional development programmes.

The lack of an appropriate intermediary level has also led to the creation in the regions of numerous organizations involved in regional development, both deconcentrated offices of sectoral ministries and non-government organizations such as regional development agencies, foundations and micro-associations. While these organizations may, in themselves, be providing a valuable service, there is generally no coordination or cooperation between them, and no transparency as to what measures are available in a given area.

Overall, the current institutional system at local and regional government level is too fragmented, both structurally and functionally. Greater integration is required in the forms and mechanisms of association, and a more powerful regional government level could encourage regional planning, financing systems focusing on regional cooperation and integrated information systems. While some of these issues are inevitable teething problems at the start of the reform process, others, such as the role of the county, require regulatory change.

An urgent requirement linking all these institutional aspects is the need to formulate a coherent, overall strategy for regional development. This could help identify the ministerial responsibility for this policy area, bring together sectoral priorities and strategies in a more cohesive fashion, and provide the overall framework for the formulation of regional and local development plans and measures. At present, although the 1993 Decree lays out the basic guidelines for regional policy, it does not provide this comprehensive framework.

Incentive issues

The main instrument of regional policy is the Regional Development Fund (RDF). The RDF was established in 1986, but fundamentally reorganized in 1992. It has been subject to several government decisions which have widened its role and increased available funding in an attempt to incorporate regional policy as part of the overall reform effort. The RDF has a legal fund status and has its own budget, accounting in 1993–94 for ECU 45 million. The RDF provides grant assistance on a co-financing basis to the public and private sectors for individual projects. Three types of subsidy are generally offered – repayable grants, non-repayable grants and interest rate subsidies – according to a matrix of eligibility conditions to categories of assisted area (such as those suffering from structural decline and those with particularly high unemployment) covering over 15 per cent of the Hungarian population.

The RDF is only one of 26 government funds under the control of ten Ministries. While many of these Ministries have some orientation towards regional development, and a proportion of monies from the funds are utilized (directly or indirectly) for regional development purposes, there is no coordination or common principles for their utilization.

There are a number of problems related to the current operation of the RDF. There has been an over-concentration of award financing in terms of both the type of projects supported and their geographical location. Infrastructure projects have received considerably more investment support from the RDF than job creation or maintenance measures. Although infrastructure is clearly important to regional development, it should not be viewed as an end in itself, and should only be supported if clearly related to the specific regional problems of the area. Shorter term crisis management, promoting job creation and economic restructuring, for example, also have a role in the case of industrial crisis regions. Complex rural development programmes and the modernization of agriculture should be the primary targets in case of problem rural regions. In addition, one of the principal criteria for the designation of assisted areas is the unemployment rate, but too little emphasis has been placed on measures designed to combat this problem.

In spatial terms, the concentration of the RDF has been on the two counties of Szabolcs–Szatmár–Bereg and Borsod–Abauj–Zemplen in the north-east of the country, despite the existence of considerable problems in other regions. Much of this concentration has been for political reasons, and the decentralization of the RDF could help to guard against this to some extent.

Future developments

A key development for the future of regional policy in Hungary is the new Law on Regional Policy, which is intended to be adopted in the autumn of 1995. This Law should clarify in a more detailed way some of the institutional and incentive issues which have been highlighted above. The new Law will take into account the European Regional and Spatial Planning Charter and the regional policy principles of EU: decentralization; subsidiarity; partnership; programming; additionality; transparency; and concentration.

The key objectives of the Law are as follows:

1. to assist the development of a market economy in every region of the country, to create necessary conditions for sustained growth, and to improve economic conditions and quality of life through coordination between social, environmental and economic interests
2. to create conditions for self-sustaining growth
3. to reduce spatial disparities (in terms of living conditions, economic, cultural and infrastructural conditions) between Budapest and the rest of Hungary and between developed and underdeveloped regions
4. to encourage initiative by regional and local communities and to coordinate them with national objectives.

In terms of the institutional aspect of regional policy and development, the Law will also determine the tasks and competences of national and regional organizations. The current proposals include the following division of labour:

1. *Parliament*
   (a) to approve national development strategy, and principles, objectives, and long-term priorities of regional development

(b) to approve regional development and physical plans encompassing the whole country, and regions of high priority, and to determine elements of plans that are binding for local governments

(c) to determine guidelines for regional development support and designation criteria for assisted areas

(d) to determine funds for regional development

(e) to determine self-government tasks related to regional development

(f) to request a government report on the development of regional processes and the implementation of regional policy.

2. *National Council for Regional Development*

new organ to assist government, competent to make proposals, comment and coordinate.

3. *County Development Councils*

(a) to comprise representatives from county general assemblies, local government associations, economic chambers, employees interest groups, and the MERP (the proposed weak position of county general assemblies could pose future problems)

(b) to coordinate development ideas of central and local government and various actors of regional development

(c) to examine and evaluate the social and economic situation of the county

(d) to make proposals for long-term development concepts, medium-term programmes, sub-programmes and major development objectives and tasks

(e) to make proposals for development objectives and the use of financial resources

(f) to participate in formulation of decisions about allocation of local government support, and separate state funds

(g) to determine evaluation guidelines for programmes.

4. *Regional Development Councils*

(a) can be set up by county governments to implement regional development and physical planning tasks involving areas outside the county boundary

(b) the practical implementation of such councils is, however, difficult to envisage.

Two issues in particular require urgent attention in order that regional policy and regional development can continue on an effective future course in Hungary. This first is the provision of an overall, coherent strategy for regional development, as mentioned in the discussion above. This would provide a framework for the coordination of plans and funds operated by different Ministries at a national level, as well as regional and local organizations. It would also address issues such as the clarification of the overall objective of regional policy, e.g. should it be ameliorative or transformational, and the policy scope, e.g. marginal to mainstream economic policy or integrated into national economic development? It is hoped, in this context, that the new Law will put in place at least the first proper attempt at a more rigorous framework for regional policy in Hungary.

The second key issue for future regional policy development is the nature and role of intermediate regional level organizations. As with the policy framework, this issue affects many interrelated areas, such as the formulation and efficient implementation of effective regional and local development plans and the decentralization of the RDF and other central measures. Much of the success of future regional policy in Hungary rests on the solution to this current impasse.

Future Regional Policy Responses

The Hungarian case study highlights a number of key factors influencing the future development of regional policy in all the CEE countries. These include the approach taken towards regional policy at central government level, the relative weight placed on this area in comparison to other policy areas, and the financial resources available for regional issues.

The need for a coherent regional development strategy is a key issue facing the majority of CEE countries. At present, virtually all important areas related to regional development are characterized by a lack of coordination. There are poor links at central government level between different Ministries influencing regional development. There is no coordination of central funds or budgets being used to support activity in assisted areas. There are a large number of organizations operating at the regional level with little or no contact between them. For regional development policy to become an effective and powerful force in the CEE countries, greater efforts must be made to develop a clear and overarching strategy for all activities in this area.

The deficiencies in the institutional infrastructure are a further major obstacle to the development of regional development policy in all the CEE countries. This is clearly a wider problem for CEE governments trying to establish effective administrations and create (or recreate) functioning and efficient regional and local units of self-government. The institutional problems, including the fragmented local government system and lack of intermediate level, have been outlined for the case of Hungary. In Poland, a paradoxical situation has emerged whereby the democratization which has occurred has, in fact, led to a greater level of centralization. Local government reform was carried out in 1990, but the Communes remain relatively weak, relying to a great extent on central funds and with only limited powers to carry out economic activity. The intermediate level of government, the *voivod*ship, has also become increasingly dependent on central government, and there is no directly elected political representation at this level, although this level is probably still too small for effective regional policy to be carried out.

A number of specific challenges can be identified in relation to the institutional infrastructure for regional development (Bachtler 1994; Bachtler and Downes 1994; Downes, Bachtler and Horvath 1994):

1. The *territorial-administrative division* of regions and the selection of appropriate spatial units is critical, as mentioned above in the context of Polish developments. There may be practical and historical administrative units in existence in the country, e.g. the 20 counties in Hungary, but there may also be strong arguments for the creation of a smaller number of larger units which could serve as spatial units for strategic planning and be visible on the map of Europe in terms of attracting foreign investment, promoting regional companies in an international context and stimulating indigenous development. This issue is, however, often highly emotive and political. In Poland, for example, although the current 49 *voivod*ships have only existed since 1975, there is some popular identification with this administrative division, and an unwillingness in many *voivod*ships to be subsumed into larger units. There are also economic problems in the Polish case – the current division has encouraged the development of a network of medium-sized towns which has stimulated more even regional development. The creation of a smaller number of larger regions could endanger this structure and focus investment and growth on regional centres which are already economic leaders in the transformation.
2. The *ministerial leadership* of regional policy and the regulation of ministerial competences within central government. This could be addressed partly through a clearer overall strategy for the policy area, and, where this has occurred, a strengthening of the newly created ministries for regional development.
3. The structures and mechanisms of *policy implementation* must be addressed – should regional policy be administered centrally through a government ministry (as in the UK), through specialist boards or agencies (such as DATAR in France), or be decentralized to a significant degree (as in Germany or Austria).
4. The role of *Parliament* is important, in terms of establishing and helping to maintain an overall strategy for regional development, monitoring policy operations and supervising the legislative progress relating to regional policy resources and institutions.
5. The *allocation of responsibilities*, both vertically and horizontally, is crucial for the future effective development and implementation of regional policy. This is linked to the issues of coordination at central government level, and the requirement to create strong intermediate level authorities, facilitating

the effective division of competences for regional development between central, regional and local levels.

The Exploitation of Western Experience

As a concluding comment, it is worth noting that, in the future development of regional policy in Hungary and the CEE countries in general, there is considerable scope for the exploitation of Western experience. The EU and other international organizations have already had an influence through raising the profile of regional policy and regional development in the CEE countries. Some of the emerging regional problems in CEE countries, e.g. old industrial regions and post-industrialization issues, have been evident in Western Europe countries for a number of decades, while other issues, such as the problems of inner cities, are currently being addressed in Western Europe and can be expected to develop over the next decades in the CEE region. Artobolevskiy (1994) argues that the regional problems in Western nations are more advanced than those in the East, so that the regional problems currently facing Western countries will encounter the Eastern nations in the future.

Considerable benefits can therefore be gained from flows of knowledge and information, as well as the participation of Western experts in the formation of policy, instruments and organizations. However, the transfer of experience must be treated with sensitivity and care. An attempt must be made to coordinate the efforts of numerous Western European governments and organizations, all providing regional development assistance to the CEE countries. It is extremely important that any Western European experience which is transferred over takes due account of the local conditions and environment. This is necessary to ensure that what is put in place is going to be effective in the long-term and take due account of the knowledge and expertise of Eastern European experts and policy-makers. Particular care is also necessary in relation to EU assistance to avoid the imposition of an EU blueprint, which may not be completely relevant to the situation of the transition countries at the time. Although structures need to adapted to EU requirements, this can be done within the context of a policy more customized to the individual needs of particular CEE countries.

The issue of how to develop an effective regional policy is not a problem isolated to Central and Eastern Europe – it is also a very topical question in Western Europe. A number of Western European countries are currently reviewing their regional policy frameworks, e.g. Germany, in the light of new economic conditions and developments (see Chapter 12). The new Member States of the EU, Austria, Sweden and Finland, are also re-evaluating their approach to regional development in the new context of EU controls and Structural Fund financing. The countries of Central and Eastern Europe are not therefore alone in their attempt to identify the more effective way forward – they are just at a different stage in the process.

References

Artobolevskiy, S. (1994) 'Regional policy in Western and Eastern Europe: two approaches.' In Z. Hajdu and G. Horvath (eds) *European Challenges and Hungarian Responses in Regional Policy.* Centre for Regional Studies, Hungarian Academy of Sciences, Pecs.

Bachtler, J. (1994) *European Integration and Regional Development in Central and Eastern Europe.* Paper presented at Symposium 'Regionalentwicklung im Prozeß der Europäischen Integration', Institut der Europäische Integrationsforschung e.V., Bonn, October 1994.

Bachtler, J. and Downes, R. (1994) *Developing a Regional Policy in Eastern Europe: The Case of Hungary.* Paper presented at 5th British–Russian Conference, Birmingham, May 1994.

Downes, R. (1995) *Regional Policy Development in Central and Eastern Europe.* Paper presented at Regional Studies Association Conference 'Regional Futures', Gothenburg, May 1995.

Downes, R. and Bachtler, J. with Horvath, G., Farago, L. and Palno Kovacs, I. (1994) *The Strengths and Weaknesses of Hungarian Regional Policy and Regional Development Fund.* Report to the PHARE Regional Development Programme, Budapest.

European Marketing Data and Statistics (1993) 28th Edition, London: Euromonitor PLC, p.98.

Gorzelak, G. (1993a) *Regional Patterns of Polish Transformation, 1990–2005.* Paper presented at International Conference 'European Challenges and Hungarian Responses in Regional Policy', Pecs, November 1993.

Gorzelak, G. and Kuklinski, A. (eds.) (1993) *Dilemmas of Regional Policies in Eastern and Central Europe.* Warsaw: European Institute for Regional and Local Development, University of Warsaw.

Kern, J. (1994) 'Restructuring and regional policy in the Czech Republic.' In Z. Hajdu and G. Horvath (eds) *European Challenges and Hungarian Responses in Regional Policy.* Centre for Regional Studies, Hungarian Academy of Sciences, Pecs.

Oltay, E. (1995) 'The return of the former Communists.' *Transition – 1994 in Review.* Prague: Open Media Research Unit.

Szlachta, J. (1995) *Economic Transformation in Poland – the regional dimension.* Paper presented at University of Strathclyde, April 1995.

CHAPTER 14

New Directions for Regional Development Planning in Japan

Hirofumi Abe

Introduction

The rapid economic growth in post-war Japan has caused the concentration of economic activities and population in a few metropolitan regions. Regions have been losing their economic vitality due to regional income disparities and population losses. With the aim of preventing excessive growth of metropolitan regions and correcting regional disparities, the government has previously formulated four Comprehensive National Development Plans (CNDP) since the first plan was formulated in 1962. Regional development policies under the four CNDPs have sought to tackle regional problems by adopting three particular regional development policies: first, the construction of a national network of transportation and communications which form the national land axis; second, the development of growth poles in local regions; and third, the relocation of industries from the metropolitan to the local regions. While the regional disparities still exist between the metropolitan and the local regions, each region has shown a growing tendency towards local development as well as the improvement of living conditions.

Looking towards the approaching 21st century, however, substantial socio-economic changes are foreseen: the rapid changes in the industrial structure under the progress of technological changes; the rising Japanese currency; a trend towards an information network society; needs for higher quality of life and safety for citizens with an ageing population; and the integration of Japan into international society. In order to cope properly with these issues, regional development planning in Japan is now seeking a new direction.

Following the author's previous research in this field (Abe and Alden 1988; Alden and Abe 1994), the chapter reviews the regional differentials in the post-war Japan in terms of income, employment, migration and population. The chapter

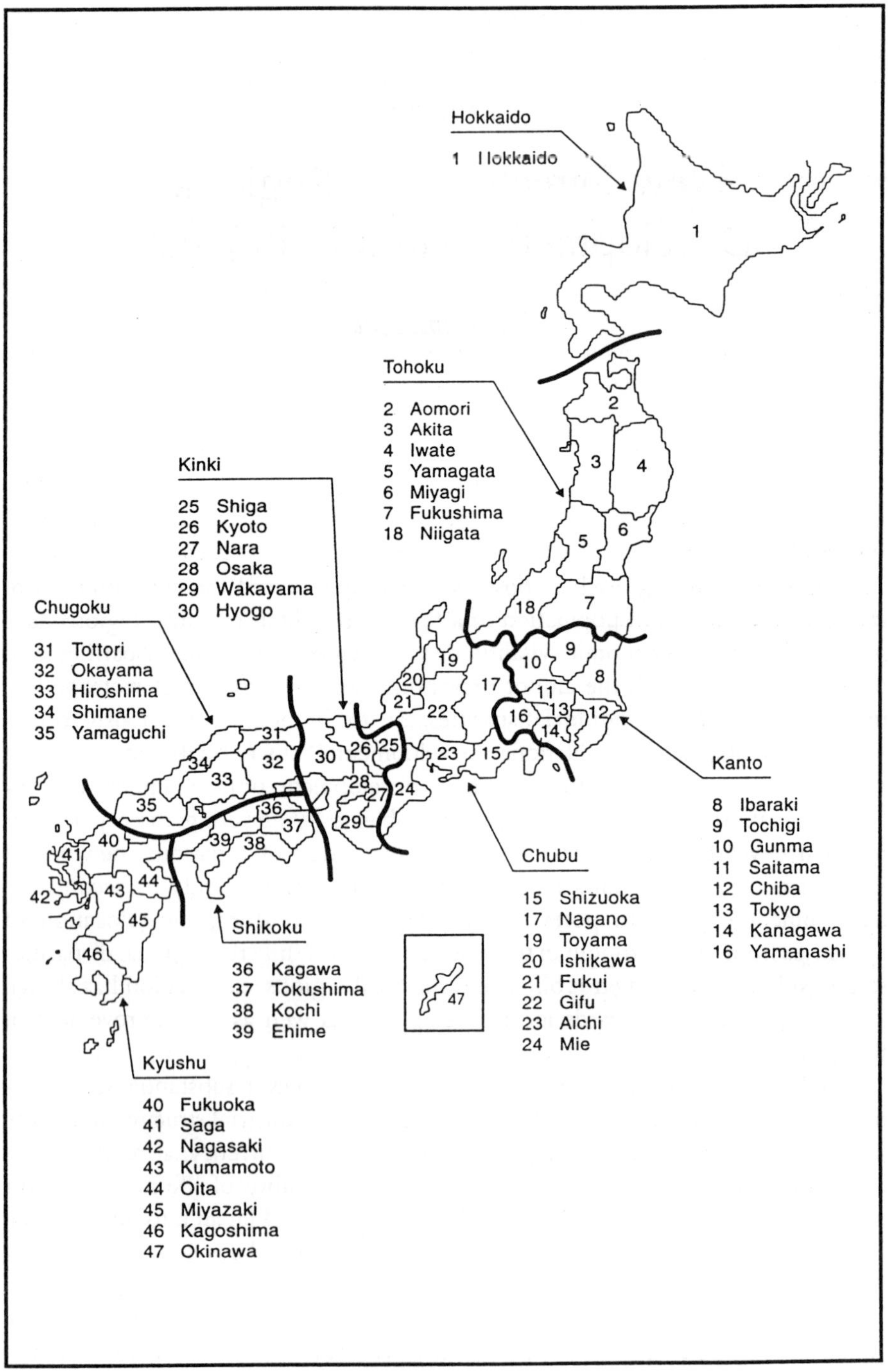

Figure 14.1 Prefectures and regions in Japan

assesses the performance of regional policies during the post-war period, focusing upon the extent to which regional disparities have been reduced. The chapter concludes by examining the current issues on regional planning and the new directions of regional policies in Japan towards the 21st century.

Administrative Areas in Japan

Japan comprises four main islands, Hokkaido, Honshu, Shikoku and Kyushu, which, together with more than 4000 small islands, have a land area of 318,000 square kilometres. Japan's population, at some 120 million, ranks it in seventh place in the world.

Japan's local government system is two-tier. The nation is divided into forty-seven prefectural areas, shown in Figure 14.1, and these are further divided into some 3000 municipalities. Each of the prefectures and municipalities has a governor and local assembly members who are directly elected by the residents. The forty-seven prefectures are aggregated on a regional basis, depending on the nature of the planning issue involved. There is no fixed or standard definition of region in Japan for statistical purposes. If the fourth Comprehensive National Development Plans of 1987 is taken as an example, the forty-seven prefectures are aggregated to nine regions (Hokkaido, Tohoku, Kanto, Chubu, Kinki, Chugoku, Shikoku, Kyushu and Okinawa), or three metropolitan regions (Tokyo, Osaka and Nagoya) and other local regions. They are illustrated in Figure 14.1 and used for the analysis in this chapter.

Post-War Regional Development Planning in Japan

Development of the post-war Japanese economy

The post-war development of the Japanese economy can be broadly classified into three periods, illustrated in Figure 14.2. During the first period (often referred to as the period of economic recovery), Japan rebuilt its economy to pre-war levels. In the period immediately following World War II, the Japanese economy was nearly devastated. Production in the mining and manufacturing industries had fallen to one-seventh the pre-war level and there were severe food shortages and inflation.

In order to demilitarize Japan and make it more democratic, the occupying Allied Forces conducted various political and economic reforms, such as the break-up of financial combines, the reformation of agricultural land ownership, the establishment of the right of workers, and so on. They had established the framework for the post-war development of the Japanese economy.

The second period continued from the mid-1950s to 1973, when the Japanese economy grew very rapidly. This rapid economic development of Japan was based on an annual average growth rate of 10.5 per cent between 1960 and 1968, followed by an average 8.8 per cent per annum from 1968 to 1973. The first oil

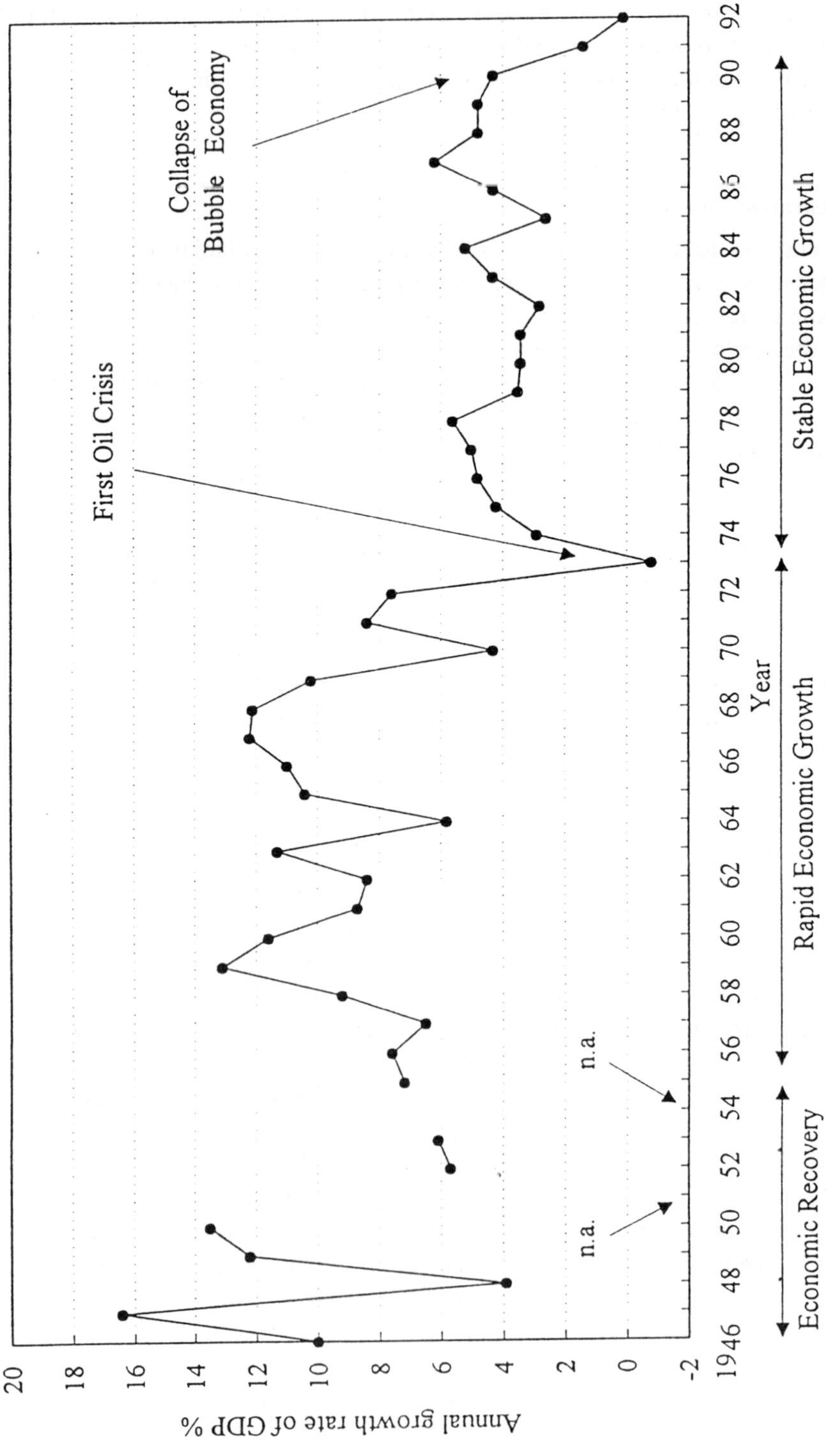

Source: Compiled from Economic Planning Agency, *Summary of Economic Statistics* 1994

Figure 14.2 Post-war economic growth in Japan

crisis slowed Japan's growth rate, but since 1973 it has continued well above the OECD average (OECD 1986a). However, in comparison to earlier growth rates, the period since 1973 is often referred to as one of low and stable economic growth.

In the late 1980s, the speculative bubble grew rapidly in Japanese economy, mainly because of the government's fiscal and monetary policy to cope with the yen's sharp appreciation after the 1985 Plaza Accord. While the Japanese economy achieved a domestic demand-led expansion during this period, land prices had drastically increased in the metropolitan regions. The soaring land prices increased the cost of housing and infrastructure provision in urban areas and significantly lowered the quality of urban life.

The growth of the Japanese economy began to slow down around August 1991, and took on a recessionary tone. The latest economic recession counts as one of the worst in the post-war Japan in terms of length and depth. The economic recession, together with the rapid appreciation of the yen, has had a major impact throughout the Japanese economy. As the government report (Economic Planning Agency 1994) has noted, this recession heightened the awareness of other long-term issues for the Japanese economy, such as concerns about the hollowing out of industries and the questions about the validity of the Japanese-style economic system.

Regional differentials in the post-war period

Various regional problems emerged during the period of rapid economic growth, namely the over-concentration of economic activities in large cities, the depopulation in local regions and regional income differentials.

Regional income disparities reached their highest level in the early 1960s, as illustrated in Table 14.1, which shows the ratio of regional income per capita to the average for Japan for the years 1955–1990. The table shows that only three metropolitan regions, Tokyo, Osaka. and Nagoya. exceeded the Japanese average throughout this thirty-five-year period. Table 14.1 also shows how the relative advantage of both Tokyo and Osaka has weakened from their peaks reached in the early 1960s. The extent of regional income differentials between the highest (Tokyo) and the lowest (Okinawa) was 88.5 index points in 1960, but this was reduced to 47.7 by 1985. The regional income differentials were therefore greatly reduced during the period of rapid economic growth.

The reduction of regional income differentials changed the goals of the CNDP. Regional income differentials were the major economic yardstick used by the first and the second CNDPs in the 1960s. In the third CNDP of 1977, however, regional disparities were defined in a broader sense, combining regional income with other factors, such as the provision of public facilities, cultural and educational opportunities, and other related factors.

Table 14.1 Per capita income by region as ratio of national average (Japan = 100)

Region	*1955*	*1960*	*1965*	*1970*	*1975*	*1980*	*1985*	*1990*
9 Regions								
Hokkaido	99.4	88.9	87.1	82.6	88.9	93.3	88.6	85.3
Tohoku	79.0	72.5	74.9	72.8	82.5	83.0	82.7	82.1
Kanto	122.3	127.3	122.3	120.6	115.9	114.7	114.6	117.5
Chubu	97.6	101.9	96.7	100.4	96.5	97.0	101.2	101.0
Kinki	119.7	120.6	119.6	115.5	106.6	105.4	104.4	101.6
Chugoku	86.3	82.8	89.2	91.2	93.2	93.3	91.9	89.6
Shikoku	84.1	79.0	80.2	83.4	84.5	84.0	80.9	80.9
Kyushu	80.5	73.4	75.3	72.9	84.5	86.1	84.3	81.7
Okinawa	63.1	55.6	53.0	51.5	73.5	69.8	71.6	68.0
3 Metropolitan Regions								
Tokyo M. R.	139.3	144.1	133.6	129.7	122.9	120.5	119.3	122.6
Osaka M. R.	126.6	128.7	126.0	120.9	110.3	108.6	108.2	104.9
Nagoya M. R.	107.6	118.1	106.1	112.4	102.0	103.1	109.0	106.8
3 M. R. Total	129.7	134.8	126.8	124.2	115.9	114.3	114.4	115.1
Local Region Total	84.5	79.5	81.6	81.3	87.1	88.3	88.0	87.1
Coefficient of variation*	0.221	0.267	0.224	0.227	0.152	0.145	0.147	0.160

* $q/x \times 100$. The coefficient is calculated using 47 prefectural data
Source: Compiled from Economic Planning Agency, *Annual Reports of Prefectural Income* (1990)

Table 14.1 also shows the coefficients of variation for prefectural income from 1955 to 1990. Regional income differentials reached their lowest level in around 1980, since when they have been increasing. This widening of income differentials has been attributed to declining public investment and changes in industrial structure following two oil crises. The excessive accumulation of advanced city functions in the Tokyo metropolitan region, which occurred in the 1980s under the internationalization of the Japanese economy and the trend towards a software and service oriented economy, had widened the regional differentials. Against this background, the fourth CNDP was formulated in 1987. With the aim of preventing the excessive concentration of economic functions in Tokyo and the growing net migration into the Tokyo metropolitan region, it proposed the formation of a multi-polar pattern of national land use through the promotion of the integrated interaction policy (National Land Agency 1987).

The growth rates of employment by sector and region for the two periods 1950–1970 and 1970–1990 show a marked contrast between the metropolitan and the local regions. The growth rates of secondary (i.e. manufacturing) industry for the two periods, shown in Table 14.2, indicate the progress achieved in terms of industrial location and development in the local regions. The growth rates from 1970 to 1990 show that the employment growth in secondary industry declined in metropolitan regions, while the total employment of secondary industry in local regions had shown a higher growth rate than metropolitan regions. On the other hand, the tertiary (service) sector shows less decentralization from metropolitan regions to local regions than does the secondary sector. Although there was significant employment growth in local regions, the Tokyo metropolitan region showed high growth rates for all periods.

Table 14.2 Employment growth rates by sector and region (%)

	Total employment		*Primary*		*Secondary*		*Tertiary*	
Region	*1950 –70*	*1970 –90*	*1950 –70*	*1970 –90*	*1950 –70*	*1970 –90*	*1950 –70*	*1970 –90*
Japan	**46.6**	**16.7**	**-41.6**	**-56.8**	**128.4**	**14.6**	**130.3**	**48.6**
9 Regions								
Hokkaido	42.4	9.3	-37.1	-43.5	57.0	0.8	159.2	33.5
Tohoku	13.6	5.2	-34.2	-57.1	90.1	46.4	99.8	38.3
Kanto	92.1	32.7	-42.0	-57.2	204.9	15.5	165.8	67.7
Chubu	43.8	16.1	-45.1	-60.5	142.8	19.2	122.0	48.2
Kinki	85.2	14.0	-44.8	-63.2	150.8	-3.4	133.9	42.7
Chugoku	22.0	3.9	-45.3	-58.5	99.7	10.8	102.3	33.4
Shikoku	10.7	-0.8	-45.3	-55.0	72.1	13.9	103.6	25.8
Kyushu	9.5	7.5	-41.2	-54.1	26.4	23.6	102.1	37.1
Okinawa	25.5	38.1	-55.2	-37.7	214.8	35.1	131.9	66.6
3 Metropolitan Regions								
Tokyo M. R.	130.0	36.4	-44.2	-54.8	224.4	9.7	182.4	68.0
Osaka M. R.	103.4	13.0	-46.8	-63.7	157.4	-7.5	143.1	39.7
Nagoya M. R.	69.9	22.6	-44.5	-59.6	159.3	17.5	143.4	53.8
3 M. R. total	109.5	26.8	-45.0	-58.4	187.7	5.4	163.3	57.2
Local region total	19.6	9.1	-40.8	-56.5	86.5	24.8	107.4	41.0

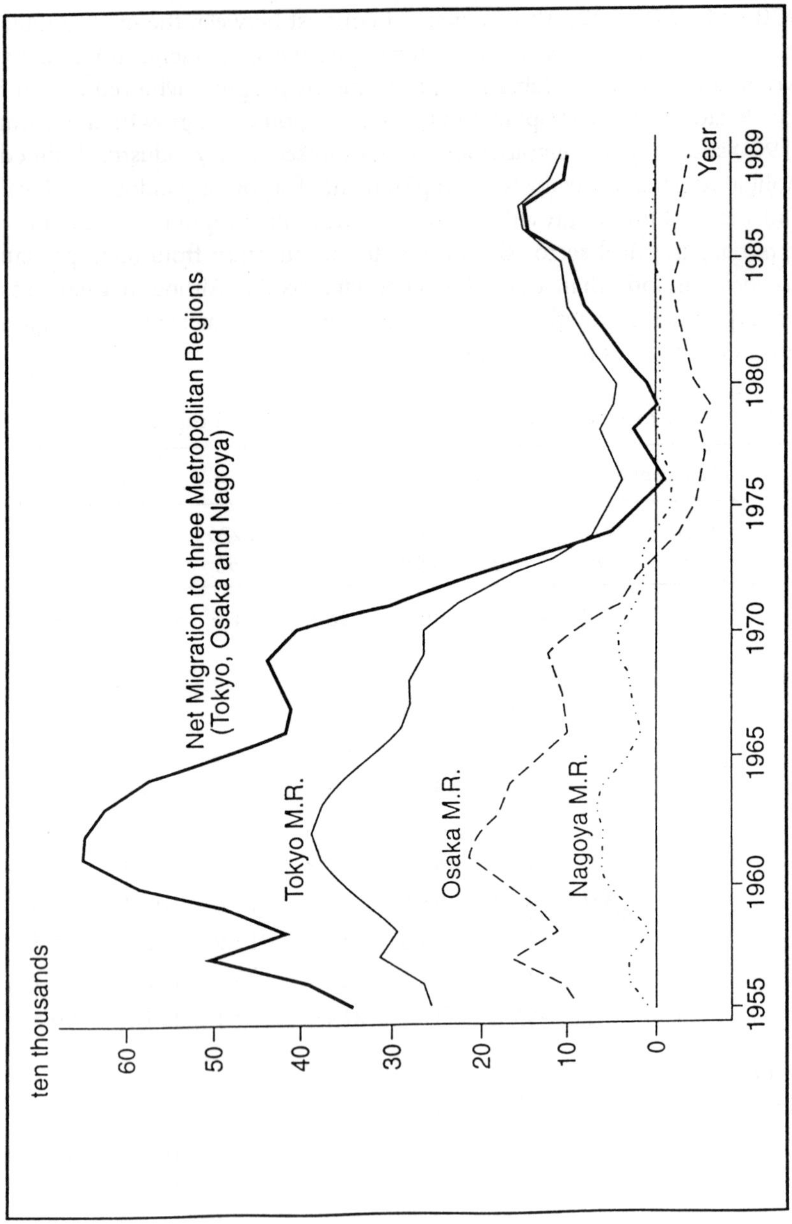

Source: Alden and Abe 1994

Figure 14.3 Trends in the net migration into metropolitan regions, 1955–1989

These trends in a changing regional employment structure have been matched by the interregional migration and the population trends for the same period. The post-war interregional pattern of migration in Japan, as illustrated in Figure 14.3, can be broadly classified into three periods. The first period up to the early 1970s was characterized by large-scale migration of young people from local regions to three metropolitan regions (i.e. Tokyo, Osaka and Nagoya metropolitan regions) for new jobs. During the second period from the first oil crisis of 1973 to the late 1980s, the return migration from metropolitan regions to local regions was dominant, and the concentration of migration to the three metropolitan regions had been reduced markedly. However, from the end of the 1980s and into the 1990s, net migration into Tokyo metropolitan region again increased, and the overcrowding of people and economic activities in Tokyo remains one of the most serious regional problems in Japan.

Table 14.3 Population growth rates by region (%)

Region	*1950 –55*	*1955 –60*	*1960 –65*	*1965 –70*	*1970 –75*	*1975 –80*	*1980 –85*	*1985 –90*
Japan	**7.4**	**4.7**	**5.2**	**5.5**	**7.0**	**4.6**	**3.4**	**2.1**
9 Regions								
Hokkaido	11.1	5.6	2.6	0.2	3.0	4.5	1.9	-0.6
Tohoku	2.8	-0.3	-2.2	-1.0	2.0	3.4	1.5	0.0
Kanto	12.6	10.9	13.4	12.2	11.1	6.2	5.4	4.7
Chubu	4.4	4.0	5.5	5.6	6.9	4.3	3.3	2.4
Kinki	10.4	9.5	12.4	10.3	8.2	3.7	2.9	1.7
Chugoku	2.9	-0.7	-1.1	1.8	5.3	3.0	2.1	0.0
Shikoku	0.6	-2.9	-3.6	-1.8	3.5	3.0	1.5	-0.8
Kyushu	6.9	-0.3	-4.1	-2.4	2.9	4.4	2.4	0.1
Okinawa	14.6	10.2	5.8	1.2	10.3	6.1	6.6	3.7
3 Metropolitan Regions								
Tokyo M. R.	18.2	15.8	17.6	14.7	12.1	6.1	5.5	5.0
Osaka M. R.	13.1	12.1	14.6	11.2	8.0	2.9	2.4	1.3
Nagoya M. R.	8.3	8.3	10.9	9.8	9.0	4.8	3.7	3.4
3 M. R. Total	14.7	13.3	15.6	12.8	10.3	4.9	4.3	3.7
Local region total	3.9	0.2	-0.9	0.5	4.3	4.3	2.7	0.8

The growth rates of population by region from 1955 to 1990 are shown in Table 14.3. Most local regions suffered population losses from 1955 to 1970. These regions supplied metropolitan regions with workers throughout the period of rapid economic growth. However, the growth of industries in local regions from the late 1960s to the early 1970s and the economic depression after the first oil crisis changed the population trends in Japan. Population increased in all regions between 1970 and 1985, and there were no significant differences in population growth between regions.

The analysis of regional income disparities, trends in regional employment and population growth and interregional migration patterns have shown the extent to which regional differentials have been reduced in Japan. Given these trends, the following section examines the statutory framework for regional development planning in Japan which has been designed to combat patterns of regional inequality in terms of income, population and employment.

Statutory Framework of Regional Development Planning in Japan

The statutory framework of regional planning in Japan has been established since the Comprehensive National Land Development Act was enacted in 1950. This remains the most fundamental law for regional development planning. As illustrated in Figure 14.4, regional plans and their related plans are broadly classified into four groups: (i) land-use plans, (ii) development plans, (iii) public investment plans, and (iv) promotion plans for special areas. This comprehensive system of regional development plans is set within the framework of a Comprehensive National Development Plan.

The first group is related to land-use plans. The National Land Utilization Plan provides the basic goals of national land use concerning the five land-use categories: urban areas; agricultural areas; forestry areas; natural park areas; and natural environmental areas. The plan is composed of a national plan, prefectural plans and municipal plans, and provides the framework of future land use for each land-use category. If the city plans are taken as an example, the urban area is further divided into the urbanization promotion areas and other city planning areas. The development of each urban area is controlled through the land-use zoning system proposed by the city plan.

The second group concerns the development plans for various spatial levels. The first level is the Comprehensive National Development Plan (CNDP), which proposes the development schemes for the whole nation and has been prepared by the National Land Agency since 1974 (the Economic Planning Agency was responsible for the plan before 1974). It is followed, secondly, by the regional plans for all regions except Hokkaido and Okinawa which have their own regional development agencies preparing their regional development plans. Regional plans for the other regions are published by the National Land Agency in association with prefectural governments in each region. The third and fourth levels are the

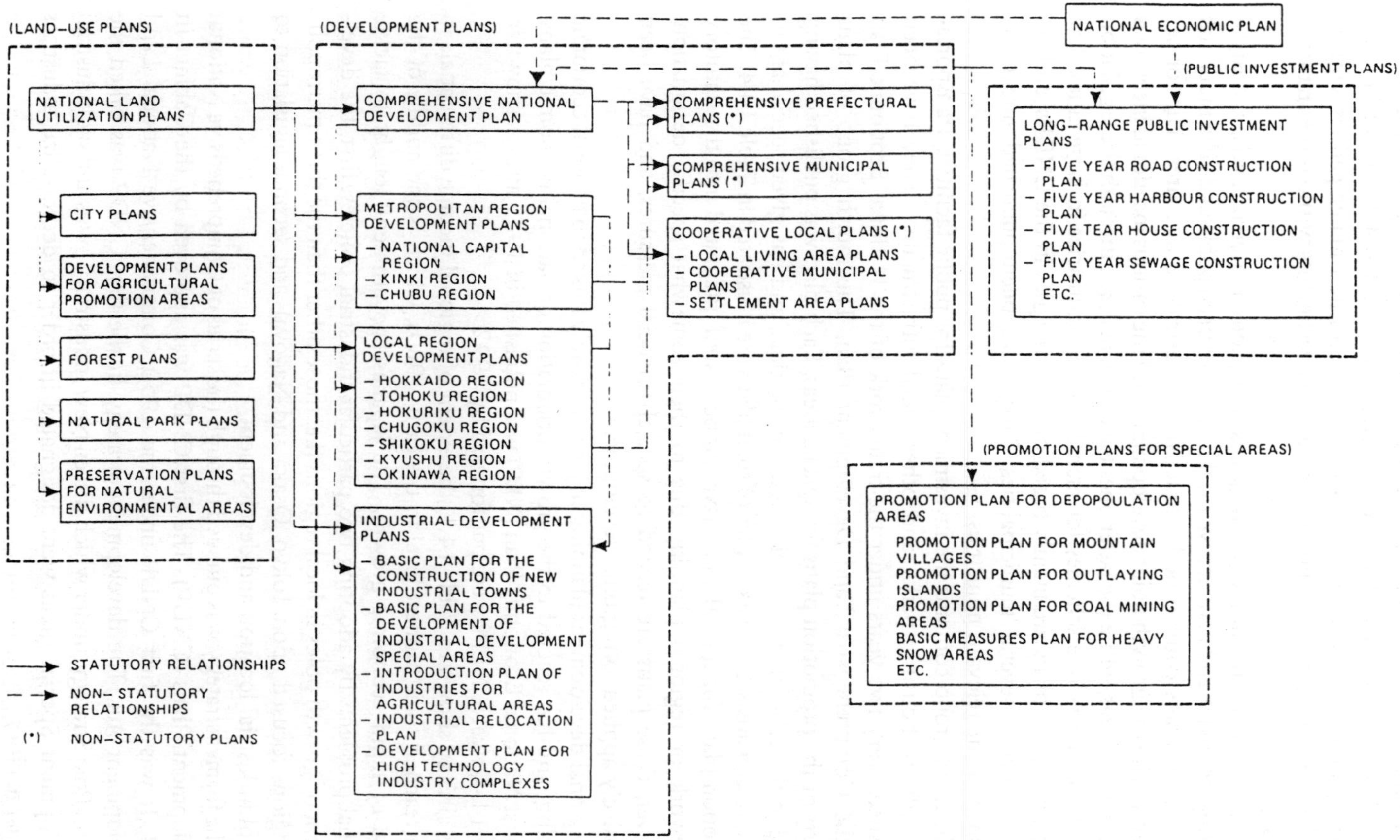

Figure 14.4 Statutory framework of regional development planning in Japan

Source: Compiled from Nishifuji and Nakayama (1983) and Abe and Alden 1988 prefectural and the municipal development plans published by the local governments. Although the 1950 Comprehensive National Land Development Act requires statutory development plans for prefectures and municipalities, current plans have been voluntarily published by local governments without the statutory process.

In addition to the development plans at various regional levels, industrial development plans and cooperative local plans have been published. The industrial development plans contain both attractive and restrictive measures. The former ones comprise the growth point developments and the various locational incentives for depressed areas, while the latter ones have been realized through the legislation of locational restrictive schemes for manufacturing industries in large cities. The cooperative local plans are mainly based on the strategies in the CNDPs, and are concerned with several municipalities. They have been published under the guidance of the relevant ministries.

The third group contains the investment plans for public facilities, transportation facilities, housing, parks, and other social infrastructure. They have been published every five years under the framework of the National Economic Plan and the Comprehensive Land Development Plan. The fourth group of plans consists of the promotion plans for special areas. Each plan was published having regard to the economic and social issues of the time, and has given special aid to the depressed areas. Some examples of such plans are illustrated in Table 14.4. The promotion plans for special areas have not been well integrated into the statutory framework of regional planning due to their somewhat specific designation. However, these plans are related to special financial measures, and have been extensively applied to regional development.

Regional development planning in Japan is closely linked to national economic planning, and has reacted to the growth orientation of national economic plans. The first National Economic Plan (NEP) was published in 1955 and, as shown in Table 14.4, twelve NEPs were put forward by 1992.

As already shown in Table 14.1, the extent of regional income differentials in Japan reached their highest level in the early 1960s, which is the middle of the period of rapid economic growth. The Japanese government sought to tackle regional problems by adopting two particular industrial policies: first, the development of growth poles in local regions (i.e. those other than the three metropolitan regions focused upon Tokyo, Osaka and Nagoya); and second, legislation to control industrial location and development.

The former strategy was pursued through the series of Comprehensive National Development Plans (CNDP). The first CNDP was approved by the Cabinet in 1962. It was the first CNDP under the 1950 Comprehensive National Land Development Act. The development strategy in the first CNDP was called the Growth Pole Strategy, under which fifteen New Industrial Towns and six Industrial Development Special Areas were designated in order to decentralize industries from large cities.

Table 14.4 Post-war National Economic Plans in Japan

Published year	*Prime Minister*	*National Economic Plans*	*Planned period*	*Growth rate of actual GNP*	
				Planned	*Achieved*
1955	Ichiro Hatoyama	Five-year plan for Economic Self-support	1956–1960	4.9	8.8
1957	Nobusuke Kishi	New Long-range Economic Plan	1958–1962	6.5	9.7
1960	Hayato Ikeda	Doubling National Income Plan	1961–1970	7.8	10.0
1965	Eisaku Sato	Medium-term Economic Plan	1964–1968	8.1	10.1
1967	Eisaku Sato	Economic and Social Development Plan	1967–1971	8.2	9.8
1970	Eisaku Sato	New Economic and Social Development Plan	1970–1975	10.6	5.1
1973	Kakuei Tanaka	Basic Economic and Social Plan	1973–1977	9.4	3.5
1976	Takeo Miki	Economic Plan for the Latter Half of the Seventies	1976–1980	6.0	4.5
1979	Masayoshi Ohira	New Seven-year Economic and Social Plan	1979–1985	5.7	4.0
1983	Yasuhiro Nakasone	Economic and Social Guideline for the Eighties	1983–1990	4.0	4.5
1988	Noboru Takeshita	Economic Management within a Global Context	1988–1992	3.8	4.0
1992	Kiichi Miyazawa	Sharing a Better Quality Life around the Globe	1992–1996	3.5	–

Source: Compiled from Economic Planning Agency, *Summary of Economic Statistics* (1994)

Despite the dispersal measures taken in the first CNDP, the concentration of activities in the three metropolitan regions continued. Therefore, in addition to subsequent CNDPs in the 1960s, various Acts for industrial relocation schemes were enacted to promote the relocation of manufacturing industry from metropolitan regions (where further development was subject to restrictions) to local regions (where further development was to be attracted). A more comprehensive industrial relocation scheme was later established under the Industrial Relocation Act in 1972.

Current Issues on Regional Development Planning in Japan

Planning issues emerged from the government review of the fourth CNDP

Various regional policies have been conducted since the fourth Comprehensive National Development Plan (CNDP) was formulated in 1987. The National Land Agency started the review of the fourth CNDP in 1992, and published the final review report in June 1994 (National Land Agency 1994). The report has identified significant socio-economic changes in Japanese regions. In this section, major issues which have emerged in the latter 1980s and 1990s are summarized.

Uni-polar concentration of economic activities in the Tokyo metropolitan region

Entering the 1980s, the population trend renewed its inflow to the Tokyo metropolitan region, coupled with the excessive concentration of economic functions there, namely the uni-polar concentration in the Tokyo metropolitan region. Table 14.5 illustrates the extent of economic concentration within the Tokyo metropolitan region.

The fourth CNDP of 1987 has been aiming at the formation of a multi-polar pattern of national land use to correct the excessive accumulation of population and economic activities in the Tokyo metropolitan region. As one of the quantitative goals of the plan, it has proposed a net outflow of migration from the Tokyo metropolitan region to other regions in the latter half of the planning period. The net migration into the Tokyo metropolitan region decreased from 160 thousand in 1987 to only one thousand in 1993, and the above goal of the fourth CNDP has been nearly achieved. The decline of youthful population and the growth of major local cities, such as Sapporo, Sendai, Hiroshima and Fukuoka, have contributed to this migration trend. Focusing upon the recent trends in migration, the final review report on the fourth CNDP has concluded that the uni-polar concentration of activities in Tokyo metropolitan region is now transferring to a new phase.

Table 14.5 Concentration of economic activities in Tokyo: shares of Tokyo metropolitan region in Japan, 1980s

Indicator	*Percentage (year)*	*Percentage (year)*
Foreign companies	82.2 (1974)	86.6 (1986)
Amount of bill clearing	69.6 (1981)	84.8 (1987)
Head offices of companies capitalized more than 10 billion yen	60.7 (1983)	62.2 (1988)
Bank loans	51.0 (1982)	55.4 (1988)
Companies listed on the Tokyo Stock Exchange	56.4 (1983)	54.6 (1988)
University students	45.0 (1980)	43.4 (1987)
Annual commercial sales	35.2 (1979)	38.6 (1985)
Bank deposits	32.7 (1982)	34.4 (1987)
Employment in finance and insurance companies	31.8 (1981)	33.0 (1986)
Employment in service industries	26.5 (1981)	27.8 (1986)
Office workers	26.1 (1981)	26.9 (1986)
Manufacturing output	26.6 (1980)	25.2 (1986)
Population	24.3 (1980)	25.2 (1988)
Offices	23.0 (1981)	23.3 (1986)
Area of Tokyo metropolitan region	3.6 (1980)	3.6 (1985)

Source: Compiled from the Economic Planning Agency, *Internationalization of Tokyo and the Vitalization of Regional Economy* (1988) (in Japanese)

Population decline and ageing society

The Japanese population, which has shown a sharp increase from 83.9 million in 1950 to 123.6 million in 1990, is now changing its trends. The total special birth rate, which represents the average number of children one woman gives birth to in her life, has shown a marked decline in recent years. The total special birth rate recorded the lowest number of 1.5 in 1992. It is far lower than the 2.08 which is required to maintain the current size of population. As a result, Japan's population will change its trend to one of decline in the early 21st century.

According to the medium-case population projection by the Ministry of Health and Welfare, shown in Table 14.6, Japan's population will level off at 130.4 million in the year 2011. Following the decline in Japan's total population, the depopulation problem in local regions might be more serious in the near future.

The age structure of population will shift rapidly to that of an aged society, since the average life expectancy has been increasing. Table 14.6 also shows the trends and prospects for Japan's age structure. The ratio of the population 65 years old and over to the total population will increase from 12.1 per cent in 1990 to 25.8 per cent in 2025. On the other hand, the population aged 15 to 65 (i.e. the labour force population) will decrease from 86.1 million in 1990 to 75.1 million in 2025, and the ratio to the total population will decrease from 69.7 per cent in 1990 to 59.7 per cent in 2025.

Table 14.6 Population trends and prospects by age, 1990–2025

	Population (1000 persons)				*%*		
Year	*Total*	*Age 0–14*	*Age 15–64*	*Age 64+*	*Age 0–14*	*Age 15–64*	*Age 64+*
1990	123,611	22,544	86,140	14,928	18.2	69.7	12.1
1995	125,463	20,103	87,134	18,226	16.0	69.4	14.5
2000	127,385	19,336	86,350	21,699	15.2	67.8	17.0
2005	129,346	20,229	84,390	24,726	15.6	65.2	19.1
2010	130,397	21,348	81,304	27,746	16.4	62.4	21.3
2015	130,033	21,244	77,404	31,385	16.3	59.5	24.1
2020	128,345	19,833	75,774	32,738	15.5	59.0	25.5
2025	125,806	18,247	75,118	32,440	14.5	59.7	25.8

Source: Compiled from Economic Planning Agency, *Summary of Economic Statistics* (1994)

The rapidly ageing population and the decrease in youthful population will lead to a decline in tax revenues and an increase in the cost of social security, which might restrict the vitality of Japanese economy. The implications of an ageing society have become a key issue in Japanese planning.

Rapidly rising yen and hollowing out of Japanese industries

The appreciation of the yen, shown in Figure 14.5, has been a principal factor for Japanese business cycles since the floating exchange rate system started in 1973. For example, following the Plaza Accord of 1985, the yen rose from a yen–dollar rate of 260.24 Yen to US$ to 127.56 Yen to US$, and the recession induced by the strong yen continued between June 1985 and November 1986. The latest appreciation of the yen recorded the rate of 79.75 Yen to US$ on 19th April 1995, the strongest level ever.

The strong yen has had a major impact throughout Japanese economy. In the short term, it worsened manufacturers' financial accounts. In the longer term, major export industries have been forced to transfer production overseas. For example, Sony recently announced its intentions to raise overseas production to 50 per cent of the total within three years from a current level of 35 per cent, and Matsushita Electric Industry has decided to shift all production of playback-only VCRs and radio-cassette players to Malaysia (*Nikkei Weekly* 1994). There is a growing concern in Japan about the hollowing-out of industries and consequent employment loss.

The situation is much more severe in local regions than in metropolitan regions due to their greater dependence on manufacturing industries.

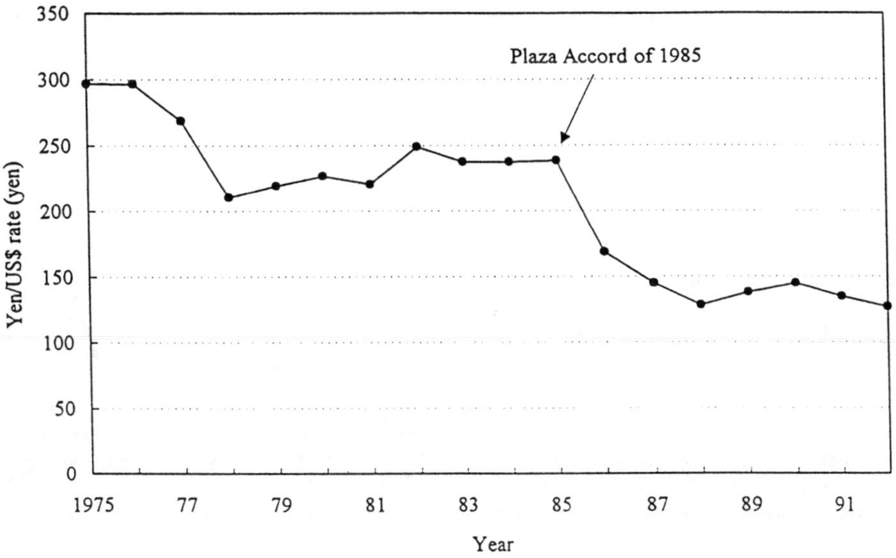

Source: Compiled from Economic Planning Agency, *Summary of Economic Statistics* 1994

Figure 14.5 Trends in the annual average of yen/dollar exchange rate

Rising land price

Land prices rose 135-fold in the 37 years between 1955 and 1992, while Japan's gross national product increased about 54 times during that period. The extent of the increases in land prices is illustrated in Figure 14.6. Based on the rise in land prices for most years, land is seen as an investment with which neither money nor any other type of capital asset can compete. The people's belief that the land price would rise indefinitely has been referred to as the Japanese land myth. It had been a dominant idea of Japanese people and companies until the collapse of the bubble economy in 1990. As the OECD report (OECD 1986b) has pointed out, the orientation of wealth formation towards the ownership of land has drawbacks for the revitalization of inner city areas, as well as on the overall effective use of land. It limited the introduction of both gradual and comprehensive schemes for redevelopment.

Land prices have showed a sharp rise over the last decade, starting with the commercial area of central Tokyo in 1983, and the rate of increase grew in 1986 and 1987. In the late 1980s, prices stabilized in central Tokyo, dropping somewhat with Japan's recession of the early 1990s. There are, however, some residential areas surrounding Tokyo where land prices continued to increase after 1988. The increase in land prices in the 1980s spread to Osaka and Nagoya, as well as to regional centres and cities elsewhere in Japan.

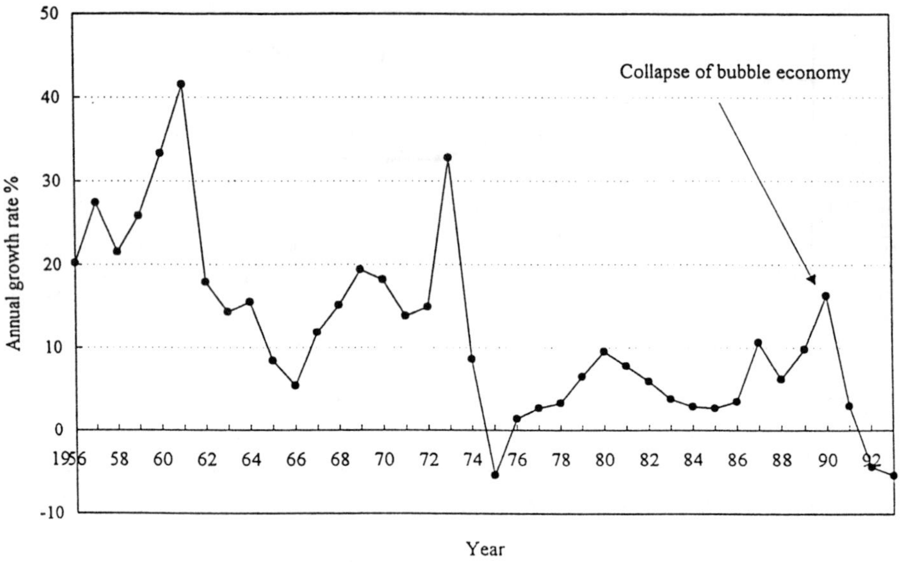

Source: Compiled from Economic Planning Agency, *Summary of Economic Statistics* 1994

Figure 14.6 Trends in the annual growth rates of land price index

This latest escalation in land prices is one of the largest scale and most serious in Japan's post-war history. A rise in land prices on a comparable scale also occurred in 1972 and 1973, as shown in Figure 14.6, but although prices came close to doubling within these two years, they dropped in 1974 in reaction to this increase. Since the early 1990s, there are now many residential and commercial districts in the Tokyo metropolitan region where land prices have fallen, and the downward trend is rippling outwards. Yet, while the recent slow-down in Japan's economic growth has softened Tokyo's land prices, by international standards they still remain extraordinarily high.

The causes of rising land prices have been examined by the government report (Economic Planning Agency 1990). In recent years, along with the advance in internationalization of the Japanese economy, economic functions have become progressively more concentrated in the greater Tokyo region. Tokyo, in particular, grew as an international financial centre, generating excess liquidity and causing the supply and demand for office space in the centre of the city to become tight. It is also believed that there have been increases in the productivity of land in Tokyo and its expected value.

The decline in land prices since the early 1990s not only represents a major change from the speculative favour of the late 1980s. It also reflects a change in thinking of both Japanese people and companies about the belief of ever-higher land prices. However, the collapse of the bubble economy and the significant fall in land prices has strongly influenced the latest long-term recession in Japan.

Improvement of the quality of urban life

The low quality of urban life, typically exemplified by the poor housing in large cities, has been an important issue in Japan. High land prices have encouraged people to live in local towns outside the large cities, and this has increased commuting for work in the central cities. While Japan has more houses than households (except in the largest cities), people are constantly demanding higher housing standards.

Japan now enjoys a high standard of living as measured by its per capita GDP. It has caught up and overtaken many other OECD countries. However, qualitative living standards remain low compared with OECD standards, as shown by the indicators in Table 14.7. Indicators used to measure the quality of urban life in Japan have focused particularly upon the physical infrastructure provision of roads, sewerage, and city parks.

Table 14.7 Japan's quality of urban life: selected indicators

Indicator	*Japan*	*USA*	*UK*	*France*	*West Germany*
Percentage of total road length paved	68 (1980)	90 (1988)	100 1988)	92 1988)	99 1988)
Length of expressway (metres/10,000 persons)	88 (1990)	455 (1988)	116 (1988)	269 (1988)	281 (1988)
Sewerage diffusion rate (per cent)	44 (1990)	73 (1986)	95 (1982)	64 (1983)	91 (1983)
City parks in major cities (square metres/person)	2.5 Tokyo (1988)	45.7 Washington DC (1976)	30.4 London (1976)	12.2 Paris (1984)	37.4 Bonn (1984)

Source: Compiled from Japan Regional Development Corporation, *Summary of Regional Statistics* (1992) and OECD data

A considerable impetus to upgrading Japan's urban and social infrastructure has recently been given by the *Basic Plan for Public Investments*, published under the US-sponsored Structural Impediments Initiative (commonly referred to as the SII) in 1990. The *Basic Plan for Public Investments* provides the framework and the basic direction of public investments during the fiscal years 1991–2000. The plan emphasizes the importance of public investments on residential environments and cultural facilities in order to achieve a better quality of life. It has proposed an estimated public investment of 430 trillion yen during 1991–2000 (recently, in 1995, this has been raised to 630 trillion yen).

Disaster prevention

The prevention of urban disasters is an important feature of urban and regional planning in Japan. Natural disasters, such as earthquakes, floods, typhoons and volcanic eruptions, have been a continual threat of life and property in Japan.

The Great Kanto Earthquake of 1923 destroyed the Tokyo metropolitan region and more than ninety thousand people were killed. More recently, the Great Hanshin Earthquake, which occurred in Kobe area on 17 January 1995, killed more than five thousand people and has ranked as the worst natural disaster in post-war Japan. The amount of damage caused by the Hanshin Earthquake has exceeded eight trillion yen. It has revealed the weakness of Japanese cities as well as the lack of crisis management by Japanese government and administration.

Deregulation and decentralization

Deregulation is one of the most important policy issues for Japan today. While the deregulation movement has spread throughout the world, the Provisional Council on Administrative Reform, which started in 1981, has proposed a deregulation programme focusing on a means of stimulating private-sector activity, achieving international harmonization and improving the quality of national life. Recently, the necessity of deregulation has received particularly strong attention because of its relationship with the latest long-term economic recession. As the government report (Economic Planning Agency 1994) has noted, public regulations, which have in the past contributed to the industrial development and the stability of national life, are today a source of rigidity in the socio-economic structure and are holding back Japan's future development and progress.

In the context of regional planning, the decentralization of political functions from central to the local governments is also a key issue. In terms of being the comprehensive administrative bodies for regions, the role of local government has been increasing to meet the needs and demands of residents seeking a better quality of life. In spite of the increasing necessity for a redistribution of roles between the central and the local governments, there exists a variety of interventions by central government in the operations of local government. These include administrative guidance, the approval of local projects, financial controls, and the transfer of central government bureaucrats to senior positions in local government. Adequate measures need to be taken to secure and stabilize the administrative and financial foundations of local government.

New Directions for Regional Development Planning in Japan

As pointed out in the previous section, substantial socio-economic changes are envisaged in Japanese regions. The government published the final review report on the fourth CNDP in 1994. The report has identified five major issues facing regional planning in the future: (i) the globalization of both the Japanese economy and society; (ii) the growing concern about environmental problems; (iii) the decline in population and an ageing society; (iv) the growing regionalism; and (v) the progress of an information network society.

In order to cope properly with these issues, the report has stressed the importance of mutual interactions and coalitions between local regions. It has proposed the formation of new national land axis and a number of local coalition axes which complement the existing national land axis, namely the Pacific Belt which connect Tokyo and Fukuoka through metropolitan regions and major local cities (see Figure 14.7).

The progress achieved in international integration and the advance of an information network society, an increase in free time and the improvement in transportation systems have all resulted in a more complex arrangement of human activities. The promotion of interaction between regions is seen as a way of revitalising regional economies through the mutual utilization of markets and resources. It may also lead to a growing recognition of each area's uniqueness in terms of natural features and cultural history. These aspects are considered to be particularly important in the ageing society and low-growth economy facing Japan in the future.

Conclusions

Japan has sought to match its economic success with similar progress in terms of urban development, infrastructure provision and the quality of life. Regional income disparities have been a longstanding issue of concern in Japan since the first CNDP was formulated in the early 1960s. This chapter has examined the extent to which regional development policy in Japan has sought to reduce regional disparities. However, under the increasing globalization of the Japanese economy, and the rapid change in industrial structure towards a more service-oriented economy, the excessive accumulation of economic activities in the Tokyo metropolitan region has been continuing. Regional income disparities have begun to widen again following similar trends in the late 1970s. Furthermore, looking towards the next century, substantial socio-economic changes are foreseen, focused upon population decline, a rapidly ageing society, a rising yen, the hollowing out of industries, and a stronger demand for a better quality of life to match recent achievements secured in materialistic living standards. These issues present a new challenge to regional development planning in Japan.

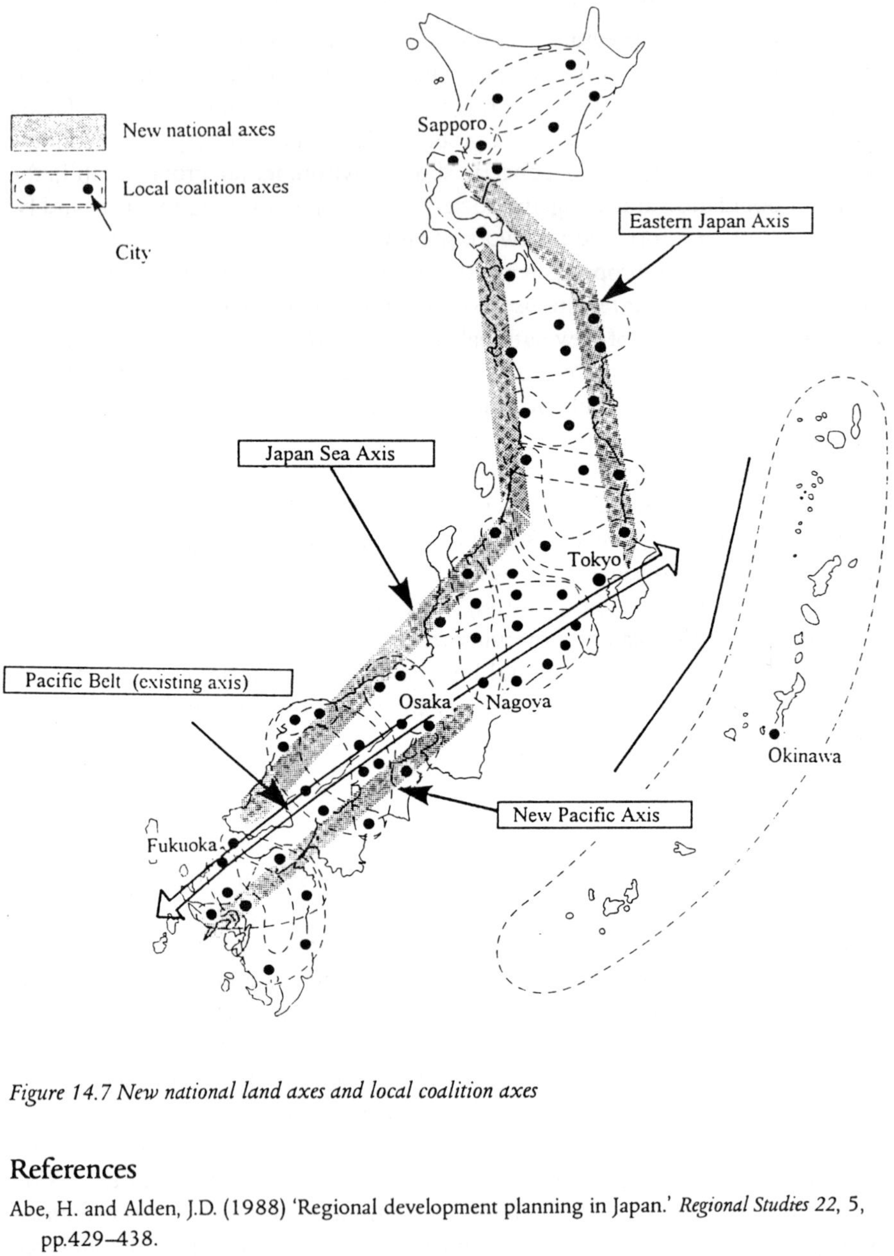

Figure 14.7 New national land axes and local coalition axes

References

Abe, H. and Alden, J.D. (1988) 'Regional development planning in Japan.' *Regional Studies 22*, 5, pp.429–438.

Alden, J.D. and Abe, H. (1994) 'Some strengths and weakness of Japanese urban planning.' In P. Shapira, I. Masser and W. Edginton (eds) Planning for Cities and Regions in Japan, A Town Planning Review Special Study, pp.12–24.

Economic Planning Agency (1988) *Internationalization of Tokyo and the Vitalisation of Regional Economy*. Printing Bureau, Ministry of Finance (in Japanese).

Economic Planning Agency (1990) *Economic Survey of Japan 1988–1989.* Printing Bureau, Ministry of Finance.

Economic Planning Agency (1994) *Summary of Economic Statistics.* Printing Bureau, Ministry of Finance.

Japan Regional Development Corporation (1992) *Summary of Regional Statistics.* Tokyo: Gyosei Publishing Company. (In Japanese.)

National Land Agency (1987) *The Fourth Comprehensive National Development* Plan. National Land Agency, Government of Japan.

National Land Agency (1994) Final Report on the Comprehensive Review of the Fourth Comprehensive National Development Plan: The Beginning of New Era and Issues on National Land Policy. Printing Bureau, Ministry of Finance. (In Japanese.)

Nikkei Weekly (1994) *Japan Economic Almanac 1994.* Nihon Keizai Shinbun, Inc.

Nishifuji, N. and Nakayama, D. (1983) *Regional Planning.* Civil Engineering Series No.48, Gihodo Publishing (in Japanese).

OECD (1986a) *Restructuring the Regions.* Paris: OECD.

OECD (1986b) *Urban Policies in Japan.* Paris: OECD.

CHAPTER 15

Regional Development Strategies in Europe

A Summary of the Key Issues

Philip Boland

Introduction

The publication of this volume coincides with a very topical and interesting discourse within academia, and beyond, on regional development strategies. The main thrust of this book has been to explicate the various regional development strategies which are currently being pursued within Europe – defined in its loosest term to include East and West. The book begins with an introductory chapter providing a detailed overview of the European Commission's views and policies on regional development, and is followed by two conceptual and theoretical chapters focusing on *regions* and *regional development*, incorporating a European angle. The main part of the book concentrates on specific regional development case studies from European Union (EU) Member States and countries not presently members of the EU, but who may accede in the near future. There is a chapter which gives a private sector approach to regional economic development, and there is also a chapter relating to Japan which provides a different dimension by examining how a very powerful economy is currently addressing regional growth disparities. The chapters have been arranged to generate both a conceptual, theoretical and empirical backcloth to regional development strategies set within a European context. The purpose of this chapter is not to provide a synopsis of the content of individual chapters, but rather to draw out and expand upon the key issues which arise out of the book, of which there are four.

The Key Issues

Reducing regional growth disparities

The first key issue concerns regional growth disparities and it is here that the guidance of the European Commission to Member States and regions is at its most direct. The three central planks of the Treaty on European Union, ratified in November 1993, and to which subsequent policy documents elucidate upon, are:

1. economic and social cohesion – denoting the need for 'regional balance'
2. the Single European Market (SEM)
3. economic and monetary union (EMU) (CEC 1994a, p.3).

The issue of *regional balance* is a recurrent theme which permeates throughout the chapters contained in this volume – of countries and regions seeking to reduce regional growth disparities by engaging themselves in policies and strategies which attempt to stimulate economic development in depressed regions, thereby generating a more balanced mosaic of regional economic development.

The European Commission's Fifth Periodic Report (1994b), *Competitiveness and Cohesion: trends in the regions*, also emphasizes the importance of reducing regional disparities within the EU – because as its title suggests, cohesion, economically, politically and socially, within the EU is a primary long-term objective of the European Commission. The Fifth Periodic Report (1994b) also describes how the 1990s have been a difficult period for reducing regional disparities because of the deep recession. A recent European Commission report, *Europe at the service of regional development* (CEC 1994c) identifies the nature and increased scale of the EU Structural Funds. It also reminds Member States how the opening up of frontiers in 1993, following creation of the SEM, has posed a further problem for the EU's most disadvantaged regions. It acknowledges that there was a possibility that the SEM would simply serve to enhance the economic strength of those regions in the strongest position to attract capital investment and the required human resources. Therefore, the aim of economic and social cohesion, i.e. the need to reduce regional growth disparities within the EU, was added to the Treaty of Rome in 1986 and so became an integral element of the SEM in 1993. The eventual outcome of these concerns was a significant restructuring in 1989 of the EU Structural Funds and a large increase in the resources allocated to them. Since Maastricht (1991) and the Treaty on European Union, the objectives of the EU have been directed towards the achievement of EMU and not simply the effective functioning of the SEM – a more ambitious and grandiose goal. To help to reduce regional disparities within the EU, total Structural Fund allocations for 1994 to 1999 have risen to 141.5 billion ECU. This clearly illustrates the commitment of the European Commission towards regional development and the need to eliminate enervating disparities in economic performance between regions of the EU.

So, following a careful and detailed analysis of the European Commission's views and policies it becomes obvious that the necessity of reducing regions growth disparities, in tandem with the promotion of sustainable regional development strategies, are the critical building blocks which serve to underpin the aims and objectives of the EU.

The case studies contained in this book replicate the above by revealing how each individual country or region appreciates the need to reduce the level of regional growth disparities by adopting coherent and focused regional development strategies. This can be seen in the United Kingdom (UK) with Merseyside, Yorkshire and Humberside and Wales; in Ireland; in Flanders (Belgium); in the Nordic countries; in Brandenburg (Germany); in Central and Eastern Europe; and also in Japan. Each of the case studies illustrates how the central, regional, and in some case even local, levels of government are increasingly pre-occupied with striving to engage their respective areas in policies and strategies which are specifically designed to reduce the extent of disparities in economic welfare between regions. The chapters reveal the importance attached to reducing regional growth disparities and the significance of regional development strategies in this process. So why has regional development become so portentous in the 1990s?

There are deemed to be economic, political and social reasons which necessitate a reduction in regional growth disparities. Economic in the sense of helping to increase the national growth rate, because if regional growth disparities are reduced, then the overall national rate of economic growth will be increased, which will then facilitate national, as well as regional, prosperity. There are also political and social factors which come into play if regional growth disparities are particularly deep and entrenched. Those regions which experience low rates of economic growth have the capacity to become fertile breeding grounds for social and political unrest. Resentment towards more affluent regions, and the government, may, over time, become translated into a potentially more vehement display of civil protest, which can threaten political and social stability. This has undoubtedly been a contributory factor in the UK in the 1980s and 1990s – providing the seeds for industrial action, riots, demonstrations, crime, etc. Other countries have suffered more severe unrest which has led to the complete dismantling of entire nations – e.g. Czechoslovakia, Yugoslavia and the Soviet Union – with one of the underlying causes being regional divergences in economic welfare. So, clearly, reducing regional growth disparities must be an essential part of any nation's regional development programme.

The role of the European Commission

A second issue pertains to the dynamic role which the European Commission is playing in striving to animate and energize regional economic development in Europe. Reference has already been made to the increased resources allotted to the EU's Structural Funds. Examples of these in operation in this book include the Merseyside Objective 1 and Yorkshire and Humberside Objective 2 regions in the UK, the Leader project in Ireland, while the recent accessions of Sweden and Finland indicate that these countries see membership of the EU as being beneficial in enabling them to enhance their economic performances by obtaining eligibility for, and access to, the EU's Structural Funds to help them reduce regional disparities. There is also the case of the nations of Central and Eastern Europe, where in recent years the EU has provided a valuable *rationale* for regional development strategies, particularly through the PHARE aid programme. A closer relationship with, and appreciation of, the EU and its polices on regional development has had the effect of encouraging, or more bluntly, compelling, these countries – who may be contemplating accession in the future – to modify both their institutions and also their regional development strategies in line with EU policy prescriptions. It is interesting to note that in recent years the EU's Structural Funds have become the major provider of regional development monies for disadvantaged UK regions The EU's Structural Fund resources are vitally important as UK regional policy expenditure consistently decreased during the 1980s and 1990s, thus providing a *financial lifeline* for many UK regions in their pursuit of regional development.

As this book has indicated, the European Commission is increasingly becoming the dominant player in regional development in both Eastern and Western Europe, as it is the main contributor of regional development funds for depressed regions in the EU. Its policy prescriptions – with their emphasis on partnership, strategies, additionality, programming and concentration – form the cornerstones of many Member States' regional development strategies.

Partnerships and strategies

A third theme relates to the ever-growing emphasis and importance attached to the role of partnerships and strategies in regional development. Partnerships between the EU and Member States, the public, private, voluntary and community sectors are seen to be order of the day, and indeed these are often prerequisites stipulated by the EU, and some national governments (especially the UK) before any financial assistance can be granted. This book has revealed how the issue of partnership, alongside additionality, programming and concentration, form the backbone of the criteria for the implementation of the EU's Structural Funds. These are particularly evident in the Monitoring Committees, Technical Panels and Secretariats and the SPDs for Merseyside and Yorkshire and Humberside; and also in the Leader Initiative in Ireland. However, these are not without controversy. This concerns urban and regional governance issues with the emergence of new actors in regional development and the creation of partnerships. The critical question appears to be: who is in control and making the vital decisions in these partnerships? In the UK and in Ireland this has led to problems of what has been termed *contested governance* and *institutional searching*. Governance issues have arisen out the increasingly contested domain of urban and regional governance – critical comment has been levied at the absence of the social partners and the private sector in many of the partnerships – their voices tend not to be heard as vocally as those of the public sector, who are accused of running the show in many of these partnerships much to the annoyance of the European Commission. Once again the UK provides the contentious arena for the ideological battle over these issues.

Institutional and governance issues have also arisen in Brandenburg and Central and Eastern Europe, examples being the unification of Germany and the collapse of Czechoslovakia. These are countries which have experienced major upheavals, and political, economic and social restructurings. This has inevitably brought many new actors in the domain of regional development and these institutions/agencies are still in the process of finding their feet. The nations of Central and Eastern Europe are continually looking to the Western counterparts and the EU for guidance on regional development.

Coherent and focused strategies, in the form of Single Programming Documents (SPDs) or Community Support Frameworks (CSFs), are regarded by the EU as the regional development model to adopt. These *regional plans* are seen to encapsulate a detailed knowledge of the economic and social ailments of problem regions, and then proffer an over-arching strategy to address them. As with partnerships, the strategies which have been adopted in the UK have been criticized for their blandness and lack of critical insight of the intrinsic problems of the regions concerned. The other case studies, pertaining to Ireland, Flanders, Brandenburg, Japan, Central and Eastern Europe and the Nordic countries all refer to the need to produce coherent, sustainable and clearly focused regional development policy strategies.

Emphasis on the private sector

Finally, the book also contains a chapter with a strictly private sector approach to regional development, which itself has striking similarities with EU proposals. The EU is seeking to create a more *entrepreneurial* climate for small and medium sized enterprises (SMEs) to operate, with emphasis placed upon innovation and technical change. This links in with Chapter 10 which provides an overview of the relevant concepts and policies which are of crucial relevance to a private sector company operating a global market place and whose host nation has recently joined the EU – Volvo in Sweden. It analyses in detail the implications of the SEM for the future of the company and how it has responded to the challenges of an increasingly competitive international market. This is set within the context of future regional development in Sweden and for a company such as Volvo. The key phrases which emanate from this chapter are competitiveness, innovation and technological adaptation – very similar to the fundamental tenets of the EU as seen in CEC (1994a–c).

As has already been mentioned, there is increasing competition between regions, within national, European and international contexts, for scarce financial investment resources. The basic target which each region has to attain is to be *competitive* and to out-compte other regions for such investment. This book has revealed that the fundamental issues which are currently occupying the minds of decision-makers in the European Commission, Member States, and indeed countries and regions not yet members of the EU, are:

1. There is need to reduce regional growth disparities.
2. The pursuit of coherent regional development strategies is essential in order to achieve the above.
3. Increasing emphasis is placed upon the integral role of partnerships and strategies in this process.
4. Increasing attention is focused upon entrepreneurship, innovation, technological change and, most importantly, competitiveness.

The way forward for depressed regions is seen to encapsulate the above and thereby foster and stimulate regional economic development. As this book has shown, regional development is now top of the European economic agenda.

Reflective Thoughts

Significance of the Japanese economy

The mere preoccupation with regional development strategies presupposes the existence of regional growth disparities. The existence of the latter necessitates the pursuance of the former. What this book has striven to articulate is how different European nations/regions are devising policies which seek to address imbalances in regional growth performance indices. The incorporation of the Japanese economy in this book is instructive in the sense that it indicates that a currently very successful economy is not immune, but can often be susceptible, to the emergence of regional growth disparities. It reveals that regional development planning in Japan today is specifically designed to control excessive economic development in the metropolitan regions, particularly Tokyo, while at the same time attempting to promote and sustain an economic revival of less economically fertile local regions. The Japanese are extremely conscious that the existence of regional growth disparities is not conducive to a successful future performance of the economy. In order for Japan to maintain its economic might in the globally competitive market it needs to generate a more balanced and cohesive configuration of economic growth.

So it is not only Western economies which suffer from regional growth disparities, even one of the most powerful economies of the world has such problems and is in the process of producing regional development strategies to ameliorate the situation. Regional growth disparities are therefore a pervasive phenomena and are not constrained or limited to the depressed countries of the EU.

EMU, the SEM and the EU

The late 1980s and early 1990s proved to be a particularly difficult period of economic adjustment and restructuring for numerous European regions due to the recession, while the creation of the SEM and the possibilities and prospects of

EMU may serve to exacerbate the plight of depressed regions in the EU (CEC 1994c). The policy response by the EU and Member States to such acute problems has been the promotion of, and engagement in, coherent and focused regional economic development strategies. As has already been mentioned there has been an ever emerging and heightening importance attached to the role of the European Commission in regional development in Member, and indeed non-Member, States. Its involvement is not only financial, in the form of the Structural Funds and other Community Initiative assistance policies, but it is increasingly becoming more *institutionally* integrated into recipient nations' regions. Explicit examples referred to in this volume include Merseyside's Objective 1 strategy, Yorkshire and Humberside's Objective 2 programme, Ireland's LEADER initiative, Structural Fund aid to Wales and the PHARE programme in Central and Eastern Europe.

As the European Commission has already acknowledged, the transition to the SEM and EMU may adversely affect many of the EU's economically less vibrant regions. It is here that the European Commission has a moral and economic responsibility to undertake for depressed regions. It is therefore seeking to enunciate what kinds of regional development strategies are, in its view, best equipped to serve to inure such regions from further decline and prevent them from entering the economic abyss. This is most evident in its aid packages, and also its direct involvement in the institutions carrying out such policies – monitoring committees, technical panels and secretariats – the ultimate aim being to satiate the avowed goal of economic and social cohesion within the EU.

Necessity rather than choice

The chapters in this book have revealed that regions receiving pecuniary support from the European Commission do so more out of necessity than choice. The case studies indicate that national governments no longer have the requisite resources at their disposal to dispense for expensive regional development strategies. The only viable alternative for depressed regions is to attempt to access the Commission's regional development resources. It can be observed that some national governments, most notably the UK being a good example in this respect, are reducing their net allocations to regional development policies, while the European Commission is in the process of augmenting its total Structural Fund spending – thereby posing serious concerns for the principle of additionality. This obviously then gives the Commission the opportunity to gain an institutional access route to regions receiving fiscal assistance. The end result is that regions within the EU, and also those regions of Central and Eastern Europe and the former Soviet Union, increasingly look to the European Commission for guidance on regional development strategies and not their respective national governments. This has led some commentators to conclude that the European Commission's Directorate for Regional Policy is more in tune with issues concerning regional economic development than are national governments.

The main tenets in regional development strategies

In today's intensely global markets the key to economic success is seen to be competitiveness. This spans many spheres such as quality skilled labour force, excellent premises and communication links, technology transfer between universities and research institutions and the private sector, high levels of innovation and research and development etc. In order for regions to attract inward investment, or to stimulate endogenous economic growth, then it is vital that they possess some, if not all, of these fundamental prerequisites. To this end the European Commission's regional development policies are intrinsically geared to achieving such targets for depressed regions within the EU. Greater emphasis is now placed upon entrepreneurship, on SMEs and supply side measures (land, labour, premises etc.), while more credence is currently assigned to the European Social Fund and training initiatives with the objective of re-skilling those out of work in order to give them more of a chance to procure employment. Merseyside's Objective 1 strategy is a good example of such policies.

Other important building blocks for any regional development strategy sponsored by the European Commission include the guiding principles of the Structural Funds: concentration, programming, partnership and additionality. These principles form the foundation upon which the European Commission's regional development strategies are constructed and so they necessitate some discussion. The concentration principle relates to concentrating measures and policies on the most economically depressed regions of the EU (Objective 1 and 2 regions); programming refers to the adoption of multiannual development programmes to correct specific social and economic problems; there is a partnership approach between all the relevant actors in regions receiving EU assistance (the European Commission, Member States' national, regional or local authorities, the public, private and voluntary sectors); and finally all EU resources are deemed to be additional to national governments' regional development spending (CEC 1994c). The latter is a very contentious issue, especially in the UK. There is also the principle of subsidiarity where decisions are intended to be taken by the lowest level of authority, i.e. placing power and decision-making with those most capable of making such choices.

Concluding Thoughts

Regional economic growth disparities within the EU remain acute and only time will reveal whether the regional development strategies outlined in this book prove sufficient to correct the situation, and ultimately lead to a more balance economic profile within Europe, especially with the likely accession of Eastern European countries in the next decade. As the 21st century approaches regional development is top of the agenda both for the European Commission and its Member States. If the Commission's aim of economic and social cohesion is to be achieved then the regional development strategies discussed in this volume will need to attain their targets and succeed. Many of them contain very ambiguous aspirations, such as Merseyside's Objective 1 programme, but as long as there exist sufficient resources and a concerted commitment and partnership towards the fulfilment of such ends then progress along that road is inevitable. The next few years will serve to be an interesting period for us all.

References

Commission of the European Communities (CEC) (1994a) *Europe 2000+: Cooperation for European Territorial Development.* Luxembourg; Commission of the European Communities.

Commission of the European Communities (CEC) (1994b) 'Competitiveness and Cohesion: trends in the regions.' *Fifth Periodic Report on the Social and Economic Situation and Development of the Regions in the Community.* Luxembourg: Commission of the European Communities.

Commission of the European Communities (CEC) (1994c) *Europe at the Service of Regional Development.* Luxembourg: Commission of the European Communities.

The Contributors

Hirofumi Abe, Professor, Department of Environmental and Civil Engineering, Okayama University, Japan.

Jeremy Alden, Professor, Department of City and Regional Planning, University of Wales, Cardiff, UK.

Dr Wilhelm Benfer, Senior Planner, Regionale Planungsgemeneinschaft Uckermark-Barnim, Eberswalde, Germany.

Philip Boland, Lecturer, Department of City and Regional Planning, University of Wales, Cardiff, UK.

Ruth Downes, Research Fellow, European Policies Research Centre, University of Strathclyde, Glasgow, UK.

Roland N-G Gustafsson, Director of Industrial Development, AB Volvo, Gothenburg, Sweden.

Rik Houthaeve, Assistant Researcher, Department of Planning, University of Ghent, Belgium.

Christian Jensen, Research Fellow, Local Government Research Institute, University of Gothenburg, Sweden.

Dr Svante Leijon, Senior Lecturer, Local Government Research Institute, University of Gothenburg, Sweden.

Peter Lloyd, Professor, Department of Geography, University of Liverpool, UK.

Richard Meegan, Senior Lecturer, Department of Geography, University of Liverpool, UK.

Lars Nordstrom, Professor, Department of Human and Economic Geography, School of Economics and Commercial Law, University of Gothenburg, Sweden.

John Shutt, Professor, Leeds Business School, Leeds Metropolitan University, UK.

Dr Hannu Tervo, Senior Researcher, School of Business and Economics, Centre for Economic Research in Central Finland, University of Jyvaskyla, Finland.

Jim Walsh, Professor, Department of Geography, St. Patrick's College, Maynooth, County Kildare, Ireland.

Subject Index

Author Index

Regional Policy and Development Series

Series editor Ron Martin, Department of Geography, University of Cambridge

Retreat from the Regions
Corporate Change and the Closure of Factories
Stephen Fothergill and Nigel Guy
ISBN 1 85302 101 6 hb
ISBN 1 85302 100 8 pb
Regional Policy and Development 1

Spatial Policy in a Divided Nation
Edited by Richard T Harrison and Mark Hart
ISBN 1 85302 076 1
Regional Policy and Development 2

Regional Development in the 1990s
The British Isles in Transition
Edited by Peter Townroe and Ron Martin
ISBN 1 85302 139 3
Regional Policy and Development 4

An Enlarged Europe
Regions in Competition?
Edited by Sally Hardy, Mark Hart, Louis Albrechts and Anastasios Katos
ISBN 1 85302 188 1
Regional Policy and Development 6

Sustainable Cities
Graham Haughton and Colin Hunter
ISBN 1 85302 234 9
Regional Policy and Development 7

Union Retreat and the Regions
The Shrinking Landscape of Organised Labour
Ron Martin, Peter Sunley and Jane Wills
ISBN 1 85302 255 1
Regional Policy and Development 8

The Regional Imperative
Regional Planning and Governance in Britain, Europe and the United States
Urlan A Wannop
ISBN 1 85302 292 6
Regional Policy and Development 9

The Regional Dimension of Transformation in Central Europe
Grzegorz Gorzelak
ISBN 1 85302 301 9
Regional Policy and Development 10

Regional Policy in Europe
SS Artobolevskiy
ISBN 1 85302 308 6
Regional Policy and Development 11

The Determinants of Small Firm Growth
An Inter-Regional Study in the United Kingdom 1986–90
Richard Barkham, Graham Gudgin, Mark Hart and Eric Hanvey
ISBN 1 85302 331 0
Regional Policy and Development 12

Unemployment and Social Exclusion
Landscapes of Labour Market Inequality
Edited by Paul Lawless, Ron Martin and Sally Hardy
ISBN 1 85302 341 8
Regional Policy and Development 13

Jessica Kingsley Publishers
116 Pentonville Road, London N1 9JB

